ANIME IMPACT

Published by Mango Publishing Group, a division of Mango Media Inc.

Cover, Layout & Design: Morgane Leoni

For permission requests, please contact the publisher at:

Mango Publishing Group
2850 Douglas Road, 3rd Floor
Coral Gables, FL 33134 U.S.A.
info@mango.bz

For special orders, quantity sales, course adoptions and corporate sales, please email the publisher at sales@mango.bz. For trade and wholesale sales, please contact Ingram Publisher Services at: customer.service@ingramcontent.com or +1.800.509.4887.

Anime Impact: The Movies and Shows that Changed the World of Japanese Animation

Library of Congress Cataloging-in-Publication has been applied for.
ISBN: (p) 978-1-63353-732-3, (e) 978-1-63353-733-0
BISAC - PER004080 - PERFORMING ARTS / Film / Genres / Animated

Printed in the United States of America

Photo Credits:
Page 9: © jointstar / Shutterstock.com / 356414120
Page 250: © Hannah Dexter Photography

ANIME IMPACT

THE MOVIES AND SHOWS THAT CHANGED THE WORLD OF JAPANESE ANIMATION

CHRIS STUCKMANN

Mango Publishing

Coral Gables, FL

Sam, thanks for noticing the DBZ shirt
I was wearing. That was a good day.

TABLE OF CONTENTS

INTRODUCTION

Anime—or Japanese animation—has been popular in Japan since *Astro Boy* appeared on Japanese television in 1963. Subsequent titles like *Speed Racer* and *Kimba the White Lion* helped spread the fandom across the country. Often adapted from popular manga (a comics style tracing its roots to the late nineteenth century), anime is as commonplace in Japan as the output of Disney or Pixar.

In the States, however, anime acceptance is playing an indefinite game of catch-up.

Back in the '80s and '90s, meeting a fellow anime geek was tantamount to connecting with a long-lost loved one. Perhaps you found yourself at a comic book store browsing the shelves for the latest horrendous—and criminally overpriced—VHS English dub. Perhaps you bumped into someone wearing baggy jeans and a black graphic T-shirt, noticed their embarrassingly large stack of anime and manga, and struck up a friendship. If so, you and your new companion had just joined the American anime underground, a shadow network built on chance encounters, early Internet chat rooms, and secretive after-school clubs.

Anime in America remained an underground art form for many years, yet a few titles pierced the public's consciousness. Katsuhiro Otomo's masterwork, *Akira*, saw limited release in the States on Christmas Day, 1989. But even that remarkable film met resistance. No lesser Hollywood luminaries than George Lucas and Steven Spielberg famously labeled *Akira* as "unmarketable." And yet, history has vindicated *Akira* as a landmark film, its animation so mind-bogglingly gorgeous that one struggles to comprehend the skill required to produce it.

Similarly, Mamoru Oshii's transcendent *Ghost in the Shell* remains one of the most influential films ever made. Filmmakers like James Cameron and the Wachowskis have cited it as a source of inspiration for their work. *GITS* even garnered attention from mainstream audiences when film critics Gene Siskel and Roger Ebert reviewed it on their show.

Akira and *GITS* are often cited as the two pioneers of anime's eventual acceptance in America, but there were others. Shows like *Star Blazers* (a.k.a. *Space Battleship*

Yamato), *Battle of the Planets* (a.k.a. *Gatchaman*), and *Robotech* all saw broadcast on American television starting from the late '70s and continuing through the middle portion of the '80s, though each was censored and altered for American audiences. Later, the Sci-Fi channel (now Syfy) aired a Saturday block of anime that included such titles as *Robot Carnival, Galaxy Express 999, Roujin Z, Fist of the North Star, Lily C.A.T.,* and even *Akira.*

Soon enough, every kid in America wanted to be "the very best!" No one was prepared for the explosion known as *Pokémon,* a show centered around capturing exotic monsters and training them to battle in arenas. *Pokémon's* success was mind-blowing. Nintendo played a major role in popularizing the anime with an ongoing string of video games and product tie-ins. It wasn't uncommon to see kids on school buses, at parks, or game stores actively trading and battling with their *Pokémon* cards. Those cards remain sought-after items today.

Pokémon became the first real multi-million-dollar anime franchise to hit the States, but it was Cartoon Network's anime block, Toonami, that changed the game forever. Toonami aired *Dragon Ball Z, Sailor Moon, Outlaw Star, Gundam Wing, Tenchi Muyo!, Yu Yu Hakusho,* and *Naruto,* among others. It dared to defy the trend of aggressive Americanization that had plagued US anime broadcasts for decades, eschewing the drastically altered storylines that robbed these shows of their Japanese cultural heritage for a closer hewing to the original material. In doing so, Toonami awakened mainstream America to the quality of Japanese animated television. Better yet, they promoted the knowledge that these shows were coming from Japan, rather than based in America. Thus, a new generation of anime fans was born, and for the first time in memory, being an American anime geek wasn't so bad.

I've had the privilege of watching this medium flourish from those early comic book store days to its viable and accepted inclusion into American culture. Naturally, anime remains more acknowledged in Japan—you won't see a giant Gundam standing outside your local 7-Eleven anytime soon—but it's no longer an underground cult here in America, either. Anime has imprinted on us, and hard. It's not going anywhere.

When I first got the idea for this book, I planned on it being a solo job. I'd research anime's history, its appeal across a broad spectrum of fans, and eventually present a well-rounded view of its impact on our culture. But one of anime's most beautiful aspects is that it speaks to and impacts upon each of us differently. My personal relationship with anime will naturally differ from the introvert who found her voice by discussing her favorite show with a fellow fan, or the man who met his future wife through their shared love of this beautiful art.

So let's make this a collaborative effort, shall we?

In the coming pages, you'll hear not just from me but from a multitude of anime fans. Some entries are penned by well-known authors or personalities, but many are written by people who've never been published before. These are computer technicians, nurses, data-entry specialists, even personal trainers. Each has their own distinctive relationship to anime, and each has a story to tell. I'm proud to include these voices here, not just because I think they're terrific writers, but because I believe it's crucial to hear from the widest swath of society if we're going to fully understand anime's broad impact.

As with my previous book (*The Film Buff's Bucket List*), the goal here is not simply to pen another "Best of" list. You don't need me for that—one quick Internet search will cover you there. Rather, my goal is to highlight the works that have moved us most. The titles included in this book are almost all hand-picked by the various writers as ones they wanted to discuss. You'll hear filmmakers describe how anime has influenced their movies, or how a certain show helped someone get through the day during one of life's rough patches. In these pages, you'll read stories of personal discovery. Many writers have detailed their experiences that led to unearthing a life-changing anime. Others have taken a more analytical approach. Each writer was encouraged to express themselves authentically, and I believe their intimate expressions have created something special. This isn't just a list of essential titles. It's a discussion of the true impact of anime on multiple generations.

Chris Stuckmann

December 26, 2017

1963 • ASTRO BOY

TETSUWAN ATOMU

— JEFFERY J. TIMBRELL —

I was a child of the '80s and, as everybody knows, Saturday morning cartoons were an essential part of the youth culture back in that time. Especially mine. My appetite for animation was voracious. I watched everything religiously. I would sometimes get my mom to buy certain kinds of cereal just because there were pictures of a cartoon I liked on the box.

I loved all of it.

Cartoons showed me a world outside of my experience, full of over-the-top characters and striking, visually dynamic imagery that stayed with me for the rest of my life. Over the years, I've often heard moralist critics bemoan the influence of animation on kids, but the biggest effect animation had on me was that it made me fall in love with storytelling, art, and filmmaking.

One of the most popular cartoons when I was a kid was the remake (and overdub) of *Astro Boy* that was directed by Noboru Ishiguro. It was a staple of my usual cartoon consumption along with *Fables of the Green Forest* (*Yama Nezumi Rokki Chakku*), *Voltron* (*Hyaku Juo Goraion*), and *Robotech* (*Super Dimension Fortress Macross, Super Dimension Cavalry Southern Cross*, and *Genesis Climber Mospeada*). Those series were my introduction to Japanese animation.

I didn't know that anime was from Japan when I was younger, but I always knew when I was watching anime because it was different from its contemporaries. Not just in visual style or the overdubbed voices but in the content of the stories; how they dealt with conflict, how they approached romance and death, and even the story structure. To me, anime always walked a fine line between being daring and realistic and being experimental and over-the-top.

Sometimes it blurred those lines.

Astro Boy was one of those animations that blurred the lines; where one second it could be dealing with really intense drama and tension and the next thing you know, you see *Looney Tunes*-style sight gags. But it was done so well that, instead of feeling like a contrast, the emotional effect felt like a one-two punch; where the show kept you on your toes wondering what was going to happen next.

I didn't have the pleasure of watching Osamu Tezuka's original *Astro Boy* until I was much older. By that time, I had watched every kind of animation I could get my hands on. From the stop-motion genius of artists like The Brothers Quay and Jan Ävankmajer to the brilliant works created by Don Bluth and Pixar to the stylistic mastery of Hayao Miyazaki and the late Satoshi Kon. So I was expecting the original *Astro Boy* to be interesting from a historical perspective, but I wasn't expecting it to blow me away or to affect me emotionally.

I was wrong.

If anything, my experience and age allowed me to have a much deeper appreciation for the original *Astro Boy*.

To look back on the scope of Osamu Tezuka's original animation—even with the hindsight of knowing just how influential it would become—*Astro Boy*'s daring inventiveness is astonishing. It's not just the story's broad strokes or the imaginative fights with giant robots who have fallen from grace, it's the details. Every single episode is brimming with this intricate world-building and rock-solid thematic consistency that takes the story of a little robot boy and gives it a powerful sense of authenticity.

For me, it was a revelation. It was a series that had a simplistic, child-friendly appearance, but underneath, it was a universe of complex ideas: moral questions about the nature of life and humanity, the differences between classes and cultures, and the conflict between our irrational fear of the "other" and a bright and advanced future.

A lot of times the story of *Astro Boy* is compared to *Pinocchio*. Where, instead of a toy-maker building a little puppet boy, it's a brilliant scientist who's lost his child, seeking to resurrect him within the body of a metallic, living robot. However, I feel the comparison to *Pinocchio* doesn't quite do justice to the ideas going on here. For one thing, Astro Boy isn't trying to become a real boy. He's always alive, from the very beginning to the very end. It's humanity who has to come to realize that, and it's humanity that has trouble seeing the truth about him and the other robots as well.

The entire concept of *Astro Boy* flips a lot of the conventional science fiction ideas about robots upside down. Where it's not really the robot who has to learn to be human, it's the humans who have to learn that the robot is alive. *Astro Boy* also has a striking rebuttal to a lot of anti-intellectualism and fear-mongering that goes on when discussing robots and technology.

Usually, in western fiction, when a scientist is stricken by grief and invents a robot to replace a loved one, it ends in horrific tragedy. These kinds of stories almost always result in the creations becoming a twisted abomination who take their vengeance on humanity for daring to play God. The narrative of the "evil robot mind that we cannot trust" is not just seen in fiction, but all over newspapers and the Internet. Where even the suggestion of an artificial intelligence is inevitably followed by comments of "Skynet" and Terminators. People imagining dystopian futures where armies of marching metal men crush our civilization underfoot at the command of some all-powerful A.I.

The funny thing is, we've built many machines in the past capable of destroying us, from weapons of mass destruction to industry that creates toxic pollution. So what makes sentient robots so particularly terrifying? The bias seems to suggest that it's not so much the nature of machines that scare us, but the nature of intelligence.

Especially an intelligence like our own.

Astro Boy is a proud and defiant rebuttal of that anti-intellectual mindset. *Astro Boy*'s imagery—especially during his creation in the first episode—mirrors the classic themes of films like Fritz Lang's *Metropolis* and James Whale's *Frankenstein*. It uses that style of imagery to build tension about the scientist inventing an artificial life. But that is where the similarities end. From the very first episode of the series, Astro Boy is not some monster or cold unfeeling android, he is the very best of us. He is innocent and curious, caring and strong; so strong in fact, that he doesn't like to fight because he doesn't have anything to prove. He's different from us, but instead of his differences setting him apart, those differences help him give us a new perspective on ourselves.

In this way, *Astro Boy* sets the classic *Frankenstein* story on its head. It takes all the paranoia surrounding technology and invention and turns it upside down, where instead of technology becoming our doom, it's our salvation.

There will always be people who live in fear, afraid of new inventions just the same as they're afraid about the effects of cartoons on kids. *Astro Boy* shows how our inventions and technology—like our art—doesn't always have to reflect the worst of us, it can reflect the best of us, too. Pretty impressive for an old cartoon about a little robot boy who flies around with jetpacks in his boots.

Jeffery J. Timbrell is a writer, filmmaker, artist, and photographer with giant space worms in his brain. He lives in Canada with his two cats, a basement full of DVDs, and a ton of regrets.

1967 • SPEED RACER

MAHHA GŌGŌGŌ

— CHRIS STUCKMANN —

Scooby-Doo and the gang are casually driving in the Mystery Machine—that flowery blue-green product of the late '60s—while a calming voiceover soothes us. They seem at peace ... but not for long. A shiny, intimidating car slams into the van, knocking the Scooby Gang off course. It's white. There's a sleek red "M" on the hood. *It's the Mach 5.*

The theme song for *Speed Racer* unexpectedly bursts forth, and the young racer, Speed—known as Gō Mifune in Japan—nods at the Scooby Gang as they *fly off a cliff and explode.*

***

This is my earliest memory of *Speed Racer*, which was airing in the afternoon on Cartoon Network. I was in elementary school at the time, and yet still recall being immediately taken by the catchy theme song, and of course, the badass Mach 5.

That sequence with Scooby and Speed ends with him staring into the camera saying "Dogs should not drive," as the Mystery Machine lays in a pile of rubble. Naturally, as an action-hungry young kid, I was intrigued. Of course, that was just one of many special intros made for the series, editing multiple cartoons together to help promote *Speed Racer*. All these years later, it serves as a striking metaphor.

This intro must've aired sometime between 1996 and 1997 when Cartoon Network was experiencing a shift. And if Cartoon Network was changing, that must've meant adolescents of the era were also. Back then, the station was dominated by Hanna-Barbera cartoons like *The Jetsons*, *The Flintstones*, and *Scooby-Doo*,

Where Are You! But just as Bob Dylan prophetically stated, times they are a-changin', and Cartoon Network was about to introduce a new generation to the life-changing block of anime entertainment: Toonami. How fitting then, that an anime legend like Speed would literally force the Scooby Gang—a well-known American animated staple—off the road.

While *Speed Racer* didn't air on Toonami, this curious anime fan can only speculate on the intentions of Cartoon Network's programmers. Were they testing the grounds by airing *Speed Racer*? Rather than performing a full cannonball into the water with Toonami, they dipped a toe in first. Who knows? Whatever the reason, that elementary-schooler was enraptured by the cars, the white-knuckle races, the music, and yes ... *that dub*. I still have fond memories of sitting down after school with my sister, crying with laughter while imitating the voice-work. Speed wasn't just fast on the racetrack, his sentences blurted out at velocities that'd make the Mach 5 jealous!

English dubs have evolved a lot over the years, and have since become considerably more respected. But back then, much of my anticipation for watching *Speed Racer* came from what new inside jokes I'd have with my sister. We'd often repeat lines to each other, likely to the confusion of our parents. Good times indeed.

Speed Racer originated in 1966 within the pages of *Shōnen Book*, a manga publication specializing in stories for boys. It goes without saying that the manga was popular enough to spawn a fifty-two-episode anime, which is often credited as one of the most influential titles ever made.

From a story perspective, *Speed Racer* isn't especially unique. Most episodes deal with Speed and his friends embroiled in an intense race or foiling some evil scheme. The overarching backstory surrounding Speed and his brother Rex, however, is surprisingly gripping. Rex disappeared years ago, much to the dismay of Speed and his family. Despite the corny trappings of the show, the way Speed's past combines with his current predicaments is actually very satisfying.

The success of *Speed Racer* was essential to the eventual acceptance of anime here in the States. While it's certainly never been as popular as titles like *Dragon Ball Z* or *Pokémon*, *Speed Racer* carved out a place in the hearts of many impressionable youngsters. For some, it was their first exposure to Japanese animation, and while it was unfortunately Americanized and altered in many ways, the simple fact that anime was airing on American television was monumental.

If you want progress, it's important to develop a "take-it-or-leave-it" mentality. Throughout this book, you'll hear many writers discuss the gradual inclusion of anime in the American landscape, and you'll read stories of their specific viewpoints of this movement. Today, we have things like Crunchyroll (a video streaming service specializing in anime), and companies like FUNimation, Sentai Filmworks, or Discotek—all doing their part to get anime delivered to our living room. But to get here, we had to make sacrifices. Sometimes that meant a horrific English dub. Other times it was drastically altered storylines. Maybe whole episodes of your favorite show weren't even aired because of some minor offensive content.

The point is, change goes about its sweet, leisurely time. You either take it, or leave it. I didn't realize then, but looking back to the '90s, a show like *Speed Racer* airing during the "prime-kid-hours" of the afternoon was huge. They took a chance, and it paid off. The show found a new resurgence of fans, and it entered into the holy realm of animated legends occupied by the likes of *Looney Tunes* or *Peanuts*. My parents—non-anime fans—know who Speed Racer is, and not just because my sister and I annoyed them over the dinner table quoting lines. He's a household name. *An anime from 1967 is a household name in 2018.*

Progress can be molasses-slow, but thanks to shows like *Speed Racer*, the anime scene in America only increased exponentially soon after. Looking back, the Mach 5 ramming the Mystery Machine off the highway was a fitting image for the '90s, and it signaled the coming era of widespread anime popularity.

"Here he comes," indeed.

1973 • BELLADONNA OF SADNESS

KANASHIMI NO BERADONNA

— BENNETT WHITE —

The important figures of anime's history are overshadowed by the towering visage of one man: Osamu Tezuka. Earning the nickname "The Godfather of Manga," Tezuka penned over seven hundred individual titles, indelibly linking himself to the very art form. His art would go on to a second life in the world of animation, where the common elements of his style would be the genesis of the "anime aesthetic" (e.g., large eyes, triangular mouths, budget-conscious animation). His 1963 directorial adaptation of his own *Astro Boy* manga was the realization of his then life's work, forever cementing his legacy as the Walt Disney of Japan.

Always a man of incredible work ethic, Tezuka further pushed the boundaries of not only anime style but how anime was made. His own studio, Mushi Production, had branched out from the waters of traditional, wholesome anime television shows—like Tezuka's own *Kimba The White Lion* (1965–1967), and into experimental, decidedly adult animated movies. In this spirit, Tezuka and his longtime collaborator, writer/director Eiichi Yamamoto, created a trilogy of erotic animated movies dubbed Animerama. While these three films were thematically related, each kept to their own story: *A Thousand and One Nights*, *Cleopatra*, and *Belladonna of Sadness*.

By 1968, Tezuka had stepped down from his role in Mushi, going back to focus on his manga work. But, his contributions to *Belladonna* were still felt, even when his pre-production input went uncredited. In his stead, Yamamoto took the directorial reigns, leading *Belladonna* in a remarkably different direction than its other two lighthearted sister films. *Belladonna* is an all-out assault on the senses; an emotional gut-check of a movie that pulls nothing back in its depictions of sexual violence. This film is not for everyone.

Loosely based on *Satanism and Witchcraft*, a largely debunked French historical fiction published in 1862, *Belladonna* is the story of Jean and Jeanne, a peasant couple in rural France in the Middle Ages. Their lives and livelihoods are under constant threat by the tyrannical Baron and Baroness of their village, who have taxed them and the other villagers into desperate poverty. As such, on the day of their wedding, when Jean is unable to pay, the fee is collected when Jeanne is brutally gang-raped under order of the Baroness. Jeanne is left in a crying, traumatized heap.

Her sorrow attracts the attention of a phallus-shaped Devil, who entices her with promises of power. Hesitant though she is, Jeanne slowly grows trusting of the spirit, who guides her and Jean down a path of relative luxury and influence. While Jean is designated a villain by becoming the village's taxman, Jeanne uses her newfound feminine wiles to become the money-lender that fuels the Baron's wartime kingdom. This sudden rise in power has the Baroness seething and she declares Jeanne a witch and an enemy of the village, forcing her to flee into the arms of the Devil. Broken, beaten, and abandoned by everyone around her, she succumbs to temptation and offers her soul to him.

When Jeanne makes her pact, she is oddly confused and disappointed that she—a God-fearing Christian—didn't turn into an ugly witch. In fact, the Devil insists she has only become more beautiful. After weeks, months, perhaps even years of unspeakable abuse from the village and the sovereignty (despite all that she has done for them), she pursues even more punishment by entering a tryst with the Devil. A life that has been predicated upon sacrifice and violence would know little else, and it takes a carnal act to shake her from the dirge of her suffering and make her realize what she can truly do.

In a stunning reversal of the typical rape-revenge story, Jeanne uses the pact she made not to punish the villagers who chased her out. The cruelty they have suffered under the pious tyranny of the Baron and Baroness, and the devastation left by The Black Death, is punishment in of itself. Instead, she uses her newfound knowledge to cure the sick and lead them to a better life free of the oppressive Christian dogma that has choked the life from them. At this point, the film takes cues from the electric acid-soaked revolution going on in America at the time and equates this better life to free love. The climax, so to speak, revolves around the townsfolk freeing themselves of restraint and releasing generations of sexual frustration. The film frames this massive orgy as both chaotic, and yet wholly good. In fact, it seems that the Devil is not so much the adversary that fell from grace, but a spirit that represents what the powerful Baron and Baroness deemed evil: lust, passion, emotional honesty, and love.

The great irony of *Belladonna* is that, while this film was created in part by the hands that typified the anime style, it is anything but typical anime. Characters aren't drawn, they are painted and etched. Jeanne's face, which the camera frequently holds onto tightly, speaks of the hardships she has weathered. The airiness and brightness of the colors almost appear in conflict with the hard-bitten story being told.

At first glance, the film feels like what would happen if Ralph Bakshi had directed *Yellow Submarine*: bold, striking, clashing uses of watercolor, all animated in a minimalist but effective manner. The scenes of the villagers unleashing their sexual angst are the crowning technical achievement of the film. Intimately connected bodies writhe and undulate, becoming like the ebb and flow of a river. Organs from both genders fold and stretch to create abstract visions of life and growth. The music is a cacophony of erratic drums, wandering bass, and free-form guitar. The music leads the revelry with every lick and shift.

This marvelous use of both color and sound also applies to the decidedly uglier scenes of the film. The many scenes of Jeanne being assaulted are not made easier to experience by its aesthetic, but they are made more thematically appropriate. During the aforementioned gang rape, we are never explicitly shown what she is experiencing, but her agony is unmistakable. A red, phallus-shaped energy penetrates Jeanne at the base of her pelvis, and it quickly shoots through her body as she cries out in anguish and pain. Along with these scenes, Jeanne herself spends much of the film's running time in a state of either partial or complete nudity. And while these segments may be considered arousing, seeing as how it is part of an erotic series of movies, the film never comes across as exploitative. The intent appears not to be titillation, but horror as viewers are made witness to what happens to Jeanne. This galvanizes Jeanne's agency as she lets go of her own personal shame and embraces her own sexuality, and inspires the villagers to do the same.

Belladonna of Sadness is a historically brave film in its willingness to break convention and push past taboo. It forces the viewer to reconsider their personal definition of what "anime" is. In film and on television, the term "anime" is a subjective, aesthetic-based one that undermines the art by forcing the whole of the medium into a single category. Good from a marketing perspective, but entirely restrictive for everything else. *Belladonna of Sadness* is an anime, but it doesn't look like it, which throws a gigantic wrench into the gears of conversation and forces everyone to reconsider what anime looks like, or rather, what could anime look like.

One could be more than forgiven if they are put off by the frankness of its sexual politics, or its depictions thereof. It is not a simple viewing, and it was never intended to be. No personal history of the art of anime is complete without at least knowledge of the film: a draining, empowering, beautiful, ugly yarn called *Belladonna of Sadness*.

Bennett White has been making content on the Internet for a decade, stretching from video games to anime, and has aggregated over twenty million lifetime views. He currently resides in Northern California.

1973 • CUTIE HONEY

KYÛTÎ HANÎ

&

1994 • NEW CUTEY HONEY

SHIN KYÛTÎ HANÎ

— JOSHUA DUNBAR —

By the time Go Nagia's original *Cutie Honey* anime debuted in 1973, the magical girl style show was well on its way to becoming an established genre in Japan. The origins of the magical girl genre can be traced back to the imported American sitcom *Bewitched*. Today, many viewers associate magical girls with things like *Super Sentai* (*Power Rangers* in the US)—cute girls fighting evil and engaging in good versus evil like operas, but this was not always the standard. Like *Bewitched*, early magical girl manga and anime series focused less on combat scenarios and more on the complications that arose from having supernatural powers in the mortal realm. One of the earliest and most notable examples, *Sally the Witch*, tells the story of a young girl from a magical kingdom who is sent to the mortal realm to make friends her own age. The original *Cutie Honey* anime was to be more along these lines, focusing more on Honey's changing ability and less on combat. However, circumstances resulted in the show being assigned to a time slot previously held by shows designed for a male audience. In an effort to retain this demographic, *Cutie Honey* was adjusted to include more action sequences and nudity during the transformation sequences.

It would be a stretch to consider the original anime's Hannah-Barbera-esque cartoon visuals pornographic-Honey resembled something along the lines of a spinning, naked Barbie doll. Limitations of 1970s animation techniques not withstanding—the show is as ambitious in its set pieces as it is sexual. *Cutie Honey* does not titter around with the usual fan-service. Often within the magical girl genre, the audience may be surprised by a sudden up-skirt shot or the heroine caught (or tied) up in some sort of compromising position. These moments can be jarring and leave viewers asking, "Did they intend it to be interpreted that way?" In the world of *Cutie Honey*, the fan-service is as blatant as it is pervasive. There is no room for the viewer to wonder or consider the intent of the writer or animator. Honey is not even safe from her school's headmistress—a bizarre mustached woman harboring a confusing romantic obsession. Honey is aware that she holds this type of appeal, and depending on her mood, can be amused, excited, and even bored by the commotion her transformative power causes.

Initiated by the words, "Honey Flash!" Honey's signature power allows her to change her attire into anything she wishes. The changes are not just cosmetic—a transformation into a biker or pilot grants superhuman operator skills. Even a transformation into a rock star comes with the ability to dance and sing far beyond the level of an ordinary human.

Certainly, Honey's ever-changing appearance makes her tailor-made for a girl's doll line, but by turns the exciting swordplay and array of monstrous villains could give *He-Man and the Masters of the Universe* a run for their money. By the 1990s, this cross-media synergy would become the norm in anime and manga. All things considered, *Cutie Honey* may have pioneered the more action-driven magical girl heroine as well as cemented the fan-service phenomena.

If the original *Cutie Honey* kicked off a fan-service craze, 1994's *New Cutey Honey* ran it into the end zone. Slickly animated and lots of bold, brassy characters, this OVA (Original Video Animation) is a huge, fun, sexy comedy everyone is invited to. A sequel to the original series, once again Honey finds herself the object of desire of both men and women alike, and this time the transformations are even more knowing and sensational—taking the form of everything from a Chun-Li look-a-like to a leather-clad, whip-wielding S&M queen. This dominatrix form is taken during a battle with the nude—except for a few well-placed diamonds—Jewel Princess. Honey seems to be having a bit of fun with both the Jewel Princess and the viewer:

"If you can call yourself a Princess, Princess, just call me the Queen!"

While some might write *New Cutey Honey* off as either tasteless nonsense or a combination of the worst sexist anime tropes, there are many aspects that elevate it beyond similar offerings and other, more traditional magical girl anime. Remarkable production values, appealing and sometimes absurd character designs (a Go Nagai trademark), beautiful color palettes, and well-choreographed action stood out in the over-inflated (thanks to the enormous success of *Sailor Moon*) magical girl market. The transformation sequences, of which there are many, are incredible. Transformation sequences are are a hallmark of the magical girl genre. Often this animation is elaborate and costly, resulting in the reuse or recycling of the same sequence many times throughout the run of a series. Unlike many magical girls shows, the animation in *New Cutey Honey*'s transformations is never recycled—each one is unique and they never fail to impress.

Of course, the degree and frequency to which her naked body is revealed also set Honey apart. The nudity in *New Cutey Honey* is certainly more realistic and gratuitous than anything presented in the original 1970s version. Although undeniably sexy, it can be interpreted as a big, cheeky, laugh at the whole genre. Magical girl series, such as *Magical Emi*, *Magic Knight Rayearth*, and *Sailor Moon* all feature varying degrees of fan-service or exploitation of their female characters. So while *New Cutey Honey* is certainly more explicit than those shows, the major difference here is that Honey is in on the joke. During a dangerous encounter with a punk-rock villainess, Honey finds herself cornered. To escape, she feigns an infatuation, professing her love and pressing her body against the woman's. Alarmed by the advance, the villainess tosses her out:

"Ugh! Get out of here—I'm not into THAT!"

Having escaped into the alley, Honey giggles and admits to herself that she enjoyed the sensation of the woman's breasts against her own:

"That was too close … but I sort of liked it too!"

In another instance, Honey momentarily breaks the fourth wall and reveals she is wearing a steel bra:

"My contract says I have to wear one of these—if my breasts were damaged, fans everywhere would be grieving!"

This lively sense of humor is also displayed in the joy she receives when teasing and mocking her opponents. Witty and self-aware, in these moments Honey is reminiscent of a female Spider-Man, though she's more self-assured than most superheroes. Many times she defeats her opponents utilizing both brain and brawn. She is a mature and principled tough girl whose kindness and empathy for others is extolled as often as her physical attributes.

The dub done by ADV Films is worthy of mention for several reasons. *New Cutey Honey* is a frenetic carnival of excesses—the scenarios range from the zany to the deathly serious. The English direction and performances capture the high energy and excitement of the material. Honey is voiced by Jessica Calvello (hand selected by Go Nagai) and the actress rubber-bands between sexy, aggressive, comedic, and vulnerable moments with an ease and understanding of anime not typical of the period (though typical of many of ADV's high quality productions). Her laugh is a pitch-perfect mischievous purr.

Sadly, the series ended after only eight episodes. The first four episodes tell a complete story arc regarding Honey's revival and her battle with Dolmeck, "The Lord of Darkness." The remaining four take a more monster-of-the-week approach, and while the episodes are clearly building toward an encounter with a revived Panther Zora (Honey's ultimate adversary), the episodic nature means that the series doesn't end on a cliffhanger despite its cancelation.

There are many other adaptations of *Cutie Honey*, most recently a 2016 live-action film. The original anime and it's OVA sequel however, are often cited as the best interpretations of Go Nagai's work. In many ways, *New Cutey Honey* feels like a culmination of every magical girl series that came before it, albeit with each genre-defining aspect ratcheted up to eleven. Many viewers may at first find themselves struggling to reconcile the voyeuristic nature of the transformations with the portrayal of a powerful female hero. It may help to consider that sex appeal and strength are not mutually exclusive, but in many ways it is these seemingly contradictory elements that make the series so exciting. Honey's combination of grit, grace, sexiness, and strength—as well as her creator's willingness to push the envelope—have established her as one of Japan's most beloved heroines.

Joshua Dunbar is a freelance illustrator and art educator and holds an MFA in Sequential Art from the Savannah College of Art and Design. A lover of all forms of Japanese media, he is currently working on his first creator-owned comic inspired by the Magical Girl genre and late twentieth-century animation. You can find his work on his Instagram at @j2dstar or joshuadunbar.com.

1979 • THE CASTLE OF CAGLIOSTRO

KARIOSUTORO NO SHIRO

— JOHN RODRIGUEZ —

My introduction to Hayao Miyazaki—to anime in general, in fact—didn't come at the movies. It didn't come via home theater, nor even through a local club. My introduction came, rather, in the bowels of a dingy video arcade, before a cabinet whose marquee read *CLIFF HANGER* in garish pink.

This was one of those newfangled laserdisc games. If you remember any of those games ... well, first, congratulations, you're old, here's a Geritol. But if you remember any of those games, it's surely *Dragon's Lair*. Yes, the one where you guide Dirk the Daring through the castle by moving the joystick in exactly the right direction at exactly the right time.

Cliff Hanger played like *Dragon's Lair*, but the similarities ended there. Whereas *Dragon's Lair* reflected the sensibilities of its creator, ex-Disney animator Don Bluth (he of *The Secret of NIMH* and *An American Tail*), *Cliff Hanger* looked like nothing I'd ever seen before. Its palette was more muted, its characters more stylized. It was also utterly incoherent in a way that *Dragon's Lair*—which featured a script written specifically for the game—wasn't. An escape from a casino! A runaway princess! Ninjas! Sword battles on a clock tower! This game had everything ... everything, that is, except story transitions that might explain what in the Sam Hill was going on. I remember walking away confused and frustrated, certain that the gorgeously animated scenes I'd witnessed held some deeper story I just wasn't grasping.

Arcades eventually faded from relevance here in America, and with them my memories of *Cliff Hanger*. But childhood memories don't die easy, as I discovered one night nearly ten years later.

"Hey, I know this!" I exclaimed to my friend just seconds after the film we'd rented—some old anime called *The Castle of Cagliostro*—began to play. And I did! There was that casino escape scene, the very one I'd witnessed in that dingy arcade. Only now we had something new: context! Sweet, blessed context! Here, at last, was the full feature I'd glimpsed only in snippets, viewable from start to finish!

Freed from the demands of dexterous joystick handling, I dug into the story with eager curiosity. Quickly, I learned that the pair of crooks who'd made off with the cash were Arséne Lupin III, mastermind thief extraordinaire, and his crack-shot partner Jigen Daisuke. What princess Lupin was chasing after was Clarisse de Cagliotros—heir to the Cagliostro family fortune and soon to be unwillingly wed to the vile Count Cagliostro—the very villain our hero Lupin would ultimately confront on that clock tower. At long last, everything was making sense!

And the ninjas? Well, they're just ninjas. But seriously ... ninjas! This film had everything!

My (re)discovery of *The Castle of Cagliostro* delighted me beyond my ability to express. It wasn't just the scratching of an old itch, the filling in of long guessed-at details. This was a legitimately excellent film, excellent in a way I wasn't yet accustomed to expect from anime. Until now, my experience with anime had mostly fallen into three categories: the heady "real" films (as best exemplified by *Akira*); the space epic melodramas (hello, *Star Blazers* and *Robotech*); and the titillating "super sexies save the world" fare (I'm looking at you, *Project A-ko* and *Devil Hunter Yohko*).

But *Cagliostro* was different from any of these. It wasn't science fiction, for one thing, and that alone came as a shock: I don't think I'd ever watched anime to this point in my life that wasn't sci-fi. Its characters were also engaging in a way that characters from other anime I'd seen weren't. Maybe it's how they were written or maybe it was just an artifact of stripping away the laser swords and mobile Gundam suits, but I genuinely liked Lupin and his pals, genuinely cared if Princess Clarisse would escape Count Cagliostro's clutches. *Akira* taught me that anime could be intellectually stimulating. *The Castle of Cagliostro* taught me that anime could be emotionally affecting.

There was something else, too: *Cagliostro* was beautiful. Not beautiful in the same way as Don Bluth's work, but distinctive like that, the kind of look that sticks with you. Indeed, there are details from that very first full viewing of *Cagliostro* that stick with me to this day.

One of those details comes during the midst of an early car chase scene (and if you haven't seen that scene, brother, put this book down now and go check it out ... it's fabulous). With a sheer drop on their left, a cliff wall on their right, and the lead car in the chase tossing grenades out the back window, Lupin decides to drive up the cliff wall (!) and into a densely wooded area. As we watch the car hurtle through trees from a backseat perspective, this colorful bird suddenly flies through the car's shattered windshield. It hovers there a moment with this "what in the hell?" look on its face before fluttering indignantly off. Did that little detail need to be included in this chase? Of course not. But it was, and it's stuck with me for years since.

After reconnecting with *The Castle of Cagliostro*, I began seeking out more tales of Lupin III's derring-do. First up was *The Mystery of Mamo*, the first *Lupin III* feature film (and the source of the only *Cliff Hanger* arcade sequence not lifted from *Cagliostro*). *The Gold of Babylon* and *The Fuma Conspiracy* followed. Each of these was fun in their own way, yet none quite resonated with me the way *Cagliostro* had. Something was missing.

In many ways, my true follow-up to *The Castle of Cagliostro* came months later when I discovered Hayao Miyazaki's *My Neighbor Totoro*. Miyazaki had by this time cemented his reputation with classics like *Nausicaä of the Valley of the Wind* and *Kiki's Delivery Service*, but I knew nothing of that. I didn't even know that *Cagliostro* and *Totoro* shared a director ... not, that is, until *Totoro* began to play. Then, the similarities struck me at once.

That might seem an odd statement to anyone who's watched these two wildly different films, but it goes back to something I mentioned earlier. *Cagliostro* was the only *Lupin* film that made me care for Lupin as a person. It had "heart," as they say, and "heart" is the common thread that ties Miyazaki's works together. You can douse us in whimsy. You can drown us in bullets. But if you don't make us love your characters as people, you've got nothing. Miyazaki instinctively understands that, and it's the way he's imbued his films—*Cagliostro* included—with such love that makes them such timeless classics.

Maybe you're a Studio Ghibli fan. Maybe you know Miyazaki's classics up and down. But maybe, just maybe, you missed the film that kicked off his career. Filling that gap in your knowledge has never been easier. You can pick up *The Castle of Cagliostro* on Netflix, iTunes, or even on Blu-ray. But if you're planning a visit to your local arcade in search of a functioning *Cliff Hanger* cabinet, take my advice and save your quarters. *Cagliostro* deserves better.

John Rodriguez is a personal trainer whose devotion to physical fitness is exceeded only by his fervor for all things film and literature. John is currently finishing his first novel—a fantasy that's sparked fantasies of a challenging new career.

1979 • GALAXY EXPRESS 999

GINGA TETSUDŌ SURĪ NAIN

— EMMA FYFFE —

In the pre-Internet era—well not *exactly* pre-Internet, but in the era of "all my friends had AOL and just talked to each other on AIM all day" while I, the child of two programmers, explored the far reaches of burgeoning fan pages via Netscape—the manner in which we were introduced to new media, particularly that which at the time was considered "niche" or "alternative," often came in the form of actual printed publications. And for a fledgling *otaku* (a fandom-obsessed person) like myself circa 1999, one such publication reigned supreme: Viz Media's monthly magazine *Animerica*.

At the Borders in that area of Southwestern Connecticut, up the street from what is now an AMC Theater (that I was never entirely sure whether it was Brookfield or Danbury), I first discovered *Animerica* amongst the other nerd magazines I'd seek out in that far corner of the wooden magazine stands: *GamePro*, *Electronic Gaming Monthly*, *Wizard*, etc. I recall browsing its pages, eagerly taking in the artwork, and searching for reviews and recommendations of anime series beyond what was currently airing on Toonami. Series I would go home and immediately search for on our recently purchased TiVo to see if there was any chance of me catching them without having to ask my parents to drive me to Blockbuster on the off-chance I could rent them.

I'm not certain if it was the first issue of the magazine that I actually decided to purchase—in fact, I know I owned Volume 7, Issue 9, which featured interviews with the staff of *Serial Experiments Lain*—but one of my earliest memories of owning and thoroughly devouring a copy of *Animerica* was June of 2000, Volume 8, Issue 5, which coincided with the limited US theatrical release of director Rintaro's adaptation of CLAMP's *X*, localized as *X/1999*, at the time. What I didn't realize then was that Rintaro was previously responsible for the film adaptation of another piece of media that appeared in every issue of *Animerica* I ever owned: Leiji Matsumoto's elegant space opera, *Galaxy Express 999* (pronounced "three nine" not "nine nine nine").

As previously mentioned, *Animerica* was published by Viz Media, who remain a major player in the world of US licensing & distribution to this day. So, Viz would publish single chapters of manga they currently had the license to, and during my prime *Animerica* reading days, that manga was *Galaxy Express 999*. Though, as an adult, I'm realizing this might not have been the original 1970s series, but the sequel which began publication in Japan in 1996. It's difficult to tell, thanks to Matsumoto's unique and consistent art style (to this day, I must admit, I blame him for my addiction to eyelash extensions), but my research tells me that the original manga series has never been released in the US in any official capacity.

Which is definitely *not* the case with Rintaro's 1979 film. Thanks to its massive success in Japan, and the steadily expanding anime fandom overseas, *Galaxy Express 999* was the first anime film ever to receive a US theatrical release, albeit in a heavily modified format, produced by Roger Corman of all people, in August of 1981. The 130 minute film was shaved down to 90 minutes, the title was shortened to simply *Galaxy Express* and several name changes, including Captain Harlock being changed to "Captain Warlock" and Tetsuro Hoshino to "Joey Smith." I wish I could say this was the manner in which I first experienced this series on screen, but I am 99 percent sure I just saw bits and pieces of the still edited 1996 Viz dub on the Sci-Fi channel, where I recognized it as "that thing I thought was kind of weird in the middle of every issue of that magazine I liked."

Because, let me be clear, I was not instantly in love with Matsumoto's work. I didn't dislike it, and I will say I was definitely intrigued by how bizarre his character designs were. Tetsuro looked like a chicken nugget wrapped in a blanket, wearing a hat. Maetel was too tall and skinny, even by anime standards, and I was extremely confused by her furry Russian Cossack hat. Also, most of the chapters I read in *Animerica* seemed to just be Maetel & Tetsuro floating around space on an old-timey looking train—remember, Viz was only publishing single chapters and we weren't getting a whole lot of story—so the action paled in comparison to other space series I was watching at the time, *Gundam Wing*. Still, something about this series intrigued me and despite not really being sure if I liked it, I did keep reading.

That was when I started noticing all the ads in *Animerica* for other series, featuring characters who looked like the ones I was seeing in *Galaxy Express 999*, but in full color and with flashier outfits. Like any self-respecting fourteen-year-old, I loved pirates, badass women, and beautiful men with good hair, and found all of these things personified in Queen Emeraldas & Captain Harlock, who at this point were just images to me. It did not take long to realize these characters existed in the same universe as *Galaxy Express 999* and thus began my now lifelong fascination with the "Leijiverse."

While the promise of "cool" characters like Captain Harlock drew me in—I'm pretty sure I bought *Harlock Saga*, Matsumoto's take on *Das Rheingold* from Wagner's *Der Ring des Nibelungen* the minute Central Park Media released it under the US Manga Corps mantle in the US—it is ultimately the complex (and admittedly, sometime convoluted) morality of *Galaxy Express 999* that forms the heart of Matsumoto's vast, frequently interconnected body of work. The reverse Pinocchio journey of tenacious Tetsuro Hoshino, who dreams of replacing his perishable human body with an immortal machine one upon reaching the Andromeda Galaxy—the final destination of the Galaxy Express 999—is full of all the emotional turmoil you'd expect in the journey of an orphaned ten-year-old who's discovering the value of a finite lifespan. His relationship with Maetel, part surrogate mother, part first love (in a one-sided crush kind of way—it's mostly not creepy) is sweet and compelling, especially as we learn more about who this mysterious blonde woman—who also bears an uncanny resemblance to Tetsuro's late mother—is.

While not every stop along this galactic train journey across the Sea of Stars is a winner (there's an episode wherein a planet commits suicide out of embarrassment after Tetsuro cuts it open), some of them are truly gut-wrenching. For example,

Tetsuro's discovery that the human bodies of people who've abandoned them in favor of machine ones are stored under the ice on Pluto. The stories of many of the more prominent side characters who were deemed important enough to appear in Rintaro's really excellent film, like the glass-bodied waitress Claire, the elegant Ryuzu, and the bandit Antares, all resonate in the hearts of the viewer as deeply as they do in young Tetsuro. The revelation of the true nature of the free mechanized bodies being offered up to those who complete the journey to get them. *Galaxy Express 999* is a coming-of-age tale that elegantly undermines childhood fantasies of the glory of immortality, addresses issues of classism, corrupt leadership, and the emotional repercussions of physically sacrificing your humanity.

Despite the original manga having never been licensed in English, all 113 episodes of the original 1978 anime series are available streaming in Japanese with English subtitles on Crunchyroll (as of this writing). The 1978 film also has some staying power, with the film finally receiving an uncut, official English-language DVD release in 2011 thanks to Discotek. This version features both the original Japanese-language version and the Viz dub, which isn't terrible, but I highly recommend watching in Japanese, if only for Masako Nozawa's performance as Tetsuro. And while you could get the DVD right now, Discotek has announced that they will be releasing the film on Blu-ray soon, so hopefully by the time you're reading this you can and absolutely should purchase it. Though I don't expect you to love every second of it, because Matsumoto's art and storytelling does take some adjusting to, it's impossible to walk away from this series without at least appreciating the amount of thought and detail behind it, and its lasting impact on the science fiction genre.

Emma Fyffe currently resides in Los Angeles where she hosts a Sailor Moon *podcast* Love and Justice *and an anime talk show* Hyper Otaku *on Hyper RPG's Facebook page. She is also the "Golden Mic" of the* Movie Trivia Schmoedown *(it says so on her IMDb) and the Captain of a ragtag crew of smugglers on Hyper RPG's Twitch-based* Star Wars *roleplaying game series "Pencils and Parsecs."*

1979–PRESENT • MOBILE SUIT GUNDAM SERIES

KIDŌ SENSHI GANDAMU

— DEREK PADULA —

Gundam is a gigantic, genuine, and glorious space opera that expresses the human condition through wars fought by young super soldiers piloting humanoid robots. It's one of the biggest pop culture phenomena in Japan and is akin to a homegrown *Star Wars*, both in popularity and revenue. Just as everyone in the civilized world knows who Darth Vader is even if they haven't seen *Star Wars*, everyone in Japan knows who Char Aznable is even if they haven't seen *Gundam*. For this reason alone, you should be curious to watch *Gundam* and discover for yourself what makes it so popular.

Like many Americans, I was first introduced to the *Gundam* franchise through the forty-nine-episode *Mobile Suit Gundam Wing* (1995) starting March 6, 2000. *Gundam Wing* was the first *Gundam* series to be televised in the United States, on Toonami. It had an attractive cast, story, voice acting, music, action, humor, political intrigue, and designs, so it became a daily treat alongside *Dragon Ball* and others. It influenced me enough that I aspired to dress like Duo Maxwell, a character who wears a black and white outfit similar to a clerical collar. He was just so cool!

I later discovered that *Gundam Wing* is one of many standalone series in the *Gundam* franchise that starts in 1979 with *Mobile Suit Gundam*. There are over 30 *Gundam* anime series, 20 movies, 113 manga, 47 novels, 220 video games, 1,000 model kits, 3 theme park rides, 1 life-size robot statue in Tokyo, and countless forms of merchandise. In 2014, the *Gundam* franchise generated ¥80 billion *yen*

($726,400,000 USD), and in almost four decades has generated several tens of billions of dollars. As a result, *Gundam* is a household name in Japan.

Mobile Suit Gundam was created and directed by Yoshiyuki Tomino, without a manga predecessor. He loved the Super Robot genre of anime made popular in the '60s and '70s. These giant robots can transform, have quasi-magical super powers, represent good or evil, have mythical origins, are made by mad scientists, or are even gods incarnate. They are controlled by young boys, often by remote control or simple one-button and a joystick controls, as they fight a cartoon-like villain of the week. Famous examples include *Gigantor* (*Tetsujin-28*), *Mazinger Z*, and *Voltron*.

But Tomino wanted to create a robot series that was more realistic. One that depicted the horrors of war, and was targeted at young adults, rather than boys. To do this, he partnered with character designer Yoshikazu Yasuhiko and mecha designer Kunio Okawara, an illustrator who is the first to ever be credited as a "mechanical designer" for anime.

Together they created the Real Robot genre. These are robots that do not transform, do not have super powers, and are not gods. Nor are they controlled by little boys from outside the robot. Instead, they are a mass-produced weapon used by soldiers for the purposes of political agendas. They are inanimate extensions of the frail men who control them from inside a cockpit. As a result, *Gundam* felt real. People died—the main characters are the ones who killed them—and there were consequences for their actions.

Gundam's signature invention is the Mobile Suit. These are humanoid tanks piloted by a single user in a cockpit that extend the user's natural abilities. Mobile Suits are inspired by the powered armor exoskeleton in the American sci-fi novel *Starship Troopers* (1959). This suit protects mobile infantry, augments their strength and movement, includes powerful weapons, and yet is sensitive enough to handle delicate objects. Tomino took this western idea and increased its size to those of Eastern robots.

The story of *Mobile Suit Gundam* is set in a futuristic earth where the world is united by a global government known as the Earth Federation. The planet is overpopulated, so they create orbital colonies in outer space—called Sides—inhabited by tens of millions of people. The main character, a young mechanic named Amuro Ray, lives on Side 7.

A colony faction called the Principality of Zeon argues the Earth Federation is corrupt, so they enact a war of independence. The story begins when Zeon attacks Side 7 with Mobile Suits and is defended by the Federation's floating carrier, named White Base. Amuro is forced to fight in a white prototype Mobile Suit invented by his father, called the RX-78-2 Gundam, and then becomes entangled in the war.

Zeon Lieutenant Commander Char Aznable leads the rebellion, nicknamed the "Red Comet" for his iconic red Mobile Suit. Likewise, through numerous battles, Amuro's nickname in the war becomes the "White Devil," because of his white Gundam that brings death. As the war rages on, Amuro falls in love with Char's ensign, Lalah Sune. Finally, Amuro attempts to kill Char, but Lalah jumps in front of his sword and dies in Char's place. Afterward, Char and Amuro become bitter rivals, and the battles continue.

The first *Gundam* is a coming-of-age story for Amuro. During his forced process of becoming a soldier, he experiences trauma, a dysfunctional family, bloodshed, and responsibility beyond his years. He discovers that he is genetically superior to normal humans, but along the way he makes mistakes, becomes humble, and finds a new family in the children he goes to war alongside. He learns that he is not an unstoppable Gundam pilot by himself. He finds hope in the idea that, together, *we* are Gundam.

By seeing that the characters are people first and soldiers second, we learn that humans are capable of compassion, sacrifice, and love, but also atrocious acts of violence. Much like Shakespearean villains and heroes, the question of what label to apply to them depends on which point of their life you happen to be looking. Over time we're able to see that the villains are not that different from the heroes.

One of the reasons for *Gundam*'s success is that it spoke to its Japanese audience. The post-World War II Japanese media created anime that was lighthearted and fun, shying away from war's consequences, but *Gundam* puts it front and center by showcasing children becoming agents of war. As a result, this war series had an anti-war message, similar to the one Japanese civilians were taught in school. Viewers learn that the conflict isn't over at the end of each episode, just as war isn't over for those who are disenfranchised by it.

Because of this, *Gundam* was one of the first anime to display serious consequences in an animated medium. Yet rather than explain a message, it presents the effects of war, poses questions, and lets you come to your own conclusions. For example, is it ever too late for redemption? What defines terrorism? Is Zeon justified in killing millions if it's for the greater good of humanity? Should children kill one another if the ends justify the means? Are enlightened dictators worth the loss of personal freedom?

The Mobile Suits are not simple tools of destruction, they are extensions of the people who build and use them. This creates a conflict of man-versus-man via machine-versus-machine. The soft humans inside the hard external manifestation of their willpower are the medium through which they express their fear, courage, hope, greed, aspiration, angst, sacrifice, love, and hate. The genetically enhanced Gundam pilots are the superhuman heart beneath the steel.

There is much more that can be said about *Gundam*'s philosophy, social commentary, and even spirituality. Parallels can be drawn between the faith and fear that men have for God, Kami, and Buddha, and the way regular people perceive *Gundam* and their closer-to-god pilots who are representations of the higher spirit within mankind. Likewise, the Zeon Army can be viewed as a fluid and celestial entity, focused on delivering harmony in the heavenly colonies, while the Earth Federation can be viewed as a rigid and grounded entity, focused on the worldly concerns of financial and global stability.

Gundam's influence on Japanese culture is vast. Aside from museums, stamps, and near-constant advertisements throughout society—including in public commuter trains such as Shibuya Station—there are real-world effects. Because *Gundam*'s science is grounded in physics, it inspires scientists and academic leaders. In 2008, the Virtual Gundam Academy was established based on *Gundam*'s principles and ideals, with a mission to bring them to reality. Even the government army loves *Gundam*. In 2007, they built a special infantry suit called the Advanced Combat Information Equipment System (ACIES), referred to as "Gundam" because that is where they hope it will one day lead. They also "seriously discussed" building a real-life Gundam in 2012, and since then, rumors about government projects for Mobile Suits have spread.

As a result of its popularity, *Gundam* inspired other anime series, such as *Macross*, *Evangelion*, *Cowboy Bebop*, and even western films. Director Guillermo del Toro cited it as an influence on his Hollywood blockbuster *Pacific Rim*, with its giant human-powered Gundam-like robots fighting monsters similar to Godzilla.

Even the face of the Gundam is a cultural icon. Each series has its own Gundam, and each of these series has its own theme that addresses particular issues. So, when fans see the face of a Gundam, they connect with its theme, as conveyed through its pilot. It's similar to how the silhouette of Goku or Vegeta's hair in *Dragon Ball* is enough to connect fans to their persona.

Gundam is so popular in Japan that they have a giant life-sized Gundam statue in Tokyo. This started in 2009 to celebrate the franchise's 30th Anniversary. The first Gundam to be placed there was an 18-meter (59 feet) tall animatronic replica of the original RX-78-2 Gundam. It was disassembled in March, 2016, and six months later a new and even taller one had been built of the RX-0 Unicorn Gundam, from the recent *Gundam Unicorn* series, standing at 19.7 meters (64.6 feet) tall.

There are Gundam café's across the country, where food is served related to the series, and hobby model kits can be built as the food is prepared. These kits that fans assemble are a big part of the *Gundam* franchise's success. Gunpla ("Gundam Plastic Model") are so popular that they make up about 90 percent of the entire plastic-model market in Japan, with stores dedicated to selling over 1,000 kits.

Outside of Japan, *Gundam* has done well, but not to the same degree. For example, *Gundam Wing* introduced the *Gundam* franchise to North America in 2000, with great success. The following year, an English dub of the original series was aired to try and capitalize on its popularity. Even though the series was heavily edited, it did well enough to almost reach its conclusion and create a new toy line. Unfortunately, the conclusion was put on hiatus because of the 9/11 attack, and Cartoon Network's decision to pull war-themed content. This killed the momentum of the series and the franchise as a whole. Subsequent attempts to introduce *Gundam* to audiences, even seventeen years afterward, have never been as successful. That said, much of the world has been exposed to *Gundam*, and the people who enjoy it are often passionate fans.

Another reason for its large following is because of its high quality animation and innovative visual techniques, especially during the battles. Likewise, the sound effects, voice acting, and music throughout the *Gundam* franchise are top-class, ranging from symphonic bellicose horns and strings, to electronic, rock, punk, tribal, choral, J-pop, jazz, and ballads. Numerous albums have been released and careers launched as the Gundam fly into battle and their pilots forge deep loves.

Where to start? To experience the full Gundam phenomenon, it's best to start at the beginning of the main story's timeline (called Universal Century), with *Mobile Suit Gundam*. Despite its age, it's worth watching because it provides the emotional context for the rest of the franchise, as each series continues the themes established in the first and adds to them. It also sets up one of the greatest rivalries in anime history, between Amuro and Char. If forty-three episodes seems daunting, then watch the better-paced film trilogy. From there, continue into *Zeta Gundam*, *Gundam ZZ*, the *Char's Counterattack* movie, and so on up to *Gundam Unicorn*.

If this feels like a tall order, then try one of the standalone series that can be watched in any order. For example, the six-episode *08th MS Team* is the most realistic *Gundam* and will give you a good impression of what the franchise has to offer. If you enjoy the premise of this series but feel it's too gritty, then I recommend *Gundam Wing*. If you want something easier to understand and melodramatic, then *Mobile Fighter G Gundam* is a good choice. It takes the idea of supernormal martial artists from movies popular in the '80s, and gives each nation on earth a Gundam piloted by a chosen fighter. It has some quasi-spiritual elements to it that you'll enjoy if you like Kung fu films. And if you want cutting-edge animation and political intrigue, then a more modern series like *Gundam SEED*, *Gundam 00*, *Gundam Thunderbolt*, or *Iron-Blooded Orphans* may interest you. Preferences vary, so beyond this, look for a *Gundam* watching guide online.

Gundam represents an entire genre of anime, so it's a must-watch. Of course, it's a given that *Gundam* will flourish in Japan for decades to come, but how will

Gundam fare in the rest of the world? I think that just as Amuro learned through his battles, Gundam are not owned by any one person or nation. Collectively, we are all Gundam. It's up to you to decide its fate.

Suit up!

Derek Padula is the world's foremost professional Dragon Ball *scholar. He illuminates the real-world historical, spiritual, and philosophical culture of* Dragon Ball *to enable readers to better understand the series and empower themselves on their own life journeys. His books include the seven-volume* Dragon Ball Culture *series,* Dragon Soul: 30 Years of Dragon Ball Fandom, *and* Dragon Ball Z "It's Over 9,000!" When Worldviews Collide. *You can find him at* thedaoofdragonball.com

---

1983 • BAREFOOT GEN

HADASHI NO GEN

— CHRIS STUCKMANN —

***Note: This article discusses the gruesome depiction of the bombing of Hiroshima as seen in* Barefoot Gen.**

Barefoot Gen was a title I'd heard of for something like fifteen years. Whispers in the corner of the comics store, fleeting mentions on those early message boards, and before long, I received a copy of it in my PO Box from a generous viewer (thank you!). Clearly, the film had made an impression. Sitting down to watch it, I had a snack and a drink, and had no idea what I was getting into. It didn't take long for the nausea to settle in. To say that *Barefoot Gen* floored me would be a legitimate understatement. This film scarred me. I've seen a lot of disturbing things in movies, but nothing quite like this. This is partially because I decided to watch the film blind, having no preconceived knowledge of the plot.

We follow young Gen, an optimistic boy living in Hiroshima, Japan in 1945. He lives in a small house with his brother, sister, and parents. Money isn't just tight, it's virtually nonexistent. The ongoing war has taken food and workers from the city, and left those remaining families on the cusp of starvation. Gen's mother is pregnant and very weak, as she requires energy for not just herself, but the child she's carrying. Gen and his brother often spend their days scavenging around the neighborhood for food, working with their father in the fields, and roughhousing like all kids do. Being awoken in the middle of the night by sirens is so common that Gen and his brother feel comfortable making jokes about it. "It's probably just another spy plane," Gen often says, dismissing the warnings.

From what we see in the first half of *Barefoot Gen*, it's clear that Gen and his brother are relentless in their pursuit to help their family. In one touching scene, a neighbor suggests that carp is the best kind of fish for their mother's health. As a result of this advice, the boys sneak into a wealthy man's garden and swipe a carp from his small pool. When they're caught by the man, they stand up to him, saying that he can hit them as many times as he wants, if they can just keep the fish for their mother. It's early scenes like this that make Gen's unrelenting spirit and idealistic confidence work later on. His passion for protecting his family is apparent, and it's one of the most beautiful aspects of the film.

Before long, the day comes. August 6, 1945.

I had become so attached to this loving family and their struggle for survival that I was dreading the inevitable. I've seen many films about nuclear war. The horror of it, the pain, the loss. But truthfully, I've never seen it depicted this explicitly. In one devastating sequence, *Barefoot Gen* goes from what appears to be a G-rated family film, to a hard R, possibly even NC-17. Before the violence though, it's the serenity, the silence of Hiroshima that's captured so heartbreakingly. Everyone in the town is going about their business. Children are in school, men and women are working in the fields. And then, one lone plane flies over the town and unleashes hellfire in the form of a single bomb and obliterates everything they ever knew. A young girl lets out a shrill cry, her balloon she's holding explodes, and we watch in sheer horror as her eyeballs melt in her sockets, her body slowly turning to ash. A dog writhes in pain as it implodes, a mother kneels to shield her baby from the blast, their bodies fusing together like a grotesque wax sculpture. Gen had bent over to pick something up, partially obscuring his body from the blast. He stands up, and looks for his friend he was just talking to, a young girl who now lies in a crumpled pile, her body shredded and burned. In one instant, Gen's entire life is altered for the worst. Suddenly, all that matters is his family. There is nothing else anymore.

The remainder of the film doesn't shy away from the after-effects of the bomb's devastation. People emerge from the smoke, stumbling forth like zombies, their skin melted and scarred. Women suffering from malnutrition no longer have breastmilk for their young. There's no attempt to censor the disturbing nature of this tragedy. Men, women, children, and yes, even infants were wiped out instantly. But the filmmakers knew that wasn't the extent of what the bomb did to Hiroshima. The aftermath of the explosion caused years of sickness and death, and this is all detailed with terrifying scrutiny. I've seen Isao Takahata's disturbing and powerful *Grave of the Fireflies*—another anime about the pain of war, and perhaps a better film—but I simply wasn't prepared for this movie. I had to pause the Blu-ray a few times to take a breath. "Holy shit," I declared aloud to no one. It's not an easy watch, in fact, I'm sure many will skip this recommendation in favor of something more uplifting. I wouldn't blame you.

As of this writing, we live in a climate that hasn't been this aware of nuclear threat since the days of the Cold War. Our conversation about it is sometimes mistakenly humorous. I'm reminded of Gen's initial dismissal upon hearing the air raid sirens. "It's probably just another spy plane." I encourage everyone reading this to watch this film. It's been released on Blu-ray for the first time, and it's more readily available than ever. Mori Masaki's film pulls no punches with its anti-war message, and that message has never been more timely.

1984 • BIRTH

BĀSU

— BRIAN RUH —

Animation has been described by the director Charlie Kauffman as "a series of still images put together to create the illusion of movement." Although this is a rather simple way of putting it, sometimes it's a good thing to keep the basics in mind when approaching an animated work. Every image, every angle was put there by a person working within a complex division of labor in order to generate the finished product flashing by on our screens.

In the best animated films, the story, narrative, and visuals come together in order to create a work that is not only visually sophisticated, but gains more depth upon repeated viewings and reflection upon its themes. However, sometimes a piece of animation is most notable for the animation itself. Such is the case with *Birth*, an OVA (Original Video Animation) from 1984 that is a standout when it comes to the craft of animation, but unfortunately falls short in the storytelling department.

There's certainly something to be said for a work that imparts the kind of visceral thrill that *Birth* does, even though it's far from the slickest or most meaningful production. However, it's a film in which you can really sense the skill of the animators. Although it was directed by Shinya Sadamitsu, this really feels like Yoshinori Kanada's film, as he was the animation director and character designer. Kanada's dynamic style would go on to inspire and influence a generation of animators, as well as artist Takeshi Murakami. Other key collaborators on *Birth* include animators Hideaki Anno (future director of *Neon Genesis Evangelion*) and Mahiro Maeda (future director of *Blue Submarine No. 6*, on which Kanada would serve as a key animator). It also features a great 1980s synth soundtrack from frequent Hayao Miyazaki collaborator Joe Hisaishi.

In its pre-title sequence, *Birth* begins on a rocky, alien world, focusing on a small blob-like creature fleeing from a larger example of the native fauna. It then takes refuge atop a spacesuit-clad girl on a hover scooter, who's later chased by a large black sphere. Unfortunately, such descriptions do not do justice to these scenes, which convey weight and movement so impressively. The camera makes full use of the variable terrain, in constant movement and motion through the chase scenes. Such animation is made all the more remarkable when one remembers that such scenes are rendered by hand, with none of the CG work that would be used if one were trying to replicate something similar these days. It's a fantastic use of perspective and flow that really showcases the kind of work possible in the medium of animation.

From this initial introduction to the central world of *Birth*, we then venture into space where we're introduced to Bao and Kim, who are in their run-down ship, chasing a mysterious glowing sword called Shade that they think will garner them a lot of money. Back on the planet, the girl we saw earlier, Rasa, is out from her village riding her floater bike (a kind of hovering scooter) to bring her brother Nam his breakfast because he'd forgotten it that morning. Nam sees the Shade sword land on their planet, but when he goes to investigate he sees a beautiful, ghostly woman called Arlia who introduces herself and promptly vanishes. A sphere that looks like the one he'd been chasing shows up and hatches an inorganic creature, who begins trying to fight Nam. Rasa is chased by a gang of inorganic bikers, meets up with Nam along the way, and is saved at the last minute by the arrival of Bao and his ship. Arlia appears again and explains that the universe is a life form, and that there is a battle between organics and inorganics for its fate. The Shade sword contains a great amount of life energy and consciousness, and it's a tool created by the universe for destroying the inorganics. After this revelation, she disappears again and another inorganic begins chasing them, calling out names of fruits and vegetables with each attack. They decide to flee to an old underground city that was destroyed in a nuclear strike, where Bao looks for the ultimate weapon against the inorganics.

As one might be able to tell from this description, the story of *Birth* doesn't really hold together, and has little internal logic. Why would the universe impart consciousness into something like a sword? What is supposed to be done with it?

And once it's been acquired, why would our protagonists need to go on another quest for a different weapon, which is so dangerous they shouldn't try to use it anyway?

Additionally, the overall conflict between organic and inorganic strikes an odd tone. At the point when the film says the inorganics need to be destroyed, they haven't been shown to be anything more than an annoyance and certainly not anything that a universal consciousness would concern itself with. Perhaps even more disturbing, in one early oddly-placed scene, we are shown the melancholy of a young inorganic after Rasa spurns his childish advances. The inorganics aren't shown as enemies of organic life as much as annoyances, and in fact have rich inner lives. This isn't to say the film necessarily needed to resolve the conflict between the two types of life as much as it needed to explain its setup, other than as a bare hanger upon which to hang a stylishly extravagant suit of animation.

In the end, while some individual scenes are well-constructed and display a fantastic use of fluid movement throughout, the film as a whole doesn't really hold together. There are sometimes baffling transitions from one scene to the next because it can't seem to settle on a single storyline to pursue. The loose plot only serves as justification for the fantastic scenes of running, flying, and exploding. However, I would argue that there is not necessarily anything wrong with that. Disdain for the conventions of narrative and storytelling in *Birth* (whether intentional or not) result in a finished work that communicates a sense of freedom through its expressive animation.

Brian Ruh is an independent scholar with a PhD in Communication and Culture from Indiana University. He is the author of Stray Dog of Anime: The Films of Mamoru Oshii.

1984 • SUPER DIMENSION FORTRESS MACROSS: DO YOU REMEMBER LOVE?

CHÔJIKÛ YÔSAI MACROSS: AI OBOETEIMASUKA

— JOHN RODRIGUEZ —

Do you remember your first crush? I do, and her name was Lin Minmei.

Wait, no: it was Lisa Hayes.

Wait … oh, darn it, I *can't decide*! Love is *hard*!

Well, sure it is. Everything requiring maturity is hard for a ten-year-old boy. But waking up at 4:30 a.m. on a school day to catch the latest syndicated episode of *Robotech* … *that* was a piece of cake. I remember those mornings: the sky still dark, the blankets warm, the reception terrible. Not so terrible, though, to block out *her*. Lin. I mean, Lisa. I mean…

Okay, I don't know *what* I mean, because I didn't know what I wanted. Perky or poised? Flashy or formal? Dainty or determined? That was the ying and the yang of *Robotech*'s Lin Minmei and Lisa Hayes, the impossible choice foisted upon dashing mecha pilot Rick Hunter and far less dashing ten-year-old me.

It was confusing as hell. But it wasn't half as confusing as *Robotech*'s convoluted lineage.

One of the pioneers of anime on American television, *Robotech* represented the Frankenstein-esque stitching together of three different mecha anime series.

The first of these series was titled *Super Dimension Fortress Macross*. *Macross* formed the foundation of *Robotech*'s tale of intergalactic war between earth and the invading Zentradi. It also established the now-famous love triangle between ace pilot Rick, pop diva Lin, and stern officer Lisa. Future seasons would completely change the cast—*Robotech* was a mish-mash of different shows, remember—but it's Lin and Lisa who've kept *Robotech* alive in my heart all these years.

But what about *Macross*, the show that birthed these memorable characters? I'm happy to report that it's alive and well. *Macross* has thrived across an array of different media, including video games, print, TV, and film. And it's the very first *Macross* film—*Do You Remember Love?*—that we'll be discussing here.

Do You Remember Love? is a reimagining of the events depicted in the original *Macross* series, yet it features all the familiar characters. There's pop diva Lynn Minmay, stern officer Misa Hayase, and of course ace pilot Hikaru Ichijyo ... hmm, something's off here. Oh, that's right: *Robotech* changed all these characters' names to better suit its American audience! Phooey, westernization!

Anyway, the core story currents of *Macross* remain intact in *Do You Remember Love?* Humanity's remnants are still on the run from alien invaders, and their base of operations is still the SDF-1, a flying fortress that's part battleship, part spacefaring city. The aliens themselves are slightly altered. There's still the Zentradi, an all-male race of giant bionoids. And like in *Robotech*, there's a counterpart race of all-female giants. Here, those women are given a name ("Meltlandi") and a backstory of strife with their estranged Zentradi kin.

Signature elements of *Macross* carry over, too. And, oh, how cool they are! Thrilling space combat! Transformable mecha! Swarms of weaving missiles that leave totally unrealistic yet utterly awesome smoke trails in their wake! This is the kind of stuff that makes ten-year-olds stand up and take notice!

Of course, mecha and missiles aren't all that ten-year-olds are apt to notice. For myself, that's about the time girls started appearing on the radar. And as it happens, *Macross* featured two of the more memorable female characters in anime history: Lynn Minmay and Misa Hayase. Both were clever. Both were courageous. And both became heartthrobs for a generation of American youths.

In some ways, the Lynn/Misa choice was like a litmus test. Did you fancy girly girls? Congratulations: You were a Minmay man! Or did you value composure and forthrightness? Well then, you were Team Hayase.

But it's safe to say that ten-year-old me wasn't digging for nuance. Ten-year-old me was too busy learning to crush. Well, maybe not just to crush—maybe learning to refine my understanding of what constitutes attractiveness, too. Lynn was lovely, of course. She was the belle of the ball and the obvious choice to dote upon. But if Lynn was beauty, then Misa was grace. She was firm. She was decisive. She carried herself with dignified bearing, and she harbored a strength that I longed to rise up and meet. Even at ten, Lynn felt like a caricature of what a woman was supposed to be. Misa, by contrast, felt like an honest-to-God person, someone I could admire and look up to.

I will never forget the epic space battles that vaulted *Macross* into the public consciousness. *Do You Remember Love?* features a couple of those, and damn if they aren't as pulse-pounding now as they were back in those early-morning *Robotech* days. They're certainly more than enough to make me forgive the film's cheeseball conclusion, where Lynn Minmay saves humanity by performing a 20,000-year-old pop tune on a shielded spaceward-facing stage while lasers and missiles whiz about her.

But it's love, not mecha or missiles, that will forever define this film for me. I think that's one of the greatest magics of art: its ability to shape a person's definition of love for a lifetime. We need those shapers in our lives. Especially when our parents—those best positioned to impart these definitions to us—are too often terrified to broach the subject.

So thank you, *Macross*, for stepping into the breach. You made me thrill to the clash of mecha versus mecha, made me cling to the edge of my seat as missiles swarmed and battleships burst asunder. But most importantly, you helped me form a definition that I still reference today. Do I remember you, *Love*? You're damn right I do.

John Rodriguez is a personal trainer whose devotion to physical fitness is exceeded only by his fervor for all things film and literature. John is currently finishing his first novel—a fantasy that's sparked fantasies of a challenging new career.

1985 • ANGEL'S EGG

TENSHI NO TAMAGO

— CHRIS STUCKMANN —

Angel's Egg reminds me of a film I would've scrolled passed on the Sci-Fi channel back in the '90s at 3:00 a.m. It feels like a drug-induced trip of psychedelic imagery while also being relentlessly meaningful. The deceptively simple story is as follows: A young girl roams a wasteland that resembles post-apocalyptic Earth. She carries with her an egg that we learn she's very protective of. She meets a man who joins her on this journey, who may be friend or foe. This plot is decidedly free of conventional drama, character troupes, or really anything we've come to expect from traditional filmmaking, let alone anime.

Some have attempted to analyze *Angel's Egg* in the past, I'm certainly not the first to do so. But there is an unfortunate lack of information about this film on the net, which is at once surprising yet also expected. I think this film is just as good as Mamoru Oshii's more well-known *Ghost in the Shell*, but I also recognize that a film this different—that barely contains any concrete answers to its philosophical questions—will likely divide audiences. Even Oshii himself was quoted as saying he "doesn't know what the film is about." It's wholly possible that *Angel's Egg* is meant to be taken purely as an art film, with no concrete interpretation actually being correct. But I have one very specific thing that I've gleaned from the film I'd like to discuss.

Faith.

While doing research on the making of *Angel's Egg*, I learned that Oshii dedicated much of his life to studying religion, specifically Christianity. He originally considered attending a seminary before he turned to directing. The large majority of his films all contain heavy religious themes. *Patlabor: The Movie* features an investigation surrounding a culprit who uses biblical phrases and passages as clues to his crimes. The Puppet Master in *Ghost in the Shell* often quotes scripture. But, for unknown reasons, he apparently had a falling out with his faith before production on this film began. Armed with this information, *Angel's Egg* took on a whole new meaning for me.

Let's break the film down piece by piece. It's important to remember that the heavy Christian symbolism is extremely important to deciphering where Oshii's head was at while he made this film. Even if there isn't a definitive answer, the film has become clearer to me when analyzed from the perspective that Oshii was dealing with a major crisis of faith while making this film.

I believe the young man in this film represents Christ, and the giant orb that shows up is likely God or the eye of God. The man carries a large device on his shoulder that's easily recognizable as the shape of a cross, and if that's not enough of a hint, his hands are bandaged in the same place Christ was likely crucified.

The young girl and her egg seem to be a metaphor for the innocence of blind faith. In one very telling scene, she says she's positive she can hear a bird inside the egg breathing, even when the man suggests that what she's hearing is just the wind. Nothing can convince her otherwise. To her, that bird is in the egg, and it will hatch. It seems that this is Oshii's commentary on religion and faith in general. The idea that belief in a higher power—despite having no tangible proof that it exists—is based entirely on faith, no matter what anyone else may tell you. The girl is very protective of her egg, as are people of their beliefs. Early on in the film, the man has an opportunity to break the egg, but instead, gives it back, stating that she should keep things precious inside her.

But later, the man breaks the egg while she sleeps. So if he planned to break the egg the whole time, why didn't he just do it then? There are many examples of God giving various assignments or tests to his servants. God allowing Satan to afflict Job, Abraham being instructed to kill his own son, or even Jesus fasting for forty days. In all cases, after being proved worthy of the test, the individual was greatly rewarded for their steadfastness.

In this case, the girl's faith is being tested. She wanders this world, collecting water, unsure of why she's doing it, unsure of the passage of time, protecting an egg that she fiercely believes will hatch. The man encourages opening the egg, and yet she still refuses. He finally suggests to her that her faith is false, that she's simply hearing what she wants to hear. When she still denies this, he breaks the egg himself.

She flees after him in horror, falling into a ravine, figuratively maturing into a woman, having been broken, her innocence and blind faith violated. She then seemingly gives birth to many more eggs, perhaps reaping her reward for maintaining faith. These eggs grow into birds, affirming her beliefs, and she's eventually memorialized on the godlike orb, having become saint-like.

There's another theory I have about these characters, one that I haven't seen discussed anywhere to my knowledge. It's possible that Oshii is exploring the belief of reincarnation, that of one's soul coming back to life after death in another person or form. There are many hints to this possibility present in the film, and one that was staring me right in the face. Both the girl and man seem to have lost memories, gaps in their subconscious. The man sees a drawing of a large tree and reflects on a vague memory of having seen it before. In what little dialogue the film has, both characters discuss the feeling of having forgotten something about themselves, as if they're both suffering from a monumental case of déjà vu. These are common traits of people who believe they've been reincarnated. Vague memories of a distant life often plague these individuals. The biggest clue, though, can be found on the film's official soundtrack, under track number thirteen. This track is the music featured in the scene where the girl dies, giving birth to many eggs, which eventually become birds. The track name, when translated into English, is literally "Transmigration." Which, if you know your theology, is simply another term for reincarnation.

So, if the reincarnation angle is correct, are we looking at a reincarnated form of Christ in the young man? He seems to have a vague memory of the Tree of Life, and when he sees the fossil of the giant bird, he undergoes some form of awakening, as if his mission has become clear, or he remembers what he must do. In the Bible, Jesus underwent a similar rebirth upon his baptism, realizing his mission on earth. Matthew 3:16 speaks of the heavens opening up to Jesus upon being baptized in water as if all had become clear to him. I don't think it's a coincidence that it's after the man steps into the water, becoming soaked by it, that he appears to come to a realization. It's after this that the man destroys her egg, as if he was recalling some assignment he was once given but had forgotten about. Was this his directive? In the start of the film, as he awaited the godlike eye, while standing on a chessboard of sorts, was he sent to meet this girl, to reaffirm her faith, and his? Is he simply a pawn of his god, as indicated by the checkered board he stands on?

This is where things split in two for me. There are two ways you can view this. The positive view is that the girl kept her faith, despite the continual testing of it. Then, the Christlike man releases her from her test, and she reaps a hundred fold what she had before, in the process realizing that her faith was true, since the birds she envisioned grow from her eggs. Eventually, she's memorialized in the godlike structure as someone to be praised or honored.

The negative view is that despite trusting in her faith and going about her tasks without question, her beliefs were betrayed nonetheless, and she's left to die after her spiritual violation. The reason that I don't give as much weight to this more cynical viewpoint is due to the ending. Despite how much of this film is left ambiguous, one thing that seems clear to me is that she is now in a position of honor.

I believe the message that Oshii is sending is simply how unclear and divisive faith can be. In his case, he seems to have dealt with considerable doubt in his beliefs and has made a gorgeous film that examines what one goes through when dealing with a crisis of faith. Just as the girl continuously asks the man who he is, it seems Oshii yearns to understand his faith, until finally, the man asks the girl the same question. Oshii is perhaps hinting that faith is simply a process of discovering who we are, what we are, and who or what we can become.

I think *Angel's Egg* is an undisputed masterpiece. There's not a single film like it in live-action, and certainly not in animation. It's a film so ambitious and unconventional that nearly any interpretation can be considered correct. There's really no right or wrong answers here. Oshii has clearly made a film steeped in heavy themes and imagery that's meant to impact everyone differently. What do you see in *Angel's Egg*?

This writing is condensed from Chris Stuckmann's video "Is Angel's Egg *an Overlooked Masterpiece?" which can be found on his YouTube channel.*

1985 • NIGHT ON THE GALACTIC RAILROAD

GINGA TETSUDŌ NO YORU

— CHRIS STUCKMANN —

A shy young cat named Giovanni awkwardly attempts to answer a question in class, much to the delight of the school bullies. The teacher is quizzing the students on the Milky Way galaxy and asks what *exactly* it is. Standing there, feeling as blue as his fur, Giovanni is unable to respond. His ignorant classmates mock and ridicule him, assuming his inability to answer reflects a lack of simple knowledge.

But no. Giovanni knows the Milky Way galaxy is made up of stars, planets, and other celestial beauties. But ... what *is* it? Amongst the astronomical wonder of space, is there ... more?

Giovanni's silence doesn't indicate any educational deficiency on his part. It does, however, speak to his reflective nature. For his classmates, the solution to the teacher's question is a piece of cake. For Giovanni, life isn't that black and white. When he gazes at the stars, endless possibilities float through his imaginative mind. This can't be explained in a straightforward manner and thus, he's bewildered by the teacher's question.

This is our hero. An introverted blue cat who puzzles over the meaning of existence. Indeed, *Night on the Galactic Railroad* is a very special film.

The story is told through a series of vignettes. Title cards appear before every major scene, splitting Giovanni's journey into a string of segments meant to convey a valuable point. Early scenes focus on Giovanni's school, the print shop that employs him, and his home environment. But as the film travels down the rickety track known as life, the story alters, inch by inch, and eventually reveals itself to be far more profound than originally suspected.

It's all the more impressive that *Night on the Galactic Railroad* avoids traversing many years of Giovanni's life. On the contrary, just as the title suggests, we experience one mesmerizing night from his perspective. But what a night it is!

A local festival is happening in Giovanni's village: The Festival of Stars. Cats young and old alike gather in the center of the town to honor this annual event. Unfortunately, Giovanni has responsibilities to care for, namely, his sick mother, and is frantically scrambling to get her some milk. This brings about more jeering from the school bullies, in particular, Zanelli, an oblivious cat who pokes fun at the disappearance of Giovanni's father. After a verbal beating from Zanelli, Giovanni flees the festival, heading toward the peak of a large hill.

He lays in the grass, staring at the vast space above him. He's at a loss for words, absorbing the grand beauty, in awe that every ball of light is a gigantic star, once again displaying his meditative nature. You can imagine his astonishment when a locomotive appears from nowhere, nearly running him down. After the shock dissipates, Giovanni boards the train without a single question.

From here on out, things get trippy. Giovanni realizes he's on board with one of his respectable classmates, Campanella, a lithe, pink cat who treats Giovanni with dignity. As they depart, they discover this is no ordinary train, and the two embark on a philosophical adventure with crushing implications for both of them.

And they're cats! Cats! God, I love anime.

Night on the Galactic Railroad is adapted from Kenji Miyazawa's classic novel, published after his death in 1934. Director Gisaburo Sugii remained mostly true to Miyazawa's vision, specifically the subtext surrounding the afterlife, and coming to terms with death, especially that of a loved one. Still, one major change was made, angering some. Miyazawa's original novel featured human characters, whereas Sugii's film turns them into cats. This is a dangerous risk, as some have seen this as an unnecessary alteration, infantilizing the otherwise intelligent material. This is understandable, but I don't think it ruins anything. Believe it or not, I'll go out on a limb and say it improves the proceedings.

Genuine surprise is a stimulant for cinema lovers. At this point in film's history, it feels like we've seen everything. This is why I'm so captivated by Japanese animation. In America, animations with cats are limited to juvenile time-wasters like *Cats & Dogs* or *The Secret Life of Pets*. But in 1985, some brave filmmakers got together and made a movie about two cats musing on the harsh realities of life while aboard a metaphysical train that roams the elusive *other side*.

Can you imagine what goes through a child's mind while watching this?

Aw, the little kitty goes to school! Oh, that's too bad, he gets bullied. Look, Dad, he's got a job! I hope he gets that milk! Wait … where'd that train come from? Huh? Is he talking with dead people? Are they gonna be okay? [cries uncontrollably]

Purists were irritated with the change from human to animal, but if the end result is a greater young audience, I'm more than fine with it. *Night on the Galactic Railroad* is the kind of mind-bending, kaleidoscopic journey into the subconscious that can truly transform you. But the journey isn't a simple one. Just as Giovanni couldn't perfectly respond to his teacher's question, there are moments difficult to fully decipher. But these sequences only serve to impart the understanding that life itself is just as confusing. The answers aren't always easy, and sometimes, you just don't have any.

Giovanni's dreamlike ride on the Galactic Railroad teaches him an abundance of life lessons, and when he reaches his destination, his outlook is one of optimism. If your child is ready for it, a viewing of this mature animation may spark a lively discussion about the intricacies of life and death.

1985 • ROBOTECH

— JEFFERY J. TIMBRELL —

Robotech deeply traumatized me as a child.

I remember being an innocent young boy in the '80s. I listened to Duran-Duran. I bought the *Thriller* album. I watched *Spider-Man and his Amazing Friends*. And all those days of innocence were washed away in a sudden blast of anime death when the Zentradi bombed the earth in an episode of *Robotech*.

There's a moment in the episode that I remember vividly where a tiny child with a panda balloon clings to a soldier just a second before the city they're standing in is bombed into so much glass.

By modern standards this is nothing. Kids nowadays have *Game of Thrones* and *The Walking Dead*. I'm pretty sure they could sit through footage of a slaughterhouse while eating popcorn and telling fart jokes. But you gotta understand you badass young folks, in my time we didn't have Jeffrey Dean Morgan caving people's heads in with a baseball bat on prime-time television. Or any-time television. Or in most films. Or in any films! In my time you rarely got to see people die in cartoons. It was a joke that used to go around the playground that Cobra and G.I. Joe intentionally missed each other with their laser rifles. When Optimus Prime died in the *Transformers* animated film it was traumatizing. Actually, no, scratch-that, it was traumatizing to see Prowl coughing up orange engine foam after getting his chest blown out in the *Transformers* movie. It was traumatizing hearing Bumblebee swear as Unicron ate a moon. Seeing Optimus Prime die was like the kid cultural equivalent of the opening scene of *Saving Private Ryan*. I can remember children stumbling out of the theater in shell-shock looking like they had been at the epicenter of a bomb. Most of my generation still gets the shakes even hearing the words "*Transformers: The Movie*" (and with the way the live-action films have been written, I imagine that's one thing our generations will have in common).

But compared to *Robotech*, the *Transformers* movie was *My Little Pony*. Seeing robots die in a cartoon was bad. Seeing kids die in a cartoon in the 1980s? *Kids*? Blown to hell by an all-out alien assault? Oh no, sir. That did not happen on the regular.

But at that point there was no turning back for me. I was already a deep *Robotech* fanatic. Are you kidding? Lisa Hayes was my first animated crush and Rick Hunter was … Rick Hunter. And who had a cooler airplane than Roy Fokker? Nobody. Ever. *Robotech* was already the bad boy. The rebel. The hard-ass who just didn't care of the Saturday morning cartoon crew. This devastating bit of television history was just them cementing their reputation. My older brother who was much cooler than me (despite also listening to Duran-Duran) loved *Robotech*. He wouldn't watch any other cartoon with me, but he sat down and watched every episode of *Robotech*.

Because *Robotech* was cool.

And it legitimately gave me nightmares.

No hyperbole. No joke.

You see, during the '80s, our culture had this little thing going on called the Cold War. It's hard to describe to people who never went through it, but I had an all-consuming fear that a nuclear war was going to happen between Russia and the United States. It seemed like it was all over the news, and the apocalyptic fall out of this inevitable war was talked about on television with the same kind of glib candor that modern day newscasters use to talk about Kanye West. You would see experts on television discussing with a smile about the effects of radiation and how, if the war happened, the chances of most people surviving was less than zero. If the blasts didn't kill us, the clouds of cancer would do the trick.

Or the entire devastation of our infrastructure.

Or the mutants.

Or the roaming gangs of Australian punk rockers.

Take your pick.

Now, it's one thing listening to that stuff as an adult and facing the potential end of the world. When you face it as a kid, it's some deeply horrible nightmare-fuel. You're powerless enough as a child that facing things like school bullies and divorce can feel like a towering monolithic challenge. But facing the realities of nuclear war at that age, with my imagination? Oh no, sir. No thank you, very much.

So Robotech took those very real, very big fears I had and made them the plot of a giant robot space opera.

And it blew my freaking mind.

For my money, there is no cartoon, no ... television show (*Stranger Things* included) that ever has or ever will better address what it felt like to be an actual kid in the 1980s than *Robotech*.

Everything in *Robotech* from the fashion and the hair styles to the pop music set against a futuristic science fiction story where fighter planes turn into flying robots. Every inch of it felt like it was honey-dipped in the cultural zeitgeist of the '80s. It was *Top Gun*, it was *Star Wars*, it was arcades and video games, it was space opera and rock opera, and big hair and bigger weapons, and pop music versus aliens! All of these elements were orbiting this epic conflict between the forces of earth and the invading Zentradi.

And at the very core of it all, there was hope. Always hope.

Oh yeah, *Robotech* has dark moments and it can get down and dirty, but the overall themes and message in the show are ones of community and friendship. It's not like *Rambo*, where the hero always wins no matter what. It's about the realities of war. It's about finding a way to survive day by day in an uncertain world. It's about facing failure and death and growing from it. Finding victories in even the worst kinds of defeat. Where even in the bleakest of situations where oxygen is running low, where heroes are trapped in enemy prisons, there's still honesty and strength and kindness.

There's still humanity.

In fact, the ultimate weapon in *Robotech* is art. While the aliens have advanced technology and overwhelming numbers, they're weak against our culture. They encounter our food and our relationships, our clothes and our music, and soon enough, they don't just like it, they fall in love with it. So much so that, what were once our enemies turn into our allies. And our friends. And even lovers.

Here is a show about apocalyptic battles that destroy worlds, whose message is what can bring an end to these conflicts isn't some ultimate gun or giant laser beam, but art, music, friendship, community. That no matter what, we can survive, we can move on. And we will. Together. For me, as a kid, that was the message I needed to hear to deal with all the fear and insecurity of that age.

I found out much later that *Robotech* was actually three shows from Japan (*Super Dimension Fortress Macross*, *Super Dimension Cavalry Southern Cross*, and *Genesis Climber Mospeada*). That made sense to me. Both in the huge dips in storytelling from the *Macross* era to *Southern Cross* eras of the show, and in the overall themes.

After all, Japan is a country that had gone through a nuclear apocalypse. They knew what it meant to rebuild, to find hope and community and to survive in the face of that overwhelming disaster. While *Robotech* was adapted for North America, and some would say butchered, I think the big ideas, the big themes, the big messages in the story, were universal. And while I can't speak for anybody else, they made an impact on at least one little Canadian kid who was scared and confused in the 1980s.

Jeffery J. Timbrell is a writer, filmmaker, artist, and photographer with giant space worms in his brain. He lives in Canada with his two cats, a basement full of DVDs and a ton of regrets.

1985 • VAMPIRE HUNTER D

BANPAIA HANTĀ DĪ

— JOHN RODRIGUEZ —

As a trainer, I'm always looking for ways to engage with clients. Sports tends to be a go-to staple. The average Joe digs sports, and my job is to relate. So I make sure to remain conversant with the latest sporting world happenings. Now, sometimes that's easy. I'm genuinely passionate about baseball anyway, and I really dig hockey. Other times, it's a drag. I can really take or leave football. And basketball? Bleh.

But my preferences don't matter. My clients' preferences matter, and there's all kinds. Most folks like talking about the big team sports, of course, but there's also devotees to cycling, track, or competitive weightlifting. I even had a Canadian client who adored curling. What's that all a-boot?

Not a single client wants to talk about boxing, however. And I never bring up boxing to clients. Which is odd, because let me let you in on my dirty little secret: I *love* boxing. Not just the big fights, mind you, but also the dinky little bouts hosted on Tuesday nights in Podunk, Iowa.

"Ugh," you say. "Boxing is barbaric." Totally, and my inclination toward it shames me. Over and over, I admonish myself for engaging with a sport that can leave its practitioners crippled by the effects of repetitive head trauma. I remind myself I should be sophisticated enough to turn up my nose at such wanton savagery, sanctioned or not.

And yet ... I still love boxing. Something about it keeps bringing me back despite my misgivings. Maybe it's my admiration for the rigorous discipline displayed by the men and women who partake in the sport's highest levels. Or maybe it's something less quantifiable and more primal: a vestigial impulse to tear off my shirt, beat my chest, and howl at the moon.

Whatever it is, I know better than to share this passion. This is the Era of Enlightenment, and boxing is so *très pas cool*. It's a guilty pleasure at best, an object of ridicule and scorn at worst. But damn if there's isn't something gripping about the sport all the same.

Vampire Hunter D is the boxing of the anime world. It's brutal. It's bloody. It's unsophisticated in the extreme. In short: it's a throwback, and not necessarily a welcome one. Rather, it's a reminder of a time when Arnold Schwarzenegger could get away with flinging Rae Dawn Chong over his shoulder while he mowed down seemingly half of Latin America with his M78. And that's not going to fly for a lot of folks today. This is 2018, damn it, and we're supposed to be woke! Yet *Vampire Hunter D* remains less woke than a narcoleptic on Ambien.

Take D, for instance. The film's bad boy protagonist, D is everything heroes of 2018 aren't supposed to be. He's all strong, silent swagger, and his answer to virtually every conflict is to whip out his ... wait for it ... *longsword* and set to hacking. No articulate empathizer here. No, sir. D is a one-man army of stabby-stabby. D is a manly man's hero. He'll crush your spine or drive a sword through your spleen, but don't be looking for him to express his insecurities.

Then there's Doris Lang, *Vampire Hunter D*'s resident heroine/damsel in distress. Right from the get-go, we watch Doris from an up-skirt perspective as she stalks down the road on a midnight werewolf hunt. Now, to be fair, it would be hard to view Doris from any other perspective, given that her skirt isn't long enough to cover her undergarments. I'd chalk this up to a sweltering sub-Saharan setting, but D goes about in a full cape and cloak. Maybe Doris has issues with underperforming sweat glands that leave her overheated? Or maybe *Vampire Hunter D* is more interested in the letters "T" and "A" than in any realistic portrayal of feminine dress.

There's more, of course. I haven't even started on the mayor's son, Greco Rohman (seriously!), that charming chap who tries to blackmail Doris after she gets bitten by the vampire Count Magnus Lee. Oh, and *then* announces to the world that

Doris got bitten when Doris won't accede to his sexual demands, thus ruining her reputation with the townsfolk.

Yet before you strike *Vampire Hunter D* from your to-watch list, consider that this film, like boxing, has persevered over the years in the hearts of its not-insignificant fanbase. There must be a reason for that, right? And there is. Because, for all its inability to measure up to 2018 standards of what constitutes acceptable storytelling, *Vampire Hunter D* is wildly inventive. Its far-flung futuristic world is one of mechanical horses, space-warping mutants, and bloody mists that can strip the skin from your bones. And, oh, the wondrous creatures! There's more biological creativity on display in just the scene where D first enters Count Lee's castle than there is in most Hollywood blockbusters!

Vampire Hunter D even manages to be narratively adventurous in a way that few blockbusters would ever dare. It goes to great lengths to humanize Count Lee's daughter, Larmica, despite the fact that she's an unambiguous villain and racist. It even ennobles Larmica by the story's end. And, let me tell you, making a self-righteous fascist seem noble is no mean trick.

But really, what *Vampire Hunter D* does best is tap into that river of machismo that soaked us in the '80s. Here is an anime that invites you to take pleasure in your primal impulses. "Why should I judge you?" it growls in your ear. "I come from the age of *Commando* and *First Blood Part II*. So my protagonist isn't a feeler. John Matrix wasn't a feeler. John Rambo wasn't a feeler. You still love them, don't you?"

And I do. God help me, but I still do. Matrix, Rambo, and yes, even D. I love them all.

Look, I could try selling you on the notion that *Vampire Hunter D* is of an artistic par with many of the anime described in this book, but I won't. It's a throwback, a luddite cloaked in gothic sci-fi garb. Yet don't write it off. Because, while it's certainly not woke, it's inventive enough to worm its way into your mind and primal enough to strong-arm its way into your heart, if only you give it the chance. And if watching it inspires you to tear off your shirt, beat your chest, and howl at the moon? Don't worry: it probably just means you're a werewolf.

John Rodriguez is a personal trainer whose devotion to physical fitness is exceeded only by his fervor for all things film and literature. John is currently finishing his first novel—a fantasy that's sparked fantasies of a challenging new career.

1985 • GOSHOGUN: THE TIME ÉTRANGER

SENGOKU MAJIN GOSHŌGUN: TOKI NO IHÔJIN

— CHRIS STUCKMANN —

We stared at the collection. The collection stared back. Two large shelves filled with anime. More anime than we could ever need. Perhaps that was the problem.

Have you ever sat in front of your collection, scanning each title, searching for one to watch? Maybe you've scrolled through Netflix for an hour, still not finding anything. You *know* you want to watch something. But what?

This was the dilemma facing my friend and me that night. Both of us agreed we felt like watching an anime, but the plethora of animated entertainment in front of us made that a daunting task.

My eyes skimmed both shelves twice, and on the second pass, they stopped at *GoShogun: The Time Étranger*—a forgotten film from 1985—directed by Kunihiko Yuyama, who later became known for directing the *Pokémon* films.

Why do I own this? I pondered, removing the Blu-ray from the shelf. Glancing at the back of the slipcover, I recalled purchasing it after seeing an advertisement from Discotek (a company that primarily distributes anime from the '70s, '80s, and '90s). Upon reading the plot, I instantly remembered why I bought it.

The Time Étranger is set forty years after the events of *GoShogun*, a "giant robot anime" from 1981 that spanned twenty-six episodes. The show follows a team of pilots who operate GoShogun, a large robot that is formed from multiple parts to battle enemies. Like many anime of that era, it was renamed for American audiences as *Macron 1*, which spliced footage from *GoShogun* and *Mission Outer*

Space Srungle to create an entirely new continuity. *Étranger* wisely forges a new path, presenting a daring story unlike anything I've seen from this specific genre.

Remy Shimada is a former member of the GoShogun team, now much older. On the way to meet her colleagues, she gets in a deadly car accident and ends up in the hospital on life support. Before long, her old friends stand over her bedside and receive the grave news that Remy is not expected to survive more than a couple days. While she lies in bed, comatose, Remy finds herself caught between life and death.

In her nightmare state, she awakes in a hotel room overlooking a dilapidated city. The buildings seem to rise in elevation, leading to a towering monument. This town is inhabited by shadowy figures and portrayed with a dull, gray color palette. They bow before the monument in submission, heads against the ground. Soon, it becomes clear that their subservience isn't out of faith, but of fear. This is the City of Fate, and their god is not one of love.

Remy discovers her fellow teammates are in the hotel as well, and everyone— including herself—looks young again. Cryptic letters arrive for each of them, detailing in gruesome ways the manner of their deaths. Remy is told that in two days, Fate will come for her, ripping her to shreds. She's even supplied photographs documenting her final moments.

Over the next two days, Remy and the team fight against the zombie-like horde. The emotionless mass plows forth, barely affected by Remy's gunfire. Grenades, machine guns, and explosives are no match for the advancing mob. Fate is coming to collect its due, and it seems that nothing can stop it.

Shuffled within this horrific nightmare are flashbacks to Remy's youth. An encounter with three young hooligans shows that her tenacity manifested at an early age. After the bullies offer money to remove her dress, she slips off her belt, and the boys think they've won. To their shock, young Remy wraps the belt around her fist, and decks each one of them, leaving them in tears on the pavement.

But the main focus of this flashback is Remy's time spent at the bottom of a cavernous pit. The ground caved in beneath her feet, trapping her in the dark. Alone and terrified, she begins to hallucinate. Ghostlike visions of other children plague her delirium, their voices echoing in her subconscious. Or ... could these visitations be literal? I admire *Étranger* for leaving this—and many other plot points—up to interpretation.

On more than one occasion, my friends and I have fantasized about the possibilities of franchise sequels. Do they all have to be the same? For instance, what if the next *Star Wars* film took place solely at a spaceport, the entire film revolving around a life-or-death game between two bounty hunters? No spaceships, no lightsabers, no Force. Just two hours in a random corner of the galaxy. The film *10 Cloverfield Lane* is a good example of how to do this properly. Most sequels don't simply continue the storyline, but also feel like they *belong* within the previously established universe. This is why *Étranger* is so special.

GoShogun was a show with a big-ass robot that blew stuff up. The only time *Étranger* even references the eponymous robot of the original show is with an insert shot of Remy's rear-view mirror. A charm of GoShogun hangs there on a string. That's it! Do you realize how incredible that is? Imagine a *Transformers* movie without a single Autobot in sight. The filmmakers have risked completely alienating their audience by making a surrealistic sequel to *GoShogun* ... without GoShogun. This is the type of bold and dangerous move that warrants commendation.

Not to be overlooked is the chilling religious subtext on display. The legion of Fate's servants attack Remy and the others, forcing the team to kill and maim the assailants. Are the filmmakers offering a critique of religion, possibly suggesting that blind faith begets violence? It's not farfetched to assume. But religion isn't the only topic on the mind of the filmmaker here.

In one shocking moment, the City of Fate's police savagely gun down a crowd of rioters who attacked Remy and the GoShogun team. When the team demands justification for this violence, the officer's response is telling: "We protect the city from rioters." Is this a scathing critique of police brutality?

When the film ended, my friend and I agreed we'd picked a good one. *Étranger* forgoes its origins, providing a fresh and singular take on the franchise. The eerie, hypnotic visuals pinned us to our seats, and the penetrating metaphors haunted us. *GoShogun: The Time Étranger* has been forgotten by time. For a while, dusty VHS copies were likely buried in the corner of thrift stores, begging to see the light of day. Thanks to Discotek, there's now a Blu-ray release. Even still, as of this writing, there are only three user reviews on IMDb, with very little information available about this gem.

Let's change that.

1986 • CASTLE IN THE SKY

TENKŪ NO SHIRO RAPYUTA

— AUGUST J. BABINGTON —

Alright, what you are about to read may come off as cheesy and even melodramatic. However, this isn't written with my hands, it's written by my heart and with love. See what I mean?

A late summer's evening is when we found each other. The night you entered my soul and opened it up like a book. The pages that would be written from here would become the story of my life; the chapters that still continue to this day are inked from when *Castle in the Sky* became my dreams.

My father had opened a restaurant; of course, I became the dishwasher. It was my first job. I was around the ripe age of fifteen, that impressionable age for movie lovers that awakens something in them when the right film comes along, the right magic.

It was opening night of the restaurant, a busy night indeed. Not arriving home until close to 1:00 am, I was truly exhausted from the first long workday I had ever experienced. Little did I know a life-changing experience was soon to follow. Ready to collapse and sleep the night away, my younger brother came to me with a rented video. "I got you *Castle in the Sky*," he said. "I remember we always saw previews of this and know you always wanted to see it," he continued. Visiting our grandmother's house, a tradition we had would be to watch *Kiki's Delivery Service*, a film by Hayao Miyazaki and Studio Ghibli. Before the VHS would start, a preview of *Castle in the Sky* would play. It was always kind of a mystery to us because we were young and never knew how to find the film to watch it. So now, on this night, the night I could barely keep my eyes open, I decided to fall asleep to this movie. I popped in the DVD with the full intention of falling asleep in minutes. Two hours and five minutes later, this became the first movie I had ever applauded. With tears in my eyes, and no one around, I applauded this movie. *Castle in the Sky* was the movie that awoke something in me, as cheesy as that may sound. I fell in love for the first time.

The story sucked me in the instant it started. The art of this film is breathtaking, and as soon as the first frame came into vision I knew I was in for something I wasn't prepared for. A thrilling action scene ensues, a mysterious young girl seems to be abducted on an airship for unknown reasons, air pirates invade and attempt to take over and, in the chance to escape the overwhelming situation, the mysterious girl falls from the ship possibly to her death. What came next was the moment I began to grow true feelings for *Castle in the Sky*. The opening credits began to roll and the most beautiful music I've ever heard started playing. The score by Joe Hisaishi is masterful. The theme of this movie is truly transportive and took me away to the magical place this movie was meant to be in. He managed to create a character in sound that helps to carry the story. The music Joe Hisaishi provides makes each scene so potent and adds a lot of heart to literally every frame.

If I get down to it, the true reason I fell in love with this story is the characters. Sheeta the innocent heroine with a mysterious crystal necklace, Pazu the unlikely hero with a delightful trumpet and a heart of gold, Muska the suave yet despicable villain with malevolent goals; I adore these characters. So much care went into their creation, and it shows. You truly get a sense of who they are as people; their agendas, goals, dreams, are all explored nicely. I've always liked a story where the apparent villains come to the aid of the protagonists, and you get that in *Castle in the Sky* with the Dola Gang. These airship pirates initially come off as antagonists with a dastardly agenda. However, through their goofy fumbles and silly failed attempts to capture Sheeta and steal away her crystal, you find yourself growing fond of this group of bumbling pirates. So, when it finally comes time for Pazu to reluctantly ask for their help to rescue his friend from the true evil of the story, these "bad guys" you were secretly rooting for join the battle for good and it's very satisfying to see what comes next. The Dola Gang helps to flesh out Pazu and Sheeta and also adds a nice levity to the story. All of these characters are the vessels that carry this story and make it truly mesmerizing.

It wasn't long after watching *Castle in the Sky* that I knew I had begun a life journey. I wanted to create my own characters that would go on adventures; characters that would experience heartache, experience love, experience hardships, experience victories. I wanted to create worlds and tell people about them. I wanted to create my own stories. I wanted to tell a story that would concoct and bring out emotions in people. I wanted to make art in this form. I began my journey to become a filmmaker. *Castle in the Sky* was the switch that clicked on in my brain and in my heart that brought me to the realization of discovering what I want to do with my life. From here, I went on through high school. I made several short films and features. My first was a fantasy drama with as much symbolism and representational art as I could squeeze in. My movie-making would continue to my college years where I received a bachelor's degree in Digital Filmmaking and Video Production. I have Hayao Miyazaki and his creations to thank for that.

In my opinion, Hayao Miyazaki is truly one of the greatest filmmakers of all time. He is regarded as the Walt Disney of Japanese Animation. Consistently making classic movies with unforgettable characters. *Castle of Cagliostro, Nausicaä of the Valley of the Wind, My Neighbor Totoro, Kiki's Delivery Service, Porco Rosso, Princess Mononoke, Spirited Away, Howl's Moving Castle, Ponyo,* and *The Wind Rises* are some of the treasures he has brought to the world and some of the films that many hold close to their hearts. He has been able to bring life experience to us, the viewers, through these special characters and fantastical stories. Hayao Miyazaki's films are wonderful, you should see them all. Each of them are unique and special. I'm sure to many others, just like myself, his stories sparked the passion to create. Hayao Miyazaki, as a person and as a storyteller, is true magic. It is truly special to me that my favorite film of all time is Hayao Miyazaki's *Castle in the Sky*.

It was the story that made me want to tell my own. It was the first time I realized, this is what I want to do with my life, to create stories. That became my dream, to make films, to bring characters to life, to provoke feelings like the feelings that were provoked in me the first time this masterpiece came into my life. My eyes opened to the possibilities. At fifteen I started to make my own movies and short films. My mind would constantly be thinking of my next story to put to video. This led to me going to film school and pursuing a life of storytelling. I strive throughout my career to push myself and make my stories better; I always have my favorite movie in the back of my mind. I'm constantly moving on a path of storytelling. Chasing a dream, a castle in the sky.

From his love of cinema to the daily grind, August J. Babington is dedicated to storytelling with all his ventures. As a director, writer, actor, and technician, August finds happiness in evoking emotion through his art.

1986–PRESENT • DRAGON BALL SERIES

DORAGON BŌRU

— DEREK PADULA —

Dragon Ball is the world's #1 anime.

Without *Dragon Ball*, I'd be dead.

Both of these statements express *Dragon Ball's* power. But before I tell you how *Dragon Ball* saved my life, let's explore what *Dragon Ball* is and why so many fans love to watch it.

Dragon Ball is a story about a monkey-tailed boy named Son Goku and his journey for greater strength. The franchise started in 1984 as a manga, and it is still being produced. At this moment, the *Dragon Ball* franchise consists of 42 volumes of *Dragon Ball* manga, 5 volumes of *Dragon Ball Super*, and over 100 volumes of official spinoffs. There are four *Dragon Ball* anime titled *Dragon Ball*, *Dragon Ball Z*, *Dragon Ball GT*, and *Dragon Ball Super*, comprised of 639 episodes (respectively 153, 291, 64, and 131). There are 19 theatrical animated films, 8 TV specials, 3 OVAs, and 3 live-action films—but fans often wish one of these did not exist, called *Dragonball Evolution*. There have been 149 video games that have sold over 44 million units, making it one of the best-selling franchises. In Tokyo there are 2 theme park attractions, 1 museum exhibit, and 1 Dragon Ball Café. If that weren't enough, there are over 15,000 pieces of licensed merchandise, over 25 supplemental art books and data guides, 3 Collectible Card Games, an official holiday in Japan called "Goku Day," celebrated every May 9, and a global religion based on *Dragon Ball's* tenants, called Gokuism, or The Church of Goku.

Dragon Ball is the world's most-recognized anime and manga series. *Dragon Ball's* creator, Akira Toriyama, is the world's most influential living manga author and the third most famous in history. *Dragon Ball Z* is the #1 selling anime brand of all time, with over 25 million DVDs and Blu-rays sold in the United States alone. *Dragon Ball* is the #2 best-selling manga of all time, with 240 million volumes sold in Japan, and a collective 300 million worldwide. A common marketing tagline for *Dragon Ball* is that it's, "The #1 Action Anime of All Time!" While this is subjective, it's also true. In a 2017 poll of Japanese anime viewers, Son Goku's rival, Vegeta, is the #1 rival in anime history. When you include the anime's global reach, the franchises' revenue is near-impossible to calculate.

Despite its top rankings, or perhaps because of it, criticism of *Dragon Ball* abounds. For example, "It's a show about nothing but punching and screaming," and "It takes forty episodes for a single fight." We are left to wonder, "If it's so bad, then why is it so popular?" To answer this question, we have to dive into *Dragon Ball's* origin.

The story begins with Akira Toriyama as a twenty-three-year-old illustrator who is out of work and living with his parents. One day, while bumming ¥500 *yen* ($5 USD) off his mom, he goes to the café to smoke and drink coffee. There he reads a copy of *Weekly Shōnen Jump* and sees an ad for a contest where the winner gets ¥100,000 *yen* ($1,000 USD) and a publication deal. He has never written a manga, but he knows how to draw, so he enters the contest in hopes of winning the money.

He doesn't win, but a young editor at Shūeisha named Kazuhiko Torishima notices his talent and gives him a shot. Afterward, he becomes a superstar in the early '80s when his *Dr. Slump* manga becomes the best-selling manga in Japan. *Dr. Slump* is about a dimwitted inventor named Senbei Norimaki who creates a nearsighted robot girl named Arale who has superhuman strength. But after five years, Toriyama feels burned out and wants to stop. Torishima becomes frightened at the idea of losing their cash cow, so he takes a train to Toriyama's home to discuss ideas for a new story.

After several hours of conversation, they fail to produce. That's when Toriyama's wife suggests he make a Kung fu manga, because he enjoys watching Jackie Chan's

Drunken Master and Bruce Lee's *Enter the Dragon* while he works. Toriyama objects, but Torishima insists. A few months later, *Dragon Ball* is born.

Toriyama uses the Chinese legend of *Journey to the West* (1592 AD) as his framework. This is a story about a Buddhist monk who travels from China to India to retrieve scriptures. The monk is aided on his journey by a supernormal Monkey King, pig man, sand demon, and a mystical white horse. These characters are the inspiration for Bulma, Son Goku, Oolong, Yamcha, and Bulma's motorcycle. It also provides the impetus for the first arc of the series where they search for the mystical dragon balls that can grant any wish, similar to the scriptures that grant enlightenment.

Journey to the West is a fusion of Buddhist, Daoist, and traditional Chinese folklore. As a result, the ideals of Buddhist compassion, Daoist truth, and austere forbearance, are baked into *Dragon Ball*'s culture. Toriyama emulates *Journey to the West*'s content, use of a narrator, cliffhanger endings, and style of humor. He then combines this with modern Western and Japanese pop culture. These include Hollywood films such as *Blade Runner*, *James Bond*, *The Terminator*, *Indiana Jones*, and *Aliens*; Japanese films like *Yojimbo*, *Seven Samurai*, generic *ninja* movies, and *kaijū* films like *Godzilla*; plus World War II films containing Nazis, aircraft, and machine guns. He then adds his own interests of motorcycles and automobiles, Japanese comedy shows, and his childhood countryside memories. Most importantly, he incorporates East Asian concepts of martial arts cultivation that enable Son Goku to ascend from a beginner martial artist to a literal god. This cultural fusion is the main reason why *Dragon Ball* appeals to fans across the world.

Despite this winning formula, *Dragon Ball* does not start off with success. It isn't until the emphasis is placed on martial arts action and self-cultivation that *Dragon Ball* becomes the biggest pop culture phenomenon in Japan. It becomes the primary reason for *Weekly Shōnen Jump*'s "Golden Era" of sales, from the mid-'80s to mid-'90s, selling 6.5 million copies a week. As a result, an entire generation of children was impacted by this series, and they've become what I call the "Dragon Ball Generation." Their worldview is forever influenced by the worldview of Goku and his friends or, in many cases, his enemies who become his friends. In turn, *Dragon Ball* inspires future manga authors who go on to become stars. For example, the hit series of *Naruto*, *One Piece*, and *Bleach* are spiritual successors to *Dragon Ball*. To that point, the creator of *Naruto*, Masashi Kishimoto, says, "Akira Toriyama is a god to me. A GOD!"

Dragon Ball is a success wherever it goes. In many countries it was the first anime or manga to be localized. *Dragon Ball* breaks open the door, establishes anime and manga as a form of entertainment, and becomes the #1 hit that everyone has fond memories of. In the case that it's not the first, it quickly becomes the top-selling series.

The North American anime industry owes a lot of its success to *Dragon Ball*. FUNimation is the largest anime dubbing and distribution company in North America, and the first anime they acquired was *Dragon Ball*. This was possible because the founder of FUNimation, Gen Fukunaga, had an uncle who worked at Toei Animation, the producer of the *Dragon Ball* anime, and worked out a deal to acquire the license. Questionable as that deal may be, when *Dragon Ball Z* premiered in 1997, it quickly became the #1 hit throughout the country and made FUNimation into a hundred-million-dollar company. Fukunaga has said several times, "FUNimation is the house that *Dragon Ball* built." In turn, FUNimation has dubbed and distributed hundreds of anime throughout the west. The money that goes into FUNimation from fans goes back to Japan to acquire the rights for more anime, which leads to more anime being produced. So the fact is, without *Dragon Ball*, the anime industry as we know it would be nowhere near as strong, and many of the anime we love would never have been produced or reached our shores.

It's because of this that I was able to see *Dragon Ball Z* in 1997 on Toonami. As a kid influenced by cartoons, comic books, and video games, afternoon TV was part of my daily ritual. But nothing could prepare me for *Dragon Ball Z*. It was astounding in every way imaginable. The heroic figures that fight for what they believe is right, powerful villains, silly jokes, epic quests, and cosmic adventures in a fantasy realm filled with supernormal powers and science fiction. What more can you ask for? I would watch the same fifty-two episodes on repeat, then again at midnight, and once more on Saturday whenever they'd air them.

Clearly I was a nerd, and because of this I was bullied at school throughout middle school and most of high school. They made fun of me for my appearance, teased me, spit on me, and pushed me against the lockers. This caused me to dislike myself, fear and hate school, become depressed, and fail many of my classes.

But after getting knocked down at school, *Dragon Ball Z* lifted me up. It taught me to believe in myself. It has an energy and spirit to it. An optimistic ideal that people can change themselves if they work hard enough at it, and to never give up.

Nonetheless, the daily grind wore me down. I was tired, and wished life was like an anime or video game, filled with fun adventures. One day, I tried to run away from home so I could escape the pain. But that only lasted an afternoon because I live in Michigan, and it's really cold. So, with no other option before me, I tried Plan B.

While dinner cooked on the stove and my parents watched TV, I pulled out a kitchen knife, closed the bathroom door behind me, and held the knife to my wrist.

Killing myself seemed like the best way to end the pain. To end the name-calling, the bad grades, ensuing shame, guilt, arguments, screaming, and endless worry about having to face another day where it seemed no one wanted me.

As I stared into the reflection of my own eyes for one final time, I hesitated. I had the thought, *No, I'm better than this. I can do great things. Just keep going ... persevere.*

The tears rolled down my face as I fell to the bathroom floor. I still had the knife in my hands. I could still do it. Then I thought, *No, I can make it another day.* I heard my dad call out, "Dinner's ready!" I wiped away the tears, returned the knife, and acted like nothing happened. I never told anyone.

Only later did I realize what kept me alive. For one, fear. A lot rolls through your mind in that do-or-die moment. Second, I'm a born optimist, and I believe people can change; including those who cause you to suffer. Third, *Dragon Ball* taught me by example that I have value and hidden potential. That I can be big, strong, and help others. That it's possible to do great things in life, so long as you endure.

"GOKU NEVER GIVES UP!"

Goku taught me there's a small light buried underneath the lies and notions that other people project on top of us to make themselves feel better. This light can't be sullied by those types of things, and it's a light so powerful that it blasts away the darkness. If it weren't for *Dragon Ball Z* reminding me of that light, I'd be dead.

Life didn't magically improve, but after hitting bedrock, I stood back up with a more positive perspective. It was in my junior year when a friend of mine compelled me to "start living DBZ." By that he meant the martial arts. So I took a Kung fu class. This class transformed my mind, body, and spirit. I became interested in Buddhist, Daoist, and Confucian philosophy. I went to Western Michigan University and earned a Bachelor's in East Asian Studies. I studied abroad in Beijing and trained with the Shaolin monks and *tàijí* sword masters. I became a different person. Or rather, I returned to who I originally was.

After returning home, I decided to write books about *Dragon Ball* so that I could give back to the Dragon Ball community and, in turn, Akira Toriyama. By following the example that Goku has taught me, to date I have published nine non-fiction books about *Dragon Ball*; I have received an apology from the writer of *Dragonball Evolution* on behalf of the global fandom; I've written a live-action web series that gave hope to over thirty-two million YouTube viewers that live-action *Dragon Ball* can be done right if fans are the creators; I've interviewed over thirty official *Dragon Ball* writers, editors, composers, voice actors, and producers; I've discovered countless amounts of lost *Dragon Ball* lore. I'm now a leading authority on *Dragon Ball* who is active in the community, delivers lectures at pop culture conventions, and helps fans achieve their dreams every day. That's the power of not giving up.

My story is not rare. I've spoken with thousands of *Dragon Ball* fans across the world whose lives have been changed or saved by this series. I wrote a book called *Dragon Soul: 30 Years of Dragon Ball Fandom* that contains 108 stories from fans and professionals in twenty-four countries. It features illustrators, voice actors, cosplayers, musicians, actors, authors, painters, philosophers, business executives, and even a Guinness World Record holder for the largest *Dragon*

Ball collection on earth. All of these people prove that *Dragon Ball* is more than a simple anime.

Sean Schemmel is the English voice of Goku, and in 2015 I asked Sean to explain *Dragon Ball*'s popularity. He said, "I worked on *Dragon Ball Z* for years ... but I didn't understand why it was so popular. I couldn't boil it all down to Americans liking explosions. Like, 'Yeah, monster trucks are exciting!' Because not everybody loves the action part of it. 'So why is *Dragon Ball Z* more popular than monster trucks?' "

Sean went on to describe how he realized that *Dragon Ball* has morals, ethics, "Buddhist influences, such as the 'beginners mind,' and being positive, always destroying evil within yourself and the world." He says, "That's why people get hooked on it, and why you can continue to watch it for the rest of your life and still find more to enjoy. The action might pull you in, but as you grow older and continue to watch it, it's the story, the way the characters grow, and how that relates back to you, that keeps you so interested in it. And that all has to do with what it means to be human, and your own personal path. So, that's why *Dragon Ball* is an eternal series that always remains popular, and why we share it with generation after generation." Sean added: "I owe my life to *Dragon Ball*."

Sean's not alone. Ryō Horikawa is the Japanese voice of Vegeta. I asked Ryō in 2012 if he felt *Dragon Ball* was a meaningful series. He said, "I think *Dragon Ball* is something like the Bible. It has a really important philosophy to it."

Even so, *Dragon Ball*'s not perfect. Sometimes the animation can be poor, the filler is frustrating, and yes, five minutes of in-universe time can last for ten episodes. Even the author himself said he simply wrote his manga "as pure entertainment," and nothing more. But therein lies the irony. Toriyama always does the opposite of what fans expect. In this case, by trying to create a meaningless series, he created one that is meaningful. Once *Dragon Ball* enters your heart, it never leaves. This series is evergreen. That's why millions of older fans are re-watching the series with their children, nieces, and nephews, so that they can also experience *Dragon Ball*'s power.

You owe it to yourself to give *Dragon Ball* a try. It's the world's biggest anime for a reason. The art, music, sound effects, action, and martial arts intensity of the series are incredible. That's what drew me into it as well. Oh, not to mention the memes! But there's a lot more than meets the eye. So, while you're looking at *Dragon Ball*, every so often, look within. You may find a power inside that you didn't know was there, and a way to unlock your full potential.

Goku, Vegeta, and their friends teach us that if you can change yourself, you can change the world. So, get out there and enjoy the adventure!

Derek Padula is the world's foremost professional Dragon Ball *scholar. He illuminates the real-world historical, spiritual, and philosophical culture of* Dragon Ball *to enable readers to better understand the series and empower themselves on their own life journeys. His books include the seven-volume* Dragon Ball Culture *series,* Dragon Soul: 30 Years of Dragon Ball Fandom, *and* Dragon Ball Z "It's Over 9,000!" When Worldviews Collide. *You can find him at thedaoofdragonball.com*

1986 • THEY WERE ELEVEN

— CHRIS STUCKMANN —

They Were Eleven appeared originally as a three-part manga in *Shōjo Comic*, a Japanese magazine that published manga for younger girls. In 1976, the manga won the coveted Shogakukan Manga Award, and finally, in 1986, an anime film was produced. By the early '90s, a VHS transfer was released in the States by now-defunct Central Park Media. It was that VHS that I rented from my local Hollywood Video. If you're not familiar with them, Hollywood Video rose to fame during the heyday of video rental stores. The company was founded in 1988 but became known nationally in the '90s as the direct competitor to Blockbuster Video.

As a young kid, I didn't really care about any of that. What I did know was that my neighborhood Hollywood Video had the best selection of anime VHS I'd ever seen. And they were only *99 cents* a rental!

I owe much of my development as an anime fan to that old store. At the time, my anime consumption was largely at the mercy of Toonami's broadcast schedule. So when VHS tapes became available at Hollywood Video, I'd scour the shelves in search of titles like *Sailor Moon R: The Movie*, *Venus Wars*, or *Voogie's Angel*. To be realistic, most of the titles they carried were terribly dubbed products of the "Japanimation Era." The early '90s were integral to the growth of anime in the States, but we still had to suffer through some awful dubs to get to where we are today.

Back to Hollywood Video. When I saw that dust-covered plastic case labeled *They Were Eleven* sitting on the shelf, I flipped it around to read the synopsis. It sounded promising. So, 99 cents and a car ride home later, I was ready to see for myself.

They Were Eleven is about ten space cadets in the middle of a grueling examination for acceptance into a prestigious and strict academy. They've passed all the requisite tests, yet one more remains. As part of this test, the ten cadets are transported to a ship in the middle of space and left to fend for themselves. Initially, they assume this is some sort of team project, perhaps to test their ability to problem-solve as a group. But before long, a troubling mystery surfaces in the form of an eleventh crew member and possible infiltrator. And because the cadets aren't familiar with one another, the spy could be any one of them. The resulting doubt and recrimination leads to a thrilling intellectual mystery that's highly uncommon for 1980s anime.

Atmosphere is something that's always impressed me when I watch this film. The deep, cold isolation of space—used to great effectiveness in films like *Alien*—becomes the perfect setting for this chilling mystery. And the creepy, long-abandoned sections of the ship add to the ominous feeling of dread that begins to permeate the cadets. Dark corners are animated with a foreboding sense of depth, creating the perception that you could actually reach into the screen and live in this environment.

But as already stated, it's the cerebral probing of these characters that makes the film stand out. Most anime set in space are about giant robots. Nothing against *Gundam*—I love me some big-ass robots—but *They Were Eleven* dares to be a psychological thriller, which is not typically a profitable genre in anime. Rather than rely on action scenes, nudity, or gore, the film subverts expectations by exploring questions surrounding gender identity. One character in the film reflects that they aren't comfortable in their own body. The rules that society has imposed upon them make it impossible to live the life they wish to lead. These startlingly adult themes are interwoven within the mystery beautifully, shattering the assumption that anime is just cartoons with nothing worthwhile to say.

They Were Eleven never received much attention. In fact, I'm not sure I would know it if not for Hollywood Video's rental selection. The DVD is out of print and essentially impossible to come by unless you resort to Amazon or eBay. It's rarely discussed when great anime titles are referenced and, as of this writing, there's been no attempt (to my knowledge) to obtain updated release rights.

I'm often asked about anime that I find under-appreciated and, while my mind tends to jump to better titles like *Now and Then, Here and There,* or *Monster, They Were Eleven* deserves its fair share of kudos. It was a film ahead of its time. An animation more interested in the darkest corner of its character's damaged psyche is one to be admired, lauded, and shared. While much of the world's cinema was still running to catch up, this mature Japanese animation was asking the questions that few films dared to discuss.

1987 • WINGS OF HONNÊAMISE

ÔRITSU UCHÛGUN: ONEAMISU NO TSUBASA

— JOHN RODRIGUEZ —

Is technology driving you away from God?

Wow, yeah, my apologies. You weren't expecting things to get so heavy so quickly, were you? That was probably uncalled for, but roll with me for a moment, if you will. I realize my question is predicated on the assumption that you even believe in God, and that's probably an unwise assumption to make. Maybe you don't believe. It sure isn't my place to preach at you if so. But, if you do believe, then maybe think about it a moment. Does the technology ensconcing you daily leave you feeling closer or further from God?

I ask because that's the question at the heart of *Wings of Honnêamise*. And while it might seem like pointless pondering, I'd argue it's a question that's more relevant today than ever.

Wings of Honnêamise chronicles the space race between two fictional nations on an alternate-reality Earth. Not that it's shaping up as much of a sprint. The Republic, our antagonists, don't even have a space program of their own. Meanwhile, the Honnêamise nation only funds their Space Force because the general whose passion project it is has ties to the royal family. Space Force is a joke, and its members are punchlines apt to reach abrupt ends when their test rockets explode under them.

Even the soldiers of Space Force scorn Space Force, and none more so than Shirotsugh Lhadatt, a ne'er-do-well who can't even bother to show up on time or in uniform for his recently exploded mate's funeral. Space Force is just a paycheck to Shirotsugh, but things change the night he hears Riquinni Nonderaiko preaching God's word to uninterested passersby. Smitten, Shirotsugh visits Riquinni at her home, where he becomes inspired by Riquinni's vision of a peaceful future for humanity among the stars. Thus inspired, he volunteers for Space Force's ultimate test flight—one that will make him a Honnêamise hero *and* spark a war with the jealous Republic.

If there's one singular theme running through *Wings of Honnêamise,* it's this: *Ain't nothing wonderful God never made that mankind can't ef up.*

Riquinni is a particularly common delivery mechanism for this message. In one telling scene, a dispirited Shirotsugh turns off his TV and picks up the holy book given him by Riquinni. In it, he reads a story of the earliest days and a man who stole fire from God, thus causing the deaths of his seven sons. These seven become the first human deaths in the world. Death from there on became the curse of mankind—all because we couldn't leave well enough alone.

Seriously, we are the worst.

Other examples of this abound. I review Hayao Miyazaki's *The Wind Rises* elsewhere in this book, and I was struck by how *Wings of Honnêamise* can be viewed as that film's logical continuation. *Wind*'s protagonist, Jiro Horikoshi, is also engaged in the development of an advanced flying craft. But where Mr. Miyazaki abruptly ends Jiro's tale once he succeeded in building the famous Zero fighter, *Wings* carries things forward from there. Notably, it shows the ramifications of the pursuit of progress. You get to see the frustration of the unemployed watching funds that might have helped them get back on their feet get funneled into a likely pipe dream. You get to hear the concerns that, even if humanity does make it into space, it will only open the door to further militarization.

Because—repeat it now with me, friends—we are the *worst.*

There's a sense in *Wings of Honnêamise* of the technological crowding out the theological. The devout Riquinni, for instance, gets her home bulldozed out from under her just as Space Force is beginning to flourish. You can almost see the accusation in the eyes of Riquinni's *Children of the Corn*-like sister's perpetual frown. It's as if she's saying: *You did this, all of you. You and your violence. You and your progress.*

Which raises the question: is Shirotsugh really a good guy? He's the face of Space Force, after all, and for all its noble ambitions, Space Force has caused a lot of grief for a lot of souls. So, is he a good guy, or is he maybe a bad guy? It's a question Shirotsugh himself poses at one point. And now we need to talk about what prompts Shirotsugh's navel-gazing ...

That scene. Oh, that scene.

You know which one I'm talking about if you've already seen *Wings of Honnêamise*. If you haven't, then let me warn you that there's a scene midway through the film where Shirotsugh attempts to force himself on the virtuous Riquinni. It's a neck-breaker of a tonal shift, *completely* out of the blue ... and appropriate to instill the film's harsh message, I would argue.

Yes, I know this view isn't in line with many who've seen *Wings of Honnêamise*, and yes, I understand that any depiction of rape—even a failed rape—constitutes a nonstarter for plenty of people. That's fair. But I disagree with the notion that this scene has no place in an otherwise masterful film. Instead, I would argue that it's the ultimate confirmation of what *Wings of Honnêamise* has been preaching to us from the start: *You're gonna ef it up, son. I gave you something pure and good, and you can't help but ef it up.* It's a brutal means of delivery, but the message is certainly on point.

And Riquinni's reaction to Shirotsugh the next day is also on point. Rather than cast him out or fly at him with fists clenched—actions she'd be entirely justified in taking—she apologizes to Shirotsugh for hitting him. You read that right: Riquinni *apologizes* to her would-be rapist! Is this some sick joke?

Not at all. It's the other side of *Wings of Honnêamise*'s thematic coin. Yes, humanity's history is one of mucking up the good and the pure. But if there's hope for us, then it lies in our willingness to turn the other cheek, even when we're rightfully aggrieved. Because if we're not working hand in hand to craft a better future for ourselves, we're doomed to continue our perpetual cycle of build/ruin/rinse/repeat.

Space Force's new rocket ultimately provokes an all-out invasion by the Republic. Of course it does. That's partly what technology represents in *Wings of Honnêamise*: an excuse to give into our worst impulses. Yet Space Force's rocket also represents a dream of a brighter future. That rocket just might lead humanity to the stars. And once you've made it there, who says you're bound to the ugly cycles of history? Who says you can't start anew?

So much of the technology we interact with daily insulates rather than inspires. It has us looking *down* instead of *up*. That's a shame, because up is the direction where, just maybe, we'd catch a glimpse of the divine. Not that you need buy into that to take something from *Wings of Honnêamise*. Not at all. You just need to want to do your part to get people looking forward instead of back. And perhaps to be willing to forgive when your fellow man invariably ef's up your pure and good designs.

Because he will. We are, after all, the worst. But maybe we don't have to be forever.

John Rodriguez is a personal trainer whose devotion to physical fitness is exceeded only by his fervor for all things film and literature. John is currently finishing his first novel—a fantasy that's sparked fantasies of a challenging new career.

1988 • AKIRA

— JOHN RODRIGUEZ —

And with these simple words—

"NEO-TOKYO IS ABOUT TO EXPLODE!"

—an anime fan is born.

I'd never been to the then-newish Cleveland Cinematheque before and didn't know that I wanted to go, given its distance from my suburban haunt. But that one-sheet ... that was something, huh? Just that boy—I didn't yet know him as Kaneda—holding that preposterous rifle over a background of black, broken buildings. Who was this badass boy with the grim-set face? Was he this story's eponymous hero? Those five block letters at his feet—the ones screaming *AKIRA* in bloody, bullshit-less red—surely suggested so. Would he wind up the harbinger of Neo-Tokyo's imminent explosion, or perhaps serve as the city's salvation? Suddenly, a thirty-minute drive into the city seemed less a burden than a necessary fact-finding mission.

And so I learned. I learned of Kaneda and the Capsules, that gang of young misfit motorcyclists. Of Tetsuo, the Capsules' runt of the litter, chaffing at Kaneda's smothering protectiveness. Of the espers, the wizened little psychics who presage the dangerous psychic powers growing within Tetsuo, and of Colonel Shikishima, the espers' custodian and the hard case plotting to assassinate a boy in order to save a city. And, of course, of Akira, the doom and/or salvation buried under Neo-Tokyo's Olympic Stadium.

Akira certainly wasn't the first anime to leave a cultural footprint on America— those of us raised on *Robotech*, that bastard spawn of three unrelated series, know that well. Yet *Akira* was undoubtedly the tipping point, the keystone for myriad western anime fandom. So the question becomes: Why? Why this film, which didn't even receive US distribution until eighteen months after its release in Japan?

Let's start by looking at the competition. That trip of mine to the Cleveland Cinematheque took place during the summer of 1990. What kind of sci-fi fare could I have enjoyed had I chosen to stick closer to home? Well, *Total Recall* had just hit theaters. If that wasn't my thing, I could have hitched my train to the final *Back to the Future* sequel. And hey, *Teenage Mutant Ninja Turtles* was still karate-chopping its way to a $202 million worldwide gross in the local second-run theater. Cowabunga!

Is this to suggest that *Akira*'s western success is owed to a lack of viable competition? "Hardly," says this *Total Recall* apologist. But while I enjoyed getting my ass to Mars as much as the next guy, I'd never hail *Total Recall* as heady cinema. Same goes for *Back to the Future III* and *Teenage Mutant Ninja Turtles*: You can argue they're fun, but you can't argue they're thinkers. If you think I'm cherry-picking, I invite you to scan down the list of 1990s top-grossing films. Spoiler alert: They don't get any brainier.

Where, then, is the burgeoning intellectual science fiction fan to turn?

Enter *Akira*. Here's a film with something to say! You take one look at Neo-Tokyo— that crowding vertical skyline, that sea of pinprick lights, each one a window on some anonymous life—and instantly understand why Kaneda and his Capsules simply must stake their claim to their scanty strip of street. Youth cries to be noticed. It rages against the notion that it must ultimately be consumed, must become one of "The Many" who shuffle through their daily routine, fuel for the machine. Kaneda's Capsules call bullshit on that demand. And though we watch their little rebellion from cinema screens or televisions 7,000 miles away from their fictional exploits, we disillusioned young raise a cheer.

Then there's Tetsuo. The boy with all the gifts, Tetsuo's bubbling cauldron of rage and resentment is instantly recognizable to any teen. True, what's fighting to burst from most teens is different than what Tetsuo's bottling—not psychic energy but rather social angst and sexual frustration—but the principle remains the same. Of course, Tetsuo's powers destroy him in the end, not to mention his girlfriend

(R.I.P., Kaori: we hardly knew ye) and a goodly chunk of Neo-Tokyo. So, perhaps *Akira* can be read as a parable on the need for youth to reign itself in. Yet Tetsuo also transcends to something greater: a whole universe born of his personal Big Bang. Tetsuo the boy dies; Tetsuo the legend will live on until the last star in his new universe goes dark. That, friends, is a legacy. Who wouldn't want that?

And though *Akira* is often dark in the extreme, there's a fundamentally hopeful sentiment here. *Akira*'s old Tokyo wasn't much to write home about before being leveled by the explosion that triggered World War III. Yet the city that rose from the rubble became more prosperous in just thirty years than its predecessor had ever been. Tetsuo couldn't contain his powers—he literally burst apart at the seams. Yet during the film's climax, the espers intone that Tetsuo's evolution represent humanity's future. This isn't some nihilistic prophecy: it's a suggestion that we as a species are growing, that through our strife and our selfishness—perhaps because of it, indeed—we stand on the precipice of Great Things.

There's been a lot of hand-wringing over the notion of a westernized *Akira*, and that's understandable. *Akira* is in many ways intrinsically tied to its roots—note in particular the notion of "rebuilding after the bomb," a gargantuan task the Japanese understand all too well—and some of those root themes aren't going to translate. Still, *Akira* speaks to people of all cultures. You could watch this film in Big Sky, Montana with nary a skyscraper in sight (the Rockies excepted) and still come away thinking: If only I had Kaneda's bike. If only I had Tetsuo's powers. What could I do? What could I be?

Coming back around to the original question—"Why *Akira*?"—is it simply the appeal of wish fulfillment? Maybe in part, but not wholly, I think. Because *Akira* also subverts wish fulfillment. It says, "Sure, you can have super powers, kid, but don't get cocky, cause you're only gonna end up squishing your girlfriend into pink goo." (R.I.P., Kaori: that really was a lovely skirt.) Maybe that's part of *Akira*'s appeal, too. It's honest enough to admit that being The One isn't all black leather and bullet time. It means pain. It means responsibility and consequence. That's right, teens of today: there's no escaping the fact.

But it doesn't necessarily mean compromise of identity. Later in life, you'll still be you. And if "you" ends up a disembodied universe, that just means you're gonna live forever, kid. Not a bad way to go.

John Rodriguez is a personal trainer whose devotion to physical fitness is exceeded only by his fervor for all things film and literature. John is currently finishing his first novel—a fantasy that's sparked fantasies of a challenging new career.

1988 • GRAVE OF THE FIREFLIES

HOTARU NO HAKA

— ROBERT WALKER —

Grave of the Fireflies opens with its two leads—children—starving to death. And it's all downhill from there. As a film, it demands not so much to be watched, but experienced. Just what that experience is I cannot say. Words fail me even years later. In the absence of anything better, I can only cough up one word: devastating.

The inherent power of the film only intensifies when one realizes it's based on the semi-autobiographical account of its author, Akiyuki Nosaka. Written in 1967, it chronicles a similar story of an orphaned boy in wartime Japan who takes charge of his younger sister. In it, she dies, and he soon follows. In reality, Nosaka survived, and the story was written as a way to work through his survivor's guilt. In the film's opening sequence, a destitute boy passes out in a train station. Onlookers, already weary of the imminent arrival of American forces after the nation's surrender, pass him by with disgust. The boy's radiant spirit then rises from his body, looking nothing like the emaciated husk lying in a heap on the concrete. The spirit spots that of a young girl, his sister. The two ghosts then disappear happily into a field of glowing fireflies.

Set in the final months of World War II, *Grave of the Fireflies* follows fourteen-year-old Seita and his four-year-old sister Setsuko. Their mother suffers from a heart condition, and their father is a Captain in the Imperial Navy—though he hasn't written back in sometime. When an American air raid unleashes fiery hell upon the city, their mother orders them to run, knowing full well she can't.

She dies.

Horrifically.

It's this scene, where the children stumble upon the bandaged, bloodied, burned body of their mother, that sends the most chills to the heart. The camera lingers. No shying away. And in this moment, their doom is set.

From that point on, Seita takes it upon himself to watch over his younger sister. With the city in ruins, he carries her on his back to his aunt's home. The aunt agrees they can stay. At first, all seems well. Seita returns with some of his mother's belongings, and gives them to their aunt. All save for a tin of fruit drops, which he gives to Setsuko—a now infamous recurring image in the film. As the weeks slip by, though, Japan's wartime effort continues to deteriorate, taking the economy down with it. Food is rationed. The aunt now has her own daughter and a niece and nephew to feed. Tensions rise. His aunt accuses Seita of being a good for nothing freeloader. Then she sells his mother's belonging for rations. Too emotionally attached, Seita comes to blows with his aunt. He decides to run off with Setsuko.

From there, they live a seemingly idyllic life in an old bomb shelter near the woods. For a time, they seem happy. And its these rare moments of joy that catch the viewer off guard. Much like James Cameron's *Titanic*, we know what must inevitably happen. But it's a testament to Isao Takahata's direction that it sometimes slips into the background.

Sadly, grim portents foreshadow what's to come. To light their shelter, Seita lets in a swarm of fireflies. The next morning, Setsuko cries out that they're all dead. Horrified, she buries them in a grave and asks with childlike naiveté, "Why do fireflies have to die? Why did mother have to die?"

Slowly, the pair's wilderness adventure becomes a battle for survival. They run out of rice. Seita goes so far as to steal food. As Setsuko wastes away, Seita takes her to a doctor, who can only recommend she eat. Finally, not long after, he realizes in abject terror that she's been sucking on marbles while he's gone—thinking, in her hallucinogenic state, that they are the fruit drops from the little tin. He rushes to the bank to withdraw what little money his mother had left, and returns with supplies. Perhaps. We, the audience, can only beg. Perhaps—?

But we've all seen the ending.

What saves *Grave of the Fireflies* from rote sentimentality is its unflinching view of the frail human condition. People make mistakes, especially in situations of high stress. The aunt receives the blunt force of this view. She all but pushes them out by making them feel most unwelcome. Her insistence that fourteen-year-old Seita enlist smacks of unreasonable expectations. In 1945, he'd still be a year short to serve. And even if he could, it would be a virtual death sentence.

More ambiguous is her demand that Seita get a job. Possible? Perhaps. Likely in that crumbling economy? Questionable. The movie makes a wise decision not to answer that question with any certainty. Did Seita truly look? Or, as the privileged boy who lost everything, did he not want to suffer the indignity of doing factory grunt work? He idolizes his father as a military hero—an officer!—and one wonders if he thought such a move was beneath him. For Seita, lowering himself becomes an admission of defeat. His life stolen from him, he seems hell-bent to reclaim it on his own terms.

As social commentary, the whole movie plays like a condemnation of the Japanese concept of "saving face." Ever enshrining the Confucian concepts of family and honor, the whole system crumbles when faced with the reality of a disastrous war. Honor becomes a liability. Family a burden. Society frays at the edges, and this leads to bad decisions with tragic results. Sure, it's easy to lay blame on Seita. But who are the adults in the room? The aunt considers it her patriotic duty to sweep these freeloaders out in lieu of her own daughter. The doctor offers advice, but no food or medicine. A farmer beats Seita for stealing. And the onlookers at the train station look upon his frail body with disgust. Simple human revulsion? Or the realization that, having suffered a humiliating defeat, the invaders will now see Japan's shame on full display in the streets?

As for Seita—he's fourteen. Homeless. Motherless. Potentially fatherless. And now saddled with a younger sister to care for. What young teenager is equipped to deal with such a burden? Some may rise to the challenge, but Seita joins the long list of poor souls who just couldn't cut it. His pride mimics that of any teenager. But it's also a reflection of his nation's. And it kills him. His quest for nonconformity makes a mockery of the privilege and freedom enjoyed by the likes of Miyazaki's fantasy heroine, Kiki. Here, a similar quest for individuality leads to disaster.

That Miyazaki chose to pass *Grave of the Fireflies* onto Takahata makes perfect sense. And it was a master stroke. Takahata himself survived the Okayama City bombing as a child, which explains the realism of the harrowing air raid sequence. Asking Miyazaki to direct this film would be like asking Walt Disney to direct *The Killing Fields*. *Grave* isn't without whimsy, but the price is steep.

The animation reinforces this dichotomy with fire-bombings, shriveled corpses, and heaps of rubble. Yet a sort of magical realism gives it a sense of meaning. Sunsets glisten. Fireflies glow. The shadows of leaves roll across the children's faces as they sleep in the afternoon haze. The natural world offers a mystical respite from the horrors of war. Unfortunately, like the pied piper, it also takes no prisoners—leading its victims down a bucolic path from which they'll never return. Nature, too, doesn't discriminate.

Yet, it's these Eden-like passages that give *Grave* its few moments of tenderness. Takahata's world, for all its brutality, remains soft around the edges—just like in his other films, *Only Yesterday* and *Princess Kaguya*. For this film, he employed a new technique, switching out the normal black outlines for brown. This gives the universe a nostalgic, nearly sepia tone feel. It's warm. Dreamlike. Strangely spiritual. Like a memory.

It's a memory etched into the Japanese consciousness. Perhaps best reflected in the final moments, which see their spirits walking into the modern skyline of Kobe. And yet, though clearly aimed at the Japanese, it plays just as well overseas. Many critics hail it as one of the best anti-war films ever made. Ironic, since Takahata insists it is not an anti-war movie, and he didn't intend it as such. Whoops.

To a certain degree, I understand where he's coming from. None of the characters share an anti-war sentiment. Seita's father serves in the Navy. He has a vested interest in Japan "winning." The cognitive dissonance on display perhaps reflects the station in his life. Still just a boy, the idea that his father lies at the bottom of the ocean is probably more than he can bear. Better to hope for the best.

And perhaps that's why it plays so well as an anti-war film. The best anti-war movies don't pick sides. Indeed, the Americans are barely shown at all. And yet, for all the nonexistent amount of screen time they receive, every American owes it to themselves to see this film. Stripped of the sort of jingoistic demonization prevalent in most war films, *Grave of the Fireflies* simply shows the after-effects. It invites Americans to empathize with "the other" by looking directly into their eyes. No lectures or speechifying. Just experience. The message is universal because war is universal. It's a sad part of the human condition. And Takahata, whether he intended it or not, understands that it's those who have the least say in wartime that suffer the most. Nations break down. Society breaks down. People break down. It's the ultimate failure in imagination.

Like the fireflies Seita uses to light his bomb shelter, the lives of the children are equally bright and short. All too quickly they're snuffed out—used up and forgotten by an all too indifferent world. It's enough to make a grown man cry. And trust me, it has.

Because of its emotional weight, some argue that the film is overly sentimental—a well-intentioned, but very deliberately crafted tearjerker. I'd argue that if you're watching children starve, you'd damn well better be made to cry. Or at least suppress some tears. And *Grave of the Fireflies* avoids the tropes of so many other lesser films that use kids as props. The two children aren't plot devices shoehorned in with some inexplicable cancer or accident or malady designed as a last, desperate attempt to milk some eleventh-hour waterworks. It's literally the centerpiece of the whole picture. *Grave* shows its hand in the first minute, telling the viewer in no uncertain terms exactly what they're getting into. And that something is a sucker punch to the soul.

As a movie, I can't recommend *Grave of the Fireflies* in the same way I would other anime. You're not going to have a "good time." For that, I'd say go watch Takahata's other film: the nostalgic, coming-of-age reminisce, *Only Yesterday*. But don't expect the same cultural significance. That this film garnered a reputation abroad as the "Japanese *Schindler's List*" speaks to its power. And like *Schindler's List*, it comes not recommended—but required.

Beautiful, brutal, heart-wrenching, and transcendent, it achieves a catharsis that few live-action films can compete with. As a testament to the supreme mystical quality of animation, it dispels the ludicrous notion that animated films are only for kids. This movie belongs right next to the likes of *All Quiet on the Western*

Front, Paths of Glory, The Diary of Anne Frank, and the various other entries by Spielberg, Kubrick, and Eastwood.

Not bad for ink and paint.

Robert Walker is the co-writer for the hit web series The Nostalgia Critic. *As a child of the '80s, he's been watching anime imports since before he even knew what anime was. Altogether, he has watched over 300 anime series and films. Not necessarily for his job, but because he has a problem.*

1988 • MY NEIGHBOR TOTORO

TONARI NO TOTORO

— ADELLE DROVER —

A giant magical panda-rabbit is the leader of Japan's most beloved animation house, Studio Ghibli. Adorning the company logo since 1990, Totoro—a character from *My Neighbor Totoro*—is both awe-inspiring in presence and cute enough to enthuse hordes of children to buy the plushy doll. So, how did this fluffy make-believe-monster-spirit become the face of an internationally renowned film studio?

Studio Ghibli is a name synonymous with animation. It's right up there behind the powerhouse American studios of Walt Disney and Pixar. Yet the approach and tone for telling children's stories—and I do mean "children's stories" though not necessarily stories explicitly *for* children—is a cultural world apart. Ghibli's animations turn away from the glossy sheen of singing princesses and chiseled-looking princes, yet they are still tales of transformation and wonder—just of a different nature. Being grounded in the reality of time and place makes their power all the more magical. As such, they are touches of the supernatural intertwined among the real-world tough lessons of growing up. Even when the world setting is entirely fictional, the foundations of these films grow heavily from the traditions of Japanese culture, religion, and folklore. The influential father of Studio Ghibli, Hayao Miyazaki, birthed a genre through the 1980s and subsequent decades of animated storytelling, the likes of which the world had never seen.

While Miyazaki's debut feature *Nausicaä of the Valley of the Wind* is an action adventure on the environmental human impact, his second directed film *My Neighbor Totoro* takes a much lighter approach to similar themes. First released in cinemas as a double feature behind the more somber *Grave of the Fireflies*, *My Neighbor Totoro*—while not the most financially popular of his filmography—is still hailed as one of his most notable works primarily because of the lovable toothy-grinned Totoro character. A character who adds magic and lightheartedness into more mundane subject matter not commonly aimed at children. It's these fantastic elements set amongst a coming-of-age sisterhood which makes *My Neighbor Totoro* such an understated success.

Set in postwar Japan, Satsuki and her younger sister Mei arrive at their new home in the countryside, ready to play and explore as much as their hearts desire. Summer days stretch infinitely and every loose acorn in the garden is a treasure worth collecting. Their father, Tatsuo, commutes regularly to his job in Tokyo and it's revealed slightly later in the film that their mother, Yasuko, is in the hospital for an extended time. While exploring their new surroundings, the sisters discover some sneaky soot sprites hiding in the dark corners of the old house, upon which their father encourages their excited investigation. A neighbor informs the girls that she too could see the soot sprites when she was a child, alluding to the power of childhood intuition.

Later on, Mei discovers a hidden path which leads her to the lair of a giant cuddly creature she dubs "Totoro." Her father again encourages his daughters' exploration into the supernatural and tells them of the spirits who supposedly live in the forest. Totoro himself makes only a few but memorable appearances throughout the film. His presence is incidental to the story of the sisters trying to settle into a new life and come to terms with their mother's precarious situation in the hospital.

The charm of *My Neighbor Totoro* comes from its story simplicity. Characters go about their lives with everyday ups and downs, adventures and tantrums, and without any kind of plan—other than to be kids. It's this paired back narrative that leaves the audience open to follow the whims and childlike spontaneity of each sister. It is for the duration of the first two acts that the story is propelled entirely by the inquisitiveness of the girls and their interest in their new surroundings.

When Mei first spies a Mini-Totoro in its natural activities (much to its dismay at being spotted), the film follows along as Mei's resolve changes from surprise at the fluffy creature, to curiosity at what it's doing, and finally to utter determination to follow it and find out where it's going in such a hurry. As the film goes on, it continues to align with the whims of the sisters through the repeated Totoro sightings, Satsuki attending school, and everyday interactions with their neighbors. Only in the final act of the film does the tone shift when Satsuki receives a telegram from the hospital with news of their mother. This prompts Mei to secretly run away, and here, we see a more conventional story arc as Satsuki goes into crisis mode and does everything she can to find her missing little sister. She enlists Totoro's help, and the following journey on the magical Catbus is one of the most joyful scenes in the film.

Satsuki and Mei's continuing exploration of the surrounding forest brings together a perfect unity of the natural and the supernatural. The real world with the secondary overlaid spirit world as influenced by traditional Shinto beliefs of Japan. In a visit to the forest, their father introduces them to a magnificent camphor tree rooted next to a forgotten Shinto shrine. The significance of the tree is marked by rice rope and paper wrapped around its enormous trunk to which the family bow and pay their respects. As a protector of the forest, Totoro is equally magnificent and worthy of respect. While we might first be introduced to the "King of the Forest" in a funny and childish way when Mei discovers the soundly sleeping Totoro, his influence over the natural world becomes clear. The midnight scene of Totoro and his companions dancing ritualistically around a patch of acorn seeds in hopes of summoning them to grow is a fantastical and hopeful spectacle.

My Neighbor Totoro isn't a film of overcomplicated grandiose but instead a simple "slice-of-life" animation. Satsuki as the eldest sister is thoughtful and wise and Mei as the younger sister is rambunctious and spirited. They are two sides of the same coin and, while their interactions with Totoro and the spirit world are fleeting, they remain better off from the experience. Totoro is the perfect child-friendly reminder of the importance of our relationship to the natural world. This cuddly yet reserved spirit-creature embodies the core values which a lot of Miyazaki-directed Studio Ghibli films explore. *My Neighbor Totoro* is a delightful animation well cherished by fans all over the world. Magical characters steeped in Japanese folklore enrich a simple story of two sisters growing up in the world.

Adelle is a movie critic and movie fangirl in equal parts. Currently working in an Australian film production house, you can find more of her thoughts on the latest movie releases and indie cinema you should be watching over on her YouTube channel, Roll Credits, *at www.youtube.com/RollCredits.*

1988 • RONIN WARRIORS

YOROIDEN SAMURAI TORŪPĀ

— CHRIS STUCKMANN —

Middle school years were awkward for many kids, myself included. As an introverted, unpopular loner, I had a handful of acquaintances but no true friends. My day was mostly spent awaiting release from the confines of my school. I appreciated learning, but I just didn't feel welcome there.

Strangely, however, when I reflect on middle school, I mostly remember the good times. That's probably due in part to my activities outside of school, but I particularly remember one interaction with a former classmate who leaned toward me in the middle of class to ask if I was watching *Dragon Ball Z*. Perhaps the cartoon I was doodling in my notepad caught his attention—I can't say for sure. I just remember being taken aback that *someone just talked to me*.

"No, what's that?" I asked sheepishly.

"Oh, man. Just go home and watch it."

I did just that. I mean, why wouldn't I? *Someone just talked to me*.

Enter Toonami. Cartoon Network's weekly afternoon block of anime classics defined a generation. It brought many excellent shows to our shores, including *DBZ*. "Dende's Demise" was my first episode, and I was never the same again.

If memory serves, *DBZ* started at 5:00 p.m., and two shows preceded it: *Sailor Moon* and *Ronin Warriors*. My burgeoning interest in *DBZ* eventually led to *Sailor Moon* and *Ronin Warriors* becoming "must-watches." *Ronin Warriors* (known as *Yoroiden Samurai Troopers* in Japan) ran for thirty-nine episodes and three OVAs. It was in many ways the male-centric counterpart to *Sailor Moon*, so Toonami's programmers were very clever to air them back-to-back.

The plot revolves around five young men who possess mythical suits of armor with devastating powers and abilities. Like most anime of this type, the armor can transform and unite in various ways to obliterate their enemies. (Expect to hear "Flare Up Now!"—the announcement of Ryo of the Wildfire's powerful attack—often in the English dub.) Opposing these heroes are a group known as The Dynasty and its leader: the demonic Master Talpa, supreme lord of the Underworld. Talpa wants to lay waste to the mortal world, and the Ronin Warriors are all that stand in his way.

Admittedly, *Ronin Warriors* isn't terribly innovative or revolutionary. Most *shōnen* (relating to young boys) or *shōjo* (relating to young girls) anime feature intense battles with vile enemies before the hero unleashes their finishing move, annihilating the baddie with a cheeseball declaration of valor. However, *Ronin Warriors* is unique in that much of the show is about Ryo and his companion Mia searching for Ryo's fellow Warriors who've been imprisoned.

Speaking of Mia, her character subverts most clichés surrounding female anime characters. She's smart, often rescuing Ryo with needed information that helps him in battle, and she's never portrayed as a sex object. On the contrary, she's always integral to their mission. That's not just shocking for '80s shōnen anime: even popular shōjo anime of the time often depicted female characters in overtly sexual ways. I recall transformation sequences of many shōjo anime panning around female bodies from head to toe. *Ronin Warriors* doesn't treat Mia like this.

An avid anime fan might tell you that *Ronin Warriors* isn't particularly cutting-edge by any means. I wouldn't blame them for finding its inclusion in this book a little superfluous. But as this book's title suggests, I'm writing about *Ronin Warriors* because of the impact it had on me as a youth. And while *DBZ* was my gateway anime, *Ronin Warriors* was the one that cemented my love of the medium.

As I mentioned in the introduction, Toonami helped spread awareness of Japan's role in the production of anime. At the time, plenty of kids assumed that *Robotech*, *Star Blazers*, or even *Sailor Moon* were American cartoons. The

Americanization of anime was a real problem in the '90s. In retrospect, I'm grateful many shows made it to our shores, whether they were heavily censored or not. It's understandable to assume that severe cursing, graphic violence, or nudity wouldn't be allowed on Cartoon Network, but this wasn't the underlying issue. Bizarre and often offensive changes were made to many shows—most famously the lesbian relationship on *Sailor Moon*—and most of the time, it was due to a cultural gap. Foods commonly eaten in Japan were altered to American dishes, cigarettes were replaced or removed, character names were altered, and sometimes entire storylines were cut.

I bring this up because *Ronin Warriors* is one of the few shows that didn't suffer any major changes. Character names were indeed replaced with more western-friendly hero names, but besides that, the show was aired surprisingly intact and with little censorship. While *Ronin Warriors* certainly wasn't Toonami's most successful show, it did retain a large fanbase. Whether the show's relative popularity helped thwart the typical Americanization these shows usually received remains unclear. What is clear, however, is that *Ronin Warriors's* English dub is often cheesy as hell:

"SO, SEKHMET, YOUR POWER ISN'T JUST OVERWHELMING BODY ODOR BUT SLEIGHT-OF-HAND, TOO!"

Or ...

"MY SNAKE-FANG SWORD ROTS ANYTHING IT TOUCHES, INCLUDING STUPID YOUNG BOYS!"

Ronin Warriors' frequent cliffhangers encourage binging. Of course, that's much easier to do nowadays. I vividly recall sitting on my couch after school, groaning in frustration upon each episode's end as Tom (Toonami's robot host, voiced by the incomparable Steve Blum) declared, "That's it for *Ronin Warriors, Sailor Moon* is next!" Talk about frustration!

Hindsight really is 20/20 because, looking back, it's obvious why *Ronin Warriors* was the perfect anime to include on Toonami's block. If you think *Power Rangers* is successful today, you should've seen it in the '90s. Virtually any show featuring transformable characters in badass armor was a guaranteed hit. It's no surprise that it found an audience with impressionable kids, including this one. Thanks *Ronin Warriors*. You may be adorably cornball, but I still love you.

1989 • KIKI'S DELIVERY SERVICE

MAJO NO TAKKYŪBIN

— ROBERT WALKER —

Kiki gets in your head.

Really, I could just leave it there. It wasn't always this way. While the 1998 Disney rerelease was the first Miyazaki film I had ever seen, there were years where *Kiki* slept at the bottom of my list as, "Oh yeah, *that* one." Now, two decades later, it sits on top again.

Just what is this mysterious spell she casts?

Well, she's a witch. I suppose that helps. Kiki starts her journey at home. The tweenage daughter of the local town witch, she spends her first moments in the movie staring up at the sky—perhaps dreaming of new opportunities. For Kiki, life is quaint. Mom mixes medicinal potions. Dad works a nine to five job. They have a car, a phone, a little house in the country. In this universe, modeled loosely after Europe of the 1950s, witchcraft simply plays like any another specialized profession.

As part of a witch's training, it's custom for a thirteen-year-old to hop on a broom and strike it out on her own in a witch-less town. Her parents, ever worried, offer her an out. She can skip the Wiccan walkabout if she wants. But Kiki refuses. She wants to become a full-fledged witch and see the world. So, after donning her traditional black witch's frock, she and her talking cat, Jiji, set out for the big city on her broomstick.

Upon arriving at the big city—a beautiful seaside port riddled with buses, cable cars, winding cobblestone streets, and clocktowers—she quickly finds herself in over her head. Literally. At one point, she winds up flying upside down while nearly getting clipped by a vehicle in a tunnel. Her cat, ever pragmatic, suggests giving up and moving elsewhere. Fortunately, Kiki discovers she has a certain skill set. She can fly. When a pregnant baker tries to chase down a mother who left her baby's pacifier at the store, Kiki offers to help. She flies it to the mother down the street. Impressed, the baker offers her an attic to stay in. It's a trade. She'll fly deliveries for room, board, and food. Kiki agrees.

Thus begins *Kiki's Delivery Service*.

From there, the film unfolds as a series of vignettes, chronicling the customers and friends she encounters on her journey of self-discovery. First and foremost, there's Osono the Baker—always lending a helping hand and a cup of cocoa. Her monosyllabic husband, Fukuo, runs the back of the house—juggling bread pans with biceps that would make Arnold Schwarzenegger drop his jaw. Ursula, a hippie painter who lives in the woods outside of town, welcomes the occasional visitor who crash lands on their broom. Then there's an old Madame who employs Kiki's help in baking a questionable fish pie for her granddaughter (shocker, the granddaughter is ungrateful). Finally, there's the striped shirted, coke-bottle bespectacled Tombo—looking suspiciously like the title character of *Where's Waldo*. A hapless goof himself, he clearly takes a liking to Kiki, though his friends view her as more of a curious novelty.

And yet, the truly remarkable thing about Kiki is how truly unremarkable she is. She has no fancy dress. No royal lineage or riches or jewelry. And yet, you'll always find someone sporting a Kiki costume at anime conventions. Its simplicity appeals to anyone on the cheap. Her love interest, Tombo, is no secret prince or swashbuckling hero. Look his name up in the dictionary and it reads, "dork." She even lacks a song. No great musical number about finding love or "wanting more." No, not Kiki. In the grand flock of animated heroines, she flies alone as the odd duck.

Contrast this with Disney's immaculate runway of glittering princesses and it's too easy. But consider her place in Miyazaki's lineup as well. Miyazaki's heroines are strong, but they still fall victim to basic fairy tale tropes. In *Nausicaä of the Valley of the Wind*, the title character's kingdom suffers an invasion. *Castle in* the *Sky* tosses Princess Sheena between not one, but two sets of captors. Chihiro from *Spirited Away* gets sold into supernatural slavery. The quest for these characters is thrust upon them by an external force. But Kiki remains the one leading heroine in the Miyazaki canon who chooses her quest. She didn't have to leave. She *decided* to. In 1989. Twenty years before Disney even attempted the same work ethic theme with *Princess and the Frog*.

As a result, Kiki enjoys the ultimate freedom to do things of her own accord. When she tidies up the attic above the bakery, it's not to clean up after seven slobbish dwarves, but because she needs a place to live. She delivers packages not on the orders of an evil headmistress, but because she needs the money. Another interesting curio? No villain. If there is a villain in *Kiki*, it's simply the dreaded "R" word that strikes fear into the hearts of children everywhere: responsibility. But Kiki takes it in stride with a smile on her face. Growing up intrigues her.

It's this wide-eyed wonder that forms the heart of the movie. And Kiki isn't perfect. Oblivious to her burgeoning romantic feelings, she acts obnoxiously standoffish to Tombo. More so to his friends, whom she regards with buried jealousy. And the movie makes it clear that giving too much drains one's resources as well. One botched delivery sees her poor cat play-acting as a temporary doll until the replacement is found. She helps the elderly Madame bake a fish pie at the expense of going to a party with Tombo. After flying in the rain to deliver the package, the ungrateful granddaughter remarks, "Ugh. I hate her stupid pies." It's worth noting that the city overflows with money. And the spoiled girl is a dark reflection of Kiki herself. Kiki is a working girl. Her customers are the 1 percent. And for her troubles, Kiki succumbs to her first knock-down cold. Her reaction to the virus is adorable, with Osono laughing when Kiki asks, "Am I going to die?" To be that young and naïve.

Most troubling is the loss of her powers. First, she loses the ability to understand her cat. Then she loses her power to fly. One could read this as a metaphor for maturing, puberty, self-doubt, whatever. Her artist friend, Ursula, sensing a kinship with a fellow creative soul, takes it upon herself to help Kiki out. On a retreat in the woods, she explains that the same thing happened to her when she began to paint. "Sometimes you have to find your own style." Lost in a new world with snooty customers and first-time crushes pulling her in every direction, Kiki struggles to find her way.

In the end, a disaster forces her back on her broom. This time, it's a beau-in-distress that has to be saved by the damsel. This finale at the hands of a mechanical disaster might feel shoehorned in, but again, it's not an unreasonable idea. Stuff happens. Life is its own challenge. And Kiki, ever pragmatic, rises to it.

Assisting her is Miyazaki's team of animators. Kiki soars above an island city that feels both tangibly real and fantastical. Not satisfied with initial sketches, Miyazaki took his animation team to Stockholm. From there, they designed a fantasy metropolis with whimsical nods to Paris, Lisbon, Madrid, and San Francisco, among others. As Miyazaki wryly noted: "The south side of the island is on the Mediterranean. The north on the Baltic." The result is stunning. Each shot bristles around the edges with little parks, flower pots, fountains, and cafes. Even if one can't see around every little zigzagging corner, there's the sense that the winding streets continue. I know nothing to compare it to, except the meticulously crafted computer-generated worlds of modern video games. It begs to get lost in. And looks equally gorgeous from the air. If this were a real city, there would be cruise ships parked there 24/7.

Little flourishes also fill in the edges. Kiki braces herself with her hand as she stumbles, the hairs stand on her head as a gust of wind blasts her into takeoff, and her broom glides dreamily down a hill as her magic sputters out. All of it hand-painted. Joe Hisaishi's score adds the finishing touch with plucky strings and whirling woodwinds.

As a whole, *Kiki's Delivery Service* provides the perfect alternative to the stranglehold of Disney princesses. Slow, deliberately paced, and meditative, it nevertheless entrances with its *Anne of Green Gables* style slice-of-life narrative. Any child who loved the inherent cool factor of the *Ghostbusters* starting their own business will easily identify with the same idea here. And identifying with Kiki herself is even easier. Neither warrior or domestic goddess, she's just an ordinary kid. Strip the film of all its fantasy trappings, and it's simply about a child who grows up, gets a job, and deals with love, life, and customer service. That this isn't the most terrifying anime ever made is a testament to Kiki's worldview. She proves that all it takes is a good heart and a lot of elbow grease to survive in the world. Of course, adults know there's a little more to it than that. But as a starting point for kids, I can think of no better role model.

It's ironic, then, that Miyazaki claimed he made *Spirited Away* as a film specifically targeted for ten-year-old girls. While a superior "technical" achievement, one wonders why he bothered to fix that which wasn't broken. He already made a perfect film for young girls. It's *Kiki's Delivery Service*. But perhaps, like the rest of us, he forgot. Because Kiki is just … Kiki.

She doesn't stick out.

She just gets in your head.

Robert Walker is the co-writer for the hit web series The Nostalgia Critic. *As a child of the '80s, he's been watching anime imports since before he even knew what anime was. Altogether, he has watched over 300 anime series and films. Not necessarily for his job, but because he has a problem.*

1989 • RANMA ½

— SAM LIZ & CHRIS STUCKMANN —

The following is Sam Liz's story:

When I was fourteen, my doctor diagnosed me with a nasty case of mononucleosis. Beyond the obvious discomfort, the next five months were particularly taxing. I was a pretty good horseback rider, and that was out of the question for a while, so as a result, I turned to my books.

My love for reading is unparalleled and I was devouring my supply at a rapid rate. With my stacks of books disappearing daily and only having the energy to make it to the library for brief trips, I had to find other avenues of entertainment. So there I was, perusing the lesser-traveled corners of the Internet. *Sailor Moon* had stoked my love of anime, and all of Toonami's programming that followed only heightened my desire for more. But where to turn? Purchasing anime was absurdly expensive, and even if you came across a good deal, odds are fellow fans had snatched it up already.

This was how I discovered *Ranma ½*. Before services like Crunchyroll made anime easier to access, anime fans had to make do with whatever they had. In my case, this was brief clips of *Ranma ½* uploaded across the net at random fan sites. With that illness keeping me mostly bedridden, I encountered many an anime that helped pass the time. One of my favorites was *Ranma ½*.

The show's main character, Ranma Saotome, is having a tough time. While on a training journey with his father, Genma, they accidentally fall into the cursed springs of Jusenkyo. This spring has a legend: those who fall into it are cursed to take the physical form of whatever creature drowned there years ago. This switch occurs whenever you're doused with cold water. Contact with hot water will reverse the curse, but you'll still switch back as soon as you touch cold water again.

Unfortunately for Ranma and Genma, this legend turns out to be true. When Ranma touches cold water, he transforms into a girl! Genma however, isn't quite as lucky. Cold water turns him into a giant panda bear! When Ranma and Genma take up residence with Soun Tendo at his dojo, Ranma discovers that Genma and Tendo had made a pact long ago: that Ranma would marry one of Tendo's daughters. As you might expect, Ranma's newfound ability to randomly switch genders makes getting to know Tendo's three daughters extremely difficult.

This show was refreshing in a way unlike any I'd seen at the time. The subject of gender identity was still taboo when I was fourteen, and it's hard to imagine what Japanese audiences thought in 1989 during its initial run. In the earlier episodes, Ranma views his predicament very negatively. He's constantly embarrassed and highly secretive about this part of himself. But eventually, over time, Ranma begins to see the benefits of both genders. He understands the better qualities of both sides, and learns how to live with this "curse." It was a refreshing message, and one that I needed to hear.

The following is Chris Stuckmann's story:

I wish mine was as cool as hers.

It's easy to relate to my wife's *Ranma ½* tale, but there's one specific aspect I zeroed in on: the desperate yearning and frenzied hunt for anime before it was easy to find. If it wasn't on TV, your options were some weird, poorly-constructed fan site, or insanely expensive and exclusive stores that carried anime. Remember those ads in *Animerica*?

"Available now at Suncoast, Coconuts, and your local comics store!" Ah, good old Coconuts. My last resort for *DBZ* VHS releases when they were sold out everywhere else. They were so overpriced.

Ranma ½ never aired on Toonami or Adult Swim, but I'd seen countless ads for the show in magazines and pamphlets at JC Comics & Cards, my local comics shop. Similar to my wife, after discovering anime, I found myself scrounging for more. *Where were the video games?* I often pondered. Before *Dragon Ball Z: Budokai* was released, us button-mashers and anime fans didn't have much in that arena. That said, I was surprised to find a PlayStation game at Blockbuster called *Dragon Ball GT: Final Bout.*

My God ... was it ever terrible.

This can't be the only anime video game option I have.

Nope, it wasn't. Enter *Ranma ½: Hard Battle*, a fighting game actually released for the Super Nintendo in America in 1993—unheard of at the time. This was the second *Ranma ½* video game, the first being brutally Americanized and released as the hilariously-titled: *Street Combat.*

Stateside game companies were just as stumped by anime as television networks back then. The prospect of marketing them to American kids baffled them. The game *Dragon Power* for Nintendo is another apt example.

This is why the release of *Ranma ½: Hard Battle*—with the proper character designs and names, no less—is so remarkable. The game pretty much sucked, don't get me wrong, but it was a step in the right direction for anime acceptance in America.

After we got married, I recall being smack dab in the middle of an epic anime nerd debate with my wife. When the topic of *Ranma ½* was broached, I was ashamed to admit I'd never seen it, to my wife's shock of course. Cut to a few years later, and we have the entire Blu-ray collection, including the OVAs.

Side note: Speaking of those Blu-rays, Viz's transfer is one of the best improvements these eyes have ever seen for an older anime.

Over the years, my wife and I have enjoyed watching the show together many times, and it's only brought us closer.

And just for the heck of it, I recently tracked down a complete-in-box copy of *Ranma ½: Hard Battle* to play, and yup ... it still sucks.

Sam Liz is a longtime anime fan, bibliophile, and nerd. She enjoys quiet, relaxing days with her husband and dogs.

1990 • CYBER CITY OEDO 808

SAIBA SHITI OEDO 808

— ERNEST CLINE —

One of the most frustrating aspects of being an anime fan living in the United States during the '80s and early '90s was the scarcity of information. There were very few online anime databases or review websites to consult—and even fewer that were available in English. Most fans in North America had to wade through the uneven ocean of imported anime VHS tapes on our own, with nothing but the box artwork and recommendations from local friends to guide us. But this scarcity of information had a way of making you feel like a brave explorer venturing into unknown territory in pursuit of hidden treasure. And when you finally managed to stumble across one of these treasures on your own, it could be a uniquely triumphant experience.

That was how I felt when I first saw *Cyber City Oedo 808*. It was in at the Gen Con gaming convention in the mid-'90s, in one of the anime screening rooms they had at the event. These screening rooms were open twenty-four hours a day during the con, and they were one of the few places where you could see new anime films and series that still hadn't been released outside of Japan. When someone put on a tape of *Cyber City Oedo 808* my eyes were immediately riveted to the screen, even though it was a copy with no English subtitles or dubbing. It was an OVA comprised of three forty-minute-long episodes, but they were screened back-to-back as a single two-hour movie. I adored every frame—and as soon as it was over, I immediately ran up to the Dealer's Room to seek out a copy of it. By the grace of Crom, I lucked out and located a VHS copy of the UK version of *Cyber City Oedo 808*, which has a hilarious over-the-top profanity-laden English-language dub track that is now the stuff of otaku legend. The UK release also features a propulsive rock/ambient/proto-synthwave score by Rory McFarlane that manages to elevate the gorgeous animation to even greater heights.

Set in the year 2808, *Cyber City Oedo 808* is about three hardened criminals, Sengoku, a wise-cracking nihilist, Gogol, a Mohawk-wearing hacker with Cyclops-style shades, and Benten, an androgynous bishōnen badass whose martial arts skills are only matched by his fashion sense. All three of these convicts are currently serving out three-hundred–year-long prison sentences in an orbital penitentiary—exotic accommodations that still suck, despite the fantastic view they have from their cell windows.

In the opening scene, Sengoku, Gogol, and Benten are all offered the opportunity to have their sentences drastically reduced by going to work for the Oedo Cyber Police. For every criminal they apprehend, they'll get a few years knocked off their prison term. And just like Eddie Murphy in *48 Hours*, they reluctantly accept the offer, because anything beats rotting in an orbital prison where no conjugal visits are allowed.

Once they agree to work for the man, Sengoku, Gogol, and Benten are each given a *jitte*, the traditional weapon and symbol of guards and policemen during Japan's Edo period. Each of our heroes are also fitted with an electronic collar that can be triggered to explode remotely if any of them decides to disobey an order or step out of line—just like the exploding prison collar Arnie is forced to wear in *The Running Man*. Then they're each sent down to Cyber City on their own separate impossible mission. These interconnected adventures play out against the backdrop of the sprawling overcrowded vertical cityscape of a futuristic Tokyo.

In the first episode, Sengoku has to solve a hacker-orchestrated hostage crisis inside the world's tallest skyscraper—and he has to do it in less than twenty-four hours, or the cops will kill him, Snake Plissken style. In the second episode, Gogol is tasked with hunting down a murderous military cyborg, and in the final sequence, Benten faces off against cybernetic sabretooth tigers and a genetically engineered space vampire. These plotlines don't really hold up under close scrutiny, but they don't need to, since the story is really just a delivery system for dazzling visuals and action sequences.

That's one of the many things I love about the overall style and tone of *Cyber City Oedo 808*—it's like a fantastic mash-up of a dozen different '80s sci-fi and action flicks. Imagine *Escape From New York* thrown into a cinematic blender with *Robocop*, *Die Hard*, *Hardware*, *Highlander*, *Cobra*, *Lifeforce*, and a liberal helping of *Blade Runner*. It all makes for a delicious cyberpunk cocktail. The animation by Madhouse is a wonder to behold, and the immense care and attention to detail that went into the design of the characters, city, ships, weapons, and vehicles shines through in every frame. It's like a collection of Syd Mead concept artwork come to life, and then set to a pulsing synthwave soundtrack.

The film was directed by the great Yoshiaki Kawajiri, who also directed *Lensman: Secret of The Lens*, *Wicked City*, *Ninja Scroll*, and *Vampire Hunter D: Bloodlust*. But *Cyber City Oedo 808* is Kawajiri's under-appreciated cyberpunk masterpiece. If you haven't seen it, give it a chance. It's the sort of diamond in the rough that could end up becoming one of your all-time favorites.

Ernest Cline is the bestselling author of Ready Player One *and* Armada. *He also co-wrote the screenplay for Steven Spielberg's adaptation of* Ready Player One.

1991 • ONLY YESTERDAY

OMOIDE PORO PORO

— MARK CRILLEY —

I had the good fortune to be living in Japan when *Omoide Poro Poro* was released in July of 1991, but the bad fortune of being too stupid to go out and see it. I had arrived in Japan about four months earlier to begin a two-year stint teaching English in Iwate Prefecture, a part of Japan that is not so far away from Yamagata, where much of the film is set. So you might say I kind of lived *Omoide Poro Poro* before I saw it: I encountered in real life the thatched-roof farmland world depicted in the movie, and taught English to little kids that were not so different from Taeko, the child whose stories are the heart and soul of the film.

I'll bet a lot of people haven't seen *Omoide Poro Poro* (I refuse to use its instantly forgettable English name, *Only Yesterday*), as it remained the sole Ghibli film unreleased in America until 2016. So perhaps I should take a moment to say what it's about. It tells the story of a Japanese woman in modern day Tokyo who takes a trip to visit distant relatives in the idyllic countryside of Yamagata. As she travels she begins reliving memories of her childhood in 1966, which are fully dramatized in the film, taking up as much as half of its running time. This series of highly vivid memories allows her to contrast her current self with her childhood self, and in so doing come to a new understanding of who she is and what she really wants in life.

If that sounds like a movie without a plot, that's because it very nearly is. But thank goodness. Because the outpouring of memories (which is pretty close to what *Omoide Poro Poro* really means) is the true joy of this film, and a conventionally intricate plot would only have detracted from them. More than any other anime film I've seen, and possibly more than any film *period*, it conveys the power of childhood memories: how they stick with you, can make you laugh, or wince, or feel genuinely sad many years later.

I first saw the film in the late 1990s, having bought a VHS tape of it—pirated, I cannot doubt—that someone was selling at a comic book convention. This would have been right around the time I met Miki, a Japanese woman here in Michigan who I fell in love with and soon asked to be my wife. We watched the movie in its original Japanese-language incarnation, which I implore you to do also. (Dubbed versions of any anime are inferior to the originals, but they are particularly damaging to the experience of viewing films that are set in Japan, as everyone suddenly sounds like they came from Santa Monica.) So as I watched the film, I had the double benefit of having lived in Japan for two years, and also having a kind of real-life Taeko there at my side to help me understand the full cultural context of what I was seeing.

It was a delightful experience. Here was a film that let me view Japan from the point of view of someone raised there. It allowed me to more fully imagine what life in Japan was like back in the 1960s, and to better understand what makes a childhood in Japan different from—and sometimes surprisingly similar to—a childhood in America. In a certain way, it helped me to know my wife better: it was as if I were being allowed to watch some of Miki's childhood memories, brought to life in anime form.

What really sets *Omoide Poro Poro* apart from other movies about childhood is the specificity of the memories depicted. There's a wonderful series of scenes involving a pineapple being brought into Taeko's home, a fruit so unusual in Japan at the time that the various family members treat it like some kind of amazing treasure box from a foreign land. When they finally learn the proper way of cutting it open, everyone sits down with massive anticipation for this, their first taste of fresh pineapple. The disappointment is crushing: no one likes it at all. Taeko is so determined to enjoy it, she forces herself to keep eating.

There are not many films that would choose to present a scene like this, one that lacks a clear dramatic climax or side-splitting punchline. But that's the genius of it. It's a weird, quirky memory: the very thing that sticks in your mind, decades later, for reasons you can't explain. Even Pixar, in all its mastery of storytelling, would never devote such care to capturing the mysterious resonance of this strange little real-life experience. Ghibli, under the guidance of Isao Takahata, brought the full force of their artistry to every last beat of it, ensuring that it would ring true in all its details. If you're like me, the scene will stick with you, until it almost seems to have become one of your own memories, making you nostalgic for a childhood experience you never actually had.

Omoide Poro Poro is filled with such scenes, especially in the parts of the film devoted to Taeko's childhood. The parts set in modern Japan, when Taeko is in her late twenties, are a bit less successful: There are talky scenes in which there is an awful lot of telling instead of showing. But there is so much power in those childhood memory scenes that, for me, this remains one of the great achievements in anime. If you are among the many people who have never seen it, I would encourage you to seek it out. The anime titles that get people talking tend to have mind-blowing visuals and a twisty narrative hook. But few of those films depict real life with the power and quiet artistry on display in *Omoide Poro Poro*.

Now, just to be clear, I want you to know that you don't have to be married to someone from Japan to enjoy this movie. But hey, if you're still single, and you're thinking of seeing this movie, and there's a Japanese person that you've fallen in love with ...

... well, it worked out really nicely for me, that's all I'm saying.

Mark Crilley was raised in Detroit. After graduating from Kalamazoo College in 1988, he taught English in Taiwan and Japan for nearly five years. A fourteen-time Eisner nominee, his work has been featured in USA Today, Entertainment Weekly, *and on* CNN Headline News, *and his popular YouTube videos have been viewed more than 350 million times. He lives in Michigan with his wife, Miki, and children, Matthew and Mio.*

1991 • ROUJIN Z

RŌJIN ZETTO

— CHRIS STUCKMANN —

If you were an anime fan in the '90s, odds are you saw the poster for *Roujin Z* somewhere. Whether it was an advertisement in *Animerica* or even the occasional comic book, you couldn't escape the image of a geriatric man emerging from a mech.

For myself, I first saw the poster for Hiroyuki Kitakubo's 1991 film in a catalog at my local comic shop, JC Comics & Cards. Before the Internet, perusing these pamphlets was my only way to learn about new anime. Convincing my parents to allow a subscription to *Animerica* was a formidable task (covers like the February 1996 issue featuring a half-nude Motoko Kusanagi ensured that), so my outside knowledge of anime was limited to whatever information was published in those little booklets. The same films were often featured: *Ghost in the Shell, Ninja Scroll, Armitage III, Akira,* and *Roujin Z.*

While I appreciate anime of all genres, I'm especially drawn to titles that explore deeper themes or promote a message on morality. *Roujin Z* accomplishes both, while also staying within the confines of what most anime fans expected back then: Robot action and *weird shit.*

Haruko Mitsuhashi is a young nurse providing care for an elderly widower named Mr. Takazawa. In contrast to most portrayals of nurses in film, Haruko is totally sincere when she says Mr. Takazawa's health and happiness is her primary concern. She feels a strong moral obligation to his well-being and is just trying to make his final days tolerable.

One day, to Haruko's horror, men storm into Mr. Takazawa's room, removing him from his bed and transporting him to a science facility. There, Mr. Takazawa becomes the unwilling guinea pig for the Z-001, a new piece of technology meant to revolutionize eldercare. It's a gargantuan bed, capable of meeting a patient's every need. If you're hungry, it feeds you. Feel like going for a stroll? The Z-001 can simulate a walk down the street. Gotta use the facilities? It's able to deal with that.

While for some, this breakthrough might be considered an advancement, Haruko makes herself very clear: it's a regression. She feels that without a flesh-and-blood person caring for the elderly, they will lose touch with humanity. Can a machine feel love? Can it understand what someone *really* needs?

Roujin Z offers a wry commentary on society's view of senior citizens, often mocking the disrespectful attitude of many. The script was written by none other than Katsuhiro Otomo, famed director of *Akira*. His outlook on the unfortunate dismissal of our elderly is gratefully filled with biting satire. When the robotic bed is introduced for the first time, its many uses are demonstrated to an electrified crowd. One man remarks that with the Z-001, he'll finally be able to leave his mother and take a vacation. Otomo's vision of a world where the elderly are cast aside and nurses are replaced by machines is so tangible, I struggle to refer to it as "futuristic."

As you may expect, before long, the Z-001 becomes sentient, taking on a personality of its own. The lumbering mechanical bed plows through the city, destroying everything in its wake. The most amusing moments in *Roujin Z* involve the bed crushing an entire street, emerging from the desolation, the sleepy Mr. Takazawa barely aware of the danger in front of him. Curiously, these sequences during the finale have attracted criticism.

What starts as a parody on the populace's rejection of the elderly, eventually becomes two robots battling in the street. For some, this development forsook the original setup and reverted to stereotypical anime tropes. Normally, I'd agree, if not for the aggressively batshit reason for this conflict.

The two main figureheads behind the creation of the Z-001 are Takashi Terada and Yoshihiko Hasegawa. It's clear from the start that while their intentions may be good, their end goal is selfish. Neither men are prioritizing the care of the infirm over their own fame. But during the third act, Yoshihiko reveals he is a traitor, having developed a combat version of the Z-001 in secret. His goals to militarize what they initially created to help people offer yet another astute observation on the part of Otomo. When science is put in the wrong hands, its value for the good of mankind is often tossed aside for financial gain, and sometimes, utilized for war.

So as these robots duke it out, thematically, it's richer than most mech-on-mech battles. It isn't just about explosions and epic takedowns. We're witnessing two creations of science clash, both formed from one idea, then split with differing ideologies. In this way, Otomo offers a scathing dissertation on science and technology. Use it to help humanity, not to destroy it.

Roujin Z can be a little uneven, and the targets of its parody are sometimes missed, but Otomo's script and Kitakubo's sure-handed direction make the ride an entertaining one. Despite an odd subplot with elderly computer hackers and some hilariously improbable technology involving Mr. Takazawa's deceased wife, in the end, the film's message is a noble one: Don't forget our old folks, they need us.

1992 • TENCHI MUYO!

TENCHI MUYŌ!

— EMMA FYFFE —

Being an anime fan in the late 1990s—who was not simply satisfied with watching whatever was in the Toonami lineup or randomly aired on the Sci-Fi channel—I often found myself in the position of renting whatever they had at Blockbuster. This resulted in me watching some strange titles, like the first half of the 1994 *Final Fantasy* OVA—Blockbuster didn't have the second half—and every ninety-minute anime film adaptation of a fighting game on the market (side note: *Street Fighter II: The Movie* is actually pretty good). To avoid the disappointment of discovering a series I liked only to be left with a massive episode-three cliffhanger, I often found myself gravitating toward titles that included "The Movie" in them. Even if I was somewhat confused because said movie expected you to already be familiar with and care about the characters from the series, at least I was getting a complete story.

I used to rent movies to gauge whether or not the series they were side-stories of/ prequels to/retellings of were worth investigating further. After all, anime titles were *not* easy to come by in the late '90s. You were almost certainly looking at a monetary investment, and even about half the titles recommended in *Animerica* weren't legally available here. I was not alone in this endeavor, being fortunate enough to have a couple of other friends who were into anime and, like me, wanted to get a taste of what was out there beyond what was included with our parents' cable packages. So the first time I was ever exposed to anything Tenchi was *Tenchi the Movie: Tenchi Muyo in Love*, which one of those friends had rented, already seen, and suggested we watch during a sleepover.

As an adult, of course I realize that *Tenchi Muyo!* and all of its associated titles are technically harem anime—series wherein a bunch of lady characters exist basically to be in love with the same guy. Additionally, the first OVA is largely considered to be the very first occurrence of this sub-genre. However, as a thirteen-year-old, that thought didn't even cross my mind. Sure, there was a whole bunch of women who seemed to be inexplicably interested in the rather underwhelming Tenchi, but that was secondary to the fact that ... there were just *that*, a whole bunch of women. And because there were a lot a of women, they were all allowed to have unique personalities, flaws, and to be good at different things. Plus the plot of *Tenchi Muyo in Love* is basically *Tenchi's* take on *Back to the Future* and the series already borrows a lot of elements from *Star Wars*, so I was hooked. Doubly so, because there were ladies fighting with what were essentially lightsabers, something we had yet to see in *Star Wars*, even in the animated series, as this predates even Genndy Tartakovsky's *Clone Wars*. Released in Japan in April of 1996 and, surprisingly, the US in August of the same year, it actually predates the *Star Wars* prequels all together, but I saw it not long after *The Phantom Menace* was released in 1999, so I was definitely hungry for some sweet, sweet Jedi or, in this case, Jurai action.

To my shock and delight, within about six months of me having seen *Tenchi the Movie*, the first of the *Tenchi* OVAs—the original *Tenchi Muyo!*—was airing on Toonami. Finally, I could see more adventures of these fabulous women I had been instantly fascinated by in this ninety-minute film. And sure, maybe the fact that these episodes were heavily edited to meet American broadcast standards—a.k.a. toned way down in the fan-service department—continued to keep me ignorant of the fact that this was intended for a male gaze. Or maybe not so much ignorant, as it made it very easy to ignore and again focus on the personality traits, rather than the physical ones, of this amazing cast of women.

There was Ryoko, a tomboyish, blue-haired space pirate who fought with an energy sword and ki blasts, something I'd seen primarily men do in the *Dragon Ball* series, and who had a cute little sidekick/mascot who could transform into a spaceship. Her main rival for Tenchi's affections, Ayeka, a refined and well-mannered princess, who would still absolutely decimate anyone who dared try to harm Tenchi or her sister Sasami. Like Ryoko, she was way more powerful than Tenchi in his usual not-manifesting the power of some boundless universal entity/royal sentient tree state (this was retconned in later iterations of the story and is about as weird as it sounds).

Mihoshi, who admittedly suffered a downgrade to "dumb blonde" once *Tenchi Universe* rolled around, but was somewhat redeemed by the addition of her extremely competent partner Kiyone, two members of the Galaxy Police who's conflicting personality types provide much of the the series comic relief. And who could forget the notorious mad scientist/sometimes Ryoko's mom/creator of weapons of mass destruction and/or actual super deities, Washu?

Is Tenchi Masaki the hero of all the versions of the "a bunch of alien girls come live at the Masaki shrine" story? Sure. Are most of the women who live there varying degrees of in love with him? Also yes. But are these women complex individuals with motivations and stories beyond being in love with Tenchi? Most definitely.

Tenchi Muyo roughly translates to mean "No Need for Tenchi." While Tenchi is not a bad guy, he certainly isn't necessary for us to care about the women around him. In fact, I would argue we care about Tenchi *because* of the women around him and their stories of terrorizing the galaxy as a space pirate, or fleeing their home planet in search of their missing brother. Their stories are what set the foundation for making Tenchi's story even remotely interesting. In the first *Tenchi Muyo!* OVAs, there would be no story without Washu, who indirectly sets the entire plot in motion, in more ways than one. While the various *Tenchi* titles may technically qualify as harem anime, they are so much more than that, with a cast of nuanced women creating the backbone of the universe and driving the story forward. Tenchi is just along for the ride.

Emma Fyffe currently resides in Los Angeles where she hosts a Sailor Moon *podcast* Love and Justice *and an anime talk show* Hyper Otaku *on Hyper RPG's Facebook page. She is also the "Golden Mic" of the* Movie Trivia Schmoedown *(it says so on her IMDb) and the Captain of a ragtag crew of smugglers on Hyper RPG's Twitch-based* Star Wars *roleplaying game series "Pencils and Parsecs."*

1992 • SAILOR MOON

BISHÔJO SENSHI SÊRÂ MÛN

— JOSHUA DUNBAR —

"Sailor Moon you've just got to believe in yourself-please-don't let the Negaverse win! Everyone's counting on you!"

"I hear you, Luna. I am not afraid anymore."

For a generation of kids reared on typical Saturday morning buffoonery, these lines of dialogue hit like a thunderclap—the whiny, fearful yet lovable crybaby had transformed into a warrior princess, and along with her, transformed a legion of '90s kids into lifelong anime fans.

To understand why *Sailor Moon* is such a watershed moment for so many American anime fans, you have to understand the cartoon landscape in the US at that time.

Though not exactly a wasteland, the anime market in the US was undeniably dry. Anime was still largely untried in the US Apart from Sci-Fi's (now Syfy) Saturday Anime program block, the only exposure came through expensive (even by today's standards) VHS tapes that usually had to be special ordered by way of a trip to the mall and a visit to Suncoast Motion Picture Co. A daunting set of circumstances for most seven- to nine-years-olds with very little pocket money and less than sympathetic parents. Parents were not the only unsympathetic eyes and ears—so unsure of the appeal of anime in the west that, despite *Sailor Moon*'s monumental success in its home country, a notorious live-action/animation hybrid was produced and briefly considered. Thankfully, it was determined it would simply be more cost-efficient to dub the original animation into English and to quote the original DiC dub, "and so our story begins … "

What made *Sailor Moon* stand out?

Female characters supporting one another at school, at home, and in crisis situations. These situations were foreign and familiar. The background art was consistently stunning and conveyed a rich sense of place. There was an air of sophistication and insight—complicated villains who were not one-note "black hats." Villains for whom the show goes great lengths in explaining their thought processes and motivations. On more than one occasion, the villains repent and are saved. In one of the most memorable moments of the series, one of the villains reaches a new level of understanding and expresses a desire to change—only to be executed for his thought crime. The pursuit of reality in the setting, the mature character development, and intricate story arcs packed a narrative punch not found in western series.

The inclusion of gay and lesbian characters also set the show apart from anything in the west at that time. Though these relationships were originally downplayed or altogether altered in the west, it wasn't long before viewers began to read between the lines. Over time, these aspects of *Sailor Moon* have been disproportionally discussed in media—though they may have initially been censored or adapted in a way to hide them, they were not central to the narrative and very little is actually lost in regards to the overall viewing experience. Nevertheless, the presence of homosexual and gender-fluid characters certainly did and continues to provide reassurance to generations of young people.

To the casual viewer, *Sailor Moon* can prove to be a highly uneven viewing experience. The show seems to have two different types of episodes, generally reflected by the art style. There are "filler" episodes that generally have a more comedic or lighthearted tone. In these episodes, the characters appear crude at times, frequently falling off-model. These episodes usually contain more gag sequences, slapstick, and feature far less refined animation. One such episode, in which the girls discover and return a lost plesiosaur to its mother, traveled so far into the realm of the absurd that it was disavowed by the *Sailor Moon* creator, Naoko Takeuchi. Viewing one or more of these filler episodes out of context, it would be difficult to believe that the characters in *Sailor Moon* also engage in heated ideological discussions (Sailor Moon's altruistic views often placing her at odds with the other sailor soldiers), find love, face loss, and experience deep regret—but they do.

Typically, the episodes that deal with the most critical plot developments are also the best looking, and feature animation that is both expressive and anatomically accurate. Episode 68, "Protect Chibiusa! Clash of the Ten Warriors" contains some of the best art of the series. In Japanese or English, this episode features gorgeous animation, an inspired soundtrack, a child in danger, and a showdown between the Black Moon Clan and the Sailor Soldiers. This episode also highlights many of the issues Sailor Moon initially faced when adapting to the US market. In the DiC dub, the song "She's Got the Power" replaces the Japanese song "Ai no Senshi" (Warrior of Love). "She's Got the Power," performed by Stan Bush (of *Transformers: The Movie* soundtrack fame) is the sort of sock-it-to-'em rock-anthem usually reserved for male superheroes. This co-opting of elements of boys media is fascinating and exhilarating, but in the 1990s this presented a major marketing problem. Is this a show for boys or girls? Young children or young adults? These problems would follow *Sailor Moon* throughout the west, as it is continually one of the most talked about yet misunderstood properties. However, gorgeous, emotional episodes such as "Protect Chibiusa!" are able to transcend the confusion casual western viewers may have about not only *Sailor Moon* but anime in general.

The animation in this episode was directed by Ikuko Itoh, who was responsible for some of the most dramatic moments in the series. Among them, the finale of the *Super S* series, an episode that culminates in an impressively realized and suspenseful free fall above Tokyo. For fans of the show, however, the most unforgettable episode is the two-part finale of the first season (The first half being handled by Itoh). DiC, who was responsible for the original English dub, has long been criticized for their handling of this episode. Confusing edits are made to the animation and dialogue in an effort to soften the impact of the violence. The Sailor Senshi are said to have been "captured" instead of killed—though the on-screen images contradict much of what is being said. In defense of DiC's decisions regarding the content, when the first part of this episode aired in Japan the on-screen deaths of these beloved characters proved highly traumatic for many viewers. So much so that following the initial broadcast, TV Asahi (which aired the show), was inundated with calls from concerned parents demanding to know the outcome of the following weeks episode so they could calm their children. Their upset is understandable. In those moments, *Sailor Moon* is less a children's show and more an honest depiction of war, with death being a real and possible consequence of battle. Strong presentations of universal themes such as good vs. evil are why the anime continues to endure and thrive throughout the world and across many cultural lines.

While it deals universal themes of love, friendship, and good vs. evil, it also presents a lovingly accurate glimpse into contemporary Japanese life. For these reasons, *Sailor Moon* not only fosters a love for Japanese animation, but also for Japan. There is a romantic view of the mundane—a quick game at the arcade before school, the falling rain on an umbrella while waiting on the bus, lunch in the schoolyard under a tree. The magic of *Sailor Moon* is that these ordinary images are as indelible as the cosmic effect-laden battles. This is reflected in Sailor Moon's dying wish in Episode 46, after the defeat of Queen Beryl:

> "When I wake up in the morning, I can see the breeze rustling the curtains. The cuckoo clock in my room tells me it's seven o'clock. Then I hear my mom say, 'Get out of bed or you'll be late!' But I'm still sleepy, so I think to myself, 'Let me sleep another three minutes.' Everyday, I'll be late to school as always. The teacher makes me stand out in the hall and my tests are covered with red marks. We all go for crêpes on our way home from school. I stare longingly at the party dress on display in the store window .... It's those fun simple things that bring me joy. That's ... that's the ordinary life I want to ... go back to."

Fortunately for us, the final season of the original *Sailor Moon* anime, *Sailor Stars*, manages to stick the landing in terms of the heroine's wish for a peaceful life. Unlike the superheroes of the western landscape-destined to repeat and endure their suffering over and over, *Sailor Moon* trusts her instincts and achieves her goal of victory through love and understanding.

Physically and emotionally exhausted, surrounded by friends, she is finally able to embrace her Prince. He reassures her and the audience:

"YOU DID WELL USAKO—IT'S FINE NOW, EVERYTHING IS OVER."

Joshua Dunbar is a freelance illustrator and art educator and holds an MFA in Sequential Art from the Savannah College of Art and Design. A lover of all forms of Japanese media, he is currently working on his first creator-owned comic inspired by the Magical Girl genre and late twentieth-century animation. You can find his work on his Instagram at @j2dstar or joshuadunbar.com.

1993 • NINJA SCROLL

JŪBĒ NINPŪCHŌ

— CHRIS STUCKMANN —

Ninja Scroll. The name struck fear into the hearts of timid anime fans like myself during its heyday. Tales spread amongst wide-eyed youth, telling of extreme violence and gore, and as a result, the stories eventually reached my parents. If that wasn't enough, the warning of violence, nudity, and language on the VHS all but confirmed I wouldn't be allowed to see it.

As a result, an aura of mysticism surrounded *Ninja Scroll*. It became more than just an anime. There was something ... *wrong* about it. I'd often chance upon the VHS—usually at Blockbuster Video—peering over my shoulder as I reached for it. *Is Mom looking? Okay good, she's way over there .... Now let's see here. Recommended 18+? I'll never get away with this.*

Gratefully, my parents were fairly lenient on what entertainment they permitted in the house. Most R-rated films were okay, but they preferred I watch the TV edited versions. Because of this, the mystery of who "Mr. Falcon" was in *Die Hard 2* plagued me for years. (Look up the old TBS edit of *Die Hard 2* and have a good laugh.) But still, like *Ninja Scroll*, there were plenty of films that were simply not allowed.

A wonderful time in my life began upon reaching adulthood. A mental list of films my parents never green-lit was suddenly within reach. After the joyous realization that I could, in fact, be my own person, I spent a few months absorbing films like *Ninja Scroll* that had previously been banned.

Experiencing *Ninja Scroll* for the first time could be likened to my initial viewing of *The Exorcist*. Both were films surrounded by years of hype and rumors, and both were absolutely not allowed in our home. So before even setting eyes on the first frame, *Ninja Scroll* benefited from its reputation as a highly violent, sexually explicit film. In short, it had me in its grasp before I even saw it. All these years later, that first viewing is still a searing memory.

A whirlwind blade slices through limbs as if they were paper. Bursts of crimson explode into the air. A massive, beastly hand intercepts the blade. The hand belongs to one of the Eight Devils of Kimon. The demon tears a man's arms off, drinking the blood dripping from the stumps. Jubei—a vagabond ninja—slices the demon's fingers to bits. The entity falls on his own blade. His skull splits in two. Brain matter pools beneath him.

All within the first ten minutes.

It's safe to say ... *Ninja Scroll* earned its reputation.

Manga Entertainment successfully released the film in America in 1995 and subsequently marketed it heavily as one of their flagship titles. A trailer for *Ninja Scroll* was featured at the start of nearly every anime VHS I rented, and the poster was plastered all over catalogs and copies of *Animerica*. Advertisements for it were impossible to avoid. And with good reason! Not only does the film work as a looking-glass into the '90s "Japanimation Era," but its status as a hyper-violent samurai epic is well-deserved.

The story follows Jubei, a wandering samurai who finds himself poisoned by a deadly virus. A spy named Dakuan blackmails Jubei into locating and eliminating the Eight Devils of Kimon, and if he succeeds, Jubei will be granted an antidote. So, with the help of a skillful warrior named Kagero, Jubei journeys across the land in search of the Eight Devils, hoping to kill every last one of them.

The film was directed by Yoshiaki Kawajiri, known for his depictions of stylized violence, rampant nudity, and over-the-top gore. His previous efforts, *Wicked City*, *Demon City Shinjuku*, and the disregarded *Goku: Midnight Eye* all but solidify his status as anime's resident purveyor of animated carnage. Looking beyond the severed limbs and massive body count, however, it's clear that Kawajiri possesses a great deal of skill as a visual storyteller.

The opening image of Jubei emerging from a cloud of dust. The silhouettes of ninjas leaping from tree branches. The glimmer of light on Jubei's sword. The hypnotic gaze of the snake tattoos lining Benisato's body, one of the Eight Devils. Visual wonder is bursting at the seams in *Ninja Scroll*, and plenty of sequences still drop my jaw to the floor, even after multiple viewings.

The film is rightfully considered essential amongst anime fans, even though the central story isn't really anything special. Plenty of anime involve a wandering samurai and a lineup of baddies waiting to be sliced and diced. What made *Ninja Scroll* noteworthy—beyond the stunning animation and intense musical score—is what it did for anime.

This isn't *just* another samurai movie. By May of 1996, the VHS from Manga Entertainment had sold more than 70,000 copies, making it one of the most popular anime films in America. As stated at the start, *Ninja Scroll* developed a reputation. Whispers of its extreme violence and frequent nudity filled comics stores. If you were hip to the anime scene at the time, films like *Ninja Scroll* were responsible for a major surge of popularity for the medium, and you recognized that. Censorship was a big problem in America, as is discussed in other articles in this book. Manga Entertainment releasing *Ninja Scroll* uncensored was a gamble, but it paid off. The favorable reception—and the number of copies sold—ensured that more uncut titles would make it to our shores, instilling hope that the forceful censoring of anime would eventually come to an end.

Without *Ninja Scroll*, where would anime be in America today?

1993 • SAILOR MOON R: THE MOVIE: THE PROMISE OF THE ROSE

GEKIJÔ-BAN – BISHÔJO SENSHI SÊRÂ MÛN R

— CHRIS STUCKMANN —

As detailed in many other entries, if you were a rabid anime fan at the turn of the century—like me—you devoured whatever was available. And I'm here to tell you, that wasn't much ... unless you were rich. The average anime VHS was priced anywhere from $20 to $35. If you were looking for a more obscure title, and *especially* if you were picky about only watching the subtitled version, then some expendable Andrew Jacksons burning a hole in your pocket was a necessity.

My first job was working as a custodian at a truck parts warehouse when I was fourteen, and it was *definitely* a minimum-wage job. A work permit was required from your principal—and good grades—to get a job that early. Throughout the next few years, I found employment at places like Taco Bell, McDonald's, and the local supermarket: Marc's. It was good to work and learn responsibility, but Andrew Jacksons were at a minimal for a very long time, if you catch my drift.

So, I turned to the video rental stores nearby: Blockbuster, Hollywood Video, and from time to time, I'd find something previously-owned at The Exchange (a Midwest chain of used electronics stores). One day, while browsing at Hollywood Video, I happened across the gigantic clamshell VHS of *Sailor Moon R: The Movie*. Naturally, I'd seen the show on Toonami but was unaware of any movie spinoffs.

I miss those days. Blissful hours dissipating away at the video rental store. Beyond the fond memories, I also miss Hollywood Video's prices. While Blockbuster rented anime for the same cost as everything else, Hollywood Video considered the medium niche enough to only charge 99 cents! Even if I had just one Andrew Jackson, I could rent a ton of anime! Which is why I brought that heavily-censored version of *Sailor Moon R: The Movie* home.

The movie tells the tragic story of Fiore, a young boy who promises his friend Mamoru that when they get older, he'll bring him a flower. After that, Fiore disappears. When Mamoru is much older, he's in a relationship with Usagi, and Fiore appears once more, ready to keep his promise. Naturally, this awkward situation becomes an issue amongst the three of them. What's worse, Fiore is now in control of a deadly flower monster, and an asteroid is hurtling toward Earth. Usagi, Mamoru, and the Sailor Guardians will have to fight against Fiore if they wish to save the planet!

After rocking out to the cheeseball English-version song, "The Power of Love," it was clear I'd become a fan. In fact, the film entertained me so much, I requested my parents drive me back to Hollywood Video to ask the manager a question. Surprisingly, I remember our conversation quite well:

"Hi, I just rented this Sailor Moon movie, and I was curious about something."

"What can I help you with?"

"Could you please tell me how many people have rented this recently?"

She began typing furiously on the large, boxy computer. "Hm ... looks like ... just you."

This was exactly what I wanted to hear. "I'd be willing to purchase this if you'd sell it to me."

"Hm." She considered the offer on the table. "I'll sell it to you for $9.99."

"Great!" We made the exchange of an Alexander Hamilton, and just like that, I owned *Sailor Moon R: The Movie* ... for considerably cheaper than I would've paid anywhere else.

At the time, I owned a pile of *Dragon Ball Z* VHS (my allowance was spread between anime VHS and N64 video game rentals) and now *Sailor Moon R: The*

Movie, so you can probably guess that this ginormous dork watched it quite often. The chunky, pink case rested proudly on my desk for years.

As my knowledge of the Americanization of anime increased over the years, it became a goal of mine to see the uncensored original film. The DVD had gone out of print, making that a daunting task. Before long, Viz announced they'd release the film theatrically in 2017, and by that time, I'd married the love of my life, who also had fond memories of renting anime from Hollywood Video. For all we know, we may have even bumped into each other at the same store, awkwardly exchanging glances.

So, we made our way to the Cedar Lee theater in Cleveland Heights, and upon arriving, we were overwhelmed by the amount of fellow fans present. The theater was packed to the edges with cosplayers and otakus, in fact, almost every single chair was occupied. Nevertheless, we found our seats and sat down, ready to finally see the long-awaited uncensored version.

It didn't disappoint. Fiore's love for Mamoru was tragic, and Usagi's concern for her own relationship with Mamoru was side-splitting and even sincere. It became clear throughout the showing that many others present had never seen the uncut version. Loving chuckles arose from pockets of the theater at the delicate subtext on display, and eventually everyone in attendance seemed to embrace the humor and romantic embarrassment.

It's amazing how much times have changed in the past two decades. I still recall the excitement I felt when the manager of Hollywood Video accepted ten bucks for that VHS. When my wife and I were dating, and we both figured out we'd browsed for anime at the same store, I knew the universe was trying to send me a message. And finally, sitting with her in a theater filled with fellow anime fans, a realization swept over me: the anime scene had evolved out of the shadows and into American culture. My wife and I no longer felt alone in our shared love for the medium.

1994 • STREET FIGHTER II: THE ANIMATED MOVIE

SUTORĪTO FAITĀ TSŪ MŪBĪ

— JOSHUA DUNBAR —

It is safe to assume that if you were a teenage boy with a pulse in the early 1990s then you were a *Street Fighter II* fan. A worldwide phenomenon, the competitive, two-player matches sparked a fighting game boom that would keep arcade cabinets overflowing with quarters for the better part of the decade. With that kind of monumental success, it was inevitable that a misguided, bewildering Hollywood feature film would soon follow.

Like the film adaptation of *Super Mario Bros.* released the year prior, 1994's live-action *Street Fighter* strays so far from its source material it leaves the viewer wondering why they bothered to acquire the license in the first place. Some reevaluations of the film praise Raul Julia's campy, over-the-top performance as series villain, M. Bison. In reality, Bison's and much of the film's lines are delivered with a wink and nod—exhibiting either a complete misunderstanding of the source material or a cynical and dismissive view of video games all together. For fans, it was a painful and disappointing experience.

In 1994, I saw the live-action *Street Fighter* movie in theaters with my father. I remember him making an effort to understand my growing obsession with gaming and Japanese media. I'm certain the live-action *Street Fighter* left him more confused than ever. It is unfortunate the film's far superior Japanese counterpart, *Street Fighter II: The Animated Movie*, wasn't released instead, as I'm sure he would have enjoyed that far more.

Developed by Japanese anime studio Group TAC and released in Japanese theaters in August of 1994, the plot of *Street Fighter II* has M. Bison using monitor cyborgs to scour the globe and gather data on street fighters. His ultimate goal is to brainwash those deemed the strongest, creating an army of street fighters-turned-terrorist soldiers. Though there are some brief, incidental exchanges concerning the villains' political motivations and allusions to personal tragedies that motivate the heroes, the story is largely unmemorable. The robotic villain sent to gather data would become somewhat of a trope within anime based on fighting games, with adaptations of *Virtua Fighter* and *Battle Arena Toshinden* employing similar narrative devices. Admittedly, it is a good method to ensure each member of the cast gets a chance to fight on screen, which is really what the audience wants to see. It is here that *Street Fighter II: The Animated Movie* exceeds all expectations, with surprisingly realistic and unforgettable action sequences that continue to influence the genre.

The animation staff was assisted by K-1 founder Kazuyoshia Ishii and renowned-heavy weight kick-boxer Andy Hug. As a result of this partnership, the fight sequences exude a level of realism that you might not expect—especially considering the fireball tossing antics of the games. Those fantastical elements, though downplayed, are very much present, and they are implemented in meaningful and impactful ways. Capcom would have less success in this regard with their *Night Warriors: Darkstalkers' Revenge* anime, with many of that game's signature characters and moves appearing insignificant and buffoonish on screen. This is not the case here, as even the most preposterous moves from the game, such as Chun-Li's Spinning Bird Kick, carry an air of weight and believability. Rightly so, the fight scenes are truly the highlights of the film. Matchups between series rivals Ryu, Sagat, Guile, and M. Bison are executed brilliantly, but it is the vicious, bloody duel to the death between Chun-Li and Vega that provides the film with its most memorable moments. It is a surprising section-rich with feminist subtext in an otherwise straightforward "good guys save the world" martial arts narrative.

Beginning with *Psycho* in 1960, audiences had experienced three decades of watching this type of scenario play out in thrillers and horror films: a female character undresses or engages in sexual activity before being hacked and slashed to death by a masked assailant.

In a sequence intercut with Vega's lurking shadow, Chun-Li, while showering in her apartment, is shown nude. Viewers have been trained that women in cinema will be punished for this behavior. In these scenes, *Street Fighter II* seems to throw many genre conventions into a blender. Vega can be viewed as a sort of anime mix of Freddy Krueger and Jason Voorhees—hulking, masked, with long, bladed claws. Unlike Freddy and Jason, Vega is a beautiful man and, by turns, narcissistic and vain. Ultimately, these personality traits typically assigned to female characters are his downfall, as Chun-Li is ultimately able to exploit his psychosis by damaging his face, throwing him off balance and allowing her to gain the upper hand. This fight places Chun-Li at severe disadvantage. Stalked and the victim of a surprise attack, unarmed and in only a night shirt, she flips the script and kills the slasher—the force of her kicks sending him through the wall and plummeting to the streets below. Chun-Li's victory over Vega displays a female heroine as both a powerful and a sexual being, and redeems generations of exploited cinema victims.

The film also features some quiet moments. The flashback sequences that reveal the seeds of Ryu and Ken's lifelong friendship and rivalry are among the most beautiful scenes in the film and are surprisingly touching given the limited context and dialogue provided. You can certainly file Ken cruising through Seattle in his convertible while listening to "Israel's Son" by Silverchair under great moments in English dubs. Chun-Li and Guile's brief discussion concerning their common ground makes you wish there was more time available to expand on the connections the many characters have with one another. Ryu giving (presumably) all of his money to a homeless mother and child further elevates and displays another side to his heroism. These character moments coupled with the quality of the fight scenes are why so many fans view these representations as the definitive versions of the *Street Fighter* characters, and it is easy to see why an entire generation of gamers embraced and fell in love with them.

Initially, a PG-13 version of the film was released in the US that removes the harsher language, blood, and Chun-Li nude scene. Over time, many different cuts of the film would be made, altering the violence and nudity to varying degrees. The definitive version of *Street Fighter II: The Animated Movie* has been released on Blu-ray via Discotek Media. This release collects every version of the film in English and Japanese, as well as the option to mix and match the different soundtracks with the different cuts of the film. It would be remiss not to mention the English version's soundtrack—an early '90s time capsule mix of nu metal, alternative, and grunge that works much better than you would expect.

The film also greatly impacted the direction of the game series. The flashback scenes depicting much younger versions of Ryu and Ken are considered the origin of the *Street Fighter Alpha* (*Street Fighter Zero* in Japan) series, which serves as a prequel to *Street Fighter II*. In a fantastic bit of fan-service, Capcom included ways for players to recreate iconic scenes from the movie. The original *Alpha* hides a secret, two-on-one mode (a first for the series) inspired by the film's climatic battle. This mode allows two human players to control Ryu and Ken and challenge a computer-controlled M. Bison. Alpha 2 Sagat players were able to challenge Ryu to a rematch in the same grassy field from the opening of the movie, once again a thunderstorm raging in the background. By the third entry in the *Alpha* series, Capcom had explored and expanded the back stories and motivations of every character in the *Street Fighter II* series, with Ryu's character path loosely following the events of the animated movie.

Joshua Dunbar is a freelance illustrator and art educator and holds an MFA in Sequential Art from the Savannah College of Art and Design. A lover of all forms of Japanese media, he is currently working on his first creator-owned comic inspired by the Magical Girl genre and late twentieth-century animation. You can find his work on his Instagram at @j2dstar or joshuadunbar.com.

1995 • GHOST IN THE SHELL

KŌKAKU KIDŌTAI

— CHRIS STUCKMANN —

The year is 2029 and humanity has become integrated with technology. It's normal to have enhancements or even entire cybernetic body parts. And since most people are interconnected within the Net, they're vulnerable to hackers who can seize control of their bodies and force them to commit crimes. This is precisely the aim of the Puppet Master, a rogue program using the Net's anonymity to commit acts of terrorism. It's up to covert counter-terrorism task force Section 9—led by Major Motoko Kusanagi, an almost fully cyborg policewoman—to hunt down this criminal AI.

Like *Akira*, *Ghost in the Shell* was part of the tidal wave of anime washing up on American shores during the early to mid-'90s. It's on every list of required viewing for anime fans, and rightfully so. This eighty-three-minute masterpiece isn't just gorgeously animated: it's a thought-provoking, cerebrally exhaustive study of mankind and what it means to be human. In a world where the human brain can directly access the Internet, even physically reside there, what really are our limits? Like Stanley Kubrick's ingenious *2001: A Space Odyssey*, *GITS* becomes a prophecy for a future that seems frighteningly probable.

GITS is also the rare example of an adaptation that improves upon its source material. Shirow Masamune's original manga was highly influential and remains a reference point for many artists attempting to capture the gritty, filthy realism of a futuristic society. But for myself, it too often focused on the bodies of its female characters, presenting them more as the objects of fantasy-fulfillment rather than people with history and stories. In Mamoru Oshii's film, Motoko and other women are often portrayed nude, but his direction is carefully calculated. Nudity is rarely depicted as sexual but simply anatomical. The question of sexuality and gender identity is one that Oshii is clearly fascinated with.

Motoko doesn't seem to consider her form from a sexual perspective. She will often disrobe, wearing a skin-tight suit that allows her thermoptic-camouflage to be more effective, and she seems blissfully unaware that others may view this clothing as inappropriate. Her partner, Batou, appears to have retained more of his humanity than Motoko. In one telling scene, after Motoko attacks and disarms a shooter, Batou approaches her and wraps his coat around her shoulders, covering her revealing outfit. In another scene, Motoko emerges from the ocean after a swim, climbing onto the boat where Batou is waiting. She begins to change out of her swimwear right in front of him, and Batou looks away.

Does this mean Batou is more human than Motoko? Or perhaps the answer is more complex. It's likely that Motoko no longer considers her body from a sexual perspective. She may not even identify as a female anymore—nor, possibly, as human.

What's so beautiful about these story elements is that Oshii leaves so many hanging in the air. One could analyze this film to death, but as with Oshii's *Angel's Egg*, it's going to come down to personal interpretations. No two people will walk away from *GITS* with the same feeling. It leaves you with a sense of euphoria that's hard to find in film, let alone anime.

Also impressive is *GITS*'s subversion of movie villain tropes. The elusive Puppet Master is often referenced during the film's first act, building a sense of dread around it. Typically, we'd expect an epic showdown to forestall some dastardly plan to wipe out the earth. But the Puppet Master doesn't come to us fully formed. It's sentient, yes, but it's still unsure what it is. That's why it "ghost hacks" people: It's attempting to discern the meaning of existence—not just its own, but humanity's. So, while the Puppet Master appears outwardly to be villainous, one could argue it's merely a confused infant life form desperately grasping for answers.

Even more compelling is the disconnect that Motoko feels with society. In one incredible sequence, we see her traveling through the city, awestruck by her surroundings. She passes a woman who looks just like her sitting in a restaurant, and later a store mannequin with her exact appearance. She realizes she is not unique, that she's in fact made from a mold. You can see this disconnect reflected in her eyes, which rarely blink. This wasn't due to laziness on the part of the animators. Oshii wanted Motoko to appear less human and more doll-like: hence, her facial expressions are often emotionless.

It's particularly impressive that these sequences are so impactful with little to no dialogue supporting them. But you don't need to hear it from Motoko's mouth that she feels torn between humanity and technology, that she's unsure of her place in the world. Those truths really do live behind those blank eyes.

GITS has inspired countless filmmakers over the years, including the Wachowskis (*The Matrix* trilogy) and Alex Proyas (*Dark City*). It's one of the few films I've seen that truly does live up to the hype. And yet I didn't fully appreciate *GITS* on first viewing. It's so much to take in, so much to process. It took three or four watches to really sink in. Yet I can say now that *GITS* is an unprecedented masterpiece. It's given—and continues to give—to so many people the world over. If you've never seen it, you're missing one of the all-time greats.

1995 • GUNSMITH CATS

GANSUMISU KYATTSU

— JOSHUA DUNBAR —

Few anime have managed to convey a stronger sense of place than *Gunsmith Cats*, a crime drama inspired by American action/crime thrillers such as *The French Connection* and *Gone in 60 Seconds*. An immaculate presentation of the city of Chicago, extensive field research was conducted by creator Kenichi Sonoda and the art staff during the production, and nearly every location seen in the anime exists. The irony, of course, is that gun-controlled Japan could produce an animated series that's quality and realism rivals, and in many instances exceeds, the live-action American films that inspired it.

At a glance, with its three female leads cruising around in a Shelby Cobra, you may think this is a Japanese anime version of *Charlie's Angels*. Thankfully, the similarities to that show end there. While *Charlie's Angels* has a campy "let's play bounty hunters" vibe, *Gunsmith Cats* is not only entertaining, but as realistic as crime dramas get. The creator's passion for American crime drama and encyclopedic knowledge of cars and firearms is instantly apparent. Though the direct-to-video release is only three episodes long, over one hundred different types of weapons are featured during the action sequences. The fanatical attention to detail is also present in the sound design—nearly all of the SFX for the cars and weapons featured in the anime were recorded using the actual items. Impeccable set dressing aside, the anime features such excellent writing and compelling characters that even viewers with no interest in cars and guns will find value in the series.

Gunsmith Cats refers to the gun shop run by markswoman and gunsmith Rally Vincent and bomb expert Minnie May Hopkins. Together, the two women operate as bounty hunters outside, and occasionally alongside, local law enforcement.

Along with the Chicago PD, the Bureau of Alcohol, Tobacco, and Firearms (ATF) is featured heavily in the story. Rally and May are also assisted peripherally (for a price) by Becky Farrah, a bookish informant who prefers to stay out of the action and remain in the background.

Although *Gunsmith Cats* began as a manga, the OVA series features a completely independent storyline. Here, the ATF enlists Rally and May to investigate and infiltrate a gun-running operation, and an original villain is introduced in the form of a female ex-KGB assassin, Natasha Radinov. Radinov is a frightening presence, a vision of Rally—sans humanity. The story elevates these two women and their skills to forces of nature—the finale playing out almost like a contemporary western. A duel to death must take place between these women as a matter of pride—they simply cannot exist in the same world together.

Though brief, *Gunsmith Cats* is a series that demands repeat viewings. You'll want to watch the high-speed chase on the Chicago freeway—one of many adrenaline-fueled set pieces—over and over. This sequence is heavily inspired by the revolutionary car chase in the 1968 Steve McQueen film *Bullitt*. Fans of that film will no doubt notice some similarities in the shot selection as well as in the selection of firearms used by the antagonist. Free from the limitations of live-action, *Gunsmith Cats'* car chase scene achieves even greater heights than that of its source material. In an inspired character turn, circumstances during this scene place Becky in the passenger seat of Rally's Shelby Cobra GT 500. Though an invaluable part of the team, Becky's anxious and fearful nature is best suited behind a computer—her hilarious reactions during the many sideswipes and near-misses inject a layer of humor into an already electrifying scene.

Some sequences can only be fully appreciated in slow motion. In one such instance, the male detective lead slides to grab a pistol from the ground, and in doing so, narrowly avoids a shotgun blast. He escapes injury, but the buckshot reduces the tail of his trench coat to a mess of tatters and shreds. This manner in which a master 2D animator can emphasize such minutiae is not possible in live-action or 3D animation.

Though all of the action takes place in male-dominated arenas (i.e., the police force, gun shops, etc.), the women never ask what should be done or need to ask men for guidance. Their movements are self-assured and made without hesitation. Like many female anime characters, Rally is composed of many opposing forces—strong and assertive, feminine yet masculine. She's not a young girl, but you would not consider her a mature woman either. Although tomboy would be a too simplistic evaluation of her personality, Rally does reject certain feminine trappings. Late in the anime, the girls are invited as guests of honor at their state senators campaign rally. On May's urging, Rally considers wearing high heels to the event.

"If I wear these things I won't even be able to move!"

The opening sequence shows the heels of these bright red pumps being broken. Stylish and symbolic, this actually foreshadows a critical moment during the final act, but to say more would spoil part of the nail-biting finale.

Over the course of its three thirty-minute volumes, *Gunsmith Cats* overflows with more excitement and believability than most American crime dramas are able to develop over the course of years. Thick with detail, it is remarkably elevated even further by a knock-out dub by ADV Films. Amanda Winn Lee's performance as Rally Vincent is transcendent—a standout performance within a stellar career. Mr. Sonoda and his staff went so far to create the believability of an American setting that this is one anime you will definitely want to watch in English.

The *Gunsmith Cats* manga ran from 1991 to 1997. The story was continued in a sequel, *Gunsmith Cats Burst*, which ran from 2004–2008. The manga contains compelling, at times shockingly gritty crime drama, as well as the exquisitely drawn cars and weaponry you would expect from watching the anime. Though be forewarned, the anime is relatively tame compared to the manga, which features a much higher level of violence and some eye-brow raising sexual situations involving underage characters. Also worth checking out is *Riding Bean*, an earlier Kenichi Sonada anime also set in Chicago. The lead character of *Riding Bean*, Bean Bandit, is a major player in the *Gunsmith Cats* manga. *Riding Bean* can be viewed as a sort of prototype to *Gunsmith Cats*, featuring an early, blonde version of Rally Vincent in a supporting role.

Joshua Dunbar is a freelance illustrator and art educator and holds an MFA in Sequential Art from the Savannah College of Art and Design. A lover of all forms of Japanese media, he is currently working on his first creator-owned comic inspired by the Magical Girl genre and late twentieth-century animation. You can find his work on his Instagram at @j2dstar or joshuadunbar.com.

1995 • NEON GENESIS EVANGELION

SHINSEIKI EVANGERION

— COMIC BOOK GIRL 19 —

Neon Genesis Evangelion is like a gummy vitamin; sure, it's sweet, but it's also filled with shit that's actually good for you. This anime boasts some serious eye candy; namely the badass giant bio-mechas known as Evangelions and a harem of sexy female characters. But at the center of all this sugar is a frustrated adolescent boy on a philosophical journey through the valley of the shadow of existential crisis.

The original series aired in Japan from 1995 to 1996 and was an instant classic, winning the Best-Loved Anime award at the Anime Grand Prix three years in a row. Part of its success is that it spoke to the depression that the people of Japan felt after the economic collapse they suffered in the early '90s (fun fact: the '90s sucked so bad for Japan that they call it the "Lost Decade"). During this recession, *Evangelion* came like a light in the darkness spurring a flagging Japanese animation industry to new heights of sophistication. *Eva*'s massive popularity quickly spilled overseas and had a direct hand in the global commercialization of anime that helped boost the pride of a disheartened nation. *Neon Genesis Evangelion* is a love letter to the lost soul in all of us, whether we be an individual or a national collective, who search for meaning in the chaos.

The mastermind behind the series, Director Hideki Anno, talks openly about how this series was a vehicle for an expression of his own personal battle with depression and how every character in it is a reflection of himself. Anno funneled the most of himself into *Eva*'s main character Shinji Ikari, and this overabundance of humanity is perhaps why this character is considered one of the most relatable male anime characters of all time.

Shinji is a stressed out fourteen-year-old with serious daddy issues who is pressured by said shitty dad into piloting the mysterious Evangelion Unit-01 to fight a race of even more mysterious kaijū known as the Angels who are hell-bent on annihilating humanity at large. After much prodding, he goes along with it, but not for some ideal of saving the world. He does it to gain his distant father's approval. Shinji is the opposite of the traditional anime hero, instead of fearlessly plunging himself into danger, he is shown panicking in high-pressure situations repeating the phrase, "I mustn't run away," to himself over and over again.

When Shinji was a small child, his mother disappears/dies, and his father abandons him shortly after that; as a result, he feels worthless. The pain inflicted by his father was so great that he shut himself off so that he won't ever get hurt again. Becoming an Eva pilot only exasperates these emotional wounds, and fighting the Angels adds new layers of physical and mental trauma onto the pile; oh yeah, and don't forget about puberty! A bevy of beautiful females surrounds this tortured teenage boy, and he finds himself particularly attracted to the enigmatic pilot of Unit-00, Rei Ayanami.

To say that Rei is popular with the boys is an understatement. Not only does she give Shinji the tingles, but she's also one of the most popular female anime characters of all time with the bandaged figurines of her wildly outselling all other *Evangelion* merchandise. There's a rumor that she has 1,000,000 men who worship her in a subconscious religion. To them, this expressionless damaged girl is a goddess; an icon of Japan itself! Rei's wounded fragility combined with her icy decisive mind makes for a perfect symbol of a recovering Japan post-crash. Like Shinji, she is the opposite of the traditional anime heroines that came before her in that she is frighteningly detached to the point of being robotic; but in her wake, there came a wave of emotionless female characters who take direct inspiration from her.

Shinji's other love interest, the fiery Asuka Langley Soryu provides the perfect counterbalance to the cool, dispassionate Rei. Where Ayanami is blue-haired and red-eyed, often shown against the moon, Soryu is red-haired and blue-eyed, originally introduced silhouetted by the sun. In her personal life and as the pilot of Eva Unit-02 she is overly aggressive, marked by an excess of pride. She is obnoxiously competitive with both Rei and Shinji for being the "best" pilot and is disgusted by Rei's mechanical indifference toward personal sacrifice. In contrast to Rei, Asuka finds herself attracted to Shinji which causes her internal conflict because she also views him as a rival for attention.

In comparison to Shinji beta-ness, Asuka is the Alpha. The yang to his yin. Where Shinji shrinks, Asuka inflates. It's beautiful how these two characters experience analogous emotional childhood traumas and illustrate equal and opposite ways of dealing with it. As the introverted Shinji struggles with his estranged parent's death, Asuka is still reeling from the dark experiences she went through with her mother who went insane and committed suicide when she was small. Her bold personality stems from an obsession to become as independent as she possibly can to protect herself from ever again being hurt by someone she loves.

These two aren't the only ones fumbling with the "Hedgehog's Dilemma," a.k.a. the challenge of human intimacy and the unavoidable mutual pain that arises from it. Every character we get to know in this show is broken and despairing, caught in a loop repeating the themes of their own childhood traumas, just like we do.

Neon Genesis Evangelion explores myriad psychological themes, many derived from the works of Sigmund Freud such as Thanatos (the Death Urge), The Oedipus Complex, Separation Anxiety, and more. It also invokes philosophical questions about free will, the nature of consciousness, and the meaning of life. But wait! There's more!

Eva also incorporates esoteric ideas from occult mysticism; namely Christian Gnosticism and the Judaic Kabbalah. Even though the show's religious references and iconography are less about the religious traditions themselves and more about adding an exotic flavor for a Japanese audience, one can still find interconnections between the anime's plot and the sacred mythologies it borrows from.

Consummate over-thinker and professional crazy person, CBG19 has parlayed her obsessive love of art and storytelling into a full-time career. She is known for hosting the Comic Book Girl 19 Show on YouTube as well as producing other documentary series centered on a myriad of pop-culture topics with her co-creator and director, Tyson Wheeler.

1995 • THE SLAYERS

— EMMA FYFFE —

In the year 2000, in addition to surviving an apocalypse that never was—I *vividly* remember picking up the phone right after midnight and being met with the expected dial tone which, to me, confirmed that we had in fact *not* experienced a complete technological collapse—I also started playing my first ever *Dungeons & Dragons* campaign. A fellow fourteen-year-old otaku friend of mine had a dad who was itching to DM (Dungeon Master) a campaign, and the "Satanic Panic" associated with the game in the 1980s had long since dissipated. In myself, his daughter, and another equally anime-obsessed young teen, he had eager participants with a bunch of original characters created for fan-fiction purposes that were dying for a more effective outlet than unfinished epics that lay forever dormant in the depths of Microsoft Word.

This was also during the era wherein, if you liked anime, you would (a) watch whatever was on Toonami, (b) rent literally whatever they had at Blockbuster, or (c) scroll through everything on the Sci-Fi channel and record anything with primarily Japanese names in the credits because it might be anime. In this case, we're dealing with option B. On one of the many weekends upon which I slept over at my friend's house—who's dad was DMing our little campaign—she and I decided to rent the first VHS of the series *Slayers*. I wasn't completely unfamiliar with it, being a connoisseur of the magazine *Animerica* in which I had seen it advertised. But for whatever reason it had failed to capture my interest.

Being a fan of high fantasy of the Tolkien-esque variety, I was much more preoccupied with *Record of Lodoss War* and already owned the OVA (Original Video Animation, a.k.a. Direct-to-Video, a.k.a. would have been a Netflix series now). I liked it okay, but ultimately found myself a little unfulfilled. The whole thing felt very dark and serious. The heroine ended up being a damsel in distress for the latter part of the series, and not the badass lady elf I was hoping for. As an adult, I am much more forgiving of this, but during my problematic "a woman isn't a strong character unless she's kicking butt alongside the boys" phase of teenage feminism, this was a massive disappointment. Little did I know that the heroine I longed for was just around the corner in the form of Lina Inverse, the main character of *Slayers*.

I think part of my attraction to Lina, in a "I wanted to be her" sort of way, stemmed from the fact that, at the time, I didn't consider myself to be particularly feminine. Lina was short, flat chested, outspoken, cursed a lot, and could eat and drink just as much as her male counterparts. I always felt like when, early on in the series, dear, sweet Gourry, whom I absolutely adore as an adult, mistook her for a child as much because of her brash, unladylike behavior as her unwomanly appearance. Plus she had red hair and I'd had an affinity for red-haired ladies since 1989 when I saw Disney's *The Little Mermaid* in theaters. She also had a short-fused temper and made lots of bad decisions that didn't result in her getting kidnapped.

If *Record of Lodoss War* is how Dungeon Masters wish their *Dungeons & Dragons* campaigns would go, then *Slayers* is more akin to how they actually play out. I can't take credit for that quote, but the point is this is a high fantasy series full of all the elements you'd expect: dungeon crawls, mystical beasts, clashes with dark wizards, etc. But it also features many of the things I was doing for the first time as player in a tabletop RPG, like spending hours drinking in taverns, or trying to extort money from a town of hapless villagers who are actively under dragon attack. And then lighting that whole town on fire. Well, I never actually lit a whole town on fire, since my character was a rogue, but she was definitely just as obsessed with treasure as Lina was. And as fiery (personality-wise), redheaded, and underestimated due to her exceedingly adorable appearance.

I think the tape we rented had maybe the first three episodes of the first season of *Slayers* on it, but that was enough to convince me that this was a series I needed to invest in. Within those first three episodes we meet not only the magnificent Lina Inverse, but also Gourry Gabriev, a dumb, pretty, and well-meaning swordsman who gets sort of unwittingly swept up in Lina's antics and the mysterious chimera Zelgadis Graywords, who is way too sexy for someone who looks like he has a weird skin disease. And of course, being the resourceful Internet-savvy young teen that I was, I discovered the basic existence of all the other major recurring characters in the first season and printed multiple reference images so as to redraw my *Dungeons & Dragons* character in the *Slayers* style. I also found there was a prequel OVA which they thankfully had on DVD at the video store at the mall. Though I have to admit, I was a little off-put by it due to the fact that Naga, the other main character besides Lina, was *very* well endowed (like more than is actually plausible) and wore a very skimpy bikini.

Incensed as I was by a woman going into battle wearing very impractical clothing, the *Slayers* OVA did naught to mar my love for the main series. The following year when I stumbled across what was almost certainly a bootleg peddling website of questionable legality that had the entire twenty-six-episode seasons of anime available for about $20 a piece, *Slayers* was one of the first series I purchased. And I do mean series, as I blindly bought the subsequent seasons *Slayer Next* and *Slayers Try* without having finished the first one. I definitely did not regret this decision.

Despite never really receiving a widespread, well-promoted stateside television release, *Slayers* was still considered one of the more popular series of the 1990s, even in the US, and I felt like I couldn't be considered a real anime fan without having seen it. And having seen it, I totally understood why people liked it so much. Much of my anime watching was done in the company of my brother, and *Slayers* was definitely one of those shows that we enjoyed watching together. After all, it was technically shōnen, and thus, my eleven-year-old brother was the target audience, but I—and I'm sure I'm not alone in this sentiment—identified so strongly with Lina that I actually think I enjoyed the series just a little bit more than he did. Or, at the very least, just as much.

Thankfully, *Slayers* is very, very readily and legally available to US audiences. All three seasons of the original '90s anime, as well as the latter two seasons from 2008–2009 are available on DVD and streaming on FUNimation's streaming service FUNimation Now (as of this writing). The first season is even available on Hulu for any fledgling anime fans who haven't quite taken the plunge into the realm of anime specific streaming subscriptions. If you're a fan of fantasy, comedy, or just some damn good storytelling complete with relatable—if slightly over-the-top—characters, I have a feeling you'll fall in love with this series as quickly as I did. Plus, you might pick up some inspiration for future tabletop RPG campaigns.

Emma Fyffe currently resides in Los Angeles where she hosts a Sailor Moon *podcast* Love and Justice *and an anime talk show* Hyper Otaku *on Hyper RPG's Facebook page. She is also the "Golden Mic" of the* Movie Trivia Schmoedown *(it says so on her IMDb) and the Captain of a ragtag crew of smugglers on Hyper RPG's Twitch-based* Star Wars *roleplaying game series "Pencils and Parsecs."*

1995 • WHISPER OF THE HEART

MIMI WO SUMASEBA

— DOUG WALKER —

One of two options usually pops in a person's head when they hear the term "coming-of-age film," a subtle, in-depth look at the trials and passions of growing up, or a corny melodrama riding more on clichés than real life experiences. *Whisper of the Heart* is somewhere in between, but surprisingly it balances out, giving us a spectacular film. Don't get me wrong, it's overly romanticized and filled with moments so sappy you could pour it on pancakes, but its genius is that it reflects an age where that is what many young people not only believe in but also seek out. Even the title *Whisper of the Heart* sounds hokey, but it properly reflects what the film is about; trying to accept the lessons of real life while still listening to the faint sound of your true passions. Many of us struggled with which path to follow in life, grounded reality or flights of fantasy, and this film brings us the perfect combination of the two. Uncertain, risky, fearful, but also exciting, whimsical, and reassuring.

The film centers around Shizuku, a bookworm who enjoys learning American songs, writing, and getting lost in her favorite stories. When she discovers someone has been checking out the same library books she has, her brain spirals into romantic overload trying to figure out who it could be. As par the course for stories like this, it's a boy she cannot stand. His name is Seiji, and your first guess is correct; they hate each other at first but over time learn to love each other's differences. Shizuku even discovers Seiji is a talented violinist and helps her learn her favorite American song "Country Roads." In most movies, this would be the focus of the entire story, with comedic pratfalls and one-liners being tossed around until it's realized that the snooty mate each of them is with isn't right for them and run to their true love during an auto-tuned song of the week. This film, thankfully, has more substance than that.

Shizuku befriends a kind old antique store owner named Shiro, and one of his statuettes of a cat he named "The Baron" captivates her. She can't quite explain it ... it just fills her with an instant passion she's never felt before. With her love of writing growing, she decides she wants to address this passion in her and write a story around the cat ... *really* write a story. She spends days concluding that this is her dream and she wants to drop out of school to pursue it. Her parents, while surprised, see how serious she is about it and agree to her request. To many this would seem outrageous, pulling a child out of school to write a fairy tale, but the film knows where to focus its time and atmosphere. Though there is little talk about it, there are several quiet moments that clearly demonstrate much thought about what she wants to do with her future. Moments of contemplation, rest, and observation represented purely through visuals. The time spent between Shizuku and her parents also demonstrate the close understanding they have, so when the choice to drop out is made, it's amazingly not surprising. Their trust in each other shows how far they can let her go without going necessarily too far.

Much of the movie works this way, relaxing your senses and making you think what you're watching is filler, but the truth is it's establishing connections between Shizuku, the people around her, and her own dreams. The film is almost meditative when she is alone partaking in simple activities, like wandering the town, thinking of ideas, or even following a chubby cat to see where it goes. It reflects a mindset that many of us had as children and young adults, conjuring a future that you're certain will come true because you're passionate about it. What *Whisper* shows over time, though, is that many people have the same dream and the same passion (if not more), but it is not harsh with its message. If anything, it welcomes that passion because this is the age when it is the purest and unfiltered. It does not force a person's reality to destroy their dreams, but rather have their reality and dreams meet face to face, leaving the dreamer to decide what needs to change and what needs to stay the same.

Everybody in this movie seems to have gone or is currently going through something similar. From the parents, to the antique shop owner, to Seiji, all of them balance a compromise between their dreams and their realities, but none of them seem bitter or angry at their outcome. None of them got exactly what they wanted, but they also realized what they wanted wasn't always what was realistic. Everyone seems comfortable with the mistakes and choices they've made, and live in an environment where they accept it as a part of life. The film still acknowledges the mistakes, though, as well as the consequences of them and how others will be made in the future. Rather than shaming mistakes, however, it invites us to learn from them and gives us characters and situations that want to do exactly that, even if they don't always know how. *Whisper* calmly and gently allows reality and dreams to coexist—they just have to take turns in the spotlight. Sometimes a dream can be made into a reality, but other times it must remain a dream. Because there is such respect for both, the corny scenes are all the livelier and the realistic scenes are more relatable. Shiro dreaming of his true love walking into his store is magic fading to reality, but Shizuku singing "Country Roads," only to have a group of musicians hear her and play alongside her is reality fading to magic. Both often get a warm sigh of emotion.

Whisper of the Heart does have many clichés about being young, but they're worked into a world that has respect, understanding, and love for growing up. It knows when to let a dream fly and when to let it melt back to reality. It quietly and subtly mixes everything that is scary, delightful, confusing, yet riveting about getting older. It's as if you're seeing many of these clichés for the first time because they're being represented by characters in a world that seems welcoming and familiar. It's a world where you can see a beautiful sunset like in movies, but slightly cutoff through the buildings in an alleyway, making it feel more real and plausible. It's a perfect collide of what is and what can be, done not with a bang but with a soothing song. Many will recognize these emotions from when they were younger, and if you're like me, they're emotions you'll often come back to visit.

Doug Walker is known for his character, the Nostalgia Critic.
His beloved movie reviews can be found on his YouTube page,
Channel Awesome.

1996 • DETECTIVE CONAN

MEITANTEI KONAN

— CHRIS STUCKMANN —

The Chapel Hill Mall in Akron, Ohio. That old building played a major role in my shopping experience when I was younger. On non-school days, my parents dropped me off at the movie theater, I'd watch a film, then walk over to the mall. This became routine.

Over the years, my favorite stores in the mall began to disappear: Waldenbooks, Coconuts, K.B. Toys, Camelot Music ... all gone. It's strange, you don't realize how many memories you have attributed to a building until it isn't around anymore.

A few years ago, yet another store announced they were closing: FYE. While this was disappointing, the "50% OFF ANIME SALE" certainly wasn't! Wanting to take advantage of this deal, I dashed to the mall to browse their selection. On the way there, my wife texted me a few titles she wanted.

Dragon Ball Season Five?
There's a chance.

Shattered Angels?
I don't even know what that is.

Detective Conan?
There's no way they'll have that.

I quick-stepped to the store and entered, blurring past a dozen red signs blinding me with gigantic font: STORE CLOSING! EVERYTHING MUST GO!

Approaching the anime section, I knelt down and began thumbing through the titles. To my displeasure, most of the Blu-rays were gone, leaving only a smattering of random titles no one wanted. But would you believe it? Season Five of *Dragon Ball* was there. Even *Shattered Angels*!

Detective Conan, though? I remembered one late-night viewing of an episode during its run on Adult Swim back in 2004 but didn't know much else.

To my legitimate surprise, the first three seasons were tucked away in the corner. The sets were, unfortunately, those garish S.A.V.E. (Super Amazing Value Edition) DVDs, with the ugly green cases that all look the same. Nitpicks aside, about $30 got us the first seventy-eight episodes of *Detective Conan*.

My wife watched most of the episodes that aired on Adult Swim, becoming a fan. Since she piqued my interest, I decided to pop in Season One, even though I bought them for her. Many episodes later, we've got yet another show that's brought us closer together.

Detective Conan—or *Case Closed* as it's known in America—is one of the longest-running television shows in history. Beginning in 1996, new episodes are still releasing today. There are over forty seasons, nearly nine hundred episodes, and that's just the anime. As of April 2018, twenty-two feature films exist. The manga is nearing one hundred total volumes. There's no doubt that, in the history of anime, *Detective Conan* occupies a special spot in the hearts of many fans. So, what's it about?

Shinichi Kudo is an accomplished detective, adept at solving grueling cases that leave even seasoned professionals confused. Even more impressive, he's only in high school—much to the chagrin of Kogoro Mouri, a competing detective who frequently gets left in the dust by Shinichi. Mouri's daughter, Ran, has feelings for Shinichi but is embarrassed to admit them. Shinichi feels the same way about her, and like Ran, is too shy to say anything.

On one fateful night, Shinichi is attacked by members of a crime syndicate known as the Black Organization. He's forced to swallow an untested poison, but he doesn't die. Instead, he wakes up a child again! After getting over the initial shock, he adopts the pseudonym, Conan Edogawa (inspired by Sir Arthur Conan Doyle) and finds a way to continue solving cases by living with the Mouri's and subtly helping Kogoro bust criminals and break cases.

Naturally, his childlike appearance makes things difficult with Ran, who misses Shinichi, wondering where he disappeared to. Shinichi—pretending to be Conan—decides to keep this transformation a secret, navigating life once again as a young boy. This means going back to elementary school, making friends with other kids his "age," and pretending he doesn't secretly love Ran.

Detective Conan is much funnier than I anticipated. Shinichi's justifiable annoyance at the ignorance of his detective colleagues creates some hilarious back-and-forth, and the constant dodging of Ran's questions makes him squirm uncomfortably. Most surprising though, are the mysteries. They're actually very clever!

One of my favorites is "Moonlight Sonata Murder Case," which finds Conan, Kogoro, and Ran investigating a string of bizarre murders on a secluded island. Kogoro is summoned there by an untraceable note with pasted letters. They soon discover that the islanders are living in fear of a curse.

Twelve years prior, a distinguished pianist murdered his whole family, set his home ablaze, and played Beethoven's "Moonlight Sonata" on the piano as he burned to death. Just that backstory alone is intriguing enough to fill an entire feature! Indeed, this special episode was an hour long, double the length of a normal show.

After nightfall, murder victims appear at a local community center, accompanied by a tape player broadcasting "Moonlight Sonata" throughout the building. The townspeople become increasingly fearful of the "curse," while Conan attempts to solve the case. It's an exciting, suspenseful episode, and one of the best.

Admittedly, the show requires strong suspension of disbelief. For instance, rather than openly solve cases himself, Conan shoots a tranquilizer dart in the necks of nearby adults, then uses a voice changer in his tie to imitate the unconscious individual. The first few times he did this I shrugged it off, *Detective Conan* is a very tongue-in-cheek show, after all. But after relying on this plot device for multiple episodes, it got old fast. Rather than deal with the difficulty of explaining what happens when the unconscious person awakes—receiving praise for solving a case that Conan actually solved—the episode usually ends before that. It's a bit lazy. In addition to this issue, it's beyond belief that no one questions the presence of a young boy at crime scenes. Despite his ability to point out small details, you'd think more people would cover his eyes or tell him to leave.

Besides those gripes, it's easy to see why *Detective Conan* has remained a staple of anime and manga for so long. The episodic adventures—relying on well-crafted mysteries and suspense—are a blast, and the central conceit of a man struggling to maintain the illusion of boyhood is ingenious. The first five seasons are attainable through FUNimation on DVD, and I'd recommend checking them out, especially if your local electronics store is having a "going-out-of-business-sale."

1996 • RUROUNI KENSHIN

RURÔNI KENSHIN

— JOHN RODRIGUEZ —

"I am the hero of my life's story." It's a positive, life-affirming sentiment. And, in my case, it's a bald-faced lie.

I was introduced to *Rurouni Kenshin* by my then-girlfriend, who herself discovered it through an anime club at the University of Pittsburgh. Some club member had procured an import DVD box set compiling the show's ninety-five-episode run, and my partner invited me to attend a binge-viewing during one of my visits. I agreed readily enough, but the show didn't exactly grab my attention. At least not initially.

The story chronicled ex-manslayer Himura Kenshin in the years following Japan's bloody transition from its isolationist Tokugawa shogunate to its new Meiji government. I found the show's setting appealing. Its writing? Less so. There's a writing maxim that goes: "show, don't tell." *Rurouni Kenshin* flipped that maxim on its head. *Everything* got told, usually through voiced inner monologues employed as stage-setters for the show's inevitable *mano a mano* combat. Characters, meanwhile, were walking, brawling clichés. Marvel at the heroes who retain their agility despite their oversized hearts of gold! And the villains? Please. Serial child-kickers who draw the line at infant punting would look noble next to these cackling mustachio-twirlers.

There were high points, to be sure. The introduction of Shinomori Aoshi, brooding leader of the Oniwabanshū spy network and now an enforcer for an opium dealer, caught my attention. And the blossoming not-quite romance between Kenshin and fiery-tempered dojo instructor Miss Kaoru certainly had its charm. But the majority of *Rurouni Kenshin*'s twenty-seven-episode first season contained more filler than a goose down blanket. That wasn't doing it for me, and I suggested leaving to my partner during our brief post-season-one break.

"Stay," she suggested. "It gets better." I did, and it did. Oh wow, did it ever.

Rurouni Kenshin's thirty-five-episode second season is called the "Kyoto Arc," and it singlehandedly justifies the show's placement among anime's "essentials." Its overarching story turned on a villain: megalomaniacal Shishio Makoto, bent on the overthrow of Japan's fledgling Meiji government. Shishio changed the game. He provided Kenshin's first credible opponent, one that would take a full season to overcome. He introduced complex new characters such as Seta Sōjirō, the traumatized child who became Shishio's most deadly assassin. He elevated former antagonists like Aoshi, now driven mad by his earlier defeat at Kenshin's hands. And he opened the door for ambiguous allies like Saitō Hajime, the Meiji government agent who might kill Kenshin as soon as aid him.

What made all this so fascinating was Kenshin's vow never to take another life. Holding to that vow was easy when Kenshin's opponents were all "fools o' the week" just begging to be knocked senseless by his reverse blade sword. But Shishio was no fool. Defeating him would require deadly earnestness. And now that I'd grown familiar with Kenshin, I found I hated the idea that he might abandon his vow and revert to his violent ways. Even for so noble a purpose as the defense of Japan's future, I wanted him to triumph over the demons within.

And the romance! Good God, *Rurouni Kenshin* was romantic! Truly, madly, wildly romantic, not just in its "Will they, won't they?" relationship between Kenshin and Kaoru but in its readiness to redeem even its most irredeemable villains. People (myself included) often use "melodrama" as a pejorative. But melodrama is an art like any other. Many of its practitioners are amateurs. Some are respectable. A very few make their art form sing. *Rurouni Kenshin* made its melodrama sing. It touched you. It broke your heart. It made you want to grow as a person so you might know its brand of love, be *worthy* of that love.

Unfortunately, *Rurouni Kenshin* doesn't conclude with the Kyoto Arc. But the show's thirty-three-episode "Return to Fillerland" final season didn't detract from the Kyoto Arc's brilliance. My partner and I left that binge-viewing hand in hand, this new shared passion binding us tighter than ever. And as I walked her home, I thought about Himura Kenshin. How he earned his friends' respect with his unwavering nobility. How he commanded attention despite his sparse speech. How he was, in many ways, the embodiment of those excellent qualities I saw in myself.

I am, if you recall, the hero of my life's story.

We never re-watched *Rurouni Kenshin* in the years following that viewing, though we often referenced it. I find that ironic in retrospect. Ironic because, despite my continued instance on drawing parallels between myself and the show's dashing protagonist, I was essentially his antithesis. Where Kenshin was diligent, I was lazy. Where he was unflappable, I flapped as easily as hummingbird wings. Where he was magnanimous, modest, and merry, I was petty, bossy, and moody. That, and a whole heap of other *y*'s, not a one of them flattering. The hero I'd imagined myself turned out to be a greater fiction that any tale told during *Rurouni Kenshin's* three-year broadcast run.

The happy ending to this fiction arrived the day my partner finally left me. And thank heavens she did! I had it coming, and she deserved far better. Not that I saw it that way initially. But when my bulwark of excuses finally crumbled, you know what struck me first?

Rurouni Kenshin.

Maybe because the show had become so entwined with my ex in my memory, I began once again seeing myself through its lens. This time, however, the image projected back looked very different. It showed the truth of me, and that truth looked foul. I was no Himura Kenshin. I was Shishio Makoto. A tyrant. A bully. I wasn't the hero of my life's story. I was its villain.

That could be the depressing conclusion to a depressing tale, but that wouldn't do. This is a *Rurouni Kenshin* retrospective, after all, and *Rurouni Kenshin* is about nothing if not redemption. Its hero is a former mass murderer, for crying out loud! And that's hopeful, isn't it? Too few people in this world seek penance and too few show readiness to forgive. Yet it's nice to believe that even the worst of us can be redeemed, if only we wander long enough.

Kenshin's road to redemption began with a vow never to kill again, and it lasted ten years. My own path also began with a vow—*I will not love again until I'm the man I envision myself to be*—and my wanderings have stretched several years longer than Kenshin's. I've held to that vow so far. It hurts like hell, but I've held. And maybe, just maybe, there's a dojo waiting for me at the end of the road. A dojo, and a Kaoru.

I'm still hopeful.

John Rodriguez is a personal trainer whose devotion to physical fitness is exceeded only by his fervor for all things film and literature. John is currently finishing his first novel—a fantasy that's sparked fantasies of a challenging new career.

1997 • PERFECT BLUE

PAFEKUTO BURU

— CHRIS STUCKMANN —

Reach a high enough level of fame in this world and all eyes fall upon you. Whether you're a movie star, an athlete, or a musician, suddenly everyone's watching. Every move you make is judged, every decision debated. In the unbalanced, these judgments and debates can become dangerous micro-obsessions. Which brings us to Satoshi Kon's powerhouse film *Perfect Blue,* an exploration of the horrors of celebrity, the perils of obsession, and the pain of crippling self-doubt.

Perfect Blue examines the life of Mima Kirigoe, a pop singer turned actress who begins suspecting that she's being stalked by an obsessed fan when the same odd-looking fellow beings appearing wherever she goes. At first, he just stares, raising his hand as if he were cradling her from his point of view. But soon, horrific murders and bloody, mutilated corpses begin piling up, and the very nature of Mima's reality begins to fall into question.

One of the legends behind *Perfect Blue* is that it inspired Darren Aronofsky's film *Black Swan.* Some go as far as accusing Aronofsky of plagiarism. There's evidence to suggest Aronofsky had the film in mind while creating his thriller. For one, he bought the rights to *Perfect Blue* simply to pay homage to the bathtub scene where Mima screams underwater—detailed comparisons between that scene and Aronofsky's recreation in *Requiem for a Dream* can be found online. Returning to *Black Swan,* both Mima and Nina (Natalie Portman's obsessed dancer) go through similar psychotic breakdowns. Both catch disturbing glimpses of doppelgängers, often seeing them reflected in glass. Even their names are similar.

Now don't get me wrong. I'm not suggesting that Aronofsky plagiarized Satoshi Kon. But there's no denying *Perfect Blue's* influence on *Black Swan's* director.

And, given that, it's a shame so few have seen the brilliant animation that inspired Aronofsky's near-masterpiece.

Perfect Blue also examines fear as it relates to technology: specifically, the Internet. This was a somewhat new idea in 1997, as the Internet was still in its relative infancy. Yet Kon captured the essence of the issue perfectly.

After retiring from her pop group, Mima learns how to access the Internet and stumbles upon a fan page entitled "Mima's Room." For a few moments, she's flattered. But this initial excitement quickly disappears upon reading detailed descriptions of what she does every day, including where she shops and what she buys. There are even audio recordings of her practicing lines on the set of her new film. This prompts a disturbing realization that her life has been intimately violated and that privacy no longer exists for her.

These concerns were cutting-edge in 1997, and they have proven frighteningly prescient. Celebrities in the social media age have never been easier to contact. Fan obsession is nothing new—the surviving members of The Beatles could tell you that—but now that everyone has a camera in their pocket, privacy is quickly becoming a thing of the past. Kon was tremendously ahead of his time with *Perfect Blue*, crafting a dark and realistically horrifying thriller that Hitchcock would've praised.

Perfect Blue isn't for the faint of heart. Its subject matter is deeply disturbing and Kon doesn't shy away from horrific violence. There are multiple moments that make my stomach turn every time I watch it. One of those involves Mima being brutally raped on stage in front of a cheering crowd. It's just a scene for Mima's new acting role, simulated with fellow actors, but this doesn't make it any less humiliating for Mima. Soon after, she finds herself haunted by a ghostly doppelgänger that maligns and insults her for performing the scene. Is this apparition real? Or is it a manifestation of Mima's self-conscious, an externalized embodiment of her fears and agonizing self-doubt?

The only time *Perfect Blue* slips is when Kon tries to answer that question in the finale. He gives face and form to the ghost, one that doesn't entirely make sense when earlier sequences are recalled. It's an ending that feels unearned and a rare misstep for Kon.

Despite the rushed conclusion, *Perfect Blue* is a dreadfully suspenseful and darkly violent exploration of celebrity culture. At a time when filmmakers didn't know how to utilize the Internet in their stories—1995's *The Net* being a prime example—Kon seemed capable of seeing into the future. He observed where obsession could lead and made a frighteningly believable film that has inspired a generation of filmmakers. It's rare that a talent like Kon's walks this earth, able to swerve between heart-wrenching drama like *Millennium Actress*, cerebral science fiction like *Paprika*, or lighthearted comedy like *Tokyo Godfathers*. But what's most impressive is that *Perfect Blue* was only his first film!

Rest in peace, Mr. Kon. You are missed.

1997 • POKÉMON

— DEREK PADULA —

Pokémon is a show about cock fighting for eight-year-old boys and thirty-four-year-old gamers. At the same time, it's a show about the power of friendship in achieving your dreams! Between these two extremes lies the wonder of *Pokémon*.

Pokémon is one of the world's most-recognized anime, and it's a must-watch series if for no other reason than to understand the phenomenon. It's an adaptation of the video game series of the same name. Since the first *Pokémon* game premiered on the Nintendo Game Boy in 1996, there have been seventy-six games that have sold over 300 million units and earned more than $70 billion in revenue; an anime series with over 1,001 episodes and twenty-five movies; and a smart phone game with over 750 million downloads—standing as the most downloaded app in history. This success has combined with an anime-centric merchandise machine to turn *Pokémon* into a household name that has hundreds of millions of people playing its games, watching it on TV, wearing its clothes, and owning its toys.

The first anime series is the most famous, spanning 274 episodes. Just called *Pokémon*, it tells the story of Ash Ketchum, a young and aspiring Pokémon trainer with the goal of becoming a master. As he does this, he competes against his rival Gary, and a trio of nefarious Pokémon thieves named Team Rocket. This is the series I watched, as did most Americans my age when it first aired from September 7, 1998, to October 25, 2003.

The premise of the *Pokémon* game is that you're a young monster-catcher out to fulfill your dream to "Catch 'em all." That is, all 151 monsters. You do that by finding monsters in environments across the world, defeating them with your own, and adding them to your collection. The anime follows the same premise with a main cast of characters.

When the game first arrived in '96, it was so popular among children that it was often banned from school. This is because of the game's social mechanic, where players connect their Game Boy's and battle their Pokémon, with the result being that the winner takes their pick from the player's stable. This led to controversy among parents and teachers who were afraid their children would become used to gambling with their Pokémon, and then transition to harder drugs, like poker. A 1999 article in the *Chicago Tribune* titled "Gotta Ban 'Em All Is Many Schools' Pokémon Response," described how children were buying and trading the monsters for real money before and after school and during recess. Most children weren't familiar with the idea of betting and losing, and it became difficult for those who grew emotionally attached to each of their Pokémon.

For two years, this game was the obsession of millions of kids, so when the anime premiered, it hit an audience eager for more. I remember when the first episode aired, because I skipped school to watch it. The show catered to children and they put it in a 2:30 p.m. time slot, preceding other shows for teens, such as *Power Rangers*. That was a problem for me because I was in high school. What's a teenager to do when he needs to watch a children's cartoon? I knew that I'd get in trouble the next day with my teachers and parents, but as an avid *Pokémon* player, I had no choice. I ditched my seventh-hour art class and ran home like a prisoner making his escape.

I turned the TV on, kneeled in front of it, and experienced one of the greatest intros of all time. The catchy lyrics sung, "I wanna be the very best, like no one ever waaas. To catch them is my real test, to train them is my caaause. I will travel across the land, searching far and wiiide. Teach[1] Pokémon to understand, the power that's insiiide! Pokémon!"

GOTTA CATCH 'EM AAALLL! ...

---

1   Unsuccessful attempts have been made to verify the accuracy of this lyric. Sources conflict, citing this word as either "each" or "teach."

As the song carried on, I became transfixed by the colorful imagery and the way the anime brought to life what I had only imagined while playing the game. Once this intro enters your heart, it will never leave you. This American original intro has gone on to be remixed by composers, sung by professional artists, and played by live orchestras across the world. But back then, all I knew is that I was going to have an incredible adventure. In many ways, better than the game it was based on.

The reason why is sentimental storytelling. The game starts you off with one of three "starter Pokémon," where you choose from the plant-based Bulbasaur, water-based Squirtle, or the fire-based Charizard. The anime takes a more dramatic path. Here, ten-year-old Ash shows up late to the lab of Professor Oak, and as a result, he receives the only Pokémon left: a strong-willed yellow mouse with red cheeks named Pikachu (Japanese for "electric mouse"). Pikachu is cuter than the other three monsters and has more human-like characteristics, including an expressive face. In the game, he was just one of many monsters and warranted no further attention, but here he takes a central role.

The thing about Pikachu is that he doesn't like going inside his master's Poké Ball—as other Pokémon do—because he will be put to sleep. In the first episode, Pikachu is reluctant to travel with Ash, and the new trainer is forced to attack a wild bird-like Pokémon by himself in order to capture it. Pikachu simply climbs a tree and laughs at him. But in response, Ash gets attacked by a flock of birds, and when Pikachu also gets attacked, Ash puts himself in harm's way to save his first Pokémon. For what kind of a trainer would he otherwise be? In a climactic turn, as a thunderstorm brews, Pikachu sees the valiant effort his master makes to protect him, runs up his back as the birds approach, and jumps off of Ash's shoulders to zap the birds away—right when the lightning strikes!

From that moment onward, Ash and Pikachu form a bond that takes them across the world, where they make new friends and enemies and win championship battles as Ash climbs his way to the top. But it isn't without sacrifice, and during their journey, you become attached to this little yellow mouse with an innocent and enduring heart. In fact, the adoration for Pikachu reaches such heights among fans that Pikachu goes onto become the icon of the series and a star in his own right.

This success comes in part because Pokémon can only talk by saying their own name in different forms of inflection. For example, "Pikachu," "Pika," "Pi," "Ka," "Chu," and "Kachu" each mean different things depending on the context and pitch. This would seem like a drawback, but by listening to the talented voice actor's subtle inflections of a single word, you're able to hear emotions emanate from these monsters on a level that is rarely found in humans acting with a full lexicon. In turn, the monsters become more than cute creatures that do battle for their masters. They become your friend. When Pikachu feels pain, you feel pain. When Pikachu wins a battle, you feel victorious. When Ash and Pikachu hug one another, you feel joy. This is why watching *Pokémon* is such a treat.

Even so, despite loving the initial episodes, I feel *Pokémon* becomes tiresome because it follows a standard formula. For example, Ash explores a new area, discovers a new Pokémon, tries to capture it, is interfered with by Team Rocket, and then either defeats Team Rocket and retrieves the Pokémon, or it escapes and he tries again with a different monster in the next episode. In this sense, *Pokémon* has the Japanese anime quality of being like a soap opera with long story arcs, and the western cartoon quality of wrapping up a self-contained story in a single episode.

They do a decent job of adding new characters and tournaments for Pokémon badges, but what keeps you watching is the character progression, the challenges Ash goes through, and the new Pokémon left to be discovered. Of course, it's the Pokémon themselves who do most of the changing, as they evolve to the next level of battle-hardened monster, better able to do their master's bidding.

As I mentioned at the top, *Pokémon* is a series where mutated animals are captured, trapped inside a personal prison until their master summons them, and are then forced to battle for the pleasure of onlookers. In turn, they are allowed to return to their prison, where they will nurse their wounds and slumber until summoned once again. This is the absurd reality of *Pokémon*. But as the intro theme states, the series is really about being your personal best, chasing a dream, and overcoming great difficulties to achieve it. This message is conveyed through a formulaic and cute approach that makes *Pokémon* a perfect anime to watch with your children, or as a grown adult (without shame). It's safe, fun, and teaches valuable lessons about teamwork, friendship, and perseverance. That's the charm of *Pokémon*.

I will now leave you with the simple yet profound words of *Pokémon's* true hero:

"PIKA ... PIKA ... PIKACHUUUUU!!"

Derek Padula is the world's foremost professional Dragon Ball *scholar. He illuminates the real-world historical, spiritual, and philosophical culture of* Dragon Ball *to enable readers to better understand the series and empower themselves on their own life journeys. His books include the seven-volume* Dragon Ball Culture *series,* Dragon Soul: 30 Years of Dragon Ball Fandom, *and* Dragon Ball Z "It's Over 9,000!" When Worldviews Collide. *You can find him at thedaoofdragonball.com.*

1997 • PRINCESS MONONOKE

MONONOKE-HIME

— ALICIA MALONE —

Watching *Princess Mononoke* for the umpteenth time, it's hard to believe the film is over twenty years old. If the film were a person, it could just about drink in the United States, and definitely could in Australia. And it's quite apt that the film is old enough to be an adult, because *Princess Mononoke* is definitely not made for children. Though director Hayao Miyazaki does spin quite the epic fairytale.

Set in medieval Japan, the story begins with young Prince Ashitaka, who is confronted by a demon-god in the form of a boar. Their fight ends with the Prince victorious, slaying the frightening beast before it reaches his village, but in the process, his arm has been cursed. Ashitaka gains super-strength, but knows the curse will soon spread and kill him. So, he heads west in search of a cure from the Great Forest Spirit, and to discover how that boar became a demon in the first place.

His travels take him to Iron Town, where he meets Lady Eboshi, who is in the middle of a fierce war with the animal gods of the forest. In an attack on the town, led by the wolf-god Moro and her human "daughter" San, Ashitaka saves two men, and is welcomed to the village. But peace is soon disrupted once more by San, who is set on killing Eboshi. After fleeing to the woods, Ashitaka is met by the Forest Spirit, and begins a friendship with San, the wolf-princess.

As you can see, *Princess Mononoke* is by no means simple. This is not a black-and-white, good versus evil tale, in fact, each side has shades of both. The humans are hardworking, yet they exploit the forest for its resources. That's why the animals are angry, but they can also be monstrous and violent. Each of the characters is richly drawn (pun intended) and the story is full of action, which keeps you engaged throughout the 134-minute runtime.

Although *Princess Mononoke* was released in 1997, its birth was much earlier than that. Miyazaki first conceived this idea in the 1970s, drawing pictures of a girl living with a beast in the woods. Almost two decades later, his producer Toshio Suzuki urged him to start work on the film, which he believed would be his last action movie. The making of *Princess Mononoke* took about three years, with each of the 144,000 cells hand-drawn and painted. Rumors say that Hayao Miyazaki personally drew about 80,000 cells himself. He also oversaw the entire production, despite being in his mid-fifties at the time. Some of the effects were achieved with computers, but Miyazaki insisted the digital animation not exceed 10 percent of the entire film. And that the new technology only be used to enhance the hand-drawn animation.

It's this combination of human and computer which makes the animation in *Princess Mononoke* truly come alive. You notice this from the very first moments of the film, in the fight between Ashitaka and the demon boar, where the swirling, crawling tentacles of black chase him down the hill. It's a striking scene, and just one of many in *Princess Mononoke*. The animation is beautiful, particularly the painterly landscapes. There are moments where you feel like you could pause the film, and hang the frame on your wall as a piece of art.

And it's not only the animation of *Princess Mononoke* which remains revolutionary all these years later. The message remains vital, and even more relevant today. At its big, beating heart, *Princess Mononoke* is a look at man versus nature, or civilization versus wilderness. How humans are destroying the planet with our endless need to consume. It's a big theme that by a different director may have come across as a whack to the side of our heads. But in the hands of Miyazaki, a love for the environment is weaved into the complex story with much nuance and care, ending with somewhat of a hopeful note for both humanity and the natural world ... as long as we heed the warning.

Princess Mononoke is part folklore, part true to life, and partly feels like a western movie. The character of Ashitaka is the type of mythic, loner hero we've long seen in westerns, thanklessly fighting a war. And if the village of Iron Town also seems ripped from a Western, it's with good reason—reportedly Miyazaki was very inspired by John Ford. But unlike those westerns, *Princess Mononoke* has a fierce undercurrent of feminism. Both sides of the war are led by women. When I first watched the film, many years ago, that was what stuck with me the most. In particular, the character of San. She is a human brought up by wolves, and though she is ruthless in her views toward the humans of Iron Town, San also has a compassionate side. She cares for Ashitaka, for the forest, and for the animal gods who live in it. San may be a princess, but a Disney princess she ain't. Not with the slash of blood across her lips and the fierce look in her eyes.

When it was released in Japan, *Princess Mononoke* was a huge hit, critically and commercially. It rapidly broke the record for the highest-grossing film in Japan (soon to be dethroned by *Titanic*) and became the first animated movie to win Best Film at the Japanese Academy Awards. When it came to the English-language version, producers approached director Quentin Tarantino. But Tarantino had another idea, recommending an author of books and graphic novels in his place—Neil Gaiman. Gaiman stepped up to oversee the English translation, throwing himself into studying Japanese folklore and adjusting the script to suit American audiences. He was also determined to hire the right voices for each of the characters, and found a wonderful mix with Claire Danes, Gillian Anderson, Billy Bob Thornton and Billy Crudup.

In the twenty years since it was first welcomed into the world, *Princess Mononoke* remains one of Hayao Miyazaki's best, for its striking animation, unique characters, and socially conscious story. It was also supposed to be his last, with Miyazaki determined to retire. Luckily for us, that didn't happen. And after four years of absence, the godfather of animation returned to birth another classic anime, *Spirited Away*.

Alicia Malone is a film reporter, host, author and self-confessed movie geek. Born in Australia, she now lives in Los Angeles, working with Fandango, Turner Classic Movies and Criterion. Her book Backwards & in Heels *chronicles the history of women in Hollywood.*

1997 • REVOLUTIONARY GIRL UTENA

— COMIC BOOK GIRL 19 —

Is it possible for a girl to transform herself into a prince? If so, what magic would it take for her to become a masculine ideal? Going in, know that this series gives no easy answers and is so philosophically deep that I've been thinking about it for over fifteen years and *holy shit* ... I still haven't found the bottom. *Revolutionary Girl Utena* is jam-packed with layer upon layer of symbolism that just keeps getting more profound the more I concentrate on it; an authentic allegorical all-you-can-eat buffet!

This series begins with a fairy tale; once upon a time, a small princess was grieving over the death of her parents, when suddenly, she meets a handsome prince on a white horse who kisses away her tears. Before he leaves, he gives her a ring telling her if she doesn't lose her noble heart, this ring will lead her back to him someday. So impressed was she by this gallant figure that she vows to become a prince herself! The end of the fable becomes self-aware and asks us a rhetorical question. Is this princess's quest really such a great idea? Our heroine's crusade is strikingly similar to that of the alchemist pursuing the seemingly impossible task of turning lead into gold. Whether it's attainable or not, our girl earnestly devotes herself to finding out.

Another thing to be aware of going into this series is that it's *queer AF*. It's as queer as it's flamboyant father/director Kunihiko Ikuhara, who openly likes to dress up in Sailor Mars drag and rubber fetish outfits. Google it. He's as sensual and gloriously weird as the colorful cast of ambiguously bisexual characters that populate this show.

One of the things I love about this series is that it's a surrealist deconstruction of the "magical girl" genre. It takes all the tropes from *Sailor Moon*, which Ikuhara had been previously directing, and turns them inside out and backward. For example, Usagi—the lead in *Sailor Moon*—is a normal girl who finds out she's the reincarnation of the Moon Princess and must use her magical powers to protect the earth. All she wants to do is go back to leading a normal life, get through school, marry her boyfriend, and start a family. Utena is the mirror opposite; she is a normal girl who has committed herself to transcending gender expectations with no clear vision of her future outside of hopefully one day finding her prince whom she is not even sure is real. The only power she possesses is that of her conviction and her extraordinary force of will.

Fun fact: *Revolutionary Girl Utena* is the direct product of an unrealized *Sailor Moon* storyline Ikuhara developed that featured the lesbian Sailor couple Uranus and Neptune at its core. He was forced to abandon the project when he quit Toei Animation, but so smitten was he with this idea, he assembled an artistic collective known as Be-Papas who developed the lost vision into this anime as well as a manga with a follow-up movie and accompanying manga a few years later. (Warning! The *Adolescence of Utena* movie is completely incomprehensible unless you have watched all thirty-nine episodes of the original series and even then, it's still so avant-garde it'll make your head spin. They don't call Ikuhara the David Lynch of Japan for nothing! Seriously. Utena turns into a pink dick car at the end.)

I adore the insane amount of thought Be-Papas put into every aspect of this intellectual property. Take for example the elegant introduction of our aspiring teenage prince Utena Tenjou. Through the "Rule of Three," it's made very clear that this character isn't here to placate anyone and firmly follows her own moral code despite peer pressure. In the opening few minutes of the first episode, she is shown besting a series of everyday challenges posed by the people all around her on the first day of the new school term at Ohtori Academy with both style and grace. She pays no mind to the silly expectations of her best friend. When a teacher confronts her on her "outrageous" choice to dress in a boy's uniform jacket and shorts instead of the traditional girl's uniform, she effortlessly bucks authority. And then she goes on to rebuff an offer to join the boys' basketball team as a sure thing to help them win regionals. Through these brief interactions, we immediately understand that Utena is a rebel who respectfully refuses to be boxed in—or pretend to be something she isn't—to make other people more comfortable.

In a twist of fate, Utena challenges the vice president of the student council to a sword fight after he publicly humiliates her bestie and she accidentally stumbles into a hidden ritualistic dueling game orchestrated by a shadowy figure known as "The End of the World." The winner of these duels is automatically "engaged" to the Rose Bride, a peculiar girl named Anthy Himemiya, who becomes the victor's property. She moves in, cooks, cleans, will tolerate domestic abuse, is seemingly totally submissive, and most importantly she can summon a magical sword that pops out of her chest for her fiancé to wield in their duels.

Utena becomes morally outraged at the idea of this meek girl being passed around like a wrestling belt and wins in her first duel. Now engaged to Anthy, Utena feels duty-bound to continue participating in this weird game; not for any vague promises of "The Power to Revolutionize the World," but to save this odd damsel! To protect Anthy and help free her from whatever binds her to the unhappy role of the Rose Bride. The quest to be Anthy's prince leads Utena onto a path of darkness where she must brave shocking depths of cruelty, manipulation, and betrayal.

And all this is just the tip of the iceberg! *Revolutionary Girl Utena* is the ultimate tale of self-actualization through the expression of unconditional (a.k.a. divine) love. It speaks of the human condition; of the wounds we all carry in our hearts and how that pain defines us. It explores how the greatest fight is not with others but within ourselves. It illustrates that through selflessness we can become a receptacle of divinity. How we find freedom from illusion when we strip away our ego, find humility, and ask for forgiveness.

The word "revolution" immediately suggests the idea of change and Utena does indeed courageously seek to be the change she wants to see in the world. But it's important to remember that the word "revolution" also refers to a completed cycle. Utena is meant to inspire us in our own cycles of change, to boldly ascend that spiral staircase to the dueling arena and face our demons rather than go in circles, doomed to repeat the past forever. In the words of Ohtori Academy's student government, "If we don't crack the world's shell, we will die without ever truly being born! Smash the world's shell! For the revolution of the world!"

Consummate over-thinker and professional crazy person, CBG19 has parlayed her obsessive love of art and storytelling into a full-time career. She is known for hosting the Comic Book Girl 19 Show *on YouTube as well as producing other documentary series centered on a myriad of pop-culture topics with her co-creator and director, Tyson Wheeler.*

1998 • CARDCAPTOR SAKURA

KĀDOKYAPUTĀ SAKURA

— CINDY CARATURO —

Cardcaptor Sakura was not the first anime I'd ever seen as a child. (That honor belongs to *Pokémon*.) The anime I watched, of course, wasn't exactly *Cardcaptor Sakura*. *Cardcaptors* (as it was called at that time) aired on the Kids' WB cartoon block, which I parked myself in front of every Saturday morning. *Cardcaptors* differed substantially from the original show, from names being changed to certain subtexts being removed. Kids' WB made further changes, including rearranging the episode order so that Syaoran, the main male character in the show and Sakura's rival, appears in the first episode (to appeal more to their male demographic). They didn't even air the whole series; only thirty-nine episodes were broadcast.

I, however, knew none of this at the time. Heck, I didn't even know it was from Japan! Despite their attempts to cater to their male demographic, it was clear to me that the true star of the show was Sakura, and I was enamored with her adventures. It was also apparent to me that *Cardcaptor Sakura* was the only show I watched back then that had a girl as the main character. That's not to say I didn't like shows starring male characters; I watched plenty of those. That's also not to say that I didn't like the female characters that appeared in them: I liked Misty from *Pokémon*, and Téa from *Yu-Gi-Oh!* was … well, she was inoffensive. I remember wondering why they were always sidelined: why didn't Misty battle more, or catch more Pokémon? When she left, why did none of Ash's other female companions ever collect badges? Why didn't Téa ever really get to duel? Shows like *Tiny Toon Adventures* and *Animaniacs* had female characters that shared the lead with male characters, and *The Powerpuff Girls* had three female leads. While I enjoyed watching these cartoons, I didn't want to pretend to be those characters and have adventures in their respective worlds. Whatever the case, *Cardcaptor Sakura* had made a special home for itself in my heart.

And boy, did I want to be in Sakura's world. When I first watched it, I thought the backgrounds made her environment seem so real, as if they were based off of places that actually exist. At the same time, there was something appealingly different about them. One of the best examples is the park she frequents. How different it was from any of the parks I'd been to! The penguin-shaped slide from that park is such an iconic image from the show, and it still stands out in my mind.

Sakura herself was also appealingly different, from the hair accessories she wore, to her cute school uniform and the rollerblades she used to get to school. I remember searching my sister's box of hair accessories, looking for anything that remotely resembled what Sakura had in her hair. To my young self's utter joy, she did in fact have some! I tried tying pigtails in my hair like I'd seen Sakura do, and although it wasn't quite like her hairstyle, I'd be happy nonetheless.

When one of my neighborhood friends had a pair of old rollerblades that she was looking to get rid of, I jumped at the chance to have them. I would rollerblade back and forth on our backyard porch, practicing so I could be as good as Sakura. My mom even bought me a replica Clow book with all of the Clow cards inside. I loved pretending that I was Sakura. I didn't have her key staff, so I would use this sparkly dark blue baton with shiny rainbow streamers coming out of the end in its stead. Removing the Windy card, I placed it on the floor and said the magic incantation I heard in every episode. Then I'd pretend to use that card to retrieve the others and add them back into my book. Each episode I watched expanded my own adventures with the Clow. Then again, just holding the book in my hands and taking the cards out to intently examine them was enough for me. That singular item illustrates another point of departure between *Cardcaptor Sakura* and the other things I watched at that time.

While I may have pretended to catch Pokémon and battle with my friends, the designs for the merchandise I had were rather simple. That's not to knock those designs; the Pokéball, for example, is one of the most iconic designs in the world. But I was never content just looking at a Pokéball. The design of the Clow book and each and every card entranced me. They were so detailed and intricate. It felt like I was truly holding something magical in my hands. That excitement of finding magic in the real world is a feeling that I've always treasured and still do.

As time passes, and you learn more about this real world of ours, those bits of magic you once thought were present all around you start to deteriorate: the characters at Disney World are just people in costumes; Santa doesn't exist; magicians don't really know magic, just illusions. The kind of entertainment we're fed changes, too: romantic comedies that usually end up being neither romantic nor comedic; adventures where the male characters are involved in all the action while the females are there to stand on the sidelines and look attractive; dramas that delve into life's harsh realities (though not always so realistically).

And what of animation? Comedies. American cartoons aimed at adults are overwhelmingly comedies, at least primarily. That's what makes anime special, and it's what makes *Cardcaptor Sakura* so important to me. It helped develop the foundation of my desire to find magic in the world around me. As I try and view my own world through a more wondrous but grounded lens, I also want to provide others with that sense of wonder. With the rise of people feeling nostalgic for their childhood lately, perhaps it's not only children who want to experience a bit of magic in their everyday lives.

Cindy Caraturo has been living and working in Japan since 2016. In her spare time, she writes and edits for the Japanese culture site Yatta-Tachi. She aspires to be both a translator and novelist, while simultaneously wondering if she's trying to wear a few too many hats.

1998 • COWBOY BEBOP

KAUBŌI BIBAPPU

— CHRIS STUCKMANN —

I sunk into the faux leather couch, emotionally exhausted. It was late in the day and my parents and I were visiting some family friends. I was trying my damnedest to be respectful of their adult conversation, but all my thirteen-year-old brain could think about was the VHS tape waiting at home with the latest episode of *Cowboy Bebop* ("Jupiter Jazz, Part II") recorded from Adult Swim. Would Spike survive his encounter with Vicious? What happened to Faye and Gren? Would Jet save them in time? I needed to know.

Needed.

It was October 2001, and *Cowboy Bebop* was airing for the first time in America. I didn't realize back then, but thinking about it now, it's apparent how much *Bebop* changed my life for the better. The nation was very confused at the time. Part of me feels like we're still confused, and maybe always will be. But as a kid just old enough to understand the implications of what happened the previous month in New York City, I was simply looking for some solace. And in the months following that disaster at the Towers, what provided me that solace was Adult Swim and its lineup of shows: *Home Movies*, *Sealab 2021*, and, of course, *Bebop*.

After returning from our visit—and after frantically confirming that the VCR had recorded the episode—I continued my *Bebop* journey. The year was now 2071. My heroes were a ragtag group of bounty hunters scavenging for scraps around the galaxy, just scrambling to make ends meet. I was pleased to learn that Spike (one of those aforementioned bounty hunters) did indeed survive his standoff with former friend Vicious, and that there would be many more adventures to come.

I certainly wasn't prepared for the adventure's end—which I won't spoil—but I recall staring at the screen for many minutes as Yoko Kanno's gorgeous song "Blue" floated through my ears. Finally, I dashed to my gigantic iMac and activated our molasses-slow Internet to scour the old IMDb message boards in hopes of learning if those brilliant twenty-six *Bebop* episodes I'd just watched were all there was. Gratefully, no: there was a movie too!

Seventeen years later, Faye and Spike—the notorious do-they-or-don't-they bounty hunters—are inked into my right arm, a permanent reminder of how influential this show has been on my life. It affected the way I view anime and, truthfully, the way I view film.

Bebop creator Shinichirô Watanabe has been very upfront about his inspirations, many of which originate in American cinema. The episode "Toys in the Attic"—in which Spike and crew must locate and destroy an unknown entity on the ship—is akin to Ridley Scott's *Alien*. The outfit Spike wears in "Asteroid Blues" is an obvious recreation of Clint Eastwood's The Man with No Name from *The Good, the Bad, and the Ugly*. Spike practices the fighting style Jeet Kune Do, following in the footsteps of the great Bruce Lee. Even Coffee—a badass, afro-haired woman who appears in "Mushroom Samba"—is a clear tribute to Pam Grier's *Coffy*.

Star Trek is a recurring influence, as well. Faye's cryogenic chamber is labeled NCC-1701-B, a reference to the starship *Enterprise*. And the character Doohan from the episode "Wild Horses" is clearly paying homage to the actor James Doohan, who portrays Scotty on the original series.

No anime in history has the effervescent pop-magic of *Cowboy Bebop*. The euphoric themes woven throughout its iconic soundtrack fuse jazz with heavy metal, rock, electronica, and blues. The opening theme song "Tank!" is perhaps the best example. Try listening to it without nodding your head. Yoko Kanno undoubtedly created one of the greatest soundtracks ever composed.

Beyond the aesthetics, you'll find characters with uncommon depth and humor. The show's exhilarating style combines drama and tension, leading to some truly electrifying confrontations. The past of Spike and Vicious—former friends turned enemies—is explored through key episodes, leading to a climactic battle in "Ballad of Fallen Angels." Their showdown in a church, followed by a jaw-dropping sequence with Spike falling from a window, is the pinnacle of what anime can do.

There's a reason Adult Swim has aired this show on and off for over fifteen years, folks. All it takes is a few glances and you're hooked. Hell, my mom loves it, and she doesn't even like anime.

When I think about it, *Cowboy Bebop* was the pebble that started the landslide. The year after this show completed its initial run in November 2001 was the most influential of my life. I discovered my love of film and was never the same again. *Bebop* played a major part in that. The stunning animation, unparalleled soundtrack, and fully-realized characters put my brain in the mindset to be inspired. This show opened my eyes to art like no other. It continues to save me over and over. If you've never experienced it, give it a try. Perhaps it will save you, too.

1998 • INITIAL D

— VINCENT R. SICILIANO —

Another day that comes along
Don't you know, don't you feel
Gettin' good power
Another night that comes along
Feeling like you're dreamin'
Feeling like you're flyin'
—"Get Me Power," Mega NRG Man

I cannot think of another show that has driven me through life like the anime adaptation of Shuichi Shigeno's manga, which is a timeless story about a teenage boy drifting his way to the top in his AE86 panda Trueno.

Forget that it's a classic underdog story about defeating those with significant technical, experiential, and financial advantages. Takumi is never a victim of his situation, he just dominates. He executes each hairpin turn with stomach-knotting aggression and complete disregard for implicit danger that would result in any lesser driver soaring into a barrel roll off Mount Akina (or local mountain). Not only does he win, for much of the series you hardly feel that he even *cares* that he annihilates the conversely arrogant competition.

Takumi is far and away the most modest of the catalog of self-assured racers he encounters, which is somehow just the really cool way to be—any time you're good at something. Takumi's approach makes me wonder: is *not caring too much* a major component of mastering one's craft? I still believe that anime characters can be good role models for kids, and I believe we should all strive for the integrity and resilience exemplified by the Fujiwara family, just with slightly less fried tofu and cigarettes.

Initial D taught me the nuances of excelling at a craft. To this day, I don't believe one's abilities are defined by the quality of a tool they are given, but that it's the skill of the user that defines the tool's value. As a kid, my friend was perplexed as to why I wanted to purchase an '86 Corolla for my first car. He thought it wasn't fast. We had a conversation that went something like this:

> ME. I'm going to buy an '86 Corolla so I can race other people and give them a good walloping.
>
> FRIEND. Dad, is an '86 Corolla fast?
>
> FRIEND'S DAD. It is … if it's up against another '86 Corolla.

You know what? He was right. An '86 Corolla is not a fast car. But that's what makes it so special, right?

Thinking about my freshman year of high school in 2004 when I first discovered *Initial D*, there were some seniors who used to roll up to the campus in the coolest drift cars. We had a turbo MR2, a Supra, an S2000, and a Miata. I got to hang out with this elusive group of street racers only because I was a pretty good *Dance Revolution*-er, and incidentally, these seniors presided over an after-school club for tearing it to the tune of *DDR Max 2* and *StepMania* (which included many *Initial D* Eurobeat songs). I wasn't sure if they *actually* were into *Initial D*, but I'm veritably certain that if they were, they'd be far too cool to admit it. However, my senior friend who introduced me to *Initial D* (who resembled Iketani in many charming ways), used to take me for perilous jaunts throughout the foothills of Northeast Ohio in his old Chrysler, and he'd yell, "Street racers don't need girlfriends," whilst inducing an oversteer at dangerous velocities around a curve, Eurobeat penetrating the otherwise banal air around us. This was reassuringly apropos as I think we were the most single guys in school, unlike the kids with the street cars.

Eurobeat is the genre of music that perfectly compliments and characterizes *Initial D*'s spirit, personal confidence, and destiny through laser focus and a little bit of luck. I have experienced the power that Eurobeat offers, and it has been my best friend in all things progress and self-improvement. Eurobeat accelerated me through my academic career, as I was able to do some of my best work channeling frenzied enthusiasm and passion. In fact, Eurobeat is its own form of energy and can be harnessed for the power of good. I continue to listen to the latest Super Eurobeat releases, helping me to perform my daily duties with a fiery intensity like no other.

I will always have a fondness for this anime and pretty much everything it offered me as a teenager through to today. I hope that going forward, we have a little bit of this same flavor of anime. An anime that inspires, gives you energy, and makes you want to rise to the top! *Initialize your dreams, friend.*

Vincent R. Siciliano is a software developer and lover of vintage electronics, especially video games and synthesizers. He enjoys traveling to Japan, biking in the park, and playing all the JRPGs he never got around to as a kid.

1998 • OUTLAW STAR

SEIHŌ BUKYŌ AUTORŌ SUTĀ

— DEREK PADULA —

Outlaw Star made me cry.

This anime goes to the heart of what it means to be a young man who follows his dreams, seeks adventures, makes friends, falls in love, overcomes his fears, conquers his enemies, and in turn, himself. The story is told through the vehicle of a science fiction space opera. One that mixes outer space battles featuring space ships with hands that hold guns and ancient Chinese magic. It's this combination of futuristic and archaic action—with an underlying current of sentimentality and romanticism—that makes *Outlaw Star* one of my favorites.

The show is especially relevant to young men going through similar experiences in their own lives as they watch it. As I was, from age seventeen to twenty. Granted, I've never been to outer space. Nor have I dated an artificial girl. Well, there have been some who turned out to be artificial in the end. But I do know what it's like to have a dream, to suffer for it, and to achieve it. And that's where *Outlaw Star* shines. It's the bittersweet feeling of perseverance and determination that you're left with. The idea that you can suffer for your dream, you can achieve it, and it'll cost you, but even so, it's worth it.

Outlaw Star is an adaptation of a manga called *Starward Warrior Knight Outlaw Star*, by Takehiko Itō. It's a *seinen* ("youth") manga for young adults. Because of this, *Outlaw Star* deals with more mature and darker themes than a typical shōnen series. These include murder, suicide, greed, betrayal, obsession, and existential crises.

It first aired in Japan in 1998 and premiered in the States in 2001. That's when I saw it on Toonami. I fell in love and watched it every day after school. There are only twenty-six episodes, but I watched them on repeat for several years.

So what's it all about? Gene Starwind. Our hero—though he's really more of a slacker-for-hire—runs an all-around "problem-fixing" business. His partner is Jim Hawking, the young and diminutive brains of the operations, as counter to Gene's brawn. Together they own Starwind and Hawking Enterprises on the planet Sentinel III, where they barely manage to pay the rent. In their day to day operations, Gene and Jim can butt heads like they're oil and water, but when they're on the job, they work together like hot bread and butter. One day, they take a job like any other, but it turns out their mysterious new business partner has an "item" that violent space pirates want to get their hands on. Lo and behold it's a girl, in a suitcase, and she's the key to unlocking an incredible treasure. When she awakens, Gene is introduced to a whole universe of problems.

Gene has a dream to travel among the stars, but there's a catch: he's afraid of space travel. Jim is wise beyond his years and wants to be grown up like Gene so he can enjoy adulthood's pleasures, but at the same time, likes being a kid. The girl in the suitcase, Melfina? Well, she's not sure what she wants or why she even exists. And Gene is there to help her figure it out. Along the way, the trio gets hold of an experimental, cutting-edge Grappler Ship that Gene names the "Outlaw Star." Melfina is the key to piloting the ship, and the pirates want both, because only Melfina has the coordinates to the Galactic Leyline, where, perhaps, boundless wealth awaits.

Here's where things get layered. The universe they explore is called the Toward Stars Era. It's filled with a menagerie of characters inspired by Hong Kong culture, far-out aliens, cat girls, samurai, dinosaur men, and humans. It's this interfusion of ancient and futuristic that combines together to create an engrossing space.

For example, one of my favorite elements of the series is Tao magic. It's rare to find magic in a sci-fi series, and in *Outlaw Star*, Tao magic is a form of supernormal power used to cast spells. It allows people to invoke telekinesis, levitate, teleport, increase their sensory powers, create shields, summon spirits, and more. This idea is inspired by Taoism, the ancient religion of China. When Tao magic users cast their spells, they chant, "Pagua Sanfa." A lot of fans in the west didn't know what this meant, and figured it was gibberish. But as a curious young man, I discovered that it's a romanization of the Chinese *bāguà sànfā* (八卦散發, "eight trigrams distribute"), inspired by the Daoist principles of *bāguà* and *yīnyáng*, via the *tàijí*. This series, along with *Dragon Ball*, made me interested in Dàoism, Buddhism, and Eastern spirituality. This eventually lead me to a Bachelor's in East Asian Studies and becoming an author on books about the eastern culture in anime.

This is cool by itself, but it gets better when it's counteracted by western science. That is, ancient magic in the form of science, called "casters." Prior to the Toward Star Era was the Fixed Star Era, and in this time there were magicians who used their "*mana*" to cast spells, in contrast to the Taoist "*qì*." As mana on each planet faded away, the magicians compressed the remaining mana into shells, and then created "caster guns" to fire them. Gene is one of the few people who owns a caster gun. But of course, these shells are rare, and firing them can come at a hefty price to the user's health. It's this contrast of opposites that makes *Outlaw Star* interesting.

Throughout the ups and downs, Gene struggles to find himself and understand this wild ride he's on, as does each of the others in the cast. We're soon introduced to the cat girl Aisha, the samurai "Twilight" Suzuka, the ship's A.I. (Gilliam), and the nefarious McDougall Brothers. Plus the pirate factions, interstellar law, and Gene caught in the middle with the prize that everyone wants.

I rarely recommend the English dub of a show over its native Japanese, but in the case of *Outlaw Star* I make an exception. Each of the voice actors is perfectly cast and conveys the proper emotions throughout. But be sure to watch the uncensored edition. For example, there is a man named Fred Luo, who is a billionaire acquaintance of Gene's. In the original, he clearly has a sexual interest in Gene and wants to be more than friends. Censoring this content is a shame because it adds an extra layer of tension, maturity, and sacrifice that Gene has to make in order to strike a deal with Fred and acquire the funds needed to continue his journey. On the other hand, I must also mention that the Japanese original is blessed with one of the best intro songs in 1990s anime, titled "Through the Night," and it's so good, it may lead you down the rabbit hole of J-pop.

Despite a lot of action up front, the first story arc is a slow burn. So if you're not enamored with it after five episodes, I implore you to continue, because it will grow on you. Likewise, the animation can be a bit lacking sometimes in its frames of motion. But the illustrations are high quality, and the battles are top notch. Fortunately the touching music brings it all together. It's composed by *Godzilla* film composer Kow Otani, who also composed another fan favorite, *Mobile Suit Gundam Wing*.

The exact particulars of why this show is appealing are hard to describe with concrete examples. It's not the battles, nor the space race, nor the art, nor music. There's an overall melancholy feeling of uncertainty, suffering, and matter-of-factness about life that persists in my mind. Even with the far-out scenarios and near-death situations, it comes back to humans' struggling to survive, yet doing it with a forbearing smile. People are lost, loves are lost, and fortunes are lost, but it's ultimately about how people gain, and the true purpose of being alive. Why do we do what we do? Does fate exist, or is free will the determining factor? How do we overcome evil if we can't love ourselves and others? It's this bittersweet melancholy tone that lingers.

When you combine these elements together you have a series that will leave its mark on you. And it's a timeless series that retains its merit today. Oddly enough, despite the popularity of *Outlaw Star*, the manga has never been published in English, and there have never been any direct sequels where fans can learn more about Gene's life after the climactic crescendo. This is part of why *Outlaw Star* continues to shine. It leaves you wanting more.

When you look up at the night sky, make sure you don't miss this shooting star passing through it. *Outlaw Star* is one you'll want to catch.

Derek Padula is the world's foremost professional Dragon Ball *scholar. He illuminates the real-world historical, spiritual, and philosophical culture of* Dragon Ball *to enable readers to better understand the series and empower themselves on their own life journeys. His books include the seven-volume* Dragon Ball Culture *series,* Dragon Soul: 30 Years of Dragon Ball Fandom, *and* Dragon Ball Z "It's Over 9,000!" When Worldviews Collide. *You can find him at thedaoofdragonball.com.*

1998 • SERIAL EXPERIMENTS LAIN

SHIRIARU EKUSUPERIMENTSU REIN

— TRISTAN GALLANT —

It was the fall of 2006. At two thirty in the afternoon, I had just exited my high school, boarded my bus, and proceeded to relax for the forty-five-minute ride home, where I would be spending the rest of the afternoon with my best friend to watch a new anime we had just gotten a hold of.

Serial Experiments Lain.

We didn't have much of an idea of what we were getting ourselves into. At the time, it didn't matter to us. Exchanging anime DVDs and VHS tapes was a common thing in our group of friends, and with the help of our school's anime club combined with our newfound love for this weird animation from Japan, we would watch anything that we could get our hands on. Miyazaki films, Clamp adaptations, even a few *City Hunter* films that we would quote endlessly during those moments of high school boredom.

But on this day, we had the complete Geneon collection of *Lain* in our backpacks. The plan, if I recall correctly, was to watch about three or four episodes, and then to perhaps saunter over to the N64 and play some rounds of *Banjo-Tooie* in multiplayer, or whatever else we had at the time. But sometimes—as all anime fans must know—you come across a show that you just can't stop after a certain point. A show that requires you to finish the whole thing in one sitting.

We watched it twice.

Looking back, I don't think we fully understood what the story of *Lain* was trying to tell us. Even now, many years later, I can sit down to watch *Lain* and come out of it with a new take I had not thought of previously. It's a series that really lends itself to multiple interpretations, it's just unfortunate that a more widespread belief is that the show just doesn't know what it's talking about.

Lain is a product of its time. It was produced in the late '90s by a group of people who really had no idea how technology—more specifically the Internet— was going to evolve over the next several years. And yet, their predictions are surprisingly accurate.

This is the point where I would give a brief description of the series for those who have not yet had the pleasure of watching it, but after a few attempts, I feel that a proper synopsis is almost impossible without generalizing the story too much. I said that there are a variety of ways to look at this series and I stand by that. Even trying to describe the titular character Lain herself could easily be contradicted or examined differently by others. On the outside, she seems like a fourteen-year-old Japanese girl who gets really into technology after another girl from her school commits suicide. But Lain could also be a homunculus created by some drugged up fanatic that is supposed to be a tool for his own ends. She could be a god, merely watching events unfold through an avatar that takes her form, or Lain could be a being that doesn't even exist at all.

If you think I am not making a lot of sense, believe me, I don't blame you. There is a reason that my sixteen-year-old self needed to watch the series twice in one sitting. The narrative of the show talks about the complexity of technology and how it affects the lives of those who use it. It talks about Roswell, alludes to the Knights of the Lambda Calculus, and references literary works by Lewis Carroll to Marcel Proust. It's a series that is so complex and intricate that I don't blame people for thinking that the show is really about nothing at all. But that answer was not good enough for me.

Eventually, many years later, I came across an interview done with the creators, printed in *Animerica* back in September of 1999. It gave me some insights, but still, I think that even the creators don't fully know or want to know what it is they created. However, one line from this interview stuck out to me. When asked what they thought the message of the series was, the show's producer Yasuyuki Ueda responded with: "The message is: things are simple."

Things are simple.

One of the most complicated and involved animated works that I have seen summed up as, "Things are simple." Well, you can possibly imagine how dumbfounded I was by those words. At that point I had spent countless hours going over the series, discussing its narrative with others, piecing together what I thought could be a giant narrative puzzle about the dangers of technology, or the fragility of human feelings, but no.

Things are simple.

It was a long while before I understood those words, after yet another re-watch of the series, in fact, before I grasped why Ueda would describe *Lain* that way. It's very easy to fall into a rabbit hole with *Lain*, to try and find meaning in the convoluted mess of themes that it presents to you. But when you do find the simplicity within it, it changes you. It can potentially alter your outlook on things that were once so complicated and involved. If you've never seen *Lain* before now, then I would recommend trying to find a few hours of spare time to watch it. Just be sure to view it with an open mind and see what comes out of it, what impression it leaves on you. Just don't do what I did and watch it twice in one sitting. That might have been a bad idea …

Tristan "Arkada" Gallant is a Canadian YouTuber, known for reviewing Japanese animation with his video series Glass Reflection *where he explores and determines the best (and sometimes worst) that anime has to offer, all the while making outlandish expressions and gestures.*

1998 • TRIGUN

TORAIGAN

— EMMA FYFFE —

I am starting to realize that the novelty of going to the toy store is something future generations will truly miss out on. In the very early 2000s, a series of anime figures designed by Todd McFarlane began to appear at my local KB Toy Works—of the outdoor strip mall variety—not to be confused with its smaller, indoor-shopping-center based counterpart, KB Toys. The characters represented in this series ranged from fairly predictable, Kaneda of *Akira* fame, a film which had already gained some notoriety in the US, slightly unusual, Ryoko of *Tenchi Muyo!*, a series I had recently taken a liking to and was actually airing on Toonami, and downright ahead of its time: Vash the Stampede, from *Trigun*.

I say this because, *Trigun* wasn't even close to being broadcast on US television, though Pioneer had begun releasing the series on what would ultimately be eight DVDs to complete the entire twenty-six-episode series, selling for about $30 a piece. It was expensive to be an anime fan before the days of streaming services. And while *Animerica*—Viz Media's monthly anime magazine I assume all my fellow wannabe otaku were turning to for recommendations between 1995 and 2002 when the more glamorous Japanese publication *Newtype* made its way stateside—was advertising the show pretty heavily, anyone who wasn't actively seeking it was unlikely to stumble upon *Trigun*. However—the moral of this story is it didn't really matter because I'd never seen *Trigun*—I knew it was anime and Vash was cool-looking so I convinced my mom to buy me the figure anyway, and I was probably not the only young teenager in America to do so. Or the only anime fan to blindly purchase any quality piece of anime-related merchandise they came across, because we'd never think to logon to our computers and buy it online—though had I been a bit older, I may have gotten in on that fledgling eBay market.

So I took home this spiky-haired, red trench coat, orange-glasses-wearing anime hero and displayed him on my clunky bedroom shelf next to Ryoko, with her amber lightsab-err, I mean, energy sword, and Kaneda in all his cyberpunk glory. And even in the presence of these two visions of anime badassery, he looked super cool. He had an interchangeable mechanical arm, a silver cross attached to a real chain you had to hook on to his coat, and a massive double barrel revolver. He was so cool, in fact, that when—based on how much I liked this figure—I decided to buy the first *Trigun* DVD and actually watch the show, I was kind of taken aback by how uncool Vash initially seemed.

I had already watched *Cowboy Bebop* (which I owned all of on DVD) and *Outlaw Star* was airing on Toonami by summer of 2001, so I was pretty familiar with the Japanese concept of the Space Western. But *Trigun* was more regular Western with some science fiction elements. It was also *way* more over-the-top in the comedy department than I expected, with lots of sweat drops and super deformed characters—and I didn't like the art style when Vash did go super deformed, which he did often. Yes, he was very good with that super cool gun the action figure came with, but he spent half the time running around, screaming, making weird faces and being obsessed with donuts. Definitely not the character I had envisioned based on his appearance. So I put *Trigun* on the back burner for a while and kept obsessively re-watching my recently acquired *Revolutionary Girl Utena* fansubs.

About a year later, my parents upgraded our Internet. Now, instead of having to occupy our second phone line and "dial in" to the Internet, so to speak, we had a cable modem. And not only did it not take up a phone line, it was lightning fast. So, after spending the initial days of this glorious new era downloading anime theme songs and burning them to CDs that I could listen to on my Sony Discman, I turned my attention to online shopping. I discovered what was almost certainly an illegal website selling bootleg bilingual (I was at the phase of my anime-watching career wherein I adhered to a strict "subs not dubs" policy) anime DVDs consisting of entire seasons for about $20 to $30 a piece. As I was browsing this newfound mecha for a series I'd heard about but never seen—like *Yu Yu Hakusho*—I decided I should pick up *Trigun* and give it another go.

This time I went in knowing this was not going to be the slick, jazz-score-laden space opera that *Cowboy Bebop* was. I knew that Vash was more than a little goofy, and this time, found it endearing. And since I was not busy being distracted by expectations versus reality as far as Vash was concerned, this time I could actually pay attention to and appreciate the other characters, like Meryl and Milly, and more importantly realize how hilarious the concept of Vash being trailed by a couple of insurance agents is. Or Wolfwood, the remorseless priest/assassin, who struggles to accept Vash's non-killing lifestyle, and wields a giant cross-shaped gun aptly named "The Punisher." Have I mentioned how cool the character designs in this series are?

And not surprisingly, there's a whole lot more to Vash than his outwardly quirky and cheerful personality. Including a very creepy, murderous sociopath brother named Knives who serves as the series' primary antagonist.

Something interesting to note about *Trigun* is that it was not considered particularly successful in Japan. It wasn't *un*successful with Vash's, again, ultra-cool character design inspiring tons of Japanese merchandise like keychains, plush toys, and mass-produced cosplay and the character himself ranking #2 in the 1998 Annual Anime Grand Prix Male Character Category. But it wasn't until 2003, when *Trigun* aired on Adult Swim in the US that *Trigun* truly became a hit. Maybe it's the old west setting, or themes of Christian morality, both of which are inherently more relatable to a western audience. Or perhaps it was the novelty of an anime series being marketed to adults and not toned down and marketed to children, an honor previously held by only a handful of titles, with *Cowboy Bebop* being the first to air on Adult Swim. Whatever it was, when Volume 1 of creator Yasuhiro Nightow's original *Trigun* manga was released by Dark Horse in the US in late 2003, it sold out almost immediately. Volume 2 would go on to become one of the top-grossing manga of 2004.

Trigun's legacy endures to this day, with the series being available to stream on both FUNimation's streaming service FUNimation Now and the not-strictly-anime-focused Hulu (as of this writing). So if you, too, find yourself captivated as I was by the image of the gangly blond man in a dope-looking trench coat, you need not look far to enjoy it. Just learn from my mistake and keep an open mind when you first come face to face with "The Humanoid Typhoon."

Emma Fyffe currently resides in Los Angeles where she hosts a Sailor Moon *podcast* Love and Justice *and an anime talk show* Hyper Otaku *on Hyper RPG's Facebook page. She is also the "Golden Mic" of the* Movie Trivia Schmoedown *(it says so on her IMDb) and the Captain of a ragtag crew of smugglers on Hyper RPG's Twitch-based* Star Wars *roleplaying game series "Pencils and Parsecs."*

1999 • JIN-ROH: THE WOLF BRIGADE

— BENNETT WHITE —

There is something oddly soothing about a gray, rainy day. The lack of sunlight dampens the mood, matching the pavement and concrete of the city outside, the water falling from the sky calms the nerves. It numbs you. It leaves you pleasantly, emotionally tranquilized. The rain further chills the air and cleans it of all dirt and detritus; breathing in this pure oxygen stings and invigorates the lungs.

This duality of finding comfort in the cold is like rising from a frigid river: your body shakes and shivers from the harshness of the frozen water, but only then can you truly feel the warmth that pulses through you. That feeling is the basis of a beautiful tragedy, a moniker that typifies a number of anime dramas, and nowhere more profoundly than in *Jin-Roh: The Wolf Brigade*.

The only anime adaptation of Mamoru Oshii's long-held Kerberos Saga—an alternate-history, multimedia franchise that stretches into live-action movies and manga as well as radio dramas—*Jin-Roh* centers on a radically different 1950's Japan. Here, Germany occupied Japan instead of allying with them during World War II, which causes the many social, economic, and political upheavals that tear the country nearly apart. Radical groups of anti-government terrorists have pushed Japan's leaders into a desperate situation. The government resorts to using martial law, enforced by a heavily armored police dubbed the Capital Police Special Unit.

Among the Special Unit is a young constable, Kazuki Fuse. On the night of a violent riot, during a search and apprehension mission, he comes across a young girl carrying a bomb in a satchel, meant for delivery to the terrorists in the sewers. Unable to bring himself to kill her, the girl detonates the bag, and although Fuse survives, massive repercussions remain for both himself and the precarious existence of the Capitol Police.

Fuse's inability to commit to his duties in the heat of the moment is not the only source of his growing internal struggle, as he happens to meet the girl's sister, Kei, praying at her grave. Despite the situation they find themselves in, they strike a peculiar friendship that seems to flourish into love. But even as he finds some comfort in Kei's company, Fuse remains conflicted. Trapped between the human connection he has with Kei, and his duty to his disgraced brethren, his survivor's guilt will not be abated.

From the very first frame, *Jin-Roh* assaults the viewer with brutality, which belies the delicate and careful attention paid to the character's movements by director Hiroyuki Okiura: one of the most unfairly unheralded anime figures of his generation. Hand-picked to direct by Oshii, the two had previously worked together on numerous landmark projects like the *Patlabor* movies and *Ghost in the Shell.*

Okiura's history of being a premier key animator and animation director served him well on what would be his major directorial debut. Though this is Oshii's property and story, Jin-Roh is Okiura's film, having not only directed it, but also storyboarded it, and designed its original characters. His commitment to the film stretches all the way down to the stunning fact that he, himself, performed the intensive and scrutinizing task of checking the animation cells layout.

His labor of love truly goes to show, as *Jin-Roh* is one of the most impressively animated films of the 1990s, if not the most gorgeously violent. The opening sound of an explosion that heralds the beginning of the movie greets the viewer with the grace and civility of a dive bar bouncer. The film slowly churns forward with shots of the Capital Police gunning down civilians; both old and young alike are left dead in a pool of their own blood. Tears of fire streak across the night sky as protesters rain Molotov cocktails upon a bulwark of outnumbered police. Deafening gunfire fills the brick arches and halls of the city's waterways, as the Capital Police corner terrorists who would rather impotently fight back against a superior, imposing, almost inhuman foe. The only silence to be had are slight pauses in the battle as bodies hit cold sewer water.

Though the violence is compelling and brutal, it's the quiet and somber moments that truly elevate the film. The score by Hajime Mizoguchi also deserves special commendation, as it exquisitely pairs itself with the animation to create a sensory experience that is rivaled by only a select few anime films. It is a lush orchestral suite, able to be light and airy or brooding and full of dread.

We are met with a calming, nostalgically-tinged piano and strings as Fuse and Kei slowly stroll around the nearby sea. The breeze gently sweeps Kei's hair in front of her face, causing her to smile as she pushes it back into place. She turns toward the sea to gaze upon a gull that rides a stream of air away from her. She sighs and wonders aloud that it must feel good ... to fly, to escape, to be free. The strings slowly descend down in scale before drawing to a low close, invoking a sense that while the two have managed to find a port in the storm, it will only last for so long.

Conversely, the music allows the audience to fully realize the gravitas of Fuse's night in the sewer, gun in hand and pointed at the bomb-toting girl. She is visibly terrified beyond her control, her knees shake and she trembles. Fuse, clad in his armor, is a statue with glowing red eyes, his face obscured by a gas mask and not one patch of his body is left uncovered. He is unrecognizable, almost monstrous. The strings ache in a long, low drone, accompanied by subtle, but clanging drums that tense the air further as the girl barely manages to inch her finger to the ripcord that will detonate the bomb. Tearfully, she grasps it, and with her last ounce of courage, tears it free. Time stops. The strings finally let go of the drone, and all Fuse can do is groan out a quiet question: *Why?*

Thematically, the story pins itself to the fairy tale "Little Red Riding Hood." The allegory is strongly felt both in terms of plot and visual styling; the latter much more obviously than the former. Fuse's struggle to cope with what happens reaches a fever pitch as his dreams terrorize him. He sees himself chase after Kei in her red cloak as a pack of wolves follows him in their pursuit. By framing Fuse, and by extension the story, through this lens, a realization begins to happen. Doubt becomes certainty, which slowly gives way to inevitably: as the film is keen to point out,

"IN EVERY FAIRY TALE WHERE HE APPEARS, THE WOLF HAS ALWAYS BEEN THE VILLAIN."

To match the grimness of the story and its plot, the color of the animation throughout is uniformly muted. This serves to further accentuate the visceral, violent scenes. Blood appears to be like oil as it leaves the body, splashing onto grungy brick walls. The weather is either overcast or raining heavily, desaturating the hues and colors to make every setting a tableau of tangible, grimy beauty. Simply looking at the city's backdrop is evocative enough to fog the breath.

And that chilling discontent is only tempered by the inescapable atmosphere the film constructs through its visuals and score. It is an ecosystem of constant bleakness, numbness, and finality. Yet, you are enraptured, even as you know deep down that there can only be one conclusion to such a film. It is a tragedy, one that is steeped in the sensibilities of the old-world fairy tales that refused all semblances of happy endings. The wolf is always the villain.

Bennett White has been making content on the Internet for a decade, stretching from video games to anime, and has aggregated over twenty million lifetime views. He currently resides in Northern California.

1999 • NOW AND THEN, HERE AND THERE

IMA, SOKO NI IRU BOKU

— CHRIS STUCKMANN —

Much like Isao Takahata's devastating meditation on the horrors of war (*Grave of the Fireflies*), the thirteen brutal episodes of *Now and Then, Here and There* leave a bruise on the heart. In the 325 minutes it takes to watch the series, you'll experience rage, shock, denial, and the sinking realization that the events you're witnessing are simply fictional exaggerations of the all too realistic plague of war. Slavery, genocide, human trafficking, child soldiers, dictatorship—all are explored in this powerful anime, and I admit I wasn't ready for it.

We follow Shu, a naïve and optimistic Kendo student. After losing a match, Shu climbs to the top of a tower to observe the sunset. To his right, he notices a young blue-haired girl staring off into the sky and instantly feels an unspoken connection with her. Suddenly, an unknown military force appears and snatches the girl. Shu intercedes on her behalf and winds up transported to an alternate reality. In this place, an evil man named Hamdo rules over Hellywood, a humongous warship that operates like a mobile city. Hamdo leads cowardly raids on nearby villages, stealing children from families and forcing them to become soldiers. He promises the children that they'll be returned to their villages after a few years of service, then subtly brainwashes them into supporting his ideologies. However, Hamdo's real obsession lies with the blue-haired girl, Lala-Ru, who possesses a power that Hamdo desperately covets.

NATHAT barely stops to breathe. In the moments when it does, the focus is always on the catastrophic terror of war. Its young soldiers often find frightened faces staring down the barrel of their guns. Most stories would wimp out here. But this series has an iron pair of balls, and these children kill without remorse. They feel justified, in fact, because of their brainwashing.

NATHAT strikes deep emotional chords. The most emotionally shattering story in the series is that of Sara, a kidnapped girl who was mistaken for Lala-Ru by Hellywood soldiers due to their similar appearance. Sara is already nearing the end of her rope when Shu becomes her cellmate. Shortly thereafter, Sara discovers her purpose on Hellywood: she's to be enrolled in the "breeding program."

Yeah.

Sara's storyline made this show a very difficult watch. I kept begging the creators to let her out of their crosshairs, but in retrospect, it was necessary. Hellywood bears many parallels to Nazi Germany, and Sara's story allowed *NATHAT* to explore one of the most sadistic elements of that regime. *NATHAT* doesn't hold back when depicting the gruesome details of Hellywood's breeding program. But while some anime linger on disgusting acts of violence or sexual assault for titillation's sake, *NATHAT* wisely uses these events to make a point: Don't forget our history. We must not forget what leads to events like this. If we do, we could very well regress.

There's a prevailing theory that *NATHAT*'s creators were confronting the darker aspects of Japan's history, as well. During World War II, Japan stole thousands of women from their families and forced them into sexual slavery. They were known as "comfort women," and they were lured with false promises just as the children in *NATHAT*, being told they'd receive factory jobs or the like. If it's true that *NATHAT*'s creators intended viewers—particularly Japanese viewers—to examine shameful aspects of their past, then they are to be praised. It's difficult for a generation to acknowledge the sins of their predecessors. Yet it's how we traverse this painful history that shows our true mettle.

While it certainly isn't a joyful experience, this is an anime that more should see. I can only speculate why it has become relatively unknown, beyond the fact that the DVD collection is out of print and tough to track down. For one thing, *Now and Then, Here and There* isn't a very marketable title. And the subject matter is highly disturbing, of course. But then why is a film like *Grave of the Fireflies* so widely popular? Perhaps it's the Studio Ghibli cachet. Perhaps it's the idea of braving thirteen full episodes of pure horror rather than just one movie. I'm not sure. What I do know is that this anime has been kicked under the rug when it should be right up there with the best of your collection.

1999 • ONE PIECE

— MALCOLM RAY —

In a market so heavily saturated, discovering your favorite genre of anime at the moment you discover anime is no less than good luck altogether. My all-time favorite anime will always be the the *Dragon Ball* franchise. It encompasses everything that I love; action, fantasy, and this sheer epic feel that made the world they were in seem larger than life. It has dinosaurs, space aliens, furries, and super-powered explosive martial arts action with fighters that could destroy planets using a single finger.

The one show that seemed to come close to what I had found in *Dragon Ball* was an anime epic about pirates called *One Piece*. It was a journey, however, and it took me a while to find *One Piece*. Though it never quite lived up to what I see in *Dragon Ball*, it had a lasting impact on what I came to find as a standard for anime concepts.

As an action-hungry '90s kid, *Dragon Ball Z* had me hooked the moment I first started watching. Having first seen it on Fox Kids during its initial US run, I wanted more. After a year hiatus, I rediscovered it on Toonami. Not only did this block have *DBZ*, there were other shows that satiated my need for anime. I saw show after show and none quite got close to being what I had found in *DBZ*. Sure, they had cool stylized designs and slick action sequences, but they left me pining for more *Dragon Ball*.

While mulling over multiple anime, I did find a few that piqued my curiosity. From *Yu Yu Hakusho*, to *Fullmetal Alchemist*, and *Naruto*; they were all very exciting. They had that stylized flare in their hand-to-hand action that I'd come to love in *DBZ*. However, there was something lacking.

When I first saw *One Piece*, it was on Fox's 4Kids Saturday morning block. It was then that I realized how heavily edited foreign cartoons could be, and what a poor dub was. I kept asking myself why Sanji, the crew's chain-smoking chef, constantly has a sucker in his mouth. Despite being heavily and poorly censored (I did eventually discover the unedited versions online), man did this show have everything. It had giants, sea monsters, animal people, ghosts, ghouls, drag queens, and super-powered beings that utilized the various abilities from a food called Devil Fruit.

The world was larger than life and super imaginative. They'd travel to various islands, from islands in the sky to islands at the bottom of the very ocean they sailed. It had the hero's journey, following the titular hero Luffy, a young man who wanted to become king of the pirates. Having swallowed a Devil Fruit himself, one called the Gum Gum fruit, it turned him into a rubber human, in the same vein as Mr. Fantastic from the Fantastic Four. This gave Luffy all the attributes of rubber, and coupled with his fighting prowess, made him a force to be reckoned with.

He wanted to find the ultimate treasure, known as "One Piece," and he'd stop at nothing to achieve his goal. He'd gather a crew of whoever he saw fit and he'd beat down anyone in his way who threatened to hurt him or his "*nakama*" (comrades/friends). The crew he gathered comprised of characters with even more emotionally heavy and wacky backgrounds and dreams.

There's a young navigator named Nami who wants to map out the entire world. Zoro, a bounty hunter who wants to become the world's greatest swordsman. They get an all-star chain-smoking chef named Sanji who wants to find a sea called All Blue that supposedly has the best-tasting sea salt. There's also Tony Tony Chopper, a reindeer doctor, who became anthropomorphic because of a Devil Fruit, and he wants to become the best doctor in the world.

There are others who join as well, and the crew continues to grow as the show progresses. It fits the theme of *One Piece*, which is growing and evolving to rise to occasion, and boy would they need it. Though they all fight with their personal unique skill sets and are incredibly powerful in their own ways, the enemies they come across seem even more infinitely powerful and unstoppable. It is a bit "enemy of the week" in its execution, but it's done rather seamlessly in that each enemy they encounter progresses the story forward. It was interesting; the fight scenes had that hyper adrenaline rush that was reminiscent of *Dragon Ball*, but it also had a lot of heart, detailing each of the character's motivations and why they fought. This was a detail that was sort of skimped out on in *Dragon Ball*. In each fight, *One Piece* made sure you *knew* the character's life while they fought for their own. This played to *One Piece*'s strength and weakness, however—something I'll get back to later.

The action in *One Piece* was phenomenal. All of the fights had brutal, detailed impacts and exchanges that were very similar to *Dragon Ball* and early *Dragon Ball Z*. Fists would indent the face and body, fire would singe fur, teeth would get visibly knocked out with tendrils of the gums flailing behind. In some cases there'd even be X-Ray style shots of characters having bones broken or cracks in their skulls. It was still done in a comically cartoonish way, because with most of these assaults, our heroes would bounce back, ready for more, somehow surviving these onslaughts. But the Naotoshi Shida art-direction made sure you felt every blow the characters were experiencing, to let you know what level of intensity was in their struggle. It wasn't always just a blur of arms and legs swinging at each other, or repetitive combos. There were meticulously choreographed fight sequences that reminded me of the best *Dragon Ball* animations. These battles would go on, fighters using various abilities via sword, kicking, inflating their limbs to gigantic proportions or even using elemental attacks like magma or light, and even the weather itself. And not all of their battles are about who is more powerful.

With *One Piece*, it's usually a battle of wit and skill, or pure strategy. In some cases, it is just massive luck. For example; in the "Skypiea" Arc, there is a powerful Devil Fruit user named Enel. He ate the Goro Goro no Mi fruit, which simply put, turned him into a lightning human. Not only could he use lightning like Storm from the X-Men, but he *was* lightning. His entire being had the attributes of lightning. He couldn't be touched by ordinary means, either. This follows the idea behind the various types of Devil Fruits, categorizing this specific one as a "Logia" type, which makes the elemental user intangible because of their attributes (i.e., fire, water, smoke). However there was a counter balance to all of these, such as water to fire (if the water is powerful enough).

In Enel's case, his counter balance was none other than Luffy himself. Being made of rubber, Luffy was impervious to electrical attacks. Oversimplified? Perhaps, but very freaking cool, and clever. Additionally, non-Devil Fruit users (regular humans) could use sea stone objects to nullify Devil Fruit users' abilities. This is because, for some mysterious reason, Devil Fruit powers are canceled out by sea water. This nullifying technique can also be achieved through a more recently developed concept called "*haki.*" Haki is basically *One Piece*'s version of *Star Wars*' "The Force." There are three different types: one that allows the user to sense the presence of others; another that allows the user to create a sort of invisible spiritual armor around their bodies, strong enough to injure logia Devil Fruit users; then, there's a type that only a select few ever attain, that basically enforces their will upon others, knocking them out. With all of this in mind, it was easy to see that *One Piece* offered a cornucopia of ideas that nearly made me consider it as a contender for my favorite anime next to *Dragon Ball*, if not more of a spiritual successor to *Dragon Ball*.

What really supplemented the action and fight scenes was the character development. Nothing makes a battle more epic than knowing what drives a character to fight. Holy cow, does this show know how to ramp up drama. Every character has a deep engaging story. And when you see them fight and struggle, it means so much more than its surface value.

In *One Piece*, our heroes manage to defeat whatever comes their way through their ambition and skill. Sometimes they do need to flee, and their defeat or losses are just as impactful. Now, while I was in love with all of this, it became incredibly overdone. While in some episodes of action packed *Dragon Ball* moments, the momentum gets dragged down by over-exaggerated power-ups and transformations, *One Piece* suffers from painfully tedious backstory digressions.

Some episodes would be entirely dedicated to flashback, for a story that could most certainly be summarized in just a few minutes. And now, at the time of this article, *One Piece* is at 800+ episodes ... and it's just too much. I'll now occasionally tune in to see where the story has gone, for the amazing fight scenes and because I'm still in love with the characters.

That being said, *One Piece* definitely has everything that made me fall in love with *Dragon Ball* and anime as a whole, and I'll still enjoy the original arcs. With the creative world-building, the epic story concepts, and the wildly imaginative characters of literally every shape and size, I know I'll be hard-pressed to find another anime that hits the same notes just as well.

Here's a video game and animation fanatic. From telling you about the new McCafe items at McDonald's to tormenting the Nostalgia Critic as Satan, Malcolm Ray is a SAG actor, and voice actor. He's represented as talent at the Stewart Talent agency in Chicago. As a freelance actor, he is currently hired talent for the online production company Channel Awesome, appearing in many episodes of Nostalgia Critic.

2000 • BOOGIEPOP PHANTOM

BUGIPOPPU FANTOMU

— CHRIS STUCKMANN —

Newtype is one of the longest running anime publications in Japan, releasing regular issues since 1985. At one time, the magazine was so in demand that other countries began to publish issues, and before long, *Newtype USA* was introduced in 2002. Being a certified, card-carrying anime nerd, a subscription was required.

Physical magazine subscriptions aren't as popular today, but I still hold one or two. In their heyday, *Nintendo Power*, *GamePro*, *Anime Insider*, and *Newtype USA* were a few of mine. Back then, many magazines included free gifts for their subscribers. *Nintendo Power* would routinely include a VHS that outlined upcoming game releases (I still have that Hot Newz 64 tape), and *Newtype USA* offered a free promotional disc that featured select anime episodes. The May 2003 issue came packaged with one such disc. On it, was an episode of *Boogiepop Phantom* and, in hindsight, I wasn't ready for it.

After viewing the episode on that free DVD, I was intrigued, yet thoroughly confused. If only I knew how much weirder it got from there!

It took fourteen more years before I finally decided to see what that was all about. A dozen episodes later, I was left baffled and more than a little stumped, but my befuddlement eventually gave way to admiration. This is a very, very bizarre show, but one worth viewing.

Boogiepop Phantom is about ...

Hm ...

Well ...

Um … this is going to be tough.

Perhaps it's best to start with the uncommon structure on display in *Boogiepop*. Each episode tells the story of a different high school student and a few adults. The featured characters were witnesses to an inexplicable beam of light that appeared in the city. Ever since, they've all felt something was just … wrong. Their lives are in an uproar, they're losing their minds, they can't operate like human beings anymore. Interestingly, each episode of *Boogiepop* will often have repeated scenes, just viewed from a different perspective. These people are all interconnected, and we gradually become aware of this shared bond over time as they pass by each other on the street, or interact with the lead character from another episode.

Soon enough—as is typical in horror—dead bodies turn up. Rumors spread. An old urban legend resurfaces: Boogiepop, said to be Death itself. This entity must be to blame, right? Kids are dying. Good kids. Kids who've never shown any indication to be anything other than top-notch students. Fear spreads amongst this unnamed town, paranoia seeps into the community, and maybe, just maybe, in the corner of the darkest alleyway … Boogiepop waits.

Along with repeated scenes, some storylines aren't told chronologically. This requires considerable patience and a resolute memory for small details. In the final episodes, you're asked to recall minor scenes covered earlier—well, they seemed minor at the time—the creators hoping we'll connect the dots. This can result in a great deal of frustration and head-scratching, but it's not without reward.

Few shows have successfully harnessed the sense of dread that *Boogiepop* has. Panic quietly creeps its way into the students' lives, only amplifying their fear of Boogiepop. As more lives are lost—sometimes in frighteningly public ways— the entire student body becomes anxiety-stricken and uncertainty abounds. For a select few, this foreboding terror gives way to mental instability and devastating consequences.

The entire show is presented with a muted color palette, and every single episode— except for the last—has a black vignette around the edges. Viewing the world through this perspective heightens the sense of nervous insecurity the characters feel trapped in, letting us experience their story through a warped lens.

Episode 4 is a more straightforward story, and the one I find most disturbing. Yoji Suganuma is a troubled young introvert with a domineering father and a lonely social life. He retreats to his room as often as possible, mesmerized by a simulated dating game. Within this game, Yoji has created his ideal woman: one who serves his every whim without question. Making matters worse, Yoji becomes addicted to a new drug called Type-S, a stimulant that heightens the senses and blurs reality.

This is all depressing stuff, but the real horror is what Yoji does to a new employee he's training at work. An innocent young girl named Rie is determined to succeed at her new job, and she'll do anything to make a good impression. When Yoji develops an attraction for her, his requests start small. Maybe a few suggestions. Before long, Yoji tries to mold Rie into his perfect woman, just like his simulated dating game. He traumatizes and objectifies Rie, using her as a puppet for his outlandish desires. His drug addiction combined with his fetish for manipulating women leads to a tragic outcome, one of the most painful in the show.

It's storylines like these that make *Boogiepop* stand out. Sure, there's an urban legend spreading about a savage, ghostly spirit, but the real horror lies in stories like Yoji's. Despite the supernatural trappings, despite the nonlinear storytelling, despite the confusing narrative ... *Boogiepop* works best when it's exploring the twisted side of youth culture, and the terrifying aftermath of drug addiction.

Another powerful story is featured in Episode 2, which primarily focuses on a man named Jonouchi. When he looks at someone, he sees a literal bug inside them. At first horrified, eventually, he realizes he has the ability to remove this bug. Sickeningly, he discovers that by ingesting the bug, he removes all emotional pain from whomever had the bug. But by lifting this weight from people, is he really helping? So often we want to escape our problems, but how else will we learn? Even if we could instantly remove our pain, would it really help in the long run?

There's so much I haven't covered here: the light beam, government testing, copycat phantoms. *Boogiepop* is a convoluted, exasperating mess. Some episodes are infuriatingly difficult, requiring hardened determination to get to the end. And even if you finish the series, you may need a second viewing to grasp the fragmented clues scattered throughout. Sounds great right? Joking aside, *Boogiepop Phantom* is a show that veteran anime fans should see at least once. It's unusual enough to warrant commendation and the unconventional approach to color-grading alone deserves attention. While your first viewing might require a notepad, odds are, *Boogiepop* will leave an impression on you. Whether it's good or bad remains to be seen.

2000 • FLCL

FURI KURI

— CHRIS STUCKMANN —

With this chapter, let's try something different. I'm not going to discuss the plot, the characters, the hidden meanings, or really any aspect of the show. My goal with this entry will be more subliminal. Rather than deliberate about the show at length, I'd like to take you through my initial experience viewing it.

While plenty of anime in these pages had a significant impact on me, few floored me like *FLCL*. None truly baffled me the way this show did, and few encouraged such introspection and analysis. So, this entry will be all about my initial reaction, as well as the coming weeks after.

Ready?

August 13, 2003.

What did I just watch? the kid asked himself. He was bundled in a blanket atop the living room couch. Winters are cold in Ohio, especially at night, you see.

He was fifteen, and he should've been in bed. The last episode of a show called *FLCL* had just played out before his eyes, and he was left perplexed. He'd spent the previous five episodes assuming that the next would explain the last. But now that he'd seen the sixth—and final—episode, he still had no idea what he'd watched. There was, however, at least one inescapable fact he was certain of: *he loved it.*

As The Pillows' closing theme "Ride on Shooting Star" bounced off the walls of his living room, he didn't move until long after the credits ended.

Just what in the world was that?

Of course, that kid was me, and I had just begun a new journey: one of retrospection and analysis.

We had the cheapest Internet service ever in 2003. I have traumatizing memories of the mechanical sounds our computer spewed to connect to the elusive World Wide Web. And yet, I recall impatiently sitting in front of the massive monitor, silently begging the machine to start up. (You may think I'm exaggerating, or perhaps that your computer wasn't that slow in 2003. But my family never had much money, and we always found ourselves many years behind everyone else. Thus, our computer was considered a relic.)

Once the net finally booted up, I scoured old forums and GeoCities pages (holy crap, remember GeoCities?), hunting for details on *FLCL*. I needed theories, analyses, explanations, *answers dammit*!

In the pre-YouTube world of 2003, analysis videos were virtually nonexistent. Hell, they weren't even that common before publishing my *Prometheus Explained* dissertation. Now, they're everywhere. What was once a phenomenal way to impart knowledge about odd, existential cinema, has since become "Why Did the *Star Wars* Person Do That Thing: Explained."

My point is ... I found nothing.

Nothing.

The last episode of *FLCL* had just aired in America for the first time, and there was no perceivable information to be found. Maybe I was "digging in the wrong place," as Sallah and Indy declared in *Raiders of the Lost Ark*, but odds are, most people in the States just hadn't heard of *FLCL* yet.

But we knew now.

Over the next few weeks, posts on IMDb began to trickle in, fan pages were created, and other confused anime nerds combined forces on forums to discuss the insanity on display in *FLCL*. (Side note: remember when talking about entertainment online with strangers was fun?) Before long, the mysterious veil surrounding *FLCL* lifted, and beneath it, a subversive, unusual show smashed me across the skull with a guitar.

FLCL—or *Fooly Cooly*—aired on Adult Swim in August of 2003, and its paltry six-episode run has been rebroadcast continuously since. In retrospect, the programmers at Adult Swim deserve major kudos for taking a chance on such a bizarre show. It was unlike anything they'd ever aired before, but simultaneously matched wonderfully with Adult Swim's brand of psychotic, warped humor that so many have come to love.

Truthfully, *FLCL* encouraged me to see entertainment differently. When you're younger, there's a common perception that comes with experiencing a confusing film—or in this case anime. Movies like *Under the Skin* or *Enemy* are visually entrancing, with intriguing storylines, and yet, they're pretty tough to piece together on first viewing. Because of this, plenty of audience members get angry. It's understandable, we like our stories wrapped in a bow. But the aforementioned films and anime like *FLCL* don't give us that release. They deny us that sought-after "wrapped bow." So for some, that means it's bad. For others, that means it's time to put that good ol' noggin to work.

As you may well know, my love of film revved into gear in 2002, but a year later, bundled in that blanket, confused as hell, a new desire was born within me.

Analysis.

Maybe that weird movie I didn't understand was actually quite powerful. Perhaps this peculiar anime broke so many rules it invented a new set of them? How could I know for sure?

Research.

After *FLCL*, I began frequenting forums, discussing anime or cinema with strangers, and *actually reading* about storytelling and the craft of surrealism. I learned of subliminal hints, camera trickery, and hidden metaphors that spoke volumes about a filmmakers intent. I was hooked.

For some, *FLCL* is simply a deranged, gut-bustlingly hilarious comedy, with little else to offer beyond that. For others, they recognize more under the surface. What differentiates this show from the pack are those wildly varying reactions.

One person may laugh hysterically from episode to episode, while another may discern the powerful message on teenage loneliness.

Regardless of what I think, you should see *FLCL* to find out what *you* think. Odds are, it will change you. And hey ... there's plenty of analysis videos published about it now! I'm jealous.

2000 • INUYASHA

SENGOKU OTOGIZŌSHI INUYASHA

— TYLER D. HALL —

At the turn of anime's expansion toward a westward audience, a few titles stuck out very prominently. *InuYasha* is easily one of them. *InuYasha* is a tale about a teenage girl, named Kagome, who accidentally falls into a well at which point she is transported into feudal-era Japan. In the past, Kagome meets InuYasha, a half demon whose only goal is to become a full demon. But there is a catch, InuYasha needs the Shikon Jewel to become a half demon, and Kagome possesses it. To top it off, she also looks exactly like the woman who he fell in love with and was ultimately betrayed by. The story, mostly from the view of Kagome, follows their adventure as they look for the shards of the Shikon Jewel, which was broken in Kagome's first interaction with Feudal Era Japan.

InuYasha has always been a favorite anime of mine. It ran on late night television, was easy to catch on to, and, overall, was very rewarding to watch. *InuYasha* is one of the types of stories that has a new adventure every couple of episodes, but it's okay for the fact that each adventure is new and unique. Though they start as a duo, InuYasha and Kagome's adventure brings them to encompass three more people into their party. This gives room for introduction story arcs, as well as a stronger way to create more personal ties between the viewer and the characters.

One thing *InuYasha* is not short on is a large well of imagination. From magical holes in your hand to swords that deal no damage no matter how hard you hit someone, the abilities and characters in *InuYasha* just can't be replicated.

A star focal point, for me, was the introduction of Naraku; Naraku is a mysterious and extremely powerful villain. He manipulates those around him toward his own goals, and has a plan to make himself come out on top. His character's influence on me shifted my villain perspective for the better. Takahashi did an incredible job scripting and creating Naraku, showing depths of Naraku's human emotions, his demon-like personality, and his true ruthlessness.

Another aspect that *InuYasha* truly does a stellar job with is its introduction of characters. Sango, for example, is not introduced in the popular "desperate situation" tactic most shōnen stories take. Instead, we see Sango's to-be backstory unravel before us. The viewer lives this experience and this flow of emotions with her, creating a strong tie to the character. This, Tessaiga's true abilities, and the infamous Kagome-InuYasha-Kikyō love triangle are just examples of plot devices and themes that really make *InuYasha* a fantastic story to watch unfold.

Tyler D. Hall is a young anime, manga, and film enthusiast. Finding inspiration from his life, he spends his time writing and creating manga.

2000 • VAMPIRE HUNTER D: BLOODLUST

BANPAIA HANTĀ DĪ: BURADDORASUTO

— CHRIS STUCKMANN —

In 1922, F. W. Murnau horrified the world with *Nosferatu*, a silent film like no other. Nine years later, Bela Lugosi ensured a place in horror movie history with his iconic portrayal of Count Dracula. Ever since, the popularity of vampires has seldom wavered, but that doesn't mean it hasn't evolved.

Let's jump ahead in history, shall we?

1997. Sarah Michelle Gellar is introduced as the stake-wielding Buffy, a high schooler destined to slay the bloodsuckers stalking the Hellmouth.

1998. *Blade*. Wesley Snipes in black leather, decapitating many a vampire. Now that sounds like a damn good time! And it was.

But a gradual, yet inevitable shift was occurring. Vampires were in vogue again, and Hollywood—smelling that new and improved marketability—staked us through the heart with letdowns like *Dracula 2000* and *Van Helsing*. Even the *Blade* sequels didn't have as much bite as the first. Unfortunately, the agonizingly painful death of the cinematic vampire was just around the corner, in the form of a sparkly, tree-climbing teen named Edward.

Stay positive, Chris, breathe ... okay, let's continue.

With this entry, I'd like to focus on a lesser-known chapter in vampire history, one that began in 1983 with Hideyuki Kikuchi's manga, *Vampire Hunter D*. Illustrated by the legendary Yoshitaka Amano, the manga spawned twenty-six novels, as well as two films. John Rodriguez masterfully wrote about the 1985 film elsewhere in this book, so with that, let's talk about the sequel.

Vampire Hunter D: Bloodlust arrived in Japanese cinemas in 2000, directed by the venerable Yoshiaki Kawajiri (*Ninja Scroll, Wicked City*) and animated by Madhouse. We follow D—a fabled vampire slayer—as he competes with several bounty hunters to locate Charlotte, a woman abducted by Baron Meier Link, a vampire and nobleman.

What sets D apart from other hunters is his status as a *dhampir*: the child of a human and vampire. Thus, he carries the genes of both, making him an exemplary warrior. He's endowed with the superhuman strength of his vampire father, and the grace and understanding of his human mother. Long story short, if he draws his sword, you're in for a world of hurt.

Kawajiri's prowess as a visual storyteller is indisputable. The instant *Bloodlust* starts, we float through a sleepy town surrounded by crucifixes, which begin to melt and crumble. Something evil has arrived. Charlotte's window bursts open, and from her mirror, we see her lifted into the air by a ghostly presence without reflection. Beyond this gripping opening, the film only improves. The detail on the screen is simply stunning. In one scene, ruffians in a shadowy bar are playing cards. A queen of spades seen in closeup reveals arduous effort was applied to the card's design. Truthfully, every single frame of *Bloodlust* contains some of the best compositions in anime history.

Where some animators are content with decent character designs and serviceable backgrounds, Kawajiri *conjures environments*. His locales feel so tangible it's like you could step inside them. Case in point, the graveyard confrontation between D and the competing group of bounty hunters. Borgoff—a highly skilled archer—launches an arrow across the cemetery toward the sound of D's approaching horse. We follow the arrow as it soars through the night air, coming to a screeching halt when D snatches it with his bare hand, shocking his opponents. Kawajiri doesn't simply show us gorgeous backdrops. He places his characters—and us—inside them, generating the illusion of three-dimensional space.

D is a stoic warrior who chooses his words carefully, which may seem a bit familiar at first. The mysterious, sword-wielding hero is a common trope of westerns or samurai epics. However, it's his closeted compassion—likely from his mother's side—that reveals a person underneath that oversized hat. When Leila—a bounty hunter, and D's direct competition—is injured and unconscious, D dresses her wound and keeps her alive. Later, D becomes weak due to sunlight exposure, and Leila returns the favor by partially burying him (necessary for his recovery). The two share a touching conversation underneath the shelter of a large tree and forge a bond that provides considerable emotional weight to the film's final moments.

If you're well-versed in Kawajiri's filmography, you'll likely watch *Bloodlust* with built-in expectations. His penchant for grotesque body horror and gratuitous violence has dropped jaws for years, but with *Bloodlust*, he tones it down a bit. Surprisingly, this doesn't result in disappointment, but instead reveals the filmmaker at the height of his powers. Make no mistake, heads roll in *Bloodlust*, and when they do, it's glorious to behold. However, Kawajiri seems more intent to dazzle us with surrealistic imagery and spellbinding editing.

The finale is set in a massive castle that seems to stretch on forever. Elegant gothic art drips across every frame, encasing us in a rich environment of gloom and darkness. D and Leila make their way through the castle, caught in a dream state. The dastardly Carmilla summons deadly hallucinations, trapping all who enter in a web of feverish hysteria. Especially entrancing is the haunting score provided by Marco D'Ambrosio, its stirring choral chants evocative of Jerry Goldsmith's work on *The Omen*. Without a doubt, the last fifteen minutes of *Bloodlust* are downright hypnotic.

Thanks to Discotek, this animated masterwork is finally available on Blu-ray, and obviously, I implore you to pick it up. *Bloodlust* successfully vaulted the mountain that is "sequelitis." It's the uncommon follow-up that improves upon an already revered original. So, despite the uncertain future of vampires in American cinema, we can look toward Japanese animation with hope. Kawajiri has been developing a *Vampire Hunter D* series for some time now, and with any luck, we'll get some good news soon. This enthusiastic fan is salivating for more.

2001 • COWBOY BEBOP: THE MOVIE

KAUBŌI BIBAPPU: TENGOKU NO TOBIRA

— CHRIS STUCKMANN —

How do you follow perfection? *Should* you follow perfection?

Shinichirô Watanabe dares to answer that question with *Cowboy Bebop: The Movie*, a feature-length tale set within the show's previously established universe. Released in Japan in 2001, eventually making it to America in 2003, *The Movie* takes place between Episodes 22 ("Cowboy Funk") and 23 ("Brain Scratch"). So, somewhere between the exploits of Teddy Bomber and Faye joining a cult, Spike battled Vincent and rushed to stop a deadly virus from spreading.

If you haven't seen the show, I'll avoid discussing the finale, but nevertheless, it was tough to contemplate where the characters could go from there. The choice to set this adventure between earlier episodes was a wise one. In so doing, Watanabe avoided needless exposition and kept from tarnishing his flawless ending. As a result, *The Movie* feels like an extended episode, but in the best way imaginable. Watanabe—along with writer Keiko Nobumoto—found a way to enliven their world, adding another rich layer to their character's history, without undermining what they'd already accomplished.

The story is as follows: Halloween is around the corner, and a terrorist named Vincent is planning something deadly. Tanker trucks explode, viruses spread, and a record-breaking three hundred million woolong is posted as Vincent's bounty. Obviously, this captures the attention of the Bebop crew—all of whom are starving and in desperate need of cash. Spike is tired of Cup O' Noodles for dinner, Faye worries she isn't getting any younger, while Jet concerns himself with the ship and money stress. Ed is ... well, Ed.

As discussed in the *Cowboy Bebop* entry, Watanabe was very upfront about his cinematic inspirations, so I wasn't surprised to learn that Watanabe originally envisioned his show as a movie, and treated each episode like a small feature. Perhaps this is why these characters—and Watanabe's approach to them—mesh so well with the world of cinema. The operatic motifs of "Ballad of Fallen Angels," or the haunting seclusion of "Pierrot le Fou" speak volumes for Watanabe as a visual storyteller. He translates his universe to the silver screen with panache, and even introduces some invigorating new characters.

Vicious was a deeply compelling villain in the series, sharing a personal connection with Spike that tormented them both. Establishing a new villain—one who has nothing to do with the overarching story—is a monumental task. Vincent is methodical and ponderous, often appearing to lose sanity for a time, waxing philosophical about Death and the Great Beyond. He's a frightening physical presence, a towering man clothed in black. He's the kind of cretinous existence capable of pressing a button and murdering thousands, without showing a hint of empathy. Worse yet, he feels his actions are justified, his tragic past the inciting incident that leads him down a path of butchery. As a physical opponent for Spike, he's his most formidable. Where Vicious and Spike were equals, Vincent is Spike's superior in battle. A ferocious beating on a monorail—one of the best scenes in the film—proves this.

The devastating romance between Spike and Julia gratefully takes a backseat here, and a new character named Elektra gains Spike's attention. Wisely, Elektra is never portrayed as a "love interest." In a thrilling hand-to-hand scuffle, Spike and Elektra share witty banter and adorable flirtations. Even when these characters are forced to share a space together, they just talk. Elektra and Spike seem intrigued by each other, possibly infatuated, but never in love. In so doing, the tragic storyline from the series remains unhindered, and we're treated to a refreshing new character in Elektra.

The Movie has many scenes set in Morocco, a rarity for anime. Spike travels there hoping to learn about the mysterious pathogen spreading amongst the public, and meets a puzzling man named Rashid. The two share one of the best "not-conversations" I've seen in a film. I'll elaborate: When two people need to discuss something in public, yet keep it under wraps, they'll often talk in code. They each understand the hidden language, but to everyone else, it sounds like they're conversing about everyday things. Rashid uses beans at an outdoor vendor to share secrets about his involvement with the pathogen, and the dialogue is riveting.

The final fist fight between Spike and Vincent is the stuff of anime legend. This humble fan has only seen one brawl that comes close to rivaling it (see my *Sword of the Stranger* entry). The choreography is astonishingly smooth, much like Spike's advice given in "Waltz for Venus," in which he tells a hopeful protégé, "You have to be like water!" Their fists float through the air like missiles, and when one strikes its target, you sense the aching pain on their faces. And just when you think they've beaten each other to a pulp, they stumble to their feet and clash once more. It's sensational.

Missing *Cowboy Bebop: The Movie* when it swept American theaters is one of my great regrets. To hear Yoko Kanno's spectacular music and gaze in awe at Watanabe's visual brilliance would've been a wonder to behold on a massive screen. All the same, it's still just as thrilling at home. Track down the Blu-ray and do that! You don't need preconceived knowledge of the series nor will watching the film beforehand spoil anything. It stands alone from the show, as well as the anime movie landscape. There's nothing else like it. This fan wonders if Watanabe will ever deliver more adventures with the Bebop crew ...

KEEP DREAMING SPACE COWBOY ...

2001 • METROPOLIS

METOROPORISU

— YAOCHONG YANG —

Fritz Lang's 1927 German Expressionist film *Metropolis* is incredibly influential. Its range extends from Alfred Hitchcock, to *Star Wars*, to fashion. Professor of Film David Bordwell once described it, quite poignantly, as "One of the great sacred monsters of cinema."

Surprisingly, despite *Metropolis'* reach, it has a rather limited influence on Osamu Tezuka's 1949 manga of the same name. Even more so, Lang's original work was later adapted into a hybrid piece by Shigeyuki Hayashi (also known as Rintaro) and Katsuhiro Otomo's *Metropolis*, released in 2001. For the most part, all three different versions of *Metropolis* end up depicting, through space, different ways of thinking of authority.

Lang's Metropolis

Lang's city is under the grip of industrialist Joh Frederson. His son, Freder, finds the condition of the working class in the city's underbelly. Meanwhile, mad scientist Rotwang constructs a machine, which Frederson requests to mimic Maria, a girl who's the target of his infatuation. The false Maria goes out and about, causing chaos. This leads to a series of events and eventually a revolt, ending in them burning her at the stake. At her death, the workers understand the spellbinding effect of the machine, and the movie ends with Freder reconciling Frederson (the industrialist) with Grot (the working man).

When we think of how a space renders authority, Lang's *Metropolis* is fixated with verticality and uniformity. The society of the city is split into two major sections: the clean and somewhat ostentatious upper society is where the wealthy and successful live; the lifeless, dangerous under-city is where the workers toil. Frederson is the master of the city. He's the owner of the massive tower New Babel, itself a reference to the *Völkerschalchtdenkmal* in Leipzig and Pieter Brueghel's *The Tower of Babel*. Notable about this specific version is that height is a naked depiction of the power structure in society. It looms over everything, dominating its shots. Here, New Babel is the city.

However, it's ultimately Frederson's fault that the fake Maria goes on a rampage, causing chaos. His blind eye to the plight of the working man stirs up the worker's organization against him. Yet the story never punishes him for his actions; it grounds him, weakens him, but he never comes to any harm. Here, the puppet master, remains unharmed, primarily because Frederson is one of them. Solidarity is the ultimate factor.

This begins Lang's ethnocentric depictions of otherness. Where does the fake Maria go? Earlier in the film, we see the club, Yoshiwara. Both a reference to Edo's famous red light district and a representation of foreign otherness, Yoshiwara is the nexus of negative activity in Lang's *Metropolis*. The fake Maria begins her activities there. The negative and raucous activities of the hedonists stem from there. Georgy loses himself there. The building is a representation of the city's unease with visible otherness, suggesting that a sense of cultural or social purity is necessary. Given that *Metropolis* is produced just after the first World War, German sentiment against Japan would have been incredibly negative; Japan challenged German naval control in the Pacific and Indian Oceans. Lang's use of Yoshiwara would strengthen anti-Japanese sentiment, solidifying it as a visible "other" ("Japan Gives Ultimatum to Germany"). Curiously, these sentiments are not visible in Tezuka's adaptation.

Osamu Tezuka's Metoroporisu

Tezuka's 1949 manga is a distinctly different story. Not only did Tezuka only have a perfunctory experience of Lang's *Metropolis*, it was also because of the cultural context in which his own Metropolis was published. Coming out just four years after Japan's surrender, the Tezuka's *Metropolis* is a city defined by latitudinal space and diversification rather than verticality.

Instead of a single, looming tower, Tezuka's city is a competitive space, a busy and labyrinthine network of scholars, ruffians, politicians, and personnel from all over the world, coming to visit, work, study, and discuss. Tezuka's city is a pluralistic environment, influenced by and, in turn, influencing the people around them. Like postwar Japan, Tezuka's city is horizontal. Its power structure is relatively hidden, diffused through a myriad of institutions and locations.

Nowhere is Tezuka's depiction more obvious than in the android Michi. Compared to Lang's fake Maria, Tezuka's Michi is androgynous and for most of the manga, benign. More so, Michi is both male and female. At a flip of a switch, Michi can turn from a boy into a girl, a holistically vague and hybridized being of machine and man. Furthermore, and this is much more important, Michi derives his/her life from the black spots from the sun, which was created by the manga's main villain, Duke Red.

The sun is a massive symbolic code in Tezuka's *Metropolis*. Remember the context of Tezuka's 1949 publication. The Emperor, who drew his authority from Amaterasu, the sun god, had his political power effectively neutralized. Duke Red, both in name and appearance a visible foreigner, attempts to seize power. Michi, a hybrid of human and machine, is not only a product of Red's influences, but also that of the brilliant Dr. Laughton. The space of the Tezuka's *Metropolis* is represented in Michi. She/he is both a constant fluctuation (through gender), but also a distanced artificiality.

While the identity of Lang's *Metropolis* is that of a uniform, tightly-connected hierarchy and social structure with an emphasis on wariness of the other, Tezuka's *Metropolis* is an eclectic, energetic, chaotic, and confusing space with a crisis of postwar identity. Compared to Lang's *Metropolis*, Tezuka's doesn't end on comforting words, but wariness. A warning of humanity's unbridled curiosity, a potential note to the mass of people in the city's space.

Rintaro's Metropolis

So, where does Rintaro and Otomo's 2001 film *Metropolis* stand? Compared to Tezuka, Rintaro *is* familiar with Lang's *Metropolis*, so the movie is a hybridized version of the previous two. More so, in hybridizing, Rintaro borrows both sentiments of self-other and national confusion. It hybridizes both Lang and Tezuka, and in doing so, hybridizes their visual rhetoric. Though Rintaro's *Metropolis* draws heavy narrative influence from Tezuka (with characters ripped directly from Tezuka's manga), the architecture of the city is decidedly Lang's. Rintaro's New Babel (called the Ziggurat in the film) returns as a giant tower that cuts through several layers of the city.

Instead of one self-other dynamic, Rintaro's *Metropolis* plays out two stories: the story of the working class against the wealthy, and the humans against the robots. Here, there is no gender-swapping robot, but there is a robot. Tima, the product of Rintaro's version of Dr. Laughton, is a soft-spoken girl who plays a critical role in the floating semiosis of the movie.

Tima fulfills several crucial roles in the film: she eventually sits on the throne, itself situated on a giant red orb (reminiscent of the *Hinomaru*, the flag of Japan); she shines with the wing of a dove, making clear religious connections to her power; the final climactic arc is predicated on her behavior, drawing attention to the singularity—and that singularity's invariable inability—of power of the Japanese imperial family.

Yet there is a duplicity of power in Rintaro's *Metropolis*. Though Tima represents the inability (and perhaps needlessness) of religious imperial power in postwar Japan, Rintaro's city maps out another kind of power. The rebels in *Metropolis* are not presented as entirely accommodating; they are, notably, quite untrusting of the robot workers, setting up more tension. In fact, the robot workers of Rintaro's *Metropolis* inhabit the lowest parts of the city. Here, they would eke out a state of existence in relation to the workers, a condition reminiscent of Giorgio Agamben's "bare life" concept.

With both Lang and Tezuka in mind, Rintaro's *Metropolis* borrows Lang's representations of self-other power while engaging with Tezuka's tackling of horizontal tensions. The workers in Rintaro's *Metropolis* rise and revolt against the city's rulers, a motif common to works by Katsuhiro Otomo (see *Akira*), who worked on the film's screenplay. The challenges faced by the robots in a separated, lower part of the city recalls sentiments of Japanese self-other exclusions of Korean-Japanese citizens in Japan (often called "*zainichi*"). In fact, former governor Shintaro Ishihara once referred to as immigrants (particularly Korean and Chinese immigrants) as "*sangokujin*," a derogatory term that roughly means *third world person*. In fact, Ishihara once famously declared the potential of martial law, stating, "We can expect them to riot in the event of a disastrous earthquake."

The revolution in Rintaro's *Metropolis*, with this in mind, emphasizes the dangers of Ishihara's rhetoric. At the time of production, Ishihara would have been the governor of Tokyo, and thus production and writing would have been fully primed on Ishihara's comments. Despite this, after all that, Rintaro's *Metropolis* emphasizes the futility of such vitriol, and in doing so, forces us to think about how messages translate through time and, more so, space.

Yaochong Yang is a PhD student at Trent University. He runs the channel Pause and Select.

2001 •
MILLENNIUM ACTRESS

SENNEN JOYŪ

— ROBERT WALKER —

There's a wonderful line at the end of *A League of Their Own*, when an onlooker asks at a reunion baseball game, "Who's that?"

"THAT'S DOTTIE HINSON. THE QUEEN OF DIAMONDS!"

"I don't remember her."

"Well, she only played for one year."

So goes the incomparable Satoshi Kon—the Master Illusionist of the medium. One of the greatest anime directors of all time, Kon only had four feature films and a single television series to his name before succumbing to pancreatic cancer. Yet each of these projects left an indelible mark.

Christopher Nolan's *Inception* plays like a riff on Kon's *Paprika*. Darren Aronofsky borrowed shots from Kon's *Perfect Blue* for *Requiem for a Dream*. And Kon's style crops up in everything from Wes Anderson's *Moonrise Kingdom* to Edgar Wright's *Scott Pilgrim*.

Still, for all the influence Kon had on popular culture, it's his second film, *Millennium Actress*, that stands above the rest. More than any other, it showcases everything Kon excels at. It features a simple story told in a completely unique way. All punctuated with flawless editing, gorgeous hand-painted animation, a stunning soundtrack, and an emotional roller coaster of a narrative.

Indeed, *Millennium*'s opening scene teases at the narrative tricks to come. A man watches the finale to a space opera on his TV set. As a woman blasts off in a rocket, a rumble extends into the viewing room. The man watching the television braces himself. It's an earthquake. Coincidence? Perhaps. But life has imitated art. From the get-go, the line between fantasy and reality blurs around the edges.

The viewer is Genya Tachibana, a documentarian on a quest to interview Chiyoko Fujiwara, a legendary actress who starred in countless films from the 1930s to the 1960s. It's now the dawn of the new millennium, and Chiyoko has secluded herself away in the mountains. Along for the ride is Kyoji Ida, a no-nonsense kid who seems perpetually bemused at the fuss Genya is putting over this project.

Chiyoko, now in her seventies, graciously greets them at her home. Genya then presents her with a small key. Transfixed, she says it unlocks memories long since been buried. The two filmmakers set up their cameras. What unfolds is a tale of unrequited love that spans an entire lifetime spent on and off the screen.

From the start, the first conceit is that Genya and Kyoji actually enter Chiyoko's story. As she reminisces about her childhood, we see them standing by as observers. Kyoji's camera rolls ever on as a young Chiyoko wanders about in her own flashbacks. Occasionally, they'll interact with her, asking questions that her younger self will then answer. As a metaphor for documentary work, nothing compares. And it's normally here that viewers will either accept this breakdown of the fourth wall, or reject it. Those that stick around are in for a ride. The two filmmakers, and the audience, literally witness Chiyoko's reconstructed story unfold before their eyes as she tells it.

Her story is simple enough. As a high school girl in prewar Japan, she aspires to become an actress. A talent scout makes her an offer, but she loses her big break when her overbearing mother puts the kibosh on it. The scout appeals to Mom's sense of patriotism. Japan is fighting in Manchuria, and the nation needs talent for their propaganda. But Mom remains nonplussed.

At the same time, Chiyoko encounters a young, brooding artist. An anti-government dissident on the run, she hides him in her parents' storeroom. There, she falls in love. As she nurses him back to health, he speaks highly of Hokkaido, and its snowy fields of white, lit by the full moon. He waxes poetic about how the moon is best when it's not quite full. For when it's full, it can only wane. But so long as it's not quite peaked yet, there is hope. Chiyoko then spots his key. The artist claims it's the key to the most important thing in the universe. This becomes the film's "key" MacGuffin. Both the moon and the key remain shared symbols of hope between the two. He longs to return to Hokkaido after the war is over, to paint the moon. She promises to meet him there.

Unfortunately, fate tears them apart. The artist is discovered. He flees. And Chiyoko, upon discovering this, chases after him in a brilliantly constructed montage, made all the more tense by Susumu Hirasawa's silent film era piano score. Upon reaching the train station, she realizes she's too late. However, the artist left his key behind. She vows to return it to him. And she has a lead: he was heading to Manchuria to join the resistance there. The same place the film crew was heading. Thus, she becomes an actress. From there, the film chronicles her triumphs and failures as she attempts to find her love while balancing an indomitable film career.

What sets *Millennium Actress* apart is the way Satoshi Kon tells his story. Kon's recurring theme is the search for identity. For Chiyoko, the search spans her career. And this career, which mirrors her own life's story, forces her to ask in her twilight years: was her quest worth it? Will it ever be?

On the flip side, there's Genya, the documentarian. He actually met Chiyoko as a stagehand and fell instantly in love. In the same way Chiyoko chases after her true love, he chases after Chiyoko. Both characters are reflections of each other— chasing the elusive happiness they secretly know they might not ever possess.

In a way, this calls back to Kon's earlier work, *Perfect Blue*. This was intentional. Kon considered these works sister films: one side reflects the other. While *Perfect Blue* showcased the "male gaze" in a dark light—focusing on a stalker who wishes to control its heroine—*Millennium Actress* showcases the "male gaze" as a noble force. Genya, for all his fanboy crushing, only wishes to help her fulfill her quest. As a character, he remains one of Kon's most endearing—a forefather of his later character, *Paranoia Agent's* Detective Ikari. At first a passive observer, he begins to take an active role in her reminiscing. And his insertion into Chiyoko's flashbacks are no different from the way fans "feel" they know an actor by the role they play.

This blending of on-screen and off-screen reality poses the biggest challenge for some viewers. Many seem genuinely shocked when they find out that the film is told in a completely linear way. But it's not as complicated as it seems.

Kon assists the viewer by placing real-life counterparts in the films within the film. Her mother, the artist, a dubious fortune-teller, and a scarred policeman all appear as recurring characters in her studio work. Of course, these characters could not have been actual cast members. But she remembers them that way. This conceit reveals multitudes about Chiyoko's character. Does she see the villains in her films as reflections of the people who hold her back in real life? Is she the hero of her own movie? Certainly, Genya sees himself that way—inserting himself as the dutiful sidekick in her blockbuster—the role he feels he was born to play. As audience members, do we not do the same when we see ourselves in movie characters?

It's insanely multilayered, but deftly handled. Some directors overcomplicate things by presenting their story as a puzzle with pieces given out of order, so the viewers must put it together. Kon presents his story as a colorful collage. The finished product is already there. No assembly required. But it's pasted together from different pieces: magazine pages, construction paper, old cut up photographs. Look too close and it seems like a jumbled mess. But one only needs to step back and squint to view the image as whole. It's simply an optical illusion.

The secret to this visual sleight of hand lies in *trompe l'œil* filmmaking. French for "deceive the eye," this Baroque-inspired artistic style uses perspective techniques to create the illusion of three-dimensional space. Imagine a spray-painted image of a child escaping out of a picture frame on a brick wall. Or consider a painting of a man staring at a mountain, staring at another painting of a man and a mountain, staring at another painting of the same thing—and so on and so on again into infinity. Where does one image begin and the other end?

For Kon, Chiyoko's on-screen and off-screen worlds are indistinguishable. She and the documentarians jump through her memories like Mary Poppins hops through chalk drawings. One spectacular montage transports her on horseback from a two-dimensional Ukiyo-e woodblock print, to a multi-plane rickshaw ride, to a three-dimensional bicycle sliding down a cherry blossom lined road—all within the space of sixty seconds. Transitions involve cannon smoke, wheels, trains, everything. All of it linked by Hirasawa's energetic techno-inspired world music score. One minute. A half dozen film roles. Seamlessly edited together.

Kon once stated that he dived into animation because it freed him to do what he couldn't in live-action. And it's true. Even by anime standards, he remains the only director—so far—who has best discovered how to use animation to its fullest potential. With absolute freedom, the animator removes information, uses exotic cuts, and makes giant transitional leaps at a speed that would be impossible to duplicate on a standard camera. The result warps space and time in a way that only dreams can match. For Kon, every cut provides a new jumping point. Like blinking in a dream, the viewer gets transported from day to night and a thousand miles away—all in a flash.

This gives *Millennium Actress* a sense of immediacy and urgency. It is, above all else, a "chase movie" driven by the power of love. One could almost equate it with *Run Lola Run*. Chiyoko chases the shadow of her love. Genya chases Chiyoko. Both chase their memories. Through Kon's loving tributes to Japanese cinema— from Kurosawa to Kaijū films—they blast through cinematic wall after wall like mirrors in a funhouse maze. In her final role at the studio, the chase leads her all the way to the moon—the artistic fascination of her one true love, and symbol of the hope she's always clung to. What will she find there? What *did* she find there?

Is any of it real? Or imagined? Does it matter? Don't memories work that way? Don't dreams work that way? And if so, why not films?

In the end, *Millennium Actress* defies any sort of literal interpretation. Like a waxing moon, it shines as a profound metaphor on how cinema shapes our lives.

Robert Walker is the co-writer for the hit web series The Nostalgia Critic. *As a child of the '80s, he's been watching anime imports since before he even knew what anime was. Altogether, he has watched over 300 anime series and films. Not necessarily for his job, but because he has a problem.*

2001 • SPIRITED AWAY

SEN TO CHIHIRO NO KAMIKAKUSHI

— DOUG WALKER —

The stories from our youth have a wide range of staying power. A child can be obsessed with *Power Rangers* for years and see *Alice in Wonderland* as a cute distraction. As time passes, those passions shift reflecting the material's nature. *Power Rangers* many now consider a cute distraction while *Alice in Wonderland* is still being analyzed for its timeless imagery and storytelling, despite it being over 150 years old. No matter how many reboots and spinoffs *Power Rangers* has, it will never have the long-lasting effect of Lewis Carrol's novel. Many people know the Green Ranger, EVERYBODY knows the Cheshire Cat. The first time I viewed *Spirited Away*, a similar prediction came over me. Even though it was praised by critics and audiences when it premiered, it was clear that it's staying power would last long after those critics and audiences had passed. *Spirited Away* speaks to primal emotions and imagination children often try to release and adults often try to tuck away. Fears similar to *The Wizard of Oz*, joys on par with *Peter Pan*, and characters as real as any classic fairy tale read to us for the first time.

The story centers around Chihiro, a young girl moving to a new neighborhood with her parents. She's that perfect combination of nervous and miserable children love telling you about when experiencing new things. When they get lost and stumble upon what they think is an abandoned amusement park, the sun goes down revealing a literal new world. Spirits of every shape and size transform the park into a bathhouse for demons, sprites, and gods. Within seconds Chihiro's world is taken from her: her parents, her home, even her name are now property of the bathhouse's owner, a witch named Yubaba. With the help of a boy named Haku, who takes pity on her, she is thrown headfirst into adapting to the strangest of survival methods. She must learn how to please an entire culture of phantoms, dragons, lizards, and ghosts pretending their unpredictable ways are not the least bit surprising to her.

The undiluted fear in every second of Chihiro's stay is brilliantly matched by the undiluted hilarity of the creatures she encounters. They are literally surprises around every corner, each one with a distinct design and immediately relatable character. Their flaws are all too familiar, like the No-Face spirit who becomes consumed by his environment, a flying dragon who connects his identity to his lost past, and a giant whining baby who is shrunk down to reflect the size of his humility. This is only the icing on one of the most surreal and unforgettable cakes one could witness. The world this film creates has elements of several great fantasies, ranging from Japanese folklore to children's chants sung during recess. They combine both the frightening and the silly into one visually stunning powerhouse. It's hard to predict what's going to pop up next, and most audiences cheerfully don't know whether to scream at them or laugh at them.

The overload of beauty and creativity that consumes every frame is reined in by both simple and complicated series of events. Every moment something strange and surprising occurs, whether it's trying to figure out how to bathe a Stink Spirit, returning a magic emblem to an estranged sibling, or figuring out the long-lost connection between a boy and his memories. But the brilliance in its layout is that while there are several "side quests," they all tie into experiencing this new realm of reality, and through the best way film should, by showing, not telling. There are several rules to this world, revolving around magical elements like lifting curses, altering appearances, even changing personalities, but all of them are shown through an equal combination of dialogue and action, so we never feel lost or like too much is being explained. Every action is moved forward by the character's needs, and while there are several small needs for any given moment, the major ones are never forgotten. Chihiro needs to escape with her parents, Haku needs to remember who he is, No-Face needs to belong, and everyone else needs to ... well, do their job, which is also exciting to watch.

Even with all of that going on, though, the film lets you catch your breath in some of the most beautiful yet haunting moments. There is a train ride that, in connection with the story, simply gets our characters from one place to another. In keeping with the film's incredible construction of environment, it lets you stay on the train to take in the breathtaking visuals in a mellow, quiet, soothing spectacle of comfort and discomfort. Traveling from one location to another is not always a riveting experience, but when you're allowed to reflect on the insanity going on around you in a sudden moment of silence, it can be the most important moment of clarity in a rush of maddening chaos. It's a mood all of us have felt on several occasions, and where most films would put a song or even inner monologue explaining the character's thoughts, this film is smart enough to let us feel it, not tell it. We bring our own reflections to the scene, and the same way shadowy spirits get off and on the train, we let our own shadowy thoughts get off and on.

The performances for both the Japanese version and the American version are both masterful. On top of comedic charmers like Suzanne Pleshette and Susan Egan, it finds genuine heart and intrigue with its two leads, Daveigh Chase and Jason Marsden. Both bring a believable vulnerability that rings to the reality of childhood, despite them being flung in a world of fantasy. While the world they inhabit is fantastical, the emotions they portray are perfectly human. The style and animation also bring to life a world that goes beyond words. The film could be played on mute and you'd still be able to follow through their expressions and movements what every character is going through. The backgrounds also waste no time sucking you into a beautiful yet fearful realm. The same place can look warm and welcoming one minute then dark and terrifying the next, just with a simple change of color and lighting. The only deciding factor is what emotions our characters are going through.

Spirited Away has intuition to know what to expand on and what to keep vague; what to bring to the table and what to let you bring. It opens the right doors to let raw emotion and raw imagination meet, yet knows what limitations to push giving it shape and form. It's a fairy tale that speaks to every fear, hope, and joyous longing that is searching for a home. It doesn't shy away from the dark moments, but it doesn't get overshadowed by them either. It still knows it's focus and emotions need to be simple; emotions both children and adults recognize and quickly cling to. The cliché "Magical" is thrown around often when describing corny/overly manipulative stories or products, but in the original meaning of the word, it's the only one perfect enough to describe *Spirited Away*. It projects a feeling that combines all the best contradictions: adult yet childish, familiar yet new, scary yet welcoming, complex yet simple. It doesn't always make sense, but it's not always meant to make sense, it's meant to be felt. It is an experience that has never left me since I saw it and will not leave the millions who have and will experience it in the future. It is the perfect definition of timeless.

Doug Walker is known for his character, the Nostalgia Critic.
His beloved movie reviews can be found on his YouTube page,
Channel Awesome.

2002 • GHOST IN THE SHELL: STAND ALONE COMPLEX

KÔKAKU KIDÔTAI SUTANDO ARÔN CONPUREKKUSU

— CHRIS STUCKMANN —

As my fingers pound away on this keyboard, a freshly inked tattoo is healing on my right forearm: a purple-haired, gun-toting cyborg named Motoko Kusanagi. She's my fifth tattoo, and by now, the pain isn't as noticeable as the first few. Nevertheless, observing the wonderful artist (B Hendrix) "stab away" as she calls it, was a cathartic one.

Ghost in the Shell: Stand Alone Complex was a milestone for me. Originally airing on American television through Cartoon Network's Adult Swim block, this unapologetic anime fan must admit: he saw the show before experiencing Mamoru Oshii's historic film. Like *Ninja Scroll* or *Akira*, the VHS cover art for *GITS*—and subsequent warning of "violence and nudity" on the back—made my folks leery of its content. *SAC*, however, aired late at night after my parents went to bed and, being a sneaky, scheming teen, I decided to avoid asking permission to watch it. **evil laugh**

Much like Masamune Shirow's original manga, and Oshii's film, *SAC* concerns the exploits of Section 9, a futuristic police force specializing in counter-terrorism operations. The group is comprised of former soldiers and detectives, some of which are heavily modified by cybernetic enhancements. In the case of Motoko, she is entirely robotic—save for her brain and spine. In essence, she is but a shell, although her ghost (her soul) is still intact.

Unlike Oshii's film, *SAC* delves into Motoko's past, exploring aspects of her childhood and humanity. During the intro to each episode of Season One, we are shown Motoko's point of view as she crushes a doll in her hand. A few episodes into the show, in a rare moment of reflection, Motoko addresses this memory. The simplicity of this image, and Motoko's contemplation on the event is profound.

Motoko is stern, fierce, and yet somehow ... gentle. Her team—especially Batou and Togusa—deeply respect her, not just for her abilities, but her unwavering resolve. As a physical presence, Motoko is feared, but her cognitive abilities—and unequaled dedication to others—commands admiration.

On the flip side, Motoko's innocence is explored in key episodes. In the episode "Mother and Child," Motoko assists a young boy caught in the middle of the drug trade. This fear-inspiring cyborg becomes something more in these episodes. Seeing behind those robotic eyes fosters a whole new appreciation for her. This is why the image of her crushing the doll as a child is so potent. Her empathetic, almost youthful purity is camouflaged, but her raw power is inescapable.

With fifty-two episodes in total, *SAC* has the exciting opportunity to flesh out the backgrounds of all Section 9 members, and the creators take every chance they get to do so. In the disturbing episode, "Jungle Cruise," a sadistic serial killer named Marco Amoretti is skinning women alive, savagely flaying their torsos in the form of a T-shirt. Batou—a former Ranger of the Japan Ground Self-Defense Force—shares a disturbing connection with the killer, and must fight the demons of his past to track Amoretti down.

Togusa is the most human of the team, having retained the majority of his flesh-and-bone body. He's referred to as a "natural." (This description varies between manga, film, and series.) Despite the variety of weaponry at his disposal, Togusa chooses to stick with his trusty revolver. He worries that modern weapons of this futuristic era will jam, and he states that "Six bullets is enough to get the job done." Being a family man—the only one on Section 9—Togusa carries with him the unique burden of responsibility. Scenes with him and his family bring a welcome sense of compassion to the series and help humanize the largely mechanized team.

The action scenes rival many anime of this type, particularly a rain-drenched showdown between Motoko and a massive robotic exoskeleton. Where many shows resort to cheapening the animation during these sequences, *SAC* uses fluid motion and precise editing to heighten the sense of realism. You won't see freeze-frames or "speed lines" here. When Motoko obliterates an opponent ... you *feel* it.

That being said, the creators have gone to great pains ensuring that *SAC* is not simply an "action show." As already discussed, each member of Section 9 is provided a compelling backstory, enlivening the proceedings. Even more impressive, however, is the political implications of the events depicted, and that the show doesn't shy away from discussing these topics.

Season One deals prominently with the Laughing Man case, in which an unknown hacker infiltrates the cyberbrains of many people, with the ultimate goal of revealing a devastating truth about the Japanese government. He brandishes a stylized logo of a smiley face, which eventually becomes a staple of popular culture, resulting in copycat criminals. Without giving away too many details, the investigation of this case—and the subsequent discovery of its consequences—speaks volumes about our perception of crime. If a criminal is breaking the law, using the guise of "public service" to mask his crimes, do we feel a natural, hidden appreciation for him? If the end result is positive, was there really any wrongdoing?

Season Two mostly concerns a group of refugees from the former World Wars, the dealings of a terrorist organization known as Individual Eleven, and Section 9's investigation of this extremist group. In this season, we're treated to a mysterious, more complex exploration of the blurry line between good and evil, and the horrific ramifications of war on many peoples.

SAC was imperative to my evolution as an anime fan. While *DBZ* and *Cowboy Bebop* legitimately changed my life, shows like *SAC*—and the batshit insanity known as *FLCL*—challenged me. With powerful storylines traversing elaborate politics and uncertain conclusions brought about by ambiguous endings, *SAC* didn't just entertain me, it *engaged* me. Analysis became crucial and introspection was suddenly critical to my understanding of the show. It's a brilliant reimagining of Shirow's world, and like Oshii's film, accomplishes the burdensome task of improving upon the source material.

2002 • .HACK//SIGN

— MATTHEW CARATURO —

When I was a kid, I absolutely loved video games. So much so, that there was a point in time where all I could think about during school was when I would be able to go home and play games. Myself, like many others, looked to those games as a form of escapism from the more troubling and less rewarding aspects of life. Within a game, we can take on any identity that we so choose to; however, what are the differences between this "data self" and our real-life identities? To what extent is this escapism acceptable? The series *.hack//SIGN* taps into these questions, alongside others, crafting a truly interesting narrative out of it.

The main protagonist named Tsukasa, is one who uses the MMORPG (Massively Multiplayer Online Roleplaying Game), The World, as a means to escape from her harsh life. At home, she is beaten by her father. But in the game, she takes on the identity of a male wavemaster. Initially, even in The World, Tsukasa seeks isolation from others. The game is undergoing all of these glitches, and at the forefront of these glitches is the Key of the Twilight: an item that can pretty much alter anything within the game, potentially putting players into comas. Tsukasa ends up finding this item, and it takes advantage of his desire for isolation. It leaves Tsukasa trapped within this game, unable to log out, and unlike other players, able to feel pain within The World. In order to escape, Tsukasa needs to learn how to trust others and face these real-world struggles head on.

In spite of Tsukasa playing a game, he isn't really playing it. He's not accomplishing anything. All he's doing is sitting around and letting those outside emotions get the better of him. It feels very similar to when one is so stricken by what has happened in the past that they are even unable to cope. This all changes; however, once he meets Bear and Mimiru. They befriend him and together the group start going on quests. Slowly they are able to get Tsukasa to come out of his shell, and they search throughout The World for answers on how Tsukasa can log out.

The other important character, Subaru, is the leader of a faction in the game called the Crimson Knights. Offline, she is handicapped due to a car accident a few years prior. In a lot of ways, what she does is a bit of the antithesis to Tsukasa. They both use the game as a form of escapism, but Tsukasa has the baggage he's dealing with written all over his face. Subaru, on the other hand, tries to stand strong and ignore the burdens she's dealing with. The responsibilities Subaru has, though, make her unable to see the game for what it is: a game. A means to have fun. Do the Crimson Knights have any right to police The World when they aren't moderators? To enforce their sense of justice on the other players? Is it worth getting so stressed when she's supposed to be enjoying herself? All of these questions build up to her finally disbanding the Crimson Knights. Even after this, the stress fails to cease. You have other players in the game that seek to bring her down afterwards, labeling her as some weak coward. What this ends up creating is a beautiful scene where Subaru finally vents those pent up frustrations to Tsukasa.

What *.hack//SIGN* manages to make note of, both with these two characters, as well as others throughout the show, is who they are and what they do outside the game. Bear, for example, is over forty years old and a famous novelist, while Mimiru, on the other hand, is a teenager and a high schooler. Silver Knight, Subaru's right hand man, is a twenty-three-year-old video rental store employee. You have people of all different ages and backgrounds coming together to play the game, and while that may show within the attitudes of the players (Bear acts very mature, while Sora, a fourth grader "player killer," acts very immature), there's no specific hierarchy based on age. This allows friendships to flourish in places they otherwise wouldn't.

For example, by the end of the series, Bear adopts Tsukasa and sends her to a boarding school, so she'll have an opportunity to start anew; away from her abusive father. This opportunity would have most likely never been available if not for The World. So, while the show definitely speaks against closing oneself off from the outside world, it also showcases what benefits online communities can offer to those partaking within them. Not every single benefit shown is that extreme, either.

Sometimes it's just as simple as finding a new friend to hang out with. Tsukasa meets friends like Subaru and Mimiru, who she ends up hanging out with offline. This can also be applicable to real life, too, as there are many individuals (myself included) who have found new friends through online communities, and were able to create bonds they otherwise would've never come across.

One last thing to note is how the outside world is portrayed within the show versus how the video game world is portrayed. The World is bright, colorful, cheery, it feels like an actual game many people would willingly invest their time into (and ended up being such, as *.hack* had many video game adaptations). The outside world, on the other hand, is this dark, creepy place, even colored in black and white; characters seldom talk, and rather than it being spoken, it's displayed on screen. This presents Tsukasa's perspective, as she continues to block out what's going on around her. It also serves as a callback to the old movies Tsukasa had watched with her mom before her death.

All of this changes, however, once Tsukasa unites with Subaru. The visuals go from black and white to color, because what each bring to the outside world is the same comfort that they had within the game. This scene utilizes the same on-screen text as before, but the context is different. This time, rather than Tsukasa blocking out what's going on, it instead represents Tsukasa acknowledging her past and remembering where she came from. Tsukasa may be in a better place by the end of the show, but that doesn't mean she needs to completely abandon The World. The game can still be enjoyed for what it is: a game. It's also important because back when Tsukasa was trapped in the game, she started losing her memories, and the knowledge of whether this version of her in The World was even real. By having her retain these memories in The World, it therefore validates her experiences in The World as both real and valuable.

Escapism through the online world of gaming isn't an inherently bad thing, and this escapism can lead to a lot of positive opportunities for people that may not have had otherwise. Even so, *.hack//SIGN* warns its audience to not completely trap oneself within the game and use it as a crutch to prevent one from moving forward in life; to not get too caught up in the game to the point where it stops being fun. For something produced in 2002, after generations of gaming have come and gone, technology continuing to advance further and further, it's surprisingly still just as relevant today as it was then.

Matthew Caraturo is a former animation student at the School of Visual Arts. He now runs a YouTube channel on anime called RogerSmith2004, and occasionally writes for an anime satire site called Anime Maru.

2002 • NARUTO

ナルト

— OMAR RIVERA —

I've often pondered if I were given the opportunity to ask the creator of *Naruto*, Masashi Kishimoto, a question, what exactly would I ask? Would I ask him about his secret formula for crafting new ideas while writing a weekly manga for fifteen years? This would most certainly benefit me since I am currently working on my very own fictional work that I'd love to have published one day. But if not that, then what? I think I've finally come up with one question that could very well lead into answering the rest. But before that, I'd like to look back on a few lessons that I've learned thanks to *Naruto*, most of which were subconsciously in there for many years before I even realized that they originated from this story.

One of *Naruto*'s main themes is the importance of connecting with others and the value of building relationships. When I was in middle school, a brand new game had just launched called *Naruto Arena*. It is a three players vs. three players ("3v3") online strategy game created by some passionate fans and it's extremely addicting. However, it wasn't really the game itself that was addicting. It was the forums and the boards of *Naruto Arena* that kept me coming back and spending hours upon hours on it. This site was the first thing that I checked when I woke up and the last thing I checked before going to bed. Before this, I had never really spoken to others online before, let alone on a forum. But there I was, surrounded by all these people who are just as weird as I am but didn't judge me for it. There was a completely different vibe to the conversations that we all had, we all genuinely liked being in the same place as one another even though we had no idea what each of us looked like. This really opened my eyes. Not only was this website an escape from reality, it made me take a step back and truly think about the way that I look at people.

Fast forward a few years later during my senior year when my English professor brought in his Xbox 360 and a classmate brought in a copy of *Naruto Ultimate Ninja Storm 3*! What in reality was just a small tournament between those of us in class that actually wanted to participate, meant much more to me than just that. These were some of the very same students that I didn't really feel comfortable around and here we were having the time of our lives playing video games together. I've always tried my best to get along with everyone, and I've been blessed with awesome friends, but there had always been this lingering feeling in the back of my mind that maybe, if I did something differently, more people would like me. Having experiences like this changed my way of thinking. It led me to realize that it's when I'm with those that accept me for who I am that wonderful memories are created.

Looking back on it, my favorite characteristics about the original Konoha 11 (a term used to collectively refer to the members of four Konoha teams) are all what they consider to be their weaknesses, but this is what made them unique and memorable. What I got from Kishimoto here is to be true to yourself and to accept your weaknesses. When you do that, everything else will follow.

I've spoken to many *Naruto* fans over the years, and I often hear the same things being said about multiple points in the series. One of those points is Rock Lee versus Gaara, and about how it's one of the highest points in the entire series. I remember when the episodes were first airing on Toonami, every *Naruto* fan I knew loved Rock Lee. All these years later, I ask myself ... *What is it that made this character loved by so many different people who all come from different backgrounds?*

I've come to the conclusion that it's for the same exact reason I looked up to Rock Lee as a source of inspiration, and it's because we all saw a bit of ourselves in this character. Rock Lee embodies the hard-work-is-greater-than-natural-talent mentality, and Kishimoto executed that concept to perfection. Seeing Rock Lee's flashback within that battle, showing him training from sunrise to sunset nonstop with no complaints, all for his ninja way—to prove that, even though he doesn't have any natural talent, he can become as great a ninja—is extremely inspirational.

This is a mentality that has helped me a lot, especially in college. Even though I'm very interested in the field I'm pursuing, I didn't have any prior knowledge whatsoever to the programs used in the courses. I've gone into class so many times thinking, *Just what am I doing here?* Looking around and seeing everyone do everything with little to no effort—when I couldn't even start the project—was a bit discouraging. It sucked at first, but I stuck with it, because this is something that I want to do and so, instead of taking everyone else's skills as a negative, I started to see them as teachers, as people I could learn from. Accepting one's weaknesses and working hard to overcome them … this lesson has become a part of who I am and I try to look at everything as a learning opportunity.

Out of all the wonderful lessons that Kishimoto has taught me through this series, there is one lesson that I've always known was there. One lesson that didn't take me until I became an adult to figure out where it originated from. Arguably one of the most important lessons I've ever learned from a fictional work: **To never give up, and to persevere**. What's truly impressive to me, looking back on this as an adult, is not really how I became inspired by it—for I am a person who gets easily inspired by things. It's because of the way that Kishimoto did it. At a young age, I didn't want to learn anything that wasn't on a game manual, and yet I immediately grasped this concept.

I eventually realized that it's because of the way *Naruto* is written. Every lesson Kishimoto wants to teach, he applies it to his character's personalities and places them in situations that best show it off. He always places Naruto in scenarios where he's forced to state that he's never going to give up. That is absolutely genius because it's something extremely simple that all of us can relate to. It's not something we're just being told. We're actually seeing someone struggle before our very eyes, someone who we believe in, someone we've come to love and care about as our main character, not because of his strengths, but rather … his weaknesses.

Naruto Uzumaki is filled with flaws; he's an idiot who always spouts a lot of nonsense to cover how he truly feels. All he wants is to be acknowledged. We don't relate to characters for their strengths, but rather for their weaknesses, and as a child I related so much with Naruto because we shared so many similar faults. When I saw that someone just like me would never give up, no matter what happened, I naturally started thinking the same way. This way of thinking has become a part of who I am and it's become a source of strength.

I'll never forget the way I felt when I read the final chapter of *Naruto*. It was the end of the journey, a journey that I started when I was much younger. So many memories, friendships and moments linked to this series. I remember going on an opening-theme-song-binge on the day the final chapter released and just looking back on everything, the entire journey both in the series itself and my own. When I saw the panel with *Naruto* wearing his Hokage cloak, I was filled with an overwhelming sense of joy that's so hard to explain. I recall just going around that day saying to myself, *My boy made it!*

This series showed me the impact that a work of fiction can have on people—especially at a young age—and I wish to one day do the same. To write a story that can inspire and emotionally invest readers in the same way that *Naruto* has done for me and so many others around the world.

So, if I were to ever meet Kishimoto, I wouldn't ask him a question, I would instead thank him for creating this wonderful story that inspired an eleven-year-old boy and sent him on the path he's currently on today.

Omar Rivera is an author that dreams of having his own work of fiction published one day.

2002 • PLEASE TEACHER!

&

2003 • PLEASE TWINS!

— YAOCHONG YANG —

We tend to think of a narrative as a controlled, linear piece. We think of it as a series of points from A to B with a certain clarity. If we're Campbellians and believe in the hero's journey, then many of us probably believe in the wholeness to a world. However, how might a narrative be constructed across multiple vantage points, multiple lenses of production and reception?

Many (perhaps most) people won't rate *Please Teacher!* and *Please Twins!* that highly. On the surface, they're remnants of the mid-2000s visual novel designs. The boldly colored character choices, the distinctive hatched cheeks—all hallmarks of an anime visual language that draws considerable influence from the galge (girl games) that preceded it. On its surface, *Please Teacher!* and *Please Twins!* are remnants of a early-2000s aesthetic and storytelling ethos that slowly faded out with the advent of the late aughts.

Therefore, a surface level look at *Please Teacher!* and *Please Twins!* suggests that it's about a pair of stories happening in a town. In a few ways, that is correct. Blogger Cythoplazma has made some very critical connections in his pilgrimage blog, such as noting *Ano Natsu de Matteru*'s spiritual connections (in the post "Onegai! Pilgrimage to Lake Kizaki"). However, there is a reflexivity in the two that Cythoplazma hints at, and will be the subject of this article. Let's start with *Please Teacher!*

On its surface, the show is straightforward. In *Please Teacher!,* a young man (Kei Kusanagi) is caught in a coma-like stasis (called a "standstill") for three years. After waking up, Kei leaves his old home to live with his aunt and uncle. One night, he witnesses a spaceship crash, upon which he finds a half-alien Mizuho. The show is around Kei and Mizuho pretending to be a married couple, and over the course of the series, they develop an honest affection for each other.

In general, it's a generic romantic plot. However, what's particularly important for *Please Teacher!* (in the context of this article) is the way in which space carries a specific power. *Please Teacher!* is set up as a fictional town revolving around a real general location. The lake where Kei finds Mizuho is based off Lake Kizaki in Nagano, Japan. Their high school is based on the old Matsumoto High School at Agatanomori Park in Matsumoto. A tower in the show is a tower at Joyama Park.

Please Teacher!, in short, is a media-mix franchise that co-opts real-life locations to encourage fan visitation. Often referred to as *seichi junrei* (translated to "pilgrimage"), the act consists of fans of anime works visiting locations that have been featured or referenced in those works. Here, the practice exists in a broader soft power initiative by the Japanese government, understood in promotional strategies as *kontentsu tsūrizumu* (contents tourism). Broadcasted in 2002, *Please Teacher!*'s Lake Kizaki (and its surrounding areas) would have been a significant site of pilgrimages in the early 2000s, riding what Philip Seaton and Takayoshi Yamamura would consider the "second wave" of multi-use pilgrimages.[2] More specifically, the locations of *Please Teacher!* would draw attention to the city of Oomachi in Nagano.

By itself, *Please Teacher!* would be a straightforward example of a text taking advantage of this media-mix relationship. It would be no different than the city of Nishinomiya (*The Melancholy of Haruhi Suzumiya*), the town of Shichigahama

---

2   Seaton, Philip and Yamamura Takayoshi. *Japanese Popular Culture and Contents Tourism*. Abingdon: Routledge, 2015.

(*Kannagi: Crazy Shrine Maidens*), or the town of Washimiya (*Lucky Stars*). Though early and well-known, *Please Teacher!*, Lake Kizaki, and Oomachi are hardly the earliest or the most well-known. They're preceded by Hikawa Shrine in Azabujuban, made a famous pilgrimage location by *Sailor Moon*. Popularity is eclipsed by Toyosato Elementary (*K-On!*) and Washimiya (*Lucky Star*). Akiko Sugawa-Shimada traces it even further, arguing that the beginnings of *seichi junrei* begins as early as the '70s, tracing women's pilgrimage heritage to *An-an* and *Non-no*.

Therefore, why is *Please Teacher!* a particularly important piece in the context of pilgrimages? *Because* it's a media-mix property, we should consider *Please Teacher!* on its media-mix grounds. For this reason, this article collapses both *Please Teacher!* and its follow-up, *Please Twins!*, into one.

Please Twins! happens in the same location with different characters in a different time. Though some of the original *Please Teacher!* characters return, they're mainly cameos. *Please Twins!* revolves around different characters with different motivations. What's important, however, is that *Please Twins!* begins where *Please Teacher!* left off. The very first scene establishes a location that looks very similar to Akihabara. It mixes busy lights and advertisements with computer parts, referencing the area's numerous hardware locations. There, on the display, we see the news, showing a house at Lake Kizaki, referencing the alien spaceship crash from *Please Teacher!* This connection is a link to both *Please Teacher!* as well as the awareness of its otaku audience (who consist of the majority of anime pilgrims).

The main character, Maiku Kamishiro, sees a familiar house. It reminds him of a photograph of the house where he grew up, which he then deduces is the same house. He decides to go there. However, Maiku is not alone; high schoolers Miina Miyafuji and Karen Onodera also see the broadcast, and they too decide to take a trip to Lake Kizaki. The story plays out as a generic romantic triangle between Maiku, Miina, and Karen, with the added dramatic tension that one of the girls is related to Maiku.

We cannot watch *Please Teacher!* without *Please Twins!* as a media-mix property, both *Please* works build off each other to set up a general "world" ripe for pilgrimage. Anime and Manga scholar Eiji Ōtsuka describes the way in which media materials depend on "premium-value" (*omaketsuki*) contents as a means of differentiation:

> In the field of animation [grand narratives supporting commodities] is what is known as the "worldview." [...] The ideal is that each one of these individual settings will as a totality form a greater order, a united whole.[3]

In other words, the consumption of a singular, linear narrative (like how we might see in a show) is sometimes of secondary interest to the otaku. To Ōtsuka, the text builds up a world in which a multiplicity of storytelling emerges. Various stories in various ways, complementing or challenging each other. He likens it to a game, where "The totality of the data programmed into one video game would correspond to the worldview."[4]

In this context, *Please Teacher!* and *Please Twins!* inhabit the "Lake Kizaki" world, fleshing out and depending on a sort of (to reference Ueno Tsunehiro) "augmented reality" upon which the pilgrimage might occur. However, recall the opening scene and inciting action in *Please Twins!*: Lake Kizaki, from *Please Teacher!*, is on display. The previous work is on display, and that gives Maiku the drive to visit that location because, to him, it has a punctuating reverence. He is, in other words, going on a pilgrimage.

Though hardly the first, and hardly the most popular, *Please Teacher!* and *Please Twins!* is a rare media-mix in which the two texts form a "worldview" that bears its own reflexivity. In setting up the *Please Teacher!* connection from the beginning, *Please Twins!* not only calls back to the otaku "worldview" habit, but it also references and bases its story around the otaku act of the pilgrimage.

Furthermore, *Please Twins!*, through its use of the photograph, emphasizes the sense of *furusato* (hometown). In this situation, the *furusato* is a sense of belonging space-distanced from the immediate living location of the person. It

3   Eiji, Ōtsuka and Marc Steinberg. "World and Variation: The Reproduction and Consumption of Narrative." *Mechademia*. Volume 5, (2010). 99-116. 10.1353/mec.2010.0008. https://www.researchgate.net/publication/236830699_World_and_Variation_The_Reproduction_and_Consumption_of_Narrative

4   Eiji, "World and Variation," 108.

is the "native home," the "place where I am from," always distanced. This isn't new: Philip Seaton, Takayoshi Yamamura, Akiko Sugawa-Shimada, and Kyungjae Jang note the sense of "home over there" as early as the 1960s, where Japanese tourists would describe Prince Edward Island as a "[hometown] away from home" due to the popularity of *Anne of Green Gables*.

Therefore, the sense of hometown is not unique to the *Please!* media-mix. However, in focusing its story around the photograph of Maiku, Miina, and Karen growing up, *Please Twins!* leverages *Please Teacher!* as both a diegetic text of *furusato* visitation as well as its own take on the second wave of pilgrimages. It's an early critical engagement with a sense of space that has found considerable momentum due to advances in digital technologies in the early 2000s. Through *Please Teacher!*, it sets up the conditions of pilgrimage, and through *Please Twins!*, it critically engages with those sentiments. The *Please!* media-mix, in other words, is an intriguing way of thinking about relationships of media forms, particular in the context of pilgrimages. Though it's not the most popular or the first instance of anime pilgrimage, it does have a unique place in being one of the first reflexive, pilgrimage-based media-mixes.

Yaochong Yang is a PhD student at Trent University. He runs the channel Pause and Select.

2003 •
FULLMETAL ALCHEMIST

HAGANE NO RENKINJUTSUSHI

— ROBERT WALKER —

If you could bring somebody you love back to life, would you? What if it meant breaking the very laws of nature? Sacrificing something of equivalent trade? Perhaps injuring one you hold dear? Could you live with the results? What would you do to correct your mistake? That is the fundamental precept of *Fullmetal Alchemist*, one of the best anime of the new millennium.

Edward and Alphonse Elric are two brothers living in a world where alchemy blossomed in the same way science bloomed in our world. There are rules, books, and entire schools dedicated to the craft. They live in the idyllic countryside of Resembool, far away from the capital city of Central. Their mother, Trisha, watches over them. Their father long abandoned them, though Trisha holds out hope he will return someday. For years, she watches them grow, exercising an instinctual alchemic talent that they inherited from their father. When she suddenly dies, the brothers resolve to use their alchemic skills to bring her back. But alchemy functions on one cardinal rule: the concept of equivalent trade. In order to gain something from alchemy, something of equal value must be given up.

On a fateful night, they draw an alchemy circle and perform the forbidden rights of human transmutation. But something goes wrong. A gate appears. Invisible forces on the other side seize Al. Edward, in a fit of panic, sacrifices his arm to get Al's soul back. Al's spirit now resides in a suit of armor. Edward receives a mechanical arm from his childhood friend, Winry—a mechanic who creates "automail" parts for alchemists who have lost their limbs in service. With her help, Edward is now whole again. But Al is not.

Edward knows what he must do. Find the Philosopher's Stone—the legendary alkahest that contains the power to bring Al's body back. But the only group that retains all the research is the military. So, Edward makes a fateful decision. He'll become a "dog of the military" in order to bring his brother's body back. The two then burn down their old home—no going back—and set out on a quest to right the wrongs of tampering with the forces of nature.

Along the way, they encounter a cast of colorful characters. They train with a mentor, a butt-kicking Sarah Conner type who teaches them the cardinal rules of life: the one is all and the all is one. In the capital city, Central, they meet Roy Mustang, the Flame Alchemist—a brooding colonel who becomes Edward's commanding officer. He's flanked by Maes Hughes, the wise-cracking intelligence agent who's always annoying his coworkers with doting stories about his little daughter. Then there's Riza Hawkeye, Roy's no-nonsense blond Lieutenant. And Armstrong, a musclebound strongman who's really just a big softy. They work for President King Bradley. (Yes, that's the "Engrish" term he goes by. I can only assume "God Emperor" was already taken.) The President seems amiable enough, but the country remains mired in endless skirmishes on its borders. This raises the ire of the religious fanatic, Scar. Swearing revenge against the alchemists who pervert the laws of nature, he scours the land, literally exploding alchemists from the inside out with his possessed palms.

Finally, there are the Homunculi—artificial super humans created from botched human transmutations. Amoral, sadistic, and imbued with a superiority complex, they consider themselves the next step of human evolution. They are named after the Seven Deadly Sins. And why not? For they are the result of humanity's sin against nature. Did Ed and Al play their own part in their creation? Will this lead to a reckoning they cannot win?

From the start, it's deep, heady stuff. A tragic coming-of-age story replete with themes of family, brotherhood, camaraderie, betrayal, death, regret, and sacrifice. The world they inhabit seems in flux. Alchemy, played out like a metaphor for science, seems like a cursed monkey's paw that's more trouble than its worth.

The military uses it to fight its wars. Religious countries to the south ban its use altogether. Researchers use it to splice souls and bodies together in unholy fused beings called "chimeras." Numerous side characters resonate with backstories about misusing alchemy and losing something dear as a result. Scar is the product of alchemy. Winry lost her parents to an alchemist. Tortured by PTSD, Mustang regrets committing war crimes using alchemy. The Elrics' mentor followed down much the same path they did, and it crippled her. The show's litany of villains abuse this magical system time and again, wreaking havoc on untold innocents. Alchemy acts like a drug. A quick fix to achieve mankind's desires. If it has an air of familiarity to it, think back to *Jurassic Park*: "Your scientists were so preoccupied with whether or not they could, they didn't stop to think if they should."

Into this tug of war, the Elric brothers search and battle and find themselves again. No decision comes easy. Political intrigue lurks around every corner. Friends seem like enemies. Enemies seem like friends. And the Philosopher's Stone ever beckons. But when their needs run counter to their superiors, what do they do? Who do they trust? Alchemy has a way of sweeping those around them into its storm. For every action they commit, there is an equal and opposite reaction. The sins of the father are visited upon the children. And where did their father go, anyway? This is no ordinary "cartoon." *Fullmetal Alchemist* is a young adult fantasy with a brain.

Credit first to manga writer/artist Hiromu Arakawa. But director Seiji Mizushima played his part as well. A veteran part-time director of *Evangelion*, another heady masterpiece in its own right, Mizushima took great care in the world-building. The manga's universe springs to life with ornate alchemic symbology, tattoos, books, and summoning circles. The animation glows in over-saturated primary colors that bring its European-inspired setting to life. The countryside bristles with emerald fields set against fiery sunsets. Central City, with its 1930s Berlin-style architecture, shimmers in bleached marble. The southern desert kingdom of Resembool burns with the golden hairs of a lion's mane. Edward's cape blazes in scarlet red. While the military sports uniforms of deep, azure blue. And the Philosopher's Stone glimmers iridescently in tones of deep magenta. This is a bright and vibrant fantasy world that begs to be lived in.

The same sense of color applies to the score by Michiru Oshima. *Alchemist* features a classically inspired soundtrack headlined by the showpiece, "Brothers." Written in Cyrillic, performed on violin and harp, and sung by a Russian children's choir, the haunting melody weaves a nostalgic shadow over its two main leads—always playing during the show's sentimental scenes.

For all its moody moments, *Alchemist* still finds time for comedy. This is a funny show. Edward gets constant flak for his short height. Al partakes in a lot of slapstick. And Mustang even goes so far as to promise that, under *his* Presidency, miniskirts will be mandatory for the ladies. Cut to: a visibly annoyed Hawkeye giving Mustang a death glare, while the men in his unit promise to follow him to the ends of the earth. On top of that, the show manages to devote time to blind dates, live births, and other small detours to spice up the character development.

Over time, these moments really add up. They're so effective that, when the inevitable happens, it becomes a brutal exercise in *Game of Thrones*-style shockers. An episode involving a chimera (fused from a dog and a human) remains infamous to this day. And the mid-season death of a supporting character forced countless grown men to admit they shed "man tears." The greatest shock, though, the creators saved for last. Freed from the constraints of the manga, the writers unleashed a mind-bending twist that makes the concept of equivalent trade even creepier. The finale rests on it. And fans either love it or hate it. But it certainly gets points for being unexpected.

Perhaps the final piece of the show's success lies in that "other" Philosopher's Stone story: *Harry Potter*. In fact, one could almost describe this show as, "What if Harry Potter worked for a fascist dictatorship?" *Fullmetal Alchemist* came out only two years after the first *Potter* film—the same year that *The Lord of the Rings* wrapped up. The world seemed primed for fantasy. Furthermore, international hits like *Cowboy Bebop*, *Pokémon*, and *Evangelion* were only five to seven years old, respectively. Miyazaki's *Spirited Away* nabbed an Academy Award, Pixar began a massive Miyazaki dubbing spree, and Dreamworks released Satoshi Kon's *Millennium Actress*. Out of nowhere, the west started salivating like Pavlov's dogs for more anime to fill the airwaves. And *Fullmetal Alchemist* answered the call. Yes, it rode the zeitgeist. But it managed to be a masterpiece in its own right.

Nowhere is this made more demonstrably clear than in the show's eerie prescience. Edward's attempt to affect positive regime change in the theological dictatorship of Ishval only leads to further destabilization. Released during the Iraqi invasion, *Fullmetal Alchemist* resonated with unforeseen allusions to the tragedies unfolding in the Middle East. Ishval, with its fierce civil war, may as well be Syria. Scar, whose religious lust for vengeance drives him to commit unspeakable acts forbidden by his own faith, may as well be a candidate for ISIS.

It's these universal themes—the sins of the father, violence begetting violence, the abuse of powers we cannot fully comprehend, the path to hell being paved with good intentions, and the longing for a past we can never get back—that makes the anime timeless. But it's the themes of family, friendship, and sacrifice for the ones we love that makes it transcendent. This makes *Fullmetal Alchemist* a story that will resonate for years to come.

Consider them the show's Philosopher Stone.

Robert Walker is the co-writer for the hit web series The Nostalgia Critic. *As a child of the '80s, he's been watching anime imports since before he even knew what anime was. Altogether, he has watched over 300 anime series and films. Not necessarily for his job, but because he has a problem.*

2003 • GAD GUARD

GADO GĀDO

— TYLER D. HALL —

Dreams never truly die, they just become clouded within the stress of reality. *Gad Guard* is, to me, a classic anime that can be re-watched and still experienced with the same amount of whim and amusement as before.

The story takes place 700 years into the future, at which point Earth has come close to running out of resources. It follows Hajiki, a young boy who lives in Unite Blue, a run-down and small Unit. One day, Hajiki finds himself with a mysterious stone called a "Gad." During the height of an emotionally intense moment, the Gad transforms into a Techode, a giant human-like robot.

Techodes are autonomous beings created from the Gad, filled with intense emotion by the one who finds them. Techodes feel "lost and helpless" without the person who created them, which in turn makes them not move, meaning only the creator can control the Techode. There are adverse effects to the situation as well, as Techodes are one of three possibilities for a Gad's emergence.

There are also Gadrians and A-Techodes. Both are monstrous beings made of organic and inorganic material. They are manifested by strong evil feelings, grief, or the overwhelming sense of greed within the finder. Hajiki finds himself entwined with the mystery of the Gads and where they came from, finding friends and even other Techodes in Unit Blue, and entwining himself into an even deeper secret, as well as finding out the mystery behind his late father's death.

The story is very impactful and meaningful to me, as it is truly the first anime I experienced from start to finish. The sense of wonder and the happiness I found watching the show kept my thirst for anime going, creating the love I have now.

Hajiki's growth throughout the story is astounding. He goes from a street smart "delivery boy" to a seriously knowledgeable young man. His experiences, heartbreak, and even accomplishments shape him into someone completely new by the twenty-sixth and final episode.

Their take on the way Techodes work reminds of a *Pokémon*-esque feel to a mecha-centered story. The meaning behind the Techode's existence is also a rewarding experience. The reveal is something worth ending the story on. The overall product is truly amazing. The bonds between characters, like Hajiki and Shinozuka, and characters and their Gads, Hajiki and Lightning, or Katana and Zero, really shows quality story formation.

Akio's character development, especially, is surprising and rewarding. Being the only daughter of a very wealthy family in Day Town, she has always felt lonely. Her friends give her a "ray of light" in the dark, as well as her Techode, Messerschmidt, which was created in the form of a "protector." This Techode's embodiment is most likely related to her father, who was never really present. She eventually finds more solace, even more so than with Messerschmidt, in another of the main characters, Takumi.

This relationship eventually leads on to her dreams being realized, as she no longer feels alone or unprotected. Nothing feels out of place or forced, it all flows smoothly for a series with such a small runtime. The overall feel of the anime, and the experience from watching it, is refreshing. A 2003 classic, showing beautiful art as well as fantastic models for the Techodes, truly propels the story into something I would definitely call noteworthy and memorable.

Tyler D. Hall is a young anime, manga, and film enthusiast. Finding inspiration from his life, he spends his time writing and creating manga.

2003 • GUNSLINGER GIRL

— THE PEDANTIC ROMANTIC —

An undercover military organization for the Italian government takes in girls whose medical conditions are terminal under its cover as "The Social Welfare Agency" and enhances them with cybernetic implants. Using a process called "conditioning," they wipe these girls' often deeply traumatic memories and begin training them into the perfect soldiers. At the behest of the government, "The Agency" engages in operations against the mafia, domestic terrorists, and mere political opponents with its human weapons' unthreatening appearances serving to drop the guards of their targets moments before those targets get dropped.

The synopsis for *Gunslinger Girl* lays out a pretty cool, very "anime" premise for a spy action series that—as its somewhat generic title would suggest—falls comfortably within the medium's "girls with guns" sub-genre. It's definitely the kind of series you could imagine as one that would get people into anime, this schlocky cyberpunk making for a solid entry point. It happened to be my own entry point, too—the first anime I watched and was able to recognize with an, "Oh wait, this is something distinct from 'cartoons,' " after I caught a random episode on The FUNimation Channel back when that was a thing that existed (you see, in my day we had this thing called a TV ...). What it did not happen to be was schlock, nor was it really even an action show first and foremost. Instead, *Gunslinger Girl* offers an incredibly somber, deeply affecting look into the psychology of its characters.

There is a lot of grayness to the morality of this series, but to get to the crux of the moral conflict ... the girls are happy. One of them thinks back on her extended hospitalization, a life of total paralysis where she was forced to listen to argument after argument between her parents about medical bills, and exactly how much worth she had to the two of them. Waking up in the morning, she sheds tears of joy over the simple fact that she's able to move. Of course, there's more insidious reasons for this happiness.

Each girl is given an older male "handler" in order to form a *fratello* (Italian for "siblings"), in which that agency-assigned handler is tasked with their girls' training and "conditioning." Each of them has their own methods, some opting to pump their girl full of the conditioning drug, others seeking to make those dosages as minimal as possible. But in every case, a powerful, obsessive loyalty to their handler is instilled in each of these girls. And in every case, these girls are conscious of the artificiality of those feelings; they're aware of the fact these are being induced, but that doesn't make them less real.

The sort of tenderness the series treats these girls with is striking. While so much media about trained child assassins focuses on how *dark* and *harsh* things are (among anime, something like *Kite* quickly comes to mind), this series would easily lend itself to that pathos of its cute cast suffering, it just doesn't exploit them like that. The single scene most emblematic of *Gunslinger Girl*'s approach to me is one that has been vividly carved into the backs of my eyelids since I first saw it, and it is anime's most memorable for me.

Two of the girls are sitting in the bedroom they share, one on the edge of her bed, the other at their little table, where tea and a box of pastries are laid out. As the girl at the table sits, toes at the ends of her short legs just brushing the floor, she's sewing, and there beside her, her roommate sits cleaning and reassembling her gun. No attention is called to it, no one comments upon the contrast, but in the mundane straightforwardness with which it is presented, the scene hits with an immense punch, beautiful and heartbreaking. These girls are at once so normal and so alien and a scene like this is all the series requires to convey that concept.

Even though the anime opens on an action scene, these are actually fairly few and far between over the course of the series all things considered, and those that are present often don't go for visceral satisfaction. You're almost as likely to get a scene whose climax involves a character sadly staring down the barrel of a gun at a newfound friend they'll have to take care of because he saw too much, or have focus taken away from a successful sniper assassination to the second sniper on that mission being chewed out by her handler. As is the case for so much truly great action, the emotional weight of these scenes almost always takes precedence.

The story spans the country, involves all sorts of intrigue between pretty well-established factions within the government itself, all fighting for influence, favor, and funding, but in and amongst all that, keeps things very personal. The series itself articulates this best really. As the girls sit outside, singing together while they watch a meteor shower one of the handlers chuckles and says, "Little girls who kill terrorists and speak three languages are now singing Beethoven in the bitter cold." The somewhat campy absurdity of the contrast between cutesy young girls and brutal military work that is a genre mainstay is used by *Gunslinger Girl* to brilliant effect as it shakes its head sadly about the marriage of those two things and the tragedy that they represent.

There is, however, one more tragedy you should be aware of. The series received a second season ... but four years later, and at the hands of a new studio. While the first season did air during the very awkward early 2000s, the "digipaint era" as it's called where studios were still figuring out how exactly to use digital coloring and not look terrible, that season was produced by Studio Madhouse, one of anime's strongest and most well-respected studios. The choice to go with a more grounded, realistic aesthetic for the series was a fantastic one, with muted drab colors enhancing that moody vibe and that grounded look aligning perfectly with the emotional approach taken. It looks quite similar to Madhouse's famous *Monster* adaptation if you're familiar with that.

The second season, unfortunately, came from the hands of the much lower-profile studio Artland, and opted for a brighter, more colorful palette, with rounder, more conventionally "anime cute" designs for the girls. In addition to that, it loses that focused personal approach of the first season and takes more interest in that broader scope. We get more, longer-lasting action scenes, more focus on the terrorists and their plots, on setting up clear, individual antagonists, and less introspection—less of the unfair circumstances and the system all the characters are beholden to as the true antagonist. While not particularly poor, Season Two is a fantastic demonstration of exactly what the first season was differentiating itself *from*, and why doing so was such a great decision.

The first season of *Gunslinger Girl* presents no particularly easy answers. Everyone is partially complicit in a system that preys upon their need to feel useful or to have a solid, safer job they can work after an injury, or to have a body that will function, and yes, even the need to have a task force effective against the terrorists—one made up of people who were dying (or as good as dead anyway) being perhaps the most moral option for that. Everyone feels vaguely dissatisfied with the state of affairs, but also sees no better option available to them. This, in a lot of ways, is how government agencies work—and how *governments* work—and this anime does all its exploring of that broad, macro-level topic through an intimate, character-centric approach that never fails to emphasize their humanity.

Gunslinger Girl is unsettling in the moral quandary it thrusts upon the viewer, deeply emotionally evocative with its earned, respectful tragedy, and leaves you with so much to think over and take away from it. It's a rewarding viewing experience through and through that, when I first watched it all those years ago, instilled within me the belief that, with anime, there were many incredibly worthwhile emotional and intellectual experiences to be had.

The Pedantic Romantic has been working as an anime YouTuber full-time since the age of nineteen (not particularly impressive, seeing as she is only twenty at the time of this writing, but still). She possesses a passion for anime analysis, industry research, and humbly asks people to support her work at patreon.com/ thepedanticromantic in equal measure. She thinks anime's pretty great, and you are too.

2003 • TOKYO GODFATHERS

TŌKYŌ GODDOFĀZĀZU

— JOHN RODRIGUEZ —

My introduction to Satoshi Kon came in the living room of this book's estimable author. He sat me down to watch *Perfect Blue*, and I'm going to be honest with you: it didn't click. Oh, don't get me wrong. It was plain as day the film was wildly—perhaps brilliantly—creative. I just couldn't grasp it. Doesn't that drive you mad, when you can sense you're seeing something special, but you *just can't get the shape of it*? I know it left me feeling grumpy. And in my fit of pique, I determined to be done with Mr. Kon and his frustrating genius.

So, here's a hat tip to you, Chris Stuckmann, for not allowing me my obstinacy. I'd never have known *Tokyo Godfathers* if you had, and I'd have been poorer for the loss.

Tokyo Godfathers is a screwball fish-out-of-water action-dramedy featuring three of the unlikeliest heroes. There's Gin, a former competitive cyclist who ended up on the streets when his wife and daughter tragically passed away. No, wait ... that's just the lie Gin spins to his homeless companions. Pride, it seems, lingers on even when the money runs out. Just like the money ran out for Hana, a transgender woman and former drag queen who lost the will to carry on financially when she lost the love of her life. Rounding out this vagabond trio is Miyuki, who ran away from home after a fight with her policeman father turned violent.

You can't have a screwball comedy without an agent of chaos, and *Tokyo Godfathers'* pint-sized little yowler of an agent sows plenty of chaos, indeed. She's an infant girl, swaddled in pink and screaming her head off in a dumpster. And now she's the responsibility of our three homeless heroes, who happen upon her on Christmas Eve. Should they turn her over to the police? Gin and Miyuki think so, but Hana—herself a foundling—isn't ready to let the infant go. Hana gives her a name—Kiyoko—and all the love she's been storing up for the child she can never have.

But what about Kiyoko's real mother and father? Aren't they near-frantic with worry somewhere out there in big, bright Tokyo? And isn't it our homeless heroes' obligation to reunite this estranged family? Maybe. And maybe, in the process, they'll grow to become a family of their own.

Tokyo Godfathers feels akin to *Raising Arizona*. Indeed, *Tokyo Godfathers* would fit quite nicely into the Coen brothers' *œuvre*. It's got all the requisite elements. The droll humor. The lovable loser heroes. The little moments of poignancy interspersed with bouts of madcap *Keystone Cops*-esque action. If you thought *Fargo* was great, you really need to watch *Tokyo Godfathers*.

But Mr. Kon isn't some base copycat. He makes this world his own with sublime details that bring Tokyo's seedy underside to life. Just look at the way he fills the spaces his homeless characters inhabit! There's an authenticity there that lets these ragged-edge lives pop off the screen. Backwater America may be the Coen brothers' storytelling stomping ground, but for Mr. Kon, it's the urban nooks and crannies that society's exiles call home. It's almost as if he saw the destitution of the streets with a clarity that the rest of us couldn't (or wouldn't).

Don't get the notion that *Tokyo Godfathers* is some depressing wallow through the metropolitan mire, however. Far from it. This film is often laugh-out-loud hilarious, and Mr. Kon showcases a masterful sense of comedic timing. His use of repetition is particularly effective. Be it the dying old homeless man who keeps begging Gin for one more "final request," the harried cab driver who's always being stiffed his fare by Hana, or the gossipy ex-neighbors who keep adding to their number to bolster their slanderous testimony against Kiyoko's parents ... this stuff is comedic gold.

Interspersed within the laughs are moments of touching sentimentality. Our homeless heroes are constantly at one another's throats, yet there's a sense of camaraderie beneath the conflict. And as their search for Kiyoko's parents progresses, that camaraderie develops into a love as patchwork as the heroes themselves.

Hana speaks a particularly astute line shortly after she upbraids Gin for embellishing his life's story. She says,

"BEING ABLE TO SPEAK FREELY IS THE LIFEBLOOD OF LOVE."

That's true, isn't it? Our impulse so often is to censor ourselves, to hide our imperfections lest they make us appear unworthy of being loved. But that's a trap, and it's unsustainable. Keep your truths bottled long enough and they'll eventually burst out in a blast of bitter resentment. No, better to find yourself a partner who will permit you to smear your messy truths all over the walls and help you scrub them up when you're done. Miyuki, Hana, and Gin all do that for one another at various stages of *Tokyo Godfathers,* and it makes them more a family than blood ever could.

Tokyo Godfathers is often ranked as one of Mr. Kon's lesser works. Don't you buy it. It's accessible. It's uproarious. It's brave in its inclusivity. Most importantly, it represents truths about the human condition that we all need reinforced from time to time. Life is grungy, life tends to tear apart. But find yourself a family and it can be sewn back together into something more beautiful than ever it was.

Thank you, Mr. Kon, for reminding me. And thank you, Mr. Stuckmann, for pointing me to the reminder.

John Rodriguez is a personal trainer whose devotion to physical fitness is exceeded only by his fervor for all things film and literature. John is currently finishing his first novel—a fantasy that's sparked fantasies of a challenging new career.

2003 • WOLF'S RAIN

URUFUZU REIN

— MATTHEW CARATURO —

Faith. Many times in life that is the one thing that allows us to keep going. Whether it be the faith in some divine being, the faith that things will get better, the faith that things will not get worse, or even faith in other people. Nothing really exemplifies this idea of faith to me quite like *Wolf's Rain* does, and that's part of the reason it's my favorite anime.

Wolf's Rain stars a pack of wolves, in a world where wolves are believed to be extinct, on a quest for Paradise. The wolves manage to get by due to the fact that they are divine beings. They can fool humans into believing they too are human, and they can take a lot more damage than one may expect. At the same time, in spite of them being divine beings, they all have these flaws and setbacks. So, the importance lies less on getting to Paradise, but rather the journey of getting there, and learning to overcome those flaws holding them back.

The world of *Wolf's Rain* is equal parts depressing and equal parts beautiful. The city we are introduced to within the first episode, Freeze City, is extremely gritty and impoverished. It has its fair share of petty thieves as well as people just trying to get by. Yet in spite of it being a place filled with hopelessness, this is where our protagonists all end up meeting each other and finding that one common goal. So there's this beauty and optimism to it, even if the world, on the exterior, is dark and dreary.

Now keep in mind, each have no reason to stay in the city. Kiba, so prideful, refused to disguise himself as a human, which left him open to getting captured and taken advantage of. Him staying there would only lead to being experimented on by the Nobles and becoming their pawn. Hige, on the other hand, maintains a very carefree attitude, not remembering his past self. After all, he's the one who ended up freeing Kiba and helping him escape from the Nobles. By accompanying Kiba, he's lowering the chances of getting captured, since the Nobles are tightening security. While Toboe is someone who has this fondness for humans, being raised by one himself, he can't stay here anymore knowing that the human he tried to befriend now fears him. Tsume feels this sense of inadequacy, because he was abandoned by his pack in the past. He ends up searching for this one group where he can fit in, a group of rebels, where he quickly becomes the leader, but he's not great at it. They tend to get caught quite often and they even face casualties in the form of a young boy named Gehl. When Tsume ends up meeting Toboe, however, there's this unconditional acceptance of who Tsume is. He can't help but be compelled to help Toboe and the group search for Paradise, even if he doesn't let it show.

Each have their own conflicts holding them back, even at the very end of the show, but still they keep on pressing to Paradise, maintaining this faith in action, even if it isn't in thought. Hige believes he is undeserving of Paradise after finding out about his past: that he worked for Lady Jaguara and the Nobles, and that the collar on his neck was just leading the Nobles to them this entire time. Yet even so, he continues on. Tsume still has this sense of inferiority, and having been at odds with Hige the entire show, he's forced to deliver the killing blow when Darcia (the show's main antagonist), brutally attacks Hige. Yet even so, he continues on. Blue, the pet dog of Quent, who had been trying to hunt our protagonists the entire time, believes she's unworthy of Paradise because she's only partially a wolf. Yet even so, she continues on. Toboe is too attached to the humans of this world to continue on. Quent is too stuck in his old ways of trying to take revenge on the "wolves" who killed his family to continue, even when it's been revealed that it was the Nobles who were responsible. Hubb, a former detective who had been investigating the wolves throughout the show, is too busy grieving over the loss of his ex-wife, Cher, to continue on.

The only character who has nothing holding them back from continuing is Kiba, who ends up serving as a foil to Darcia because Darcia claims that all of the other individuals accompanying Kiba were pointless. That in reality, the only person Kiba needed to go to Paradise was himself, because this was fated all along. This makes sense, considering how the show's deaths played out as if by fate. The response to this ends up being one of the most salient points the show makes: While perhaps none of them were necessary, they were worthwhile. Before meeting them, Kiba had been filled with pride, unwilling to think of anything but himself and his own goals. But by the end, not only has he swallowed his pride, he's grown to understand other perspectives besides his own. While he does have this burning faith in Paradise, he understands why the others accompanying him may not share that same passion. Darcia, on the other hand, got there all alone, but he's not viewed as the better man for it. Kiba is passionate and still feels for other people, whereas Darcia has lost that ability to feel. If anything, he's only grown worse from this journey, killing anyone in his way.

The show's conclusion has received criticism for its reset ending, however, I think it's very important that this ending is here and I feel that, without it, the meaning of the show would completely change. Multiple series in the early 2000s had very nihilistic endings, most notably *Texhnolyze* and *Gilgamesh*, both from 2003. *Wolf's Rain*, on the other hand, rejects this nihilism by having that reset. Kiba claims right before the world ends that "there is no Paradise," and it freezes over. Later restarting and forming a landscape much like our modern day city: death and rebirth. Maybe this Paradise the wolves had been searching for was unattainable but, even so, isn't there meaning in searching? After all, without this purpose in life, the wolves would be just like the humans of Freeze City: barely getting by and not understanding what the point is; trapped in this eternal hell. This isn't a story where the characters constantly have to repeat the same journey ad nauseam and grow insane from it. But rather, this is a story where their ongoing journey makes them stronger. The kind where, even if the world was destroyed and reborn again, these ideas remain true.

Even if we all have our inner insecurities, even if we cannot entirely clear our minds to attain this unachievable goal, why not search for it? *Wolf's Rain* taught me to keep going and maintain faith in achieving my own goals. To allow myself to feel and understand others, rather than grow numb to what other pain people may be feeling, as well as my own pain. It's brutal, it's beautiful, and I love it.

Matthew Caraturo is a former animation student at the School of Visual Arts. He now runs a YouTube channel on anime called RogerSmith2004, and occasionally writes for an anime satire site called Anime Maru.

2004 • HOWL'S MOVING CASTLE

HAURU NO UGOKU SHIRO

— SAM LIZ —

In the last few years, Studio Ghibli films have found their footing here in America. It's finally easy to find merchandise in mainstream stores, and just plain *watching* them is no longer a hard task. You can just pull it up on Google for rental. When I was younger, getting to watch most anime required a lot of digging. The Internet was a far different place twenty years ago. Finding some titles was like hunting for gold. I was lucky in the fact that *Howl's Moving Castle* came out in the later half of my discovery of the anime world.

At age fourteen, I discovered *Howl's Moving Castle* by Diana Wynne Jones—a book I adored—had been turned into a movie. I was excited, but dismayed to learn that it was only available in Japan. This was 2004 and the idea of getting an anime movie in America was still a new concept to me. The TV shows were slowly trickling in on Toonami, and movies felt like they were arriving even slower. Having only seen a few Studio Ghibli films at this point, I wasn't all that familiar with their body of work.

Fast forward a little over a year and, to my shock, I found a DVD of *Howl's Moving Castle*. Snatching it off the shelf, I ran to the register, immediately scrapping my plans for the day (I think it was finishing a report for school but watching *Howl's Moving Castle* was infinitely more important).

I popped the DVD into the player and sat back to watch. Predictably, as a book junkie, my first thought was, *This is very different than the book*. But despite my normal penchant for thinking, *The book was better*, I took to this adaptation with vigor. The score entranced me, the art was stunning (as with any Studio Ghibli piece) and the story drew me in. I was hooked, completely in love with this version just as much as the book.

The story is set in a country embroiled in the beginnings of a war with a neighboring kingdom. A snippet of crucial detail is slipped in, in a manner that most would overlook. You enter the world of Sophie, a demure, mousy girl working in her family's hat shop. Her differences from the other girls is quickly made clear. The ladies are all dressed in richly colored clothing and are more lively in nature. They giggle as they talk about being terrified of Howl stealing their hearts. While quiet Sophie—fashioned in more drab clothing—sits in the back, away from the group.

You follow Sophie as she leaves to visit her sister, unknowingly about to meet the elusive Howl. After rescuing her from a drunkard, Howl sweeps Sophie literally off her feet, leading to a thrilling walk across the sky while being pursued by evil henchmen.

Upon returning home to the hat shop, Sophie encounters a large woman who is under the impression Sophie is Howl's girlfriend. This meeting leads to a curse placed on Sophie by The Witch of the Waste—who's aiming for Howl's heart. With no choice, Sophie embarks on a journey to find a way to break her curse.

Now an old lady, Sophie makes the trek into the waste where Howl's castle has been seen from time to time by the villagers. Along the way, she finds a helpful scarecrow with a turnip for a head. It follows and aids her in securing a place to sleep for the night.

The aid comes in the form of a moving castle, an impressive but ugly machine. Upon entering the castle, Sophie is met by Calcifer, a cursed fire demon. A bargain is struck between the two: Sophie can stay, as long as she helps Calcifer break his curse.

After a good nights sleep, Sophie is awoken by Markl coming down to take care of customers. Of course Markl (Howl's young apprentice) is confused by the stranger in his house. He questions her about her presence, which prompts Sophie to hire herself as a cleaning lady for the filthy castle. Howl makes his appearance again and doesn't even bat an eye at Sophie being there. You find out as the movie goes along why he is so accepting of the odd situation.

I feel like this is a good place to stop describing the story. It gets more riveting and enthralling from here, and I want you to enjoy watching it for yourself. The characters will pull you into the world without my aid.

Howl is part charming, part child, with an odd twist of daring. The complex nature of his character is integral to the story. You can't help but wonder while watching the movie: What is he *really* doing? What drives him? Some answers are never really clear, and you're left with a lot of questions about him as his backstory is never fully explained.

Sophie is endearing and spunky. Her character is so delightful, with well-written dialogue and great character growth. You fall in love with her realness. Her self-doubt is a part of all us in some way. That moment you realize the real effects of the curse placed upon her is like looking in the mirror—an embodiment of our inner voice. Watching her grow and shed that self-doubt gave me hope that maybe I could someday as well. (Still working on that, wish I had her gumption.)

The rest of the quirky family never feels like side characters added for comic relief. They have their purpose in progressing the story and shaping the world that Hayao Miyazaki presents to us.

As I sit writing this, my husband is reminding me that I showed him this movie when we were first engaged. It honestly shocked me at the time that Chris had never seen this before. But then I remembered the DVD was put out by Disney—notorious for putting titles back in "The Vault"—and you had to be lucky to find a copy. His first viewing had him entranced just as much as I was. Which was a good thing, because I probably would've spent the rest of our lives bugging the shit out of him if he didn't like it.

Sam Liz is a longtime anime fan, bibliophile, and nerd. She enjoys quiet, relaxing days with her husband and dogs.

2004 • MELODY OF OBLIVION

BŌKYAKU NO SENRITSU

— MATTHEW CARATURO —

Our society has its fair share of expectations, many of which I tend to find quite binding. By the end of high school, one is expected to know exactly what direction they want to take with their life and a lot of responsibilities are suddenly thrown at them. People in charge flourish, while many times people in lower positions are left in the dust. *Melody of Oblivion* seeks to criticize this society that we're all part of through the use of absurd imagery and fantastical elements. What I find particularly interesting about this story is that, rather than simply criticizing society, it provides a far more realistic angle to those who are doing the criticizing.

The story follows Bocca, a teenage boy who ends up becoming a Warrior of Melos. Those who receive such powers are tasked with fighting the Monster Union, a group of individuals who have taken over society and left people completely unaware of the fact that they've taken over. It's almost as if the battle between the monsters and humans never happened. In this case, the Monster Union represents the system tying everyone down; Bocca and the Warriors of Melos represent those who would go against the system.

The first episode starts out with Bocca's parents complaining in the background as he leaves for school. More specifically, they are concerned because Bocca needs to retake his test, and if he doesn't do well, he might not end up like his brother, who was able to get a good job and become an upstanding member of society. Bocca is told to stay away from Mr. Tsunagi, the owner of the machine shop, because otherwise he's not going to be able to get a good job; hanging around part-time at some place like that won't look good on your resume.

One of the most pertinent scenes that represents this is the archery scene with the gym teacher. Bocca gets a perfect shot in, but is basically told that this accomplishment is useless. He can use the arrow to hit the target, but he can't use an arrow to shoot through the wall behind it. In other words, archery, as a skill, can be no more than a hobby and he won't go anywhere with it. In general, he's viewed as this outlier from society, and it's not even due to his attitude, but rather because of his test scores, who he hangs out with, and his skill at archery.

It's not even like the teachers are of any help. For example, Bocca's parents pay off his teacher to make sure that he passes the test. This showcases a society that is more concerned with appearances than actually knowing the material and applying it. Bocca's gym teacher is honestly not much better—not only for accepting the bribe—but also for selling out his students to members of the Monster Union, believing that, in this era, the only way to survive is to obey the monsters.

I see this as a metaphor for those who do anything their higher-ups tell them to, regardless of whether or not it's the right thing to do, just because they might lose their job—or even worse, lose their life—if they were to not listen. My favorite thing about these early episodes is that Bocca actually ends up proving his gym teacher and society wrong. The archery that was viewed as pointless and no more than a hobby actually ends up becoming Bocca's livelihood, since he uses a bow and arrow as a Warrior of Melos. This leads to a fantastic scene where Bocca saves a student that his teacher kidnapped by shooting the arrow onto the target and through the wall, destroying it. Mr. Tsunagi, the person he was told to stay away from by his classmate, ends up giving him the opportunity to become a Warrior of Melos in the first place, by introducing him to Kurofune, another Warrior of Melos.

Things are not all good for Bocca, as the rest of the series focuses on him going from place to place with a thief he met named Sayoko. That being said, not everything he does is necessarily beneficial to society. For example, one of the early places he goes to is called the White Night Cape, a tourist attraction that has been enmeshed in eternal darkness by the Monster Union. Bocca puts an end this darkness, but rather than being rewarded for it, he's actually berated by the townsfolk.

Prior to this, the hotels were struggling to make any business, but ever since the Monster Union came, the hotels were rewarded with tons of guests; the hordes of giant babies entering the hotel symbolizing the White Night Cape's economic prosperity. On one hand, you can't blame Bocca for wanting to put an end to it, since the Monster Union was causing trouble in that area and sacrificing children—with any citizens trying to rebel turned to stone—but on the other hand, you can't blame the townsfolk for being angry, because now their businesses will start to struggle. So neither party is really in the wrong here.

One thing the show also makes clear is that the characters going against the system are fighting an endless battle—one that neither side may win and one where they might not have an honorable death. The Warriors of Melos never seem to face off against the big members of the Monster Union, but instead against the lackeys and the underlings. Even when the characters do start facing off against more serious threats near the end of the series, these threats don't take the warriors seriously at all.

The final battle of the show takes place in space, and there's this constant visual metaphor of a karaoke room. This karaoke room contains both the protagonists and antagonists, and in particular a really silly scene wherein the main antagonists are singing the ending theme. In any other show, this battle would be taken seriously and viewed as this epic and tense fight, but the Monster Union treat it as a complete farce because, to them, the Warriors of Melos aren't a serious threat. Meanwhile, one can really tell the Warriors of Melos are giving this fight their all and trying their hardest, yet failing to make much of a dent on the Monster Union's defenses.

This viewpoint translates into how a lot of characters die in the show. It tends to be both abrupt and not very dramatic because, at the end of the day, those going against the system aren't going to be viewed as heroes. Not many remember this war against the Monster Union, and the warriors lack time to grieve. So, what makes going against such a system worth it?

By the end of the show, Bocca is still fighting and it feels like the system hasn't really changed, in spite of years and years passing. What makes things worth it, however, are those who you can end up influencing to break through the system holding them down. Like how Mr. Tsunagi and Kurofune were able to influence Bocca and Sayoko, Bocca, too, ends up influencing someone from his old high school. Bocca accepts the reality of his situation, but doesn't let that deter him from trying to make a difference: he continues on.

Melody of Oblivion understands that the system is not something that will ever be changed completely. There will continue to be monsters in power, and the people trying to stop them won't win every battle. Even with that in mind, the show encourages viewers to accept the reality of the situation, but also to not completely adhere to the system; to stand up for what they believe is right even if it's not popular to do so. For a show that is rather infamous for being absurd and insane, I find it very meaningful.

Matthew Caraturo is a former animation student at the School of Visual Arts. He now runs a YouTube channel on anime called RogerSmith2004, and occasionally writes for an anime satire site called Anime Maru.

2004 • SAMURAI CHAMPLOO

SAMURAI CHANPURŪ

— ALEXANDER RABBITTE —

Shinichirô Watanabe has produced a number of brilliant works, and as an auteur that purposefully exploits one of anime's most inherent qualities, his stylistic choices display characters and premises in a relatable yet complex fashion. In deliberately molding different genres together, Watanabe's work becomes so transfixing to watch and effortlessly differentiates itself from the confines of a singular text.

Most notably, this can be seen in Watanabe's most acclaimed work, *Cowboy Bebop,* a twenty-six-episode concept that not only fuses stylistic choices of space opera to gangster and film-noir, but threads these ideas toward characters that are equally compelling to behold. Much of the same can be seen in regards to Watanabe's *Samurai Champloo* as well. Set in an alternate version of the Edo-era, it not only mixes different genre tendencies rather noticeably, but presents an episodic narrative design that displays captivating figures like Mugen: an unconventional breakdancing swordsman whose unlawful past as a pirate keeps haunting him. Jin, a rogue samurai on the run after accidentally murdering his own teacher, and Fuu, a tea-house waitress, who are all in search for "the samurai who smells of sunflowers."

Just as *champuru*—an Okinawan dish—is savored because of its flexibility of form that allows people to experiment with personalized recipes, *Samurai Champloo* contrasts styles and differentiating cultural references across the twenty-six episodes that succeed in providing characters and a context that leaves you wanting more as each chapter concludes.

Watanabe's style perfectly executes an aesthetic that's utilized in a self-conscious and playful manner, providing an appeal that may seem the same in conjunction with other anime, but is knowingly mindful of the show's many scenarios and characters. Aside the infusion of hip-hop and the use of scratching as a transition method that separates different plot points, a notable example of clashes between east and west is Episode 5, named "Artistic Anarchy."

In this episode, the main heroine, Fuu, is kidnapped as a "model" by famous Ukiyo-e artist Hishikawa Moronobu. The paintings he produced influenced European impressionist painters, specifically impelling Vincent Van Gogh whose name is mentioned in the episode's opening monologue. As much as the story depicted within this episode is complete fiction, it's nonetheless interesting how they intertwine a form of outlandish context with actual nods to European art history.

In Episode 18, "War of the Words," the iconography of graffiti art is exemplified through characters painting words on Osaka Castle, as well as Mugen defiling Fuu and Jin's possessions near the end of the episode. This mixing of generic and historical iconographies not only enlivens a premise that fuses this historical period of feudal Japan with formal aesthetics of rapid editing, but it also serves as a construct that enriches the dramatic quality of the three characters' search for Fuu's father—the milieu that forms a deeper and meaningful connection between the trio.

Samurai Champloo also presents a dimension of awareness through its character development of Mugen and Jin which provides a whimsical approach to the proceedings. Watanabe's show follows a contextualization that's synonymous with Japanese *chanbara* films: samurai features equivalent to cowboy and swashbuckler movies. Mugen and Jin are two men who come together from opposite ends of *bushido* (code of conduct for samurai) who both have glaringly contrasting personalities. Speaking freely, acting independently, and questioning authority, the two male protagonists embody a Western archetype that challenges both Mugen and Jin's journey.

This is best exemplified in "Elegy of Entrapment," in which both Mugen and Jin are mystified and bested by Sara, a blind assassin tasked with killing the protagonists in exchange for her son's safety. Through their respective bouts with her, both men subtly change from what they were initially represented to be. Instead of likable figureheads providing the show with charm, they're a set of characters that naturally conform to the demands of the world in which they are living and fit with one of *Samurai Champloo's* lasting contextual motifs: move along with the times. Whereas *Bebop* exhibits a multitude of episodes in which characters recall their tortured pasts, *Champloo* is all about facing the future and how a lengthy journey can slowly change someone's personality.

Alongside the lovable cast of characters, the mesmerizing soundtrack significantly contributes to the tense action sequences. While *Bebop* employs jazz and distinct themes rather ironically with a transfixing sci-fi twist, *Samurai Champloo* features a soundtrack equally enveloping in the way it structures hip-hop melodies with striking fluidity. Furthermore, unlike the many anime films and shows I've come across, what makes *Samurai Champloo's* soundtrack so incredible is the way each and every distinctive jingle never plays more than one time across the episodes. Whether we're seeing the three protagonists converging with each other comically or when Jin or Mugen are fighting, it heightens those moments in a manner that's hard to forget and makes naysayers of hip-hop instant supporters.

One of the many reasons I favor anime over live-action features and TV is due to the fact that it upholds themes, complex contexts, and diverse animation styles. The best anime however, are the ones which distinguish themselves from the one-dimensional nature of acknowledgment and introduce a unique stylization that leaves you pondering and influenced long after. This was certainly the case for me with Shinichirô Watanabe's *Samurai Champloo.*

Alexander Rabbitte is a film blogger from Manchester, United Kingdom, who consistently publishes movie and anime reviews on his blog, The Rabbitte Perspective. *He graduated from the University of Salford with a BA (Hons) degree for Film Studies in 2016.*

2004 • PARANOIA AGENT

MŌSŌ DAIRININ

— ROBERT WALKER —

Fear, paranoia, anxiety. Some of the most basic human impulses. History bursts at the seams with examples of mass hysteria—cases where human imagination created greater terrors than reality ever could. Orson Welles discovered this power during his panic-inducing radio broadcast "War of the Worlds," (an adaptation of H. G. Wells' novel). But what if it were real? What if our mass hysteria made our imaginary terrors manifest? Is such a thing possible?

While I personally consider *Millennium Actress* to be Satoshi Kon's masterpiece, one cannot discount the outlier television series, *Paranoia Agent*. With three major movies under his belt (*Perfect Blue*, *Millennium Actress*, and *Tokyo Godfathers*), Director Satoshi Kon tried his hand at a thirteen-episode anime series. His intention? To fill the series with all the little odds and ends that couldn't quite fit into his larger projects. The result? An experimental kaleidoscope of characters, stories, and social commentary that all intersect at the end of a baseball bat wielded by a roller-blading boy. He is Shōnen Batto. Literally translated: "the boy with the bat." The nebulous Paranoia Agent.

But is he real?

At first it seems so. His initial target is Tsukiko Sagi, a shy graphic designer who fast became the goose who laid the golden egg. With one hit under her belt, the wide-eyed pink plushy dog, Maromi-chan, she's under immense pressure to design the next big thing. Unfortunately, the stress is getting to her. She spends most of her day crying to her imaginary friend, the Maromi pup. And if you think you know terror, nothing is quite as unsettling as watching a grown woman talk to a saucer-eyed pink plushy with the voice of a Japanese Chipette. Since the plushy's mouth doesn't move, the whole thing comes off like a David Lynch fever dream. In fact, visionaries like Lynch and Terry Gilliam may be the closest spiritual cousins to this series.

With a deadline fast approaching, Tsukiko begs for a miracle. She gets one. Out of nowhere, a creepy kid with a baseball bat skates by and whacks her on the head. She collapses. One hospital stay later and the deadline is postponed. A random assault. Case closed, right?

Enter Detectives Ikari and Maniwa. They suspect Tsukiko made the whole thing up. Perhaps, considering her overactive imagination. But then more victims begin to appear. And this is where the show truly takes off. Each victim gets a full backstory, detailing what led them to the attack. There's Yuichi, a schoolboy baseball prodigy who always wins at the game of life. When things don't go his way, he gets whacked. Then there's his tutor, Harumi Chono. A studious professional, she seems to have it together. That is, until late at night, when an alternate personality takes over. Literally the Hyde to her Jekyll. The multiple personalities fight for their right to exist. Which side will win? The courteous teacher accepted by Japanese society? Or the uninhibited call girl waiting to bust out after dark? Only Shōnen Batto can settle the score. Other episodes address every Japanese social issue, from gossiping neighbors to creepy pedophiliac otaku culture. In each case, the individual's sense of reality and fantasy is warped at best. But how does one make sense of this rogue's gallery of lost children?

It seems the closer Detectives Ikari and Maniwa get to solving the case, the more it eludes their grasp. Soon they succumb to the same unraveling fabric plaguing the other victims. An argument ensues: Should they go down the rabbit hole, like the younger Maniwa suggests? Or stick to the facts, as his superior Ikari advises? Is Shōnen Batto real? Some sort of cosmic wish fulfillment? A mass hallucination? And what of the attacker's motives? Does he ride as an angel of sleep? A sleep that Poe once called "the little death"—bringing sweet release in the form of blissful unconsciousness? Or is it something darker? As the assaults continue, why do they take a more sinister, downright deadly turn? And what, if anything, does all of this have to do with the runaway toy line, Maromi-chan, and its designer, Tsukiko? The girl who kick-started an epidemic with her first report to the police?

It's complicated, but deceptively simple. And it pulls no punches. Make no mistake—it's adult. Kon's world is not Disneyland. This is a universe populated with selfish kids, schizophrenics, and sexual predators. It's rough. But Kon balances it with great good. Detective Ikari remains one of the great unsung anime heroes of all time. Stoic and unassuming, he trudges on with his job for the sake of his sick wife. In a key episode, Kon once again taps into his love of Trompe-l'œil style filmmaking. In the midst of a mental breakdown, Ikari enters a 2-D manga representation of his childhood neighborhood. This exploration of the Japanese concept of Natsukashii (yearnings for "nostalgia") forms the moral core of the series. What should we accept? Fantasy or reality? How many of us would leap at the opportunity to return to a simpler time in our lives? The devil is in the details. And what of his wife? Can she resist the lure of the boy with the bat? It's a tall order.

Other episodes balance light and dark with the same deft hand. Episode 8, "Happy Family Planning," is my personal favorite. It involves an online suicide club looking to meet offline. Unfortunately, during the actual meetup, the gang discovers that they should have listed an age requirement. Though the club's relentless efforts are macabre, the payoff never fails to get a laugh. It's a play on the old wisdom: "Don't force things. The more you seek something, the more it slips through your fingers." It's a common theme. If you think you know where this show is going, odds are you don't. It's subversive.

And subversive is the key word here. Kon relishes in breaking down the fourth wall. And that fourth wall is these characters' lives. Nothing is as it seems in his world. A stunning talent faces failure for the first time. Teachers become secret streetwalkers. A doting daughter discovers her father is a sex fiend. Said father sees himself as the hero in his own head, even as he commits a lewd home invasion to cover his debts. Reality simply unwinds for these "ordinary people." Until, at last, it shatters the very fabric of the anime itself.

Episode 10, "Mellow Maromi, Making of the Anime," chronicles a studio's attempt to make a Maromi-chan anime. It's fascinatingly educational and all very meta.

It details the key players, processes, and stresses involved in bringing a series to the small screen. Slowly, the production derails as Shōnen Batto closes in. The result is unsettling. An unraveling anime detailing the making of an unraveling anime? Is art imitating life or vice versa?

Overall, the Madhouse Studio animation is on par with any Kon work—fluid, quirky, but with his standard Miyazakian realism in the character design. The score, by regular Kon collaborator Susumu Hirasawa, resonates with ecstasy-fueled dance club abandon. The now infamous intro, featuring the main characters laughing maniacally as a mushroom cloud blooms over Tokyo, was inspired by the show's midnight run. The constant, screaming refrain of, "Raaiiyaa Ra Ra I Yo Ra!" rings like a thunderclap. And Kon and Hirasawa claimed that was a conscious effort to wake the viewer up. The closing credits, featuring the main characters sleeping around a giant Maromi-chan plushy, fades out to an unsettling lullaby. The duo sheepishly admitted they wanted to put the viewer back to sleep. After all, their show was over. Who cares what runs next? "*Oyasumi Nasai*," as Maromi so often cryptically chimes. "Good night."

As a work of art, *Paranoia Agent* defies description. It's the perfect example of what an anime series can be when it's allowed to think outside of the box. It's mesmerizing. Unpredictable. Unclassifiable. It revels in Kon's world of magical realism, where modern day Tokyo and hallucinogenic fever dreams collide in a whirling cyclone of twists and turns. Is it a fantasy? Psychological thriller? Horror? Mystery? Satire? A giant sleight of hand trick spattered with ink and paint?

One thing's for sure: it's unmistakably Satoshi Kon.

Robert Walker is the co-writer for the hit web series The Nostalgia Critic. *As a child of the '80s, he's been watching anime imports since before he even knew what anime was. Altogether, he has watched over 300 anime series and films. Not necessarily for his job, but because he has a problem.*

2005 • EUREKA SEVEN

KŌKYŌSHIHEN EUREKA SEBUN

— CINDY CARATURO —

I came across *Eureka Seven* completely by accident. My brother and I had been watching anime on Cartoon Network's Toonami block, and I had heard that *Bleach* was going to start airing on the channel's Adult Swim block. Since that block aired later at night, I decided to tape the episodes so I could watch them the next day. Now, admittedly, my memory is a bit hazy on the particulars; however, I'm pretty sure that, while I knew how to set the VCR to start recording at a certain time, I didn't know how to tell it when to stop (at least at first). All I know is that I ended up with a tape that had the whole night's programming on it. This is how I discovered *Eureka Seven* (as well as shows like *Samurai Champloo*, but that's not the focus of this chapter).

As the opening theme played, I couldn't help but be intrigued. It was Eureka's design that really sparked my interest. The color and tidiness of her hair, coupled with the fact that she was in a giant robot, enticed me to sit and keep watching. Of course, the first episode I saw wasn't the first episode of the show, so I had no idea what was going on. At all. To be frank, it probably isn't a show you should just pick up in the middle, but that's what I did.

Up until this point, the kinds of anime I had seen had been more fantasy-based and usually took on a comedic tone (not that they didn't have their serious moments). Shows like *One Piece*, *Zatch Bell*, *Naruto*, and *Bo-bobo* have fantastic elements to them: Fruit that gives its consumers incredible powers; a book that controls a magic child so they can fight other children and become king of the world; ninjutsu that allows its user to do seemingly anything; and a world where insanity reigns supreme and comedy is king. These are imaginative shows and, at the time, I was interested in them. For some reason, though, they didn't get under my skin in the same way that *Eureka Seven* did.

So, why *Eureka Seven*? What's so special about it? I think there are two major aspects that deeply influenced me. The first is its world. I love how complete it feels. Not only did "lifting" (the show's version of surfing that essentially allows the user to fly in the sky) seem cool to me, but the fact that it was part of a subculture with its own magazine kind of blew my mind. I don't know why the existence of a magazine in the show's universe stuck with me, but it did. Maybe because it's such a real-world item that hadn't really shown up in the cartoons I'd seen before. That level of detail really impressed me. I know that's a silly thing to say. "The first thing she names is that there's a magazine?" I think I've always gravitated toward small details like that. To me, when creators include those little things, they not only enrich the setting, they show just how much those working on the project have really thought about their world as a whole. It's something that still impresses me.

Beyond that, *Eureka Seven*'s world was one I didn't understand when I first watched it. I know that can be a turn-off to people, but I think that only made me more fascinated by it. What's the Scub Coral? What exactly are Coralians? Eureka looks human, but she's also a Coralian, right? It felt like I was looking at a completely different culture, trying my best to understand it. While the show's sci-fi elements factor heavily into the main plot, there were also aspects of religion thrown in the mix. It's this expansive location, and I adored seeing as much of it as I could.

Of course, what is any story without its characters? They are, without a doubt, the second reason this show left a strong impression on me. While I tried to navigate what went on in the show's universe, the characters allowed me to understand the emotions behind every happening. Each character has a distinct personality, brought to life by the impeccable English voice cast.

Being around the same age as Renton (the male lead) when I first watched the series, I felt connected to him. Throughout the show, Renton's views of the world are challenged. I was around the age where that had started to happen. Though his personality didn't exactly match mine at the time, I still understood his way of seeing the world: from idolizing Holland, the leader of the rebellious Gekkostate that Eureka is a part of, to coming to terms with the harsh and unfair aspects that color life. Because I connected to him and sympathized with his emotions, I ended up growing closer to all of the other characters that colored his perspective and helped him grow.

That's the other thing about this show I love: its character growth. I don't think any of the characters have the same exact perspective at the end of the series that they did at the beginning. The gradual changes not only allowed the characters to personally grow, but allowed the relationships they had with others to continue to grow in complex new ways. I'm not sure if it's that I'd never seen this kind of depth to characters before, or if this was the show that got me to notice this level of depth. In either case, the sense of progression influenced my own ideas on how to write compelling characters.

Eureka Seven has remained in my heart ever since I first watched it all those years ago. I might even love it more now than I did back then. The thoughtfulness and care that emanates from it still resonates with me. They are qualities that I take into account when creating my own work. I think everyone has that one piece of work that they can point to and say, "This changed my life." I'm not exaggerating when I say that's the case with *Eureka Seven* and myself.

Cindy Caraturo has been living and working in Japan since 2016. In her spare time, she writes and edits for the Japanese culture site Yatta-Tachi. She aspires to be both a translator and novelist, while simultaneously wondering if she's trying to wear a few too many hats.

2005 • MUSHI-SHI

蟲師

— TRISTAN GALLANT —

Mushi-Shi is an anime that I find a little more difficult to discuss when deciding to whom I can recommend it. Why is that, you may ask? Well, it's quite simple. It's a very good show, seriously it is, but it's not the kind of show where you'd shout out: "HEY EVERYONE! LET'S GO TO MY PLACE AND WATCH *MUSHI-SHI*!" and they'd reply: "*MUSHI-SHI*?! WOOOOOO ALRIGHT!" Instead, *Mushi-Shi* is more so a show that you would watch on your own, after getting home from a long day at work or school, wrapping up in a warm blanket by the fireplace, and pouring yourself a glass of fine liquor to just watch calmly as the night passes by. But that kind of experience is not for everyone. It all depends on what someone wants out of an anime.

This series is very much like a collection of fairy tales containing similar elements, rather than a show with a continuous narrative plot line. This is, however, one of the things that keeps the show interesting. In deciding to not have a continuous plot line, it instead opts for a more episodic nature, which has its advantages and disadvantages. On the plus side, it means that you can literally jump into each new episode without any prior knowledge, like leaping off a diving board with a blindfold on. Nine times out of ten you'll land in a vat of completely safe storytelling fun. But the downside is that you will occasionally hit the bottom of the barrel.

Mushi-Shi is about a "Mushi Master" named Ginko, who travels around a mythological version of tribal Japan in search of Mushi. Mushi are—for lack of a more interesting and scientific word—spirits or ghosts. They are otherworldly beings that exist on a completely separate plane of existence and occasionally interact with our world, with mixed results. The general setup with any given episode is that Mushi cause a problem or an interesting scenario for random episodic characters, and then Ginko comes in to save the day with his massive amount of Mushi knowledge. He's kind of like a medieval Japanese ghostbuster.

Going back to the positives and negatives, though, the great thing about this story setup is that every tale is contained within one episode. You don't have other stories clogging up everything around it with extra information that people need to keep in mind for some sort of plot twist down the line. It makes everything neater, and as such, *Mushi-Shi* contains what I believe to be some of the best writing to come out of anime in quite some time. The show teaches us something that I feel like writers need to understand better. Having an overarching storyline is great, if you set it up well, but if you don't follow through with a balls-to-the-wall brilliant ending, then some of your audience (myself included) will be cursing you behind the palms that are pressed to their faces.

That's not to say that having one-shots all the time is the best and only thing you should do. There are drawbacks to this as well. In the case of *Mushi-Shi*, the only character we can get attached to is Ginko himself. There's not really much of an ensemble here. There are a couple characters that appear scattered about for a few episodes here and there, but by and large each new episode brings with it a whole new cast of unknown characters. What we lose out on is having more personal character-driven stories told in long form. *Mushi-Shi* just doesn't have that. Even with Ginko, the development that he receives is limited by the one-off characters with whom he interacts. His past is something rarely mentioned, and even his past experiences are briefly touched upon only when they apply to the episode's scenario. Ultimately, this leads to a very different kind of storytelling, one with a different focus.

Mushi-Shi is an anime that caters to a smaller audience and isn't always enjoyed by those who follow along with mainstream anime. But it's a series that demonstrates just how wide-ranging anime can be. To have this show be simply about ghosts and spirits and yet still end up successful—without falling into step with popular tropes of the horror or supernatural genre—is quite a sight to behold.

Some of the stories it tells are sad, depressing even, as most good tales involving spirits and the like tend to be. There's not always a happy ending. And that's why this show isn't the first one I recommend to everyone, nor is it entirely suited for every occasion. However, if you've ever been on the fence about watching *Mushi-Shi* previously, or have never heard about if before now, then I would absolutely be the one to knock you off of that fence and tell you to give it a go. On the other hand, if you were always against watching this anime before, I respect your thoughts and opinions. There is probably not much I could say to you that would get you to change your mind about it. I still feel like you're missing out, though.

Tristan "Arkada" Gallant is a Canadian YouTuber, known for reviewing Japanese animation with his video series Glass Reflection *where he explores and determines the best (and sometimes worst) that anime has to offer, all the while making outlandish expressions and gestures.*

2006 • DEATH NOTE

— ADAM MACDONALD —

For someone to leave *Death Note* out of any conversation about anime is as criminal as the actions of its lead character, Light! I'm embarrassed to say that, if you asked me about anime only a couple of years ago, I would be that someone.

I'm from the the '80s. I was bombarded with Saturday morning cartoons and bubble gum commercials. The only animation I was aware of were the ones that my eyes were glued to while eating my bowl of sugar they called cereal. *Thundercats*, *Transformers*, and *Dungeons & Dragons* to name only a few. These cartoons shaped my existence at the time. I was so obsessed with *Transformers* that I would tape an episode on VHS, watch it back and pause it on the very frame I wanted. Then I would meticulously draw that cell to the best of my ability. That drawing wouldn't leave my side for weeks.

Anime only crept into my life much later, when I was introduced to *Robotech*. It looked and felt a little different than what I was used to. There was something more "mature" about it than, say, *Transformers*. In the end, *Robotech* didn't speak to me, so I gave up on it. Fast forward to 2016—YES, 2016!—and *Death Note* finally fell from the sky and into my lap.

News broke that Netflix was in the process of making a live-action version of *Death Note*. Being a fan of the director they chose, I decided it was about time I checked it out. So I scrolled through Netflix and, to my delight, all thirty-seven episodes were on full display to devour!

PLAY.

The first thing you're hit with is the intro. Intense, quick, playful, and completely unexpected. I didn't like the intro or its song at first, but after watching only a couple of episodes, I found myself not pressing the skip intro button to intentionally hear it! I love it! It became part of the whole ritual of watching the show. I can't imagine watching an episode without its iconic opening theme. It's addictive.

I was struck immediately while watching the first episode by how far animation had come since my *Robotech* experience. If I had watched the classic *Ghost in the Shell* in theaters I would have clearly seen the great progression. And yes, I've come around and have seen *Ghost in the Shell* and, like *Death Note*, it secured me with its artistic genius.

The mythology steaming from the Shinigami Realm is so compelling, it could be a series on its own. So clever and thought-provoking. The religious undertones which start the series "This World is Rotten" as Light proclaims. In that context, the apple that Ryuk (a Shinigami "death god" character) has an insatiable appetitive for takes on a deeper meaning. How they unraveled the story with Light and his possession of the Death Note is some of the best set up I have ever read or seen, in any format. From pure storytelling, it has no equal. You can't help but get sucked in almost immediately.

Juxtaposed from the high-energy opening theme, the series settles down in an almost hypnotic way. Beautiful synth music swells, cinematic pans of the environment. In fact, the camera never seems to settle, it's always on the move— something I appreciate. In my opinion, the camera work in *Death Note* rivals any major Hollywood movie. This element probably blew me away more than anything else in the series. I absolutely loved how it would suddenly pan across Light's face at the exact moment it needed to. It would freeze, stutter, and float through every scene, leaving the impression that great care was put into every single frame. Bravo!

I must admit I borrowed this for my film *Pyewacket*. In *Death Note*, the camera would at times "vibrate" on a close-up shot of Light, a way of immersing the audience in his thoughts and state of being to great effect. In my film, the lead character Leah walks into an extreme close-up while listening to something mysterious making noise in the attic above her. At that moment I made the camera vibrate for the same effect and, to my relief, it worked.

The sound design was also clearly meticulously planned. A great moment is when they suck all the sound out of the scene while the Death Note itself falls from the sky.

After the story begins, you might think, *How could this concept not dry up in an episode or two?* This is when the series injects another layer that quenches those fears almost immediately. Once Light is "cleansing" the world of evil, the government gets involved and sees "Kira" (the figure attributed to Light's work) as a terrorist. The government then hires a secret weapon of their own simply named L. Seeing as Light needs a name to kill, the creators brilliantly introduce this nameless rival … just perfect.

Another small touch I find so interesting is that Ryuk never seems to look straight ahead. They give his strange eyes a distant, absent look. It's these details that make *Death Note* a cut above the rest.

I'll end on a recent shopping experience. After watching the series, I found myself in my local mall. I strolled by Hot Topic and, to my surprise, I stopped and stood there a moment. I decided to walk in. Slightly embarrassed, I asked an employee, "Do you guys have anything *Death Note*?" I figured if any place would, they would, being the temple of pop culture.

"Yes of course!" they replied. I didn't know what I wanted, just a piece of the show … maybe even the *Death Note* book itself!

The sales person came back and declared …

"Ah, sorry looks like we are sold out of everything." It was their most popular line and I wasn't surprised. It confirmed to me that like Light, *Death Note* latches its grip on anyone who comes across it.

Adam MacDonald is an actor, writer, and director, known for the films Backcountry *and* Pyewacket.

2006 • OURAN HIGH SCHOOL HOST CLUB

ŌRAN KŌKŌ HOSUTO KURABU

— MELISSA SEE —

Picture this: a nineteen-year-old introverted college kid who never gave anime much thought beyond *Pokémon* or *Sailor Moon*—not even realizing as she grew up that they *were* anime—being told by her friend to watch a series called *Ouran High School Host Club*, and reluctantly doing so because she was told to.

I'll remember that moment for the rest of my life, because *Ouran High School Host Club* was the series that made me fall in love with anime as a medium.

Ouran High School Host Club is about a high schooler named Haruhi Fujioka who attends the prestigious, elite Ouran Academy on a scholarship. She goes searching for a quiet room to study on one afternoon, but she instead finds the Host Club, a school club comprised of six handsome rich boys—"the Hosts"—that entertain beautiful rich girls. Upon being mistaken as a boy, she stumbles into an expensive vase and shatters it. To pay back the money she owes for the broken vase, she becomes indebted to the Host Club and starts working alongside them as a Host. And because she's such a natural at being one—even when the Host Club discovers that she's a girl—she remains a part of the club, continuing to pay off her debt, pretending to be a boy.

At the time I started watching this series, I was averse to anything that was stereotypically "girly." I didn't seek out romantic books, I didn't even like the color pink. I know it was strange thinking, especially looking back on it, but that's just how I was at that age.

So, I went into *Ouran High School Host Club* as a huge skeptic. And because of this—as would become, and still is, the norm for me whenever I watch a new anime—the characters were what drew me to this series. Each member of the Host Club is endearing in their own way, particularly the head—or King, as he calls himself—of the Host Club, Tamaki Suoh. Even after all these years of being an anime fan, I credit Vic Mignogna—the incredible voice actor of Tamaki Suoh in the English dub—for making me fall in love with anime. Because, even though I eventually grew to love every crazy, satirical part of the series, Tamaki was why I stuck around after the first episode.

As I continued to watch the show—and re-watch it, care of my requesting the DVDs from the library repeatedly and checking out other anime series in between—I learned that there was another world, entirely separate from my life in school and my penchant for dark young adult books. It was a world I could fall in love with (and was) every time I would go to the library to pick up the DVDs again.

Nevertheless, the love of anime that *Ouran High School Host Club* had given me was still relatively tiny until my college anime club was founded. I remember I was walking into a student lounge area off the library's main entrance, feeling lonely that particular day since I wasn't going to be seeing anyone I knew, and just happened to see the poster announcing the anime club's formation tacked onto the overcrowded bulletin board. Despite the fact that I feared the majority of social interactions at that age—and to some extent, still do—I decided to attend the meeting. What I found upon walking in was unlike anything I'd ever encountered.

For the first time in my living memory, I was in a place where I truly didn't feel like an outcast. Because, in the anime club, there were *no such things* as outcasts. I had, without knowing until it was happening, found my second family. And my second family was a group of unapologetic, excited nerds.

We watched various episodes of anime, feeding off of each other's energy and having spirited discussions about it. No one looked at another person strangely because of how passionate they were about something. We used everyone else's passion for the medium to become more passionate about it ourselves.

As the months went by and our club grew, we made plans to attend Castle Point Anime Convention, a small con in Hoboken, New Jersey. It was my first convention ever and I remember waking up at 6:00 a.m., too excited to sleep, my stomach a happy mess of nerves, like Christmas had decided to come in spring. That feeling continued throughout the day ... through the drive to Hoboken; the first time seeing groups of cosplayers; to going to the dealers' room; looking at everyone else's purchases on the way home; and everything in between.

And that feeling? Christmastime in spring? It has never changed, no matter how many times I attend Castle Point Anime Convention or board planes to meet up with friends as we go to conventions that are hundreds of miles away from either of our homes. I still feel the same sense of giddiness. My nervousness as I board a plane and strap myself in—readying for my stomach to swoop during takeoff—has been replaced by the excitement I have for reuniting with friends for another weekend of adventures and memory-making.

I've flown by myself. I've sung the original theme song from *Pokémon* with strangers on a perpetually crowded train. I've seen No-Face cosplayers handing out gold chocolate coins. I've seen breathtaking artwork. I've been tackled out of happiness because someone recognized my cosplay and happened to be cosplaying from the same series. I've been to Canada. I've seen cosplayers performing beautiful music on the lawn just because they felt like it. I've seen the Detroit River dappled by sunlight. I've met some of my best friends in the world.

And I wouldn't have gotten to do any of those things without first falling in love with *Ouran High School Host Club*.

Melissa See is an avid collector of far too many anime, books, and manga. Her goal is to someday work in the anime industry as a director. She currently resides in New York.

2006 • PAPRIKA

PAPURIKA

— CHRIS STUCKMANN —

Some artists go their entire life without gaining notice. They die unfulfilled, their potential never realized. Sometimes, we discover these artists posthumously and we kick ourselves for being blind to the genius that had been staring us right in the face. Conversely, some artists are blessed with lengthy careers and an impressive catalog of work, but often it's their earliest projects that contain the most vitality.

One could argue Satoshi Kon passed away in his prime. Certainly, the handful of films he left behind speak to his ability as a surrealistic genius. His final film before his untimely death, *Paprika*, is unlike any other anime. Much like his first film, *Perfect Blue*, it's a mesmerizing, psychedelic journey into the mind.

We follow a team of scientists responsible for the creation of the DC Mini, a device capable of projecting yourself into another's subconscious and manipulating it. Sound familiar? Indeed, Christopher Nolan's 2010 epic dream-thriller *Inception* features considerable similarities. Nolan has stated that his idea had been in the works for a decade, putting his screenplay in production before *Paprika* graced theater screens. Nevertheless, it's shocking that Kon's work has been compared to that of a subsequent American film twice now. (See the *Perfect Blue* entry for a discussion of how Darren Aronofsky's *Black Swan* compares to *Perfect Blue*.)

But while *Inception* was reasonably accessible, *Paprika* feels almost intentionally challenging. It's almost as if Kon purposefully omitted direct answers to puzzling scenes. Once the idea of dream-hacking is introduced, you're constantly second-guessing each moment. Is this real or a dream? Do these characters exist within a tangible environment, or are they constructs of the mind?

Then there are the ethical concerns. An invention like the DC Mini, if introduced to the public, would likely result in protest and anger from civil rights groups. Is it worth the fuss? Is it even moral to (literally) parade around someone's dream?

A major strength of Kon's films is that they're smart enough to acknowledge these questions but not arrogant enough to force-feed you answers. But *Paprika* also imbues its villain, the doubting chairman, with a sense of relatability. He's rude and power-hungry, to be sure, yet his fears seem sound initially. We might side with the scientists since they seem most human, but we also understand where the chairman is coming from. This makes *Paprika's* depiction of good and evil as elaborate as the DC Mini itself. One side may be right, but it's a razor-thin line splitting protagonist from antagonist here.

Kon is a masterful storyteller, and with *Paprika*, he draws a delicate connection between filmmaking and dreams. One character, Detective Konakawa, has a checkered past. He's plagued by flashbacks, often in dream-form, of an unsolved mystery that still haunts him. "But what about the rest of it?" A phrase uttered by a disembodied voice taunts Konakawa. On more than one occasion, he admits to not appreciating movies. They're just not his thing. Nothing in Kon's film is presented without purpose, and eventually, we learn that Konakawa's disconnect with movies stems from an experience he had as a youth. He once agreed to help a friend with a film, shooting much of it before bowing out, leaving an unfinished project and an abandoned friend behind. "But what about the rest of it?"

Is it any wonder that Kon weaves connections between movies and dreams? Both are pure invention, after all, expressions of subconscious desires and/or fears. And while dreamers create worlds of fiction in their minds, a filmmaker does that with a script and camera. Have you ever awoken from a dream (or nightmare) and immediately felt the urge to jot down the events you just envisioned? You just might be a storyteller.

Upon reflection, it becomes apparent that nearly every major character in *Paprika* is hiding something. For some, it's love. For others, it's their true motivations. One character, Atsuko Chiba, has created a persona named Paprika who she inhabits when diving into dreams. Paprika is the direct opposite of Chiba. Where Chiba is reserved and rational, Paprika is outgoing and daring. It's rather ingenious that these scientists have created a device that allows them to understand people's deepest, darkest secrets while simultaneously hiding their own true nature. It makes you wonder if their inability to connect emotionally with others is what spurred them to develop the DC Mini in the first place.

While many anime characters exist purely as mouthpieces for expository dialogue, the people occupying Kon's world feel like just that: *people*. A prime example is Kōsaku Tokita, a brilliant scientist with a compulsion to overeat. "I swallow everything," he says. And when we see him sitting alone in his office, tinkering away at something, we get a window into what his life must be like. Genius like Tokita's was likely alienated as a child, leading him to reclusiveness, depression, and, eventually, dysfunctional consumption. None of this is expressly stated, mind you, but Kon's intelligent use of visual storytelling combined with clever character design allows you to interpret these details.

Satoshi Kon was quite possibly the best anime director ever. This statement isn't meant to diminish Hayao Miyazaki in any way. Miyazaki helmed more masterpieces in the '80s alone than most filmmakers will in their entire career. But with Kon, each film he made contrasted with the rest of his works. *Perfect Blue* is nothing like *Tokyo Godfathers*, nor is *Millennium Actress* even remotely close to his work on *Paranoia Agent*. His command of surrealist imagery was unparalleled and his ability to harness our unspoken fears was unequaled in his field. There has never been another filmmaker with Kon's capacity for cinematic wonder. His stories penetrated the mind and pierced the soul.

There have been a select handful of celebrity deaths that have truly hurt me: the tragic passing of Heath Ledger directly after giving the performance of a lifetime; Robin Williams, a true luminary of joy and peace; Carrie Fisher, forever a beacon of light and resilience; and the devastating loss of Satoshi Kon, having blessed us with just four films. I consider each one a gift.

2006 • TEKKONKINKREET

TEKKON KINKURÎTO

— TYLER D. HALL —

"THEY LIVE BY THE LAW OF THE JUNGLE. THE CITY IS THEIR PLAYGROUND. UNDERESTIMATE THEM AND YOU'LL KISS ASPHALT." —FUJIMURA, TEKKONKINKREET

Tekkonkinkreet is a tale of two children, Black and White, who follow their own rules to survive in the city they believe they own. The tale follows their most recent adventure in the dying city of Takaramachi. In the midst of a crumbling economy, Takaramachi has become a city overrun by slums and the Yakuza. Black and White have a reputation in the town as "The Strays," known for causing havoc and doing what they want. The film follows their life as they make an enemy of the leader of the Yakuza, Snake, who is also planning to take control of Takaramachi and turn it into a theme park. He sends three superhuman assassins, and a hectic pursuit with many twists, missteps, and tragedies occur.

The film is refreshing to watch. It takes a fantastic approach on a brother's keeper-esque story. Black and White's character significance runs all the way to their names. Black, Kuro in the manga, portrays a stronger, more chaotic role in the story. As the older brother role, he is the fighter of the duo, the leader and strategist. His place in the story shows the struggle of stress and life on your mentality, namely on a child who was thrust into a parental-like role.

White, or Shiro, on the other hand, is on the completely other side of the page. White represents purity down to its most basic form. On top of being compassionate, caring, and having a love for anything that's done no wrong to him, he also appears to have some sort of mental disability. White is different from other childlike characters in the sense that he himself is a child, with a very prominent childlike mind and actions. They desperately need each other to survive, though they are so different. Their survival is based off of one another no matter how much it may seem they should be apart from each other.

Matsumoto, the creator of the series, does a fantastic job of interweaving storylines and different characters. Any viewer immersing themselves into this story can pick up on this fact. The way he incorporates the timeline and world perspective for the characters introduced gives a global feel to the way you experience the story.

The elimination of Snake, for example, is to show that all things come full circle, as well as a way to allude to the theme of karma. As a viewer, I found myself looking at all of the minute details, astounded by the art style and fluidity of the animation. I can watch the film over and over again, and every time I watch it, I feel as if I find another clue on how to create perfect character relationships and keep a fantastic fluidity throughout my stories.

Tyler D. Hall is a young anime, manga, and film enthusiast. Finding inspiration from his life, he spends his time writing and creating manga.

2006 • THE GIRL WHO LEAPT THROUGH TIME

TOKI O KAKERU SHŌJO

— JOHN RODRIGUEZ —

I once went to a dance club in college ...

Whoa, slow down there, Disco Stu!

Har, har. Go on and mock. You probably went dancing all the time. Not me. That kind of thing is knee-buckling when you're an overweight introvert more at home with *Dungeons & Dragons* than drinking and debutantes.

Sounds like you were kind of a coward.

That's not very kind. And besides, I went, didn't I? Damn right, I did! I marshaled my courage and marched right in there like I owned the place.

So, your friends had to drag you inside, huh? Wow, you really were *cowardly ...*

ANYWAY, I went. Even got my butt on the dance floor—a not-so-insignificant accomplishment, given the size of the butt in question. And it's funny. After all my angst, all my certainty that I'd only end the night alone ... there she was.

Who?

Her. That girl. Dancing. Smiling. Lovely. Holding her hand out. To me. To *me!* Only I didn't know what to do ...

What's to know? Take her damn hand!

I couldn't. I didn't. And then it was gone. Retracted. I actually saw the invitation expire in her eyes. It felt like watching the owner of the nicest restaurant in town flip her "OPEN" sign to "CLOSED FOREVER TO *YOU*, CHUMP."

Harsh.

Don't I know it. I've replayed that scene in my head a thousand times over the years. All I had to do was take her hand, for God's sake! If I could just do it over ...

Sorry. Life doesn't give do-overs.

That's what they say. But are you *sure* about that? 'Cause I knew this one girl, Makoto Konno—or as I like to call her, *The Girl Who Leapt Through Time*. And life *did* give her do-overs! A lot of them, actually. Every time the littlest thing went wrong, Makoto would take a running leap into the past, then patch things up to her liking.

Sounds like that'd be hard on the knees.

Hey, time travel ain't easy, especially when you're leaping in a skirt.

But life must've been a breeze for this Makoto, her being able to change anything she wanted?

Not precisely. See, Makoto didn't really *want* change. Why would she? Well, put yourself in her penny loafers. She's heading into summer break. She's got two great guys for best friends, and there's not much finer than playing catch with them in the park. Sure, there's that looming specter of having to select her college major, a choice that will of course affect her whole life to come. But basically, things were pretty great for Makoto. No, what she wanted is for life to remain as it was. Familiar. Uncomplicated.

Then why didn't she just jump back and make it so?

Well, that's the thing. It's true that the changes Makoto made usually worked out to her short-term advantage. But they also came with their own set of entanglements. Say Makoto embarrassed herself by starting an accidental fire in Home Ed. Of course, she'd just leap back, switch stations with another student, and voilà! No burn! Only now *that* classmate starts the fire, causing him to take grief from the class bullies, leading him to a nervous breakdown.

That'll teach him to take his tempura for granted.

The point is, entanglements are a natural byproduct of our daily interactions. Even a time-traveler can't avoid them. There's just no containing the collateral damage even if she can sidestep a coming blow. Kind of like how Makoto's friend ended up getting hurt when Makoto used her 20/20 future vision to dodge the fire extinguisher hurled by that classmate who suffered a nervous breakdown.

Wait, the dude chucked a fire extinguisher? You sure this wasn't the Hulk?

His skin definitely wasn't green. But it makes you think about how other people create fissures in the perfectly smooth life we're trying so hard to shape for ourselves. I mean, sometimes you just want things to stay the way they are. It's summer break and you're playing catch with your two best friends and, wow, life's fine. Let's just freeze this moment, can we?

I'm cool with that.

But then other people come and complicate things. Maybe it's the teacher warning you that there's decisions on your future to be made. Or maybe it's the best friend confessing he wants to date you. People mess everything up because people have this irritating habit of changing, or at least reminding us of impending change. So, you try to pump the brakes on that change. But that's like trying to catch a thunderstorm in a thimble. You'll get some of it, sure, but ultimately, you're just going to end up soaked.

Should have brought galoshes.

Then there are those times we want to take something back. We say something foolish or untoward. We overstep a boundary. We burn a bridge.

We miss an opportunity to take a girl's hand.

Right. And we spend a lifetime replaying those errors. We see the paths we could have taken. They look so much greener, and we'd give a kidney for a do-over.

Sorry. Life doesn't give—

I know, I know. Neither do other people, usually. They tangle up with us, make a mess of our neatly ordered lives. Then they leave it up to us to take from the wreckage what we can.

So other people suck, is what you're saying.

No, not at all! Other people are delightful! The fissures that they create in our lives are wonderful! I'm telling you, there is nothing in this world more boring than a perfectly smooth sheet of glass. But add a few spiderwebs of cracks to that pane and, what do you know? You've got art.

Is that how it worked for Makoto, then?

Kind of. Art actually plays a big part in *The Girl Who Leapt Through Time*'s story. It's a touching story, ultimately, and one well worth seeking out. Though it sure does come with a truckload of do-overs.

Speaking of do-overs … listen, I shouldn't have called you a coward earlier. That's one I'd like to have back.

Really? You mean it?

Yeah. Though partly I'm just worried you'll chuck a fire extinguisher at me if we don't get square. You wouldn't do that, would you?

If only we could see into the future …

John Rodriguez is a personal trainer whose devotion to physical fitness is exceeded only by his fervor for all things film and literature. John is currently finishing his first novel—a fantasy that's sparked fantasies of a challenging new career.

2007 • 5 CENTIMETERS PER SECOND

BYÔSOKU GO SENCHIMÊTORU

— ALEXANDER RABBITTE —

Ever since one of the great conjurers of animation, Hayao Miyazaki, departed the filmmaking scene in 2013—with his swan song feature, *The Wind Rises*—anime-enthusiasts become invested like never before in pursuing a successor that could equally maintain Japanese animation as a recognized genre for all audiences, just as the famed Studio Ghibli director had done with his craftsmanship.

Of course, throughout anime's existence in the western perspective, Japanese animation has always endorsed films and shows that saw many imaginative animators become auteurs in their own right. Whether you're looking through Satoshi Kon's spellbinding animated films, *Perfect Blue* or *Paprika*, that both purposefully interject notions of surrealism, or perceiving any of Isao Takahata's works that amalgamates spontaneous animation styles with distinctive storylines, anime has always catered to artists that imbue ensnaring imagination and ideas that provide something stimulatingly different.

Much of the same can be said of Makoto Shinkai, a unique animation director that has been dubbed by critics and audiences alike as "The New Miyazaki" due to his visually distinct animation style that flawlessly differentiates from the "norm" of traditional cell stylization and the threaded theme of "Romantic Separation" throughout his filmography. Many will look toward Shinkai's recently acclaimed cinematic outing *Your Name* as his filmmaking pinnacle. The plethora of bewildering animations that Shinkai has constructed thus far have in many ways made him the admired director that he's become, and undeniably shows what can be done with drawn animations that don't have feature-length running times.

This is certainly the case with *5 Centimeters Per Second*, Shinkai's second animated feature after *The Placed Promised In Our Early Days*. It not only does everything you would expect, considering many of the director's works, but it served to be a film that expanded my gaze and appreciative understanding of the medium that is anime.

Ever so naturally, Japanese animation has always been something that I've latched onto from an early age, and there are a number of shows and full-length animated features from my upbringing that I still love. Yet, for all the adoration I have for those films and shows, it wasn't until my own viewing of Makoto Shinkai's *5 Centimeters Per Second* (the speed of falling cherry blossom petals collapse to the ground, or a metaphorical reference to the transient nature of youth) that I saw Japanese animation in a different yet profound manner.

For sure, the subtle nuances of the characters that reside in all Studio Ghibli films and the fluid and intricate detail that's pursued throughout Satoshi Kon's filmography shows the creative and expansive nature that Japanese animation can provide. However, when watching Shinkai's second feature animation for the first time, I was experiencing an anime film that was unique from what critics and audiences alike might expect to see in a Japanese animation.

Unlike *Your Name*, which uses Shinkai's common thematic formality of romantic longing in a way that is uplifting and heartfelt, *5 Centimeters Per Second* presents this conception of young love—seen through the scenarios that the character Takaki is faced with—in a mode that feels realistic and attainable for those who've experienced similar situations. With the story divided into three separate episodes, we observe different parts of Takaki's life from being a school boy in one part, to an adult who's trying to get by whilst living in Tokyo in another. It's very much a film that is grounded in realistic notions, from the simple context to the way in which it's told, which I found surprising.

From my own perception, by viewing the many shows and films that comprise it, anime has always abided by contexts and visuals that emit a fantastical nature to the proceedings. Yet, as bewildering as the animation is consistently shown to be, there's no going around the notion that *5 Centimeters Per Second* bestows thematic and visual intricacies that feel wholly tangible. However, with this believability intact, it always paints a harsh reality that hits you hard near the end; especially for those who've experienced similar situations while in a long-distance relationship.

Of the three episodes, the first, "Cherry Blossom"—where we see Takaki trying to preserve his long-distance relationship with Akari—remains my preferred mini-story. From the moment we see flashbacks of a younger Takaki bonding with an also younger Akari, there's a sentiment that anime isn't just for those seeking the fantastical—it's also appropriate for audiences seeking something intimate and relatable at the same time.

Much of this is culminated in the ending of the third chapter that exemplifies *5 Centimeters Per Second* as one of Shinkai's most mature and complicated works to date. Whereas his films *Voices of a Distant Star* and *Your Name* try to maintain a romantic connection in their respective closing stages, *5 Centimeters Per Second* is ultimately about moving on from past acquaintances instead of just living in the past. When Akari and Takaki fortuitously pass each other where they had promised to watch the cherry blossoms together, Takaki simply smilies and walks on, acknowledging that it's better to find a new way to become happy in the present rather than yearning for what has never been established. As ambiguous as the ending may seem, Shinkai's 2007 artistic feature can thoroughly be considered as a methodical illustration that depicts romanticism in a poetic yet relevant manner.

Thematically speaking, Shinkai is something of a poet in the sense that he purposefully produces achingly beautiful tales of youthful love. Indeed, everything that *5 Centimeters Per Second* provides is like watching a poem in motion; enmeshing your gaze with sentimental ideas that harmonize with the eclipsing visual style.

However, it is within the film's animation that Shinkai's triptych stories blossom (mind the pun) into fruition and bewilderment. In using photos of actual locations as inspiration, never before have I seen another anime that presents a cityscape or an environment so filled with detail and vibrancy. Despite the places and settings being colloquial with locations in Japan, watching *5 Centimeters Per Second* is like gazing at a watercolor painting that's being brought to life, and establishes the notion that traditional cell animation is just as impactful as CG. Watching the film for the first time, everything displayed felt real to me and still does to this day. It takes your breath away. To match the bottled-up passions of his characters, Shinkai designs their whimsical drama in a dazzling palette of shimmering hues.

As much as it's pointless dubbing him as "The New Miyazaki"—bearing in mind that Shinkai follows ideas and a visual style that are strikingly different when compared to Miyazaki—it's warranted to say that Makoto Shinkai is a master craftsman of Japanese animation and is slowly rising up to Miyazaki's veteran status. While many will put his now known prestige down to the acclaimed *Your Name*, it's imperative to consider that Shinkai's past work is justification that he's always strived to be an innovator in his field. This is conclusively demonstrated within this original work, *5 Centimeters Per Second*, an animated feature that upholds a wondrous and detailed animation style that is wholly original and euphoric to behold. It's a distinctive film that displays a context which is elegiac yet brutally reflective of reality at the same time; making it an original feature, that differs from many other anime movies, and a contemporary classic from my own perspective. Ultimately, *5 Centimeters Per Second* represents what anime can offer and serves to be a film that made me realize this notion.

Alexander Rabbitte is a film blogger from Manchester, United Kingdom, who consistently publishes movie and anime reviews on his blog, The Rabbitte Perspective. *He graduated from the University of Salford with a BA (Hons) degree for Film Studies in 2016.*

2007 • GURREN LAGANN

TENGEN TOPPA GUREN RAGAN

— TYLER D. HALL —

Is it childlike wonder or foolhardy arrogance that compels you to push toward your dreams, no matter their size? *Gurren Lagann* is a wondrous mecha tale that follows Simon (pronounced Simone), a young boy following his dreams and attempting to "Pierce the Heavens!" Aided by some titular characters/role models, Simon truly finds himself and goes on an adventure much larger than anything he could have anticipated.

The anime follows many themes that seem to never overshadow one another. Responsibility, major loss and its complications, and friendship are just some of the themes/lessons to arise from this story. The blend of art, storytelling, awesome mecha-fights, and music really allow *Gurren Lagann* to pierce the ceiling and arise to a new level of story crafting. The popularity of the series spawned a manga adaption, four light novels, a video game, and two movies.

A major portion of the story follows Simon and Kamina, two dwellers of an underground village, who yearn for more, and the knowledge of what is truly on the other side of the ceiling. As their world has been destroyed long ago, humans have since retreated into the depths of the earth to find solace, peace, and safety. Kamina, Simon's brother-figure and role model, is an arrogant troublemaker in their village. He is always attempting to stage breakouts through the ceiling, in which Simon would follow. Every attempt ends the same way: Kamina caught, following with a punishment.

The story begins when Simon finds a "core drill" and a Gunmen, the type of mecha in the anime. Shortly after, a much larger Gunmen falls through the ceiling into the village, creating commotion, destroying a large amount of the area, and bringing forth the third main character, Yoko. Yoko and Kamina are the "big siblings" to Simon, Yoko also being his "first love," though it is unrequited. They provide him with insight, answers, and even the desperate help he needs in tight situations.

There are themes present in *Gurren*: the will to follow your dreams and never give up, and the realization of how significant you are and that your actions always have consequences. Simon's adventure, struggles, and eventual happiness, propel us forward, farther than Lord Genomes spiral tower, farther than space and the great nothing—beyond it, and into life lessons that are meant to be taught and loved to learn.

All in all, *Gurren Lagann* brings forth multiple layers of great storytelling. By the eighth episode, watchers are fully immersed over the significant loss of Kamina. On the outside, it seems particularly foolish to kill off a main character—especially one with so much involvement throughout the story—but to the viewers, it's much more significant, as well as necessary. Kamina's death is, in a sense, a passage of his will onto Simon. This is an effective way of creating emotional ties which further envelope you into the story. Kamina's death hits everyone in multiple ways and Kazuki Nakashima, the screenwriter, knew very well what he was doing.

You see the death take a severe impact on Simon. In most anime stories, a character's death is a serious and sometimes necessary loss, with all of the characters around showing their emotions and respects. In *Gurren*, Simon takes a hiatus from his responsibilities for nearly three whole episodes. This is so very significant because it gives the viewer many ties into the story. You bond with Simon, you feel his pain just as clearly as he does; you mourn the loss as well. But then, you're introduced to the newest main character, a character with much more significance than you can initially imagine.

Her name is Nia, and she becomes the focal point of the second season, as well as Simon's current and future love interest. Nia's significance in the second season and ending is something that will stick with me all throughout my story crafting. She was introduced quickly, almost as if she may be a key or throwaway character, but she becomes so much more, and it is executed beautifully. In an anime based around comedy, action, and cool mechas, it's absolutely amazing the way the creators of the story incorporate all of these underlying themes, different arcs and character paths, and diverge them into one whole, harmonious story.

Gurren Lagann is a personal favorite for me, and not just in terms of anime. Any list of recommended shows that I have the chance to put my hands on, *Gurren* is there. Simon's character progression is a perfect example of proper story divulgement. This can be seen in the emotion in his fight with Lord Genome, and even the fight with the all-encompassing end boss, the Anti-Spiral.

Characters followed Kamina and Simon for their charisma, only to end following Simon for his passion. To me, growth is something important and something that matters above all else. There will always be loss. There will always be pain and discouragement. But there will also be hope. There will be love, and there will be dreams. *Gurren Lagann* does a fantastic job of making you understand this, and it makes you want to continue the story to pursue the twists and questions of the world. But to me, it does something more important.

It makes me realize there is a ceiling above me. A ceiling that limits you to only that which is around you. You become aware of the "hole in the ground" that you currently exist in. From there, it makes me want one thing: to pierce the heavens and find what the world truly has to offer.

Tyler D. Hall is a young anime, manga, and film enthusiast. Finding inspiration from his life, he spends his time writing and creating manga.

2007 • MONONOKE

モノノ怪

— RACHEL L.S. CHARMAN —

Who are we? Past the skin, past the mind, and even further past the soul; who are we really? When we strip away everything that we use to personalize and identify ourselves in the eyes of others—our jobs, hobbies, passions, hatreds, and every external stimuli that allows us to be seen as a "person" in the colloquial sense—what are we left with? To plumb the deepest, darkest corners of one's being, after shedding the airs and egos to find the real "person," the real "you" within, and bring your real self to the eyes and judgments of others: that is, in essence, the heart of *Mononoke*.

Starting off as the third and final three-part *Bake Neko* segment of a 2006 anime series known as *Ayakashi: Samurai Horror Tales*, *Mononoke* is a spin-off series produced by Toei in 2007 for Fuji TV, and it is often confused with the 1997 Studio Ghibli-produced movie *Princess Mononoke*. However, other than sharing a similar title, the movie and series have nothing in common with each other. *Mononoke* is an anthology series, with no overarching narrative, that follows the exploits of various people living their lives in Edo period Japan while nursing dark and terrible secrets. The only element that connects these people together is the singular recurring character called "Kusuri-uri," or The Medicine Seller, who draws out their surreptitious sins which manifest themselves as monstrous and destructive beings known as the titular "Mononoke."

Despite its trappings as a supernatural anime, this series is more akin to a condensed mystery, since the character arcs only last two to three episodes. However, it doesn't waste a single second of its runtime with superfluous minutiae. Though this series could not technically be classified as a traditional mystery with a "whodunit" structure—as the culprit is without question in every arc—it could, rather, be classified as a "whydunit." The mystery comes from the mitigating factors and reasoning for the Mononoke's existence, not the fact that Mononoke exist at all. This structure helps keep you on your toes as you sink your proverbial teeth into the various characters' tales and twisted truths.

The protagonist of sorts, the elusive Kusuri-uri, moves the stories along with his fervent search for the Mononoke's Katachi (a.k.a. Form), Makoto (a.k.a. Truth), and Kotowari (a.k.a. Reasoning, or Regret). He ascertains these facets of the Mononoke's existence by delving deep into the psyches and souls of the people who had a hand in creating the preternatural apparitions; once he uncovers those three crucial elements, he can exorcize the demons with his powerful blade. Kusuri-uri himself, however, is a complete enigma. His origins and any detail of his character beyond what is presented to you plainly is kept extremely vague. Because, in actuality, the series is not about him. He is simply a means to an end in resolving the supernatural trouble, without much regard to who lives and who dies. His purpose seems to be entirely dependent on the Mononoke themselves, opening the doors for interpretation on just who and what Kusuri-uri truly is.

The most striking thing about this series is undoubtedly its visual style, which invokes the Ukiyo-e style of painting that was very popular in Japan from the seventeenth to the nineteenth century, yet with a more flat and stylized presentation. Its peerless atmosphere and visual style provides this series with endless unspoken personality, that makes it stand out sharply from the oftentimes repetitive and uninspired designs that anime in general can get bogged down in. The panache that this series exudes is certainly an acquired taste, and it may turn off some people for its over-exaggerated character designs and sometimes sluggish animation. However, these things absolutely feel like intentional aspects of the motif—to create an unsettling, uncomfortable ambience intercut with a bright, brash color palette in a gorgeous, yet understated visual juxtaposition.

What truly cements *Mononoke* as a worthy contender in its field is the sublime, flowing pace of the storytelling and the dark, disturbing themes therein. At the center of it all, this series is about terrible people doing terrible things, and those who seek vengeance against them for their transgressions. However, it throws many mental curveballs to keep every arc fresh and original, despite the similar structure they all share. The dialogue is brilliantly structured in such a way that not a single line spoken by anyone feels unnecessary; it serves to either move the stories along, or establish character, of which all are interesting. You can tell that this world they live in is an odd one—just a hair's breadth away from complete insanity at all times, and the only thing that keeps that insanity at bay is the tight chains and locks people shackle their secrets in.

Much in the way that repression in real life can have severe consequences to one's physical and mental state, here, repression is damaging enough to hurt and kill other people. In that regard, Kusuri-uri's intentions in exorcizing the Mononoke are most definitely open to debate—does he care more about putting the malevolent Mononoke to rest than he does about actually saving people? After all, the Mononoke are created by the subjugation, cruelty, and greed of others, so who should really be saved in the end? Like *Shiki*, the grayness of the morality is another point of elucidation that can keep the avid viewer coming back for further analysis.

If the similar anime series, *Shiki*, is about external antagonism threatening the characters, then *Mononoke* is about the threat of internal antagonism; the suppression of the unspeakable acts human beings commit when they believe that no eyes are upon them. The inexorable avarice and brutality that beats against their souls, made manifest by these paranormal phenomena, can bring one to self-introspection. The lies we enshroud ourselves in to continue with our lives like normal, shouldering the heinous acts we partake in for our own gain, will one day gnaw their way from out of our hearts like an infection, and will end up taking away everyone and everything we know. Do you perhaps have such darkness in your own heart?

Beyond its existential themes of guilt and repression, this series does a marvelous job at portraying life in Edo period Japan and manages to pull you straight into its milieu with seemingly no effort at all, even with its heavy stylization. It can bring anything from rainy village centers, to silent snowy courtyards, to a cherry blossom-filled breeze to life, which greatly helps to envelop the viewer into the twisted narratives, and ease some of the more delicate observers into the intense themes and dialogue cascades with its bold colorization.

To highlight one of the best aspects of this series in detail would be rather unfair to anyone who chooses to give it a view; however, the aspect in question is how fantastically this series builds itself up through gradual escalation of the tension and character drama, before finishing off with utterly astonishing payoffs. With a complete absence of any gratuitous violence, gore, or other lazy horror trickery, *Mononoke* supplies such pulse-pounding finales that are immensely satisfying, regardless of what side of the morality you find yourself on. Truly, there is only one word that can properly describe them, and that would be: spectacular. Upon first viewing, they may seem somewhat abrupt, but each one serves the sequence of events flawlessly without an ounce of excess.

When all is said and done, *Mononoke* is indeed a rare breed; peerless in its presentation, and completely without compare in its genre. Some aspects may not appeal to everyone, as some can't see past the admittedly odd visual designs to enjoy the narratives and revelations to their fullest extent; however, this is understandable. The only one that could potentially be considered comparable in style would be 2004's *Gankutsuou: The Count of Monte Cristo* produced by Gonzo; but even that style is considered by some to be unintelligible at times. *Mononoke* stands on its own, and never once allows its visual design to get in the way of its masterful storytelling. If this has only one failing, it's that it only has a paltry episode count of twelve. However, its short existence only serves to make the whole experience that much sweeter.

So, in this series, we see a reflection of ourselves; our own darkness that threatens to seep out from within us like ichor and consume not only ourselves, but everything around us, too. It's a series that may make you think twice before you raise your hand against the defenseless, or raise your voice against the broken soul, or kick the weak when they are down. Because, when the judgmental eyes of others turn against you, and your sins, encased in thick armor, are brought naked into the spotlight, you may find yourself devoured by the blackness that sat festering at the very core of your true being ... the real you.

Rachel L.S. Charman is a Canadian author, director, and YouTuber who has a burning passion for animation, and the dark and macabre. She adores the more serious side of life, and makes it her goal to spread the joy of animation wherever she goes.

2007 • SWORD OF THE STRANGER

SUTORENJIA MUKÔHADAN

— CHRIS STUCKMANN —

"I'll do my best not to say anything," Joe said with a sly smile.

I laughed. "It's okay, man," plopping down onto the couch beside him. "I know you get excited by these kinds of movies."

Joe is one of my greatest friends. He's an excellent screenwriter, immensely talented, humble and kind, with a natural gift for storytelling. Like myself, he adores movies. Unlike myself, he can't help but audibly express this while watching them. It's an inside joke between the two of us that when we watch a film together, I'll always know what parts he loves or hates because his body language is so loud, you can't miss it. When something amazing happens, he'll emit a tiny squeal. If a segment doesn't jive with him, you might hear a "*Hmph.*"

But tonight, Joe and I were watching *Sword of the Stranger*. I wanted to make sure the film was fresh in my mind for this chapter. Joe knew this. He knew I needed to pay close attention, and he'd resolved to reign himself in.

Yeah ... that didn't happen.

At least five times during the breathtaking opening, Joe burst out with exuberant, "Oohs!" and "Aahs!" He simply couldn't hold it in as men fell brutally to the sword, their limbs flying across the screen in sprays of blood. I didn't blame him. "Joe, your commentary makes this even better," I said. And it did. We had a blast.

Sword of the Stranger begins with Kotaro and Tobimaru—the best dog in anime since *Cowboy Bebop's* Ein—fleeing from a band of vicious warriors. Young Kotaro has a secret, you see, and he's not the only one. Soon, Kotaro and Tobimaru encounter a nameless samurai with a mysterious past. Quickly, this samurai gets drawn into Kotaro's conflict, and we learn he's a master with the sword. But what makes his demolishing of Kotaro's pursuers even more impressive is that he's tied his sword's hilt to its sheath, restricting him from drawing it. There's a very important reason for this which I won't reveal—it's more powerful to experience this emotional journey blind.

Kotaro, Tobimaru, and their new companion must ultimately work together to survive ongoing attacks from the dangerous group of samurai chasing Kotaro. This including the devilish Luo-Lang, a westerner often singled out for his striking blue eyes. Luo-Lang is almost superhuman with a sword, as he proves in some breathless action sequences. He slices through bone as if it were butter, and he does it without blinking. He's a horrifying villain, that old-fashioned kind that seems completely insurmountable. Which raises the question: Just how can Kotaro and our nameless hero defeat him?

Few animated films reach the epic heights of *Sword of the Stranger*. The backgrounds are simply some of the best in anime history. Beautiful mountains, valleys, and forests stretch out behind the characters, blending with the foreground to create an impossibly real illusion of depth. The film is over a decade old now and still looks better than plenty of today's animations.

Anime is often accused of cheapening the expression of character models by just moving the mouths while keeping the face and body still for multiple frames. Not so with *Sword of the Stranger*. This anime features such painstakingly detailed movement, it should be one of the benchmarks for animated emotional expression.

Also, *Sword of the Stranger's* fight scenes are rivaled only by the revolutionary battle between Spike and Vincent in *Cowboy Bebop: The Movie*. The climactic sword duel, inspiringly scored by Naoki Satô, is particularly gorgeous. Warring figures blur through the air as two titans of legendary skill clash swords in an epic battle of good vs. evil. These are two men in their prime, fighting with perhaps the only other person alive who matches up to them. Really, this finale can't be missed. It's anime at its pulse-pounding best.

What makes this film special, though, is that despite its technical mastery, its heart and soul remain intact. The charming not-father, not-son friendship that develops between the samurai and Kotaro is endearing. Something that struck me is the voids both characters have in their lives. They're both wanderers of sorts. They both have traumatic pasts, and they both took different routes to end up basically in the same place. They're mismatched, and yet they need each other. Kotaro needs protection and a father figure. And the samurai might not know it yet, but he needs redemption. Before their journey ends, they'll learn things about themselves they've been long afraid to admit.

WALL·E won Best Animated Feature at the 81st Academy Awards. It was in competition with just two other films: *Bolt* and *Kung Fu Panda*. I was shocked to learn that *Sword of the Stranger* was submitted ... *and not even considered for nomination*. You read that right: the Academy nominated an American Kung fu comedy about warrior animals over an authentically Japanese animation about a tormented samurai and his reclusive ward. Not that the Academy hasn't snubbed many a great film or actor, but this one's particularly bothersome. I'm a fan of all three films nominated that year, but only Pixar's lovely tale of robotic yearning deserved to be mentioned in the same breath as *Sword of the Stranger*.

This movie is an *experience*. From the opening shot to the last, it's a sumptuous visual feast featuring groundbreaking action scenes and innovative character work. Director Masahiro Andô previously worked as an animator on such titles as *Jin-Roh: The Wolf Brigade*, *Neon Genesis Evangelion*, *Wolf's Rain*, *Fullmetal Alchemist*, and even *Ghost in the Shell*. Thus, it's no surprise that his directorial debut is so self-assured.

As I sat in awe, letting the genius on display wash over me, I began registering more, "Oohs!" and, "Aahs!" from Joe. They didn't bother me in the least. It's just a shame the back of the *Sword of the Stranger*'s Blu-ray can't feature this quote:

> *"Whoa! Squeeee!"*
>
> —*Joe*

2008 • NATSUME'S BOOK OF FRIENDS

NATSUME YŪJIN-CHŌ

— RACHEL L.S. CHARMAN —

Reconciling with a traumatic past can be a very difficult thing. Whether it be from physical or mental abuse, neglect, shame, guilt, or anything that affected us profoundly during our formative years. Finding a way to move past the unpleasant and hurtful memories locked deep within our hearts is the only way we can make a path to a happier future. Because, no matter what background we come from, or how many painful actions we have committed or suffered through, we all deserve to be happy. That is the core of what makes *Natsume's Book of Friends* stand out from the crowd.

Natsume's Book of Friends began life as a shōjo manga series in 2005 before being adapted into an anime series by Brain's Base in 2008 with six seasons, and with production later being handed over to the studio Shuka for the fifth and sixth seasons. The series follows the exploits of the titular Natsume Takashi, a teenager orphaned at a very young age, who has the innate ability to see and interact with Yokai, which are a breed of supernatural and spiritual creatures from Japanese folklore. Because of his ability, Natsume is seen as weird and strange by everyone around him. As a result, he was passed from family member to family member as he grew up, until he eventually ended up living with distant relatives in the area where his grandmother, Natsume Reiko, lived. Reiko also had the ability to see Yokai, and was similarly shunned by her family and peers.

The bulk of the narrative in the series follows Natsume's trials and tribulations of trying to live peacefully with his new adoptive guardians, make friends, and live a normal life. However, his ability to see Yokai keeps dragging him back into their chaotic and complicated world, as the various Yokai that inhabit the land often take advantage of Natsume's kind nature to further their own ends. This is made even more complicated when Natsume uncovers his grandmother's "Yuujinchou," or "Book of Friends," that has a multitude of Yokai's names in it, allowing him to control them unconditionally. Because of this, many Yokai seek to have their names returned, or to take the book for their own.

To go into any more detail would be unwise at this point, as those descriptions only make up the skeleton of a story whose meat and muscle is found mostly in the title character himself, and in the absolutely breathtaking atmosphere and environmental design. To elaborate a little more, Natsume Takashi is truly the heat of the series, as his attempts to blend in with society and finally settle into a happy and prosperous life are constantly hampered by the Yokai that surround him. Still, Natsume takes all this in stride for the most part and never compromises his gentle and compassionate personality for anything, be it supernatural or otherwise.

A large part of the series' appeal comes from how Natsume interacts with the Yokai that find their way into his life one way or another. Given the breadth of diverse and unique Yokai in this anime's universe, it makes for riveting character drama, as well as tonally-appropriate comedic moments as well. Though comedy is mostly supplied through Natsume's Yokai bodyguard Madara, or "Nyanko-Sensei," as Natsume calls him, it manages to stay balanced with the more tense and dramatic moments well and never breaks the flow of the storytelling. Though, admittedly, some of the stories can get slightly repetitive, given the format, this repetition never hampers the stellar character interactions on display, allowing the viewer to make a real, genuine connection with everyone on screen.

With its utterly flooring background designs, which expertly bring the Japanese countryside to life in the bright, boiling summer sun to the frigid, silent winter, this is a series that is truly a treat to the senses. Its use of a softer color palette, and a calming piano and string-based score to accompany it, assist in bringing the world to life—both the humans' world, and the Yokai's. Now, truthfully, the overall animation quality isn't amazing, technically speaking, but it's exactly as involved as it needs to be to serve the calmer stories and relaxing atmosphere. If you find yourself in the right mood, the naturalistic beauty this series exudes can be almost overwhelmingly soothing, with a slight splash of delightful creepiness on top as well, resulting from the characteristics of the Yokai themselves.

It wisely avoids using a central antagonist, and never tries to insinuate that the Yokai are the only threatening force. While there are bad Yokai who hurt and torment Natsume, there are bad humans who are just as guilty of the same actions. It sees both sides of their respective conflicts and goes out of its way to make even the monsters sympathetic. These Yokai are not just monsters of the week, there to try and hinder the protagonist. They're living, talking, thinking creatures who are simply divided from humanity but don't have any less significance. And it is certainly very refreshing and enjoyable to have the alleged antagonists be sympathetic and relatable to a certain degree.

At the end of the ride, this series is a simple story about life, meetings and partings, and moving on from the upsetting past while etching out a happier future. However, classifying it as a "slice-of-life" series may not be the proper taxonomy for such a thing. It does have an emphasis on action in certain parts, without going overboard. In truth, this series could be described as a character drama, with elements of "slice-of-life" scattered throughout. And the reasoning for it being categorized as a "character drama" would be because of its emphasis on dissecting the defining moments in Natsume's past.

Given that Natsume grew up in a world that rejected him from every side—by the humans, who saw him as creepy and odd, and by the Yokai, who often tormented him and played with his naiveté—it would stand to reason that he would be maladjusted in his later years. Natsume finds himself having difficulties accepting affection when anyone offers it to him and always sees himself as a burden on others. To live in a constant state of fear and anxiety from a world you can neither control nor understand is a genuinely frightening prospect, and to be rejected from society for the very things that make you special is a heartbreaking notion to ruminate over. Despite his disposition of being caught between two different worlds and being unable to find his proper place in either of them, Natsume retains his caring soul, no matter how many times people and Yokai tried to stamp it out; and that is truly a thing of wonder to behold. To witness such a goodhearted young man suffer through so much, and still come out a decent person in the end, uplifts the spirit in a way that can't be described by mere words. It brings hope to the viewer that there is a way to move on from a troubled past and renew one's life, even if the scars of the past never truly fade. Again, at the end of the ride, this series is a simple story about life, meetings and partings, and moving on from the upsetting past while etching out a happier future.

Natsume's Book of Friends is a series that is an extremely good choice to turn to when you are feeling upset or anxious. Its incredibly calming effect that envelops you in a warm sense of tranquility not often felt in anime—coupled with its legitimately gorgeous and astounding environmental design—makes you develop a genuine connection with the characters and situations, be they negative or positive. It's a outwardly simplistic series that belies a delightful depth and serenity that is guaranteed to find a special place in your heart, whether you know it or not.

So, to those of us who suffered in the past ... those of us who find the memories of our darkest days banging against the walls of our minds and scratching at the insides of our hearts like an errant burrowing creature—are we doomed? Will we forever be in a position where we can't move on from the hurt and pain we endured while we journeyed our way through life? If you look close into this series, you can remain confident that the answer is: no. It is important to know that you must find your own pathway to happiness, yet it is equally important to not allow the person you are to become lost in the process. We can move on, but we shouldn't forget. For, much like Natsume and all the suffering he endured, the things that hurt us in our pasts shape who we are. So, strive to move on, but try not to turn away from your scars—in the end, they make us that much stronger in the face of the future.

Rachel L.S. Charman is a Canadian author, director, and YouTuber who has a burning passion for animation, and the dark and macabre. She adores the more serious side of life, and makes it her goal to spread the joy of animation wherever she goes.

2008 • PONYO

GAKE NO UE NO PONYO

— ALICIA MALONE —

I remember very clearly the first time I saw *Ponyo*. It was 2009 and I was still living in Australia, where I grew up. In Sydney, where I did not. I was born in the capital of the country—a small, very well planned town called Canberra. And to say I was obsessed with movies as a child was an understatement. Little Alicia spent every weekend at the local video store, carefully selecting her movies for the week ahead. There was a special deal where you could rent seven films for seven days for seven dollars. This was a challenge I took very seriously, determined to get the perfect mix of genres. The titles I picked were from film books I had devoured, and while reading up on anime there was one name which kept popping up—Hayao Miyazaki.

That was early on in his directing career, but by 2009, Miyazaki was well and truly established. He had a string of critically acclaimed movies and an Oscar to his name. Each new release from Studio Ghibli was met with breathless anticipation. *Ponyo* would be his tenth feature. As for me, I was just getting started as a film reviewer in Sydney, appearing weekly on a morning television show (creatively titled *The Morning Show*) and writing articles for movie magazines and websites. I was asked by one magazine if I would write a review about *Ponyo*. So, of course I said yes. And then instantly became nervous about doing it justice.

But any worry I had about getting all the details exactly right was quickly forgotten. As soon as *Ponyo* began I was sucked into Miyazaki's mythical world. The film opens in the depths of the ocean, with bursts of bright colors and light shimmering off the sea creatures as they swirl around in the water. Everything is alive with movement, even the bright orange hair of the king of the ocean, a former human and wizard named Fujimoto. His daughter, Brunhilde is a goldfish who desperately wants more from her life. She longs to be human. And she is no ordinary fish, with the power of the sea on her side, but her father doesn't want this to happen. He struggles to keep the ocean free of debris, and sees humans as the enemy who use his home for their garbage disposal.

Brunhilde's escape from the ocean brings her into contact with some of that garbage, getting stuck in a glass jar and washing up on shore. That's when she meets five-year-old Sosuke, who saves her life and decides to name her Ponyo. Sosuke is happy to have her as a friend, living on a small island with his overworked mother, Lisa. She is dealing with depression and anger toward Sosuke's father who is away working, on a ship far out at sea.

Despite their connection, Sosuke realizes he can't keep Ponyo in a bucket forever, so he returns her to the sea. But now that she's had a taste of human life, Ponyo's desire to be a proper girl is much stronger and she takes action to make the final transformation. This sets off a series of events, including a violent storm which puts many lives at danger and causes Ponyo's mother, the sea goddess Granmamare, to come out and try to set things right.

If you think the story sounds familiar, you'd be right. This is based on the Hans Christian Andersen fairytale, *The Little Mermaid*. But because this is Hayao Miyazaki, it's been given a subversive spin. The focus is not so much on what it takes to be human, and more on a different human quality. The pain we feel when we are separated from loved ones. At different points in the story, each of the characters have to deal with the distance between them and a person they love.

Miyazaki is not afraid of darkness, of showing and eliciting true emotion. But he balances the pain of distance in *Ponyo* with the lightness of love. The other emotion weaved throughout is pure, unadulterated joy. And that word, "unadulterated," really fits. Because this is the kind of joy you see in children. You cannot help but smile at Ponyo's willful antics, her wide smile toward Sosuke, and even wider eyes whenever she sees her favorite food, ham. It's a celebration of childhood in a movie meant to inspire the whole family, not just children.

There are more delightful characters to be found in the nursing home where Sosuke's mother works. The ladies who befriend Sosuke are eccentric, good-natured, and occasionally paranoid ... though the paranoia sometimes proves to be spot on. It's a lovely depiction of old age. Another focus for Miyazaki in *Ponyo* concerns our planet, with strong messages about looking after our home before our home turns on us.

The reminder of what we are in danger of losing—all that precious marine life—is present throughout each frame of the beautiful animation. Despite *Ponyo* being born in the age of 3-D computer-animation, Miyazaki remained delightfully 2-D, creating the film with pencils and ink. All in all, there are 170,000 frames, each one drawn by hand. There is something so special about his old-school style, and in no way does it feel old-fashioned. The movie is filled with vibrant color, with Miyazaki creating a rich and energetic world.

The version I first saw was actually the English dub. Normally, I am a bit of snob when it comes to dubbing and will choose a subtitle every time. But in 2009, I had only the one choice. And I have to say, the voice cast for this version fits the roles perfectly. I particularly enjoy the gravely tone of Liam Neeson. He's the voice of Fujimoto, and brings his natural warmth and confidence to the role. There is just something about Neeson's voice that always makes me feel ... calm. Same too with Cate Blanchett, who voices Granmamare, a fitting role for a goddess like herself. And the two main characters are played energetically by siblings of pop stars—Frankie Jonas as Sosuke and Noah Cyrus as Ponyo. She has since become a star herself, but it works that their voices aren't recognizable enough to be distracting.

After that first screening of *Ponyo*, I couldn't wait to get home and write about it. The words bubbled up in me, much like the waves in the film, and I struggled to contain it to a neat 500 words. I can't remember what I actually wrote, but I do remember that feeling. And every time I've watched *Ponyo* since, I think of that night back in 2009, where a master of anime showed me how much magic exists in the everyday. I didn't realize quite how much I needed that reminder.

Alicia Malone is a film reporter, host, author, and self-confessed movie geek. Born in Australia, she now lives in Los Angeles, working with Fandango, Turner Classic Movies and Criterion. Her book Backwards & in Heels *chronicles the history of women in Hollywood.*

2009 • FULLMETAL ALCHEMIST: BROTHERHOOD

HAGANE NO RENKINJUTSUSHI

— KATELYNN E. NEWBERRY —

Full Metal Alchemist: Brotherhood was an anime I watched by accident. I was at a low point in my life and happened across it on Crunchyroll. I liked the art style, so I thought, *What the heck? I'll see what it's about.* From the moment *Brotherhood* began, I was hooked. It was like a good book that I couldn't put down. In less than a week, I finished the series.

Brotherhood is a beautifully animated show. The comedic parts are drawn in a quirky, borderline chibi-style (small, cute, childlike), whereas the dramatic parts are drawn in a more serious manner. The tones of the colors change depending on the time of the day, which is something that impressed me. Along with each unique personality, comes a wonderfully animated character (my favorite character design being the villains). With some anime, I feel that the environments don't get as much attention as the character design; I didn't feel that way about *Brotherhood*.

Each environment was carefully crafted. It felt like they were as much a part of the story as the characters. The towns are colorful and stunning; they made me want to be there with the Elric brothers on their adventure.

The voice acting is also something that should be highlighted. Even though some of the actors played multiple characters, they did a great job creating individual voices for each role. As someone who has dabbled in voice work, I applaud these actors, not only with creating characters, but the emotion they put behind their performances. They did an incredible job with each role. Had the voice acting been subpar, I never would've gotten so invested.

The *Brotherhood* storyline is my favorite anime story to date. It never stops moving, and it didn't feel like there was a whole bunch of unneeded filler. The story, to me, is very cohesive. I enjoyed the different elements like science, religion, war and the corrupt government. Though it's clear from the very beginning that there's a lot of drama involved, there are equal amounts of comedic wit as well. Writing the main protagonists as children made the series special. I enjoyed seeing what it would be like if a child assumed a highly ranked position in the government.

The Elric brothers were very strong, likable characters, but the supporting characters were just as amazing. I wasn't attached to just one character, but each of them in their own way. You grow with these characters. You get attached to them and care for them. You also become devastated if you lose one of them.

Because of the incredible people behind the scenes, from the very first episode of *Brotherhood*, I was sold. I had quickly become emotionally attached to the Elric brothers and their friends. I was invested in their journey, rooting for them, crying with them, and laughing with them. I think one of the most appealing aspects of the show is the Elric brothers themselves. They are two incredibly intelligent and talented young alchemists. These boys can outperform most (if not all) of the adults in this universe. They are young protégés, the youngest of the state alchemists, but their success was not without sacrifice.

One of the major plot points of the story is how Edward gained the name "Fullmetal Alchemist" from the state. The two boys went through a devastating event, and in turn, tried to perform the alchemy taboo. The loss was great, quite possibly greater than the event that sparked it. Through the series, you watch the weight of this decision on the Elric brothers and how it affects their lives. You ride this emotional rollercoaster with them, as they set out to accomplish their goal. These are young boys who never had a childhood. It was ripped from them at a very young age. Their story really pulls at your heartstrings. In the beginning of the series, the adults don't know their situation, but when they learn, you can see the weight of it on their animated faces. Children or not, the Elric brothers are determined to accomplish what they set out for, along with a little help from some friends.

There are only sixty-four episodes of *Brotherhood*. Sometimes longer anime loses its luster after a while, so I liked that *Brotherhood* didn't need hundreds of episodes for the Elric brothers to finish their journey. When the series was finished, I wasn't left wanting for more. They wrapped the series up so tightly in a cute little bow so I could move on with my life, knowing what the Elric brothers had accomplished.

KateLynn E. Newberry is an actress with a love for creating art. She promises her fiancé she will finish the Buu Saga ... one day.

2009 • SUMMER WARS

— GEOFFREY G. THEW —

Summer Wars never got a theatrical release in Canada, so I pestered my parents to bring it home on VHS the day it got a home video release. Until it came out, I was listening to the soundtrack CD nonstop. That was way back in winter of the year 2000, but it still remains one of my favorite anime films to this day.

Sorry, that's a confusing way of putting this. *Summer Wars*, Mamoru Hosoda's third major feature film, was released in 2009. But it was also released in the year 2000 as a forty-minute short film called *Digimon Adventure: Our War Game!*, which was then chopped up by Fox executives, spliced together with two other *Digimon* shorts, and released into the American wilderness as the Frankenstein abomination known as *Digimon: The Movie*. Because if *Pokémon* could rake in a hundred million dollars on a shoestring licensing and editing budget, dangit, they could, too.

Except they couldn't. They really couldn't. They made less than a tenth of what *Pokémon* did.

Hollywood butchery aside, *Our War Game* could have easily remained a small footnote in the *Digimon* mega franchise. One particularly good short film whose biggest contribution to the overall franchise is the stark, white depiction of the Internet that has inspired the look of a lot of licensed video games. But then, Mamoru Hosoda, riding the success of his award-winning adaptation of *The Girl Who Leapt Through Time*, decided to go and remake it—just without any of the constraints of the *Digimon* license.

You ... really wouldn't think it would work. *Our War Game* plays heavily on the audience's nostalgia for the first season's cast, acting as a sort of "reunion special" for fans who missed them when the second season introduced a whole new team of "Digidestined." Without our emotional investment in Sora and Tai's failing relationship, or in the kids reuniting with their Digimon and coordinating over MSN video chat to save the world, the film would be little more than eye candy.

The concept of a rogue AI hijacking the Internet to spread chaos and potentially destroy the world, only to be stopped by some kids on their computers (and the overwhelming power of spam) is definitely cool. But if you take out that emotional core, it's just another modernized ripoff of the *Digimon* short's namesake, *WarGames*. So, what do you replace franchise nostalgia with to make the film work?

"Family" was Hosoda's answer to this dilemma. In lieu of Tai and Matt, the movie focuses on a high schooler named Kenji, who finds himself wrapped up in the affairs of a huge (and very old) family of samurai descendants after his classmate Natsuki ropes him in to pretending to be her fiancé. Despite being total strangers, by the end of the film, Kenji truly becomes part of the Jinnouchi family, winning Natsuki's real love and the rest of the clan's approval.

This new story doesn't just give the movie a broader appeal than "Hey, member *Digimon*?" It also speaks to how the world (and Internet) changed in the decade between the two films. Our war game is about the then-novel idea of connecting with old friends over the Internet, whereas *Summer Wars* explores the idea of getting to know total strangers intimately—an equally novel idea at the time the film was made.

See, as much as it's about family, *Summer Wars* is also about social media. Instead of the broader Internet we see in *Digimon*, *Summer Wars* shifts focus to a massive, globally integrated social media platform called OZ (which controls traffic lights, rockets, and infrastructure, because anime). Also, that underlying theme of social networking meshes quite nicely with the story of finding a family in a group of total strangers.

It seems normal to us in the age of Facebook that we can just take a peek into the private thoughts, political opinions, family troubles, and day to day lives of total strangers (and also see many, many pictures of their pets). But the technology that lets us do it is still in its infancy. Facebook had only just been opened up to the public, YouTube was less than a year old, and Twitter had just been founded when the production of *Summer Wars* began in 2006.

Yet, by the time of its release, all of that felt normal, and what Hosoda dreamed up as a crazy sci-fi concept seemed mundane (though syncing your Facebook to your pacemaker still sounds pretty nuts).

When I watched *Digimon: The Movie*, I was a little kid. When *Summer Wars* came out, I had just graduated from high school. And while it didn't "totally change my life" in quite the same way as seeing my personal favorite brand of collectible monsters in a movie did back in the day ... it definitely gave me some much-needed perspective.

In half of my lifetime, the world had become a totally different place. And while these two films are essentially the same story, looking at the differences between them makes the sheer magnitude of that change clear. It's no longer unusual to see a far-off friend through a computer screen and, in fact, they don't feel far off at all. The immense distance between the Digidestined in *Our War Game* isn't really a relevant concept anymore—because no matter where they are in the world, in a sense, our friends are now always right next to us.

The uncomfortable closeness of the Jinnouchi household is a much better depiction of the new, social-networked web, where people you've never met in person can learn everything about you, and tell you everything about themselves. Our evolving relationships with technology have changed how we relate to each other, and things have only changed more dramatically since 2009.

Now, nearly a decade has passed since then, and I almost wish Hosoda would drop the exciting new original film he's working on to revisit this story once more. Because his last two cracks at it serve as fascinating snapshots of our ever-changing digital landscape.

Geoff Thew, or "his divine holiness the anime pope" to his friends, runs Mother's Basement, a YouTube channel dedicated to the meticulous dissection of small details in anime and other media. He made a name for himself breaking down the editing, cinematography, and hidden references of anime openings in his series "What's in an OP?" But he's best known for his brutal teardowns of Sword Art Online and for his family's legendary "double shill" technique.

2010 •
PRINCESS JELLYFISH

KURAGEHIME

— MELISSA SEE —

I'd always felt like I was the "weird" person. Being physically disabled since birth, always conscious of how my disability separated me from others, would do that. Being awkward, anxious, and unapologetically excited about things as I grew older only fueled the knowledge to myself, and to the bullies throughout high school, that I was weird. It wasn't until I was much older, in my early twenties, that I started to realize that I wasn't weird at all. And it's because of the anime series, *Princess Jellyfish*.

Princess Jellyfish is about an eighteen-year-old girl named Tsukimi who has recently moved to Tokyo to try and make it as a manga illustrator. She lives in a communal apartment building known as Amamizukan with four other women who call themselves the Sisterhood. All of them genuinely fear any social interaction with those they deem "stylish," people who, unlike them, have themselves put together. And they're all otaku (people who are obsessed with a particular interest). Tsukimi loves jellyfish and has ever since she was little, when she would visit an aquarium with her now-deceased mother. Feeling overwhelmed after a failed outing in Shibuya, she decides to go to visit a jellyfish she's named Clara at a nearby pet store. Realizing that Clara is in imminent danger because she's sharing a tank with a species of jellyfish that could kill her, Tsukimi awkwardly tries to convey this to the employee, and is met with hostility due to her persistence. She ends up being rescued herself by (and rescuing Clara with) a boy around her age named Kuranosuke, the son of a politician, dressed in drag. What follows is a story about Tsukimi and Kuranosuke's budding friendship, as he teaches Tsukimi and the rest of the Sisterhood that—contrary to what they've believed—they're not weird at all. In fact, they're beautiful.

And like the Sisterhood, I learned I wasn't weird.

It took me up until my friend introduced me to this series to realize that. A long time, certainly, considering how old I was, but that's the thing about anime: you're always bound to learn something about yourself eventually. *Princess Jellyfish* was the first anime to teach me something about myself.

I am so grateful to have learned that what I believed about myself for my entire life was *wrong*. But I remember feeling so glad to realize that. Because as I was growing up, fewer things upset me more than knowing those around me thought I was weird, either due to my disability or what I was passionate about. But when I was younger, I found solace in books. As I got into college, I found solace in anime as well, with *Princess Jellyfish* adding to that solace and opening the door for me to find more series that made me feel that way. Before watching this show, I'd been using anime as a form of escapism, not as a medium where a person could actively be learning about themselves while being entertained at the same time.

And that's why the notion of people dismissing anime entirely—as either just children's shows or *hentai* (perverse)—is painful to me, not just as an anime fan in general, but as someone who knows the capabilities this medium possesses. There are anime series *marketed* to children like *Pokémon*, as a sort of ad for other products within the franchise like its games and trading cards, while teaching important values children should have. But that's not anime's entire purpose as a medium.

There are anime series that teach the people who watch and engage with them about depression; the consequences of war; the very concept of love; the emotional trauma of losing family members; determination in the face of adversity; treating people with respect and dignity regardless of their gender(s); and so much more.

Anime can be—and in some respects, certainly is—for children, but there are always going to be anime series that leave a huge impact on viewers. It's been nearly a decade since I first watched *Princess Jellyfish*. Nearly a decade since I first learned that I wasn't weird at all, and I'm still grateful for having watched that series and others like it. Sometimes, an anime can teach you the basic concept of right and wrong, but other times, it can teach you something about yourself that you should have realized all along.

Melissa See is an avid collector of far too many anime, books, and manga. Her goal is to someday work in the anime industry as a director. She currently resides in New York.

2010 • SHIKI

屍鬼

— RACHEL L.S. CHARMAN —

Seclusion—an oft-forgotten facet of horror that separates the mundane from the truly terrifying. What does it mean to be utterly, completely secluded from anyone or anything that can save you from your peril? The sensation of true, all-encompassing loneliness often evokes the primal, deep-seated fear of death that permeates our collective consciousness, throttling us with the inescapable knowledge that none of us are truly safe; from the monsters that entrap us from the outside, and the demons that gnaw away at us from the inside.

Shiki is an anime series produced by Daume in 2010 and adapted from a 1998 novel written by Fuyumi Ono that tells the story of a small, secluded village in Japan known as Sotoba. This village, hewn together in a sinister tapestry of momi fir trees, is stricken with a sudden, strange epidemic which begins killing off the denizens in droves. Toshio Ozaki, the young town doctor, seeks to quell the supposed illness plaguing the town; yet, the solution does not lie in any medicinal practice known to man. Ozaki, along with the inquisitive and haughty city boy Natsuno Yuuki, slowly unravel the origins of the illness, as the victims of the disease seemingly stalk the streets at night.

To delve into the many brilliant facets of this twenty-five-episode series would be a disservice to such a beautifully crafted narrative, which can render your heart still with the biting tension, sinister atmosphere, and intense gore. Many anime series, such as *Hellsing Ultimate* and *Tokyo Ghoul*, proudly boast that they are "extremely violent," and many use this violence as its only method of establishing the "seriousness" of their plots without any sense of subtlety or buildup. However,

Shiki does something that most other so-called "horror" anime series fail to do: earn its violence.

The essence of true fear is not the presence of gore or violence; rather, true fear comes from the unknown—what we cannot see is far more frightening than what is put right in front of our faces. In this regard, *Shiki* uses its intense violence sparingly. It understands that it needs to build a connection with its characters, of which there are scores, and establish a real atmosphere before doling out any amount of gore or violence. Its measured approach to bloodshed makes the turn to overwhelming carnage in the latter half of the series feel that much more "earned"—much in the vein of the *Silent Hill* series of video games.

Even stepping beyond the more brutal aspects of the series, *Shiki* also takes a deep, intriguing look into religious themes, such as what it means to be forsaken by God. The character of Seishin Muroi, a monk and suicide survivor, weaves a story of his own creation into the overarching narrative that perfectly mirrors the ongoing conflict between the suffering of the living, and the suffering of the dead. How would one's attempt to live with a life they have thrust into be seen in the eyes of a higher power? If you can only live by killing others, do you really have a right to life? Or is your right to exist forfeit once you take another's life?

This exploration of the themes of innocence, sin, superstition, and existentialism—all interwoven inside a thick narrative thread that gives character and purpose to all the denizens of Sotoba—truly makes for a fantastic experience. The special sauce that makes all of these singular elements work, however, is the truly foreboding atmosphere. Simply put: this is an anime that wants you to understand that everything is hopeless, and any attempt to maintain a normal life while your world is pulled out from under your feet is utterly impossible. Nobody is safe— you will die ... but not for long. The series does an exemplary job at making you feel not only for the victims of the epidemic, but for the bringers of the epidemic as well. An expertly crafted battle of morality is constantly waged throughout the series, which blends together nicely with the examination of the themes of transgression and innocence.

The tension here is real. The fear is real. The sadness of losing everyone you love, the heartbreak of knowing there is no way out of your situation, the uncertainty of just what is causing the deaths ... everything about this anime is just so intensely real. Not in a "based on a true story" way, but in that you can feel it there, crawling under your skin like a swarm of insects. It's a story and a situation that many of us fear in real life that tells of the ever-present specter of doubt and death that slowly closes in on you, cuts off every escape route, and brings you to the edge of your own limits in body and in mind. This is not anime for the faint of heart, or the fogged of mind.

In terms of the anime's actual presentation, there are minor issues in the visual design, in that some of the character designs are a little ridiculous, given the grim, terrifying situation and how well it's presented. Still, this visual design is wholly indicative of the style of anime in general, and may be par for the course for any veteran anime watchers who choose to pick this series up, which I sincerely urge you to do.

This series truly is not for the cowardly soul. It creates real dread and apprehension without the use of cheap jump scares, common horror tropes, or anything that could be seen as "gratuitous." Much like a well-baked cake, everything is measured out perfectly and it manages not to collapse under its own gravity, like so many other failed attempts at horror do. Now, visually, *Shiki* is not by any means the scariest thing in existence; anyone who is experienced in Japanese-style horror seen in media, such as *House*, *Fatal Frame*, or *Yami Shibai* to name a few, may not even bat an eye to this series. However, this series would fall more into the "psychological horror" genre, as it prefers to scare you with its subject matter rather than its visuals. After all, the most frightening thing in this world can be what surfaces from the deepest depths of the human mind itself.

The gradual unfolding of the moral duality of the characters is something you may not even notice during your first watch—the series is not trying to insinuate that any one person is better than the other. The people fighting off the epidemic are just as guilty as those spreading it, yet they are willing to resort to even more violent and aggressive methods than the infectors to get their regular, nondescript lives back. In essence, not a single person is a "hero," nor are they a "villain." Everyone is just living the only way they can, given their circumstances, and it is up to the viewer to decide who is in the right. No matter what you decide, though, you can guarantee that someone will suffer because of your judgment of them; almost as though you, the viewer, are the higher power that has judged the so-called "guilty ones" in both the series' narrative, and Muroi's fictional narrative. Truly, this is a series that makes it crystal clear that the only truly guilty one is the one who chooses to watch it—namely, you.

In summation, *Shiki* is a wholly engrossing, sometimes gut-wrenching exploration of the darkest depths of humanity, topped off with a satisfying swirl of severe sadism and sickening subject matter that leaves you floored from the first frame to the final second. This is not a series that rewards you if you shut off your brain, unlike many other anime that could be classified as "horror," yet, as stated, they only resort to immense gore and violence without any buildup, subtlety, or tension. *Shiki* stands in a league of its own, without many other worthy contenders in its genre. It truly breaks you down from the inside out and makes you genuinely question: "What would I do if I was in that situation?" A question which is made all the more tragic by the heartrending moral gray area this series boasts. However, its boasts are more than well-deserved in nearly every aspect.

And in the end, when the fires have burned out, the blood has dried, and the bus carrying the few survivors speeds away from the doomed village, all that remains is hopelessness in the knowledge that this scourge will continue to spread. A cliffhanger of sorts, for sure, yet one that is earned. Much like all of the deeper themes, the ending is left conceptually open. Depending on whose side you take, it could be a happy ending, or a terrifying one. Though, one thing remains painfully clear as the bus drives away from everyone's silent, secret sins: that in the depths of the darkness in our hearts, truly, none of us are ever safe.

Rachel L.S. Charman is a Canadian author, director, and YouTuber who has a burning passion for animation, and the dark and macabre. She adores the more serious side of life, and makes it her goal to spread the joy of animation wherever she goes.

2010 • THE TATAMI GALAXY

YOJÔHAN SHINWA TAIKEI

— BRIAN RUH —

In early 2018, director Masaaki Yuasa debuted his new series *Devilman Crybaby* on Netflix, where it quickly garnered a large audience and much discussion online. An adaptation of Go Nagai's *Devilman* manga from the early 1970s, Yuasa managed to capture the sex and violence of the original while adding a surprising amount of pathos. This recognition was heartening because Yuasa has been frequently and unjustifiably overlooked by many English-speaking anime fans for a number of years. One possible reason for this is that few of his films and TV series have a stereotypically "anime" look to them, frequently choosing a more abstracted or angular look. One can only hope that the success of Yuasa's *Devilman* leads to continued reappraisals of his works.

One of Yuasa's earlier series that deserves additional attention is *The Tatami Galaxy*. Although major American anime company FUNimation streamed the show online as it was airing in 2010, it has never received a physical DVD or Blu-ray release in North America (and was only released in the UK in 2016, although it did get a DVD release in Australia in 2011). Although still widely available via online streaming, in the past, representatives from FUNimation have expressed skepticism that a physical release would be profitable for the company.

One issue that would complicate a North American Blu-ray release is due to the popularity of dubbed anime. The vast majority of anime is put out with both the original Japanese-language track (with English subtitles) and an English-language dub. However, when compared to many other anime, *The Tatami Galaxy* would be extraordinarily difficult to dub. Much of the series is told in a first-person perspective with frequent rapid-fire voiceover narration from actor Shintaro

Asanuma. Finding a voice actor capable of pulling off his lightning delivery in English while still capturing the series' deadpan humor would be tricky indeed.

The Tatami Galaxy follows the exploits of an unnamed protagonist as he attempts to discover the life that best suits him while attending a university in Kyoto. The typical view of Japanese universities has been that the period in high school and preparing for entrance exams is the most challenging part of the educational system, and the pressure lessens once someone enters post-secondary education. Although this isn't the case for all students, it certainly seems to be for the protagonist of *The Tatami Galaxy*, who is far more interested in his campus club activities than his academic classes.

He begins by joining the tennis circle in the first episode, thinking it will allow him to relax and find the woman of his dreams. On the contrary, he is unable to make any meaningful connections, save one—another young man named Ozu who drags him (perhaps willingly) over to a dark side of mischief in which they play pranks to annoy and break up couples. The episode ends with a large crowd chasing Ozu in drag on a bridge during the Daimonji festival. After Ozu falls into the river, the crowd turns on the protagonist once they realize he's one of Ozu's friends. As they pick him up and pitch him into the river as well, he wonders what he could've done to make his life turn out differently.

The second episode begins by going back in time to the protagonist's first days on campus, and he chooses to join a different campus circle—one that makes low-budget movies. There are some large differences, but there are also quite a few similarities in his encounters with other people around him. The series keeps on repeating this pattern—the protagonist chooses a different school club (or none at all) and ends up unsatisfied.

The constant repetition of choosing different clubs might lead to a dulled viewing experience, but on the contrary, *The Tatami Galaxy* is very smartly put together. Even though the various timelines generated based on the decisions the protagonist makes have key differences, they share enough characters and events that, as the show goes on, the viewer is able to piece together more of the relationships. Events that may seem a bit odd in one episode may pop up again a few episodes later with additional context. In that regard, the structure of *The Tatami Galaxy* benefits from binge-watching all the episodes close together, rather than spreading them out across eleven weeks, as they would've originally aired.

The ideas of the show cannot all be ascribed to director Yuasa, although he also served as a writer. The series was somewhat unique in that it was based on a novel (rather than a manga or light novel) which was written by Tomihiko Morimi, who also wrote the original work on which the *Eccentric Family* anime was based. Also participating in the creative process was writer Makoto Ueda, whose 2005 film *Summer Time Machine Blues* presages some of the ideas he'd work with in *The Tatami Galaxy*. Also deserving of mention is illustrator Yusuke Nakamura, whose unique designs for the cover of Morimi's novel formed the basis of the characters in Yuasa's adaptation. (Nakamura also illustrates the album covers for the band Asian Kung fu Generation, which performs the opening theme song of the anime, adding an additional connection among the creators.)

In the end, the life lessons of *The Tatami Galaxy* aren't particularly profound. After following the protagonist along his many timelines, the viewer watches him realize that there's not one ultimate road to happiness. Life is not a mystery to be solved. The important thing is to make the most of the decisions you have made and not worry about what might have been. It's not a lesson that's particularly deep or complicated, but it's something many of us need to be reminded of. And the journey getting there in *The Tatami Galaxy* is unique, hilarious, and fantastic.

Brian Ruh is an independent scholar with a PhD in Communication and Culture from Indiana University. He is the author of Stray Dog of Anime: The Films of Mamoru Oshii.

2010 • TRIGUN: BADLANDS RUMBLE

TORAIGAN BADDORANDO RANBURU

— CHRIS STUCKMANN —

We all have our favorite neighborhood movie theater. Maybe yours has crimson fabric draped on the walls and leather recliners designed for optimum relaxation. Maybe the 7.1 Dolby Surround rumbles the floor and the IMAX projector beams pristine images to the screen.

That would've been fun when I was younger. Our neighborhood theater didn't have any of those things. Sometimes my shoes stuck to the floor. On some days, the seats had a popcorn smell caught inside the cushions. If you listened hard enough, you could hear the projector. Better yet, the employees were positive one of the auditoriums was haunted.

My neighborhood theater was Plaza 8 at Chapel Hill. Opening its doors in 1988 as "General Cinema," going there became a staple of my young life. Before a movie began, an intro featuring various concession foods watching a band perform was attached to the print (yes, the "print"). As soon as that jazzy intro played, my anticipation for whatever film I was about to see went through the roof!

Plaza 8 gave me a lot of "firsts." I saw my first film at a theater there, and much later in life—2011 to be exact—I saw my first anime in theaters: *Trigun: Badlands Rumble*. I became aware of the showing due to a poster hanging in the entryway. It listed a "two-night only special event," and, being a huge fan of *Trigun*, this was unmissable.

But what's so special about seeing anime in theaters?

I'm glad you asked. Arriving that night, I expected to walk in, pay for my ticket, sit down, and watch a movie. Instead, standing in the lobby were cosplayers, mingling with fellow fans. It felt great to be surrounded by people who *understood*. Even today, some of my best friends still playfully scoff when I broach the topic of anime. They mean nothing by it, but it brings to mind the earlier days of the fandom as mentioned in my introduction. Chatting with fellow *Trigun* fans and viewing the film with them was a pleasure. They got the humor. The in-jokes. All of it. Watching it at home ... just wouldn't have been the same.

Badlands Rumble finds the indomitably clumsy Vash the Stampede on the trail of Gasback, an obsessive robber who commits crimes not for monetary gain, but for the thrill. Twenty years ago, during one of Gasback's heists, Vash simultaneously saved Gasback from a bullet, while also foiling his robbery attempt. Now in the present, the accident-prone Humanoid Typhoon is on Gasback's heels, secretly ensuring that no one gets hurt.

If you haven't seen the twenty-six episodes *Trigun* has to offer, then you wouldn't know that Vash has a sixty billion double dollar bounty on his head. He's the most fear-inspiring, murderous, depraved, heartless man who's ever lived. Except ... he's never actually killed anyone. In reality, Vash is as innocent as they come. Unluckily, he's inflicted with the John McClane curse: always in the wrong place, at the wrong time. Whenever some disaster sweeps through a city or a bunch of people die at the hands of some psycho, Vash is unfortunately there when the dust clears. So he develops a reputation amongst the people of planet Gunsmoke, one that he doesn't really deserve.

On the contrary, Vash spends most of his time trying to avoid harm to himself, but especially to others. One scene in *Badlands* sees him adorably collecting bullets from the guns of some thugs at a bar. The image of this supposed "murdering psychopath" crouching underneath a table, cradling a massive pile of ammunition is so lovable it hurts. Vash is no doubt charmingly unaware, but *Badlands'* script is shrewd to communicate that his naïve behavior can sometimes cause more problems than it avoids.

Amelia—the tough-as-nails new girl in town—is a woman keeping her past at bay. We uncover the truth in a blistering finale, but for much of the film, Amelia's backstory remains hidden. After Vash helps Gasback escape for the umpteenth time, Amelia loses it, questioning Vash's motives. By saving Gasback—a hardened criminal with a taste for destruction—is Vash really helping? By letting someone like that get away, is Vash in turn endangering the lives of countless others?

A thought-provoking quandary indeed.

Gasback's revenge path leads him to Macca city, where he hopes to fundamentally destroy his former colleagues' lives. They betrayed him on that fateful day when Gasback originally met Vash twenty years ago, and now he's looking to settle the score. A villain-against-villain storyline with our hero caught in the crossfire is one of the reasons I love *Trigun*. Poor Vash. Always where no one wants to be.

As an anime-to-movie transition, *Badlands* is above the fold. It feels like it fits within the established universe—although a little hard confirmation on the exact episode placement would've been nice—and it generates some considerable excitement toward the final minutes. That being said, *Badlands* is a little forgettable, and sometimes feels inconsequential. It's nowhere even close to the quality of *Cowboy Bebop: The Movie*, but instead, it's more akin to something like *Sailor Moon R: The Movie*—likable, easy to digest, and dutiful in maintaining the feel of the source material.

Trigun was never graced with the level of popularity in Japan it achieved here in America—which is probably why the series still isn't on Blu-ray—so it's impressive that *Badlands* was even made. Even if I never get to experience another adventure with Vash, I'm grateful for this one, and Plaza 8 for showing a print that day.

Not long after, Plaza 8 announced they were closing their doors. Hollywood was forcing them to upgrade to digital, and they just couldn't afford it. Soon, the entire building was demolished. My neighborhood theater was gone. But the memories aren't. I've still got those. Seeing *Badlands Rumble* in a theater filled with cosplayers is one of the better ones.

2011 • STEINS;GATE

— TRISTAN GALLANT —

There are two things that generally cause me to gravitate toward any particular anime: the first is time travel, and the second is the promise of a good ending. And I will especially gravitate toward a combination of these two. Time travel anime exist elsewhere, sure, but it's a sub-genre of science fiction that—I feel—is hard to do correctly. Combined, though, with that promise—that hint—of a good, possibly even perfect ending to the overarching story? That turns my idle curiosity into captivated attention.

Now I should mention that it is very rare for me to say that any series, film, or narrative really has a "Perfect Ending." Besides being something that's entirely subjective to the viewer, it's also incredibly difficult if not impossible to fully achieve. So, when I say that something has a perfect ending, I don't want to give off the illusion that it has no flaws whatsoever. What I am getting at is that it's an ending that far makes up for its flaws in various ways.

Steins;Gate is an example of one such ending.

Its main character, self-proclaimed mad scientist Okabe Rintaro, stumbles entirely by accident upon the creation of a device that allows him to send text messages to the past, thus influencing history. The first half of the story is both the discovery of this device and its initial testing, with the second half being the complete reversal of everything to try and return back to his original timeline. Because, as most time travel stories go, when you start messing with the space-time continuum, things can get really messed up in a hurry.

It's a tale about redemption, multiple timelines, and bananas that are regarded by some, specifically me, as one of the best stories, adaptations, and endings that have been released in our ... well, I don't know if medium is the right word, but you get my point.

In my opinion, one of the greatest ingredients *Steins;Gate* has for the recipe of a perfect ending is actually the genre of science fiction itself, and more specifically how it uses time travel to great effect. In a broad sense, the narrative of *Steins;Gate* works perfectly because it has to by design. When you write a tale about time travel, especially one where the same events are revisited multiple times, you need to know where the story is going before you sit down to write its first iteration. Because what a character might do on their second, or even third time during the same event has to be kept in mind and presented as still plausible based on what's shown to the audience the first time through. You can't say that a character went back in time and then burned down a building when you have already shown us that same building standing tall past the point in time when it "burns down." Otherwise, you start getting into paradox territory, which ... is another topic for another book.

Steins;Gate works because its ending is already known and even shown to the audience within its first hour of gameplay—or episode of anime, depending on the version you are enjoying. The location and the "time" of the first few scenes is the same as those at the climax, just from a different point of view. That perspective allows the narrative to come full circle, to end where it began. Despite telling a tale that takes several hours to get through, it exists within a very carefully crafted closed loop that comes with its own innate finality once that loop is fully completed.

It not only has that, but the show brilliantly combines a multitude of different time travel tropes in plausible ways. For example, the show's infamous "D-Mail" (the messages Okabe sends to the past) is just a short form of "DeLorean Mail" in reference to the '80s time travel film series *Back to the Future*. Throughout its narrative, though, we also see alternate realities, personality changes, and even gender-swaps under the right circumstances. We watch Okabe's friends run and get gunned down by shadow organizations, only for Okabe to flip a switch, jump to a new timeline and see it happen all over again but in different ways.

All of that leads to the answer of the ultimate time travel question: how do you change a future you've already seen without making it so that you wish you never changed it in the first place?

If you were to witness an event, and you then dedicated your life to time travel so that you could go back and stop said event from occurring, how would you accomplish this without wiping away the very reason for your desire to travel back in the first place? If you stopped the event, then the "you" in the past would never have seen it, would never have had the motivation or drive to research time travel, and therefore would never have gone back in time to cancel it. Welcome to the paradox that *Steins;Gate* attempts to solve.

Okabe witnesses the death of Makase Kirisu, and then spends the next several weeks in an alternate timeline where he gets to know her as a friend, and perhaps something more than that, only to realize his time travel experiment has gone awry and he needs to return to his original timeline, where unfortunately his new friend is already dead. How can he save her life?

The answer that *Steins;Gate* shows the audience is one they had the puzzle pieces for all the way from the start. They just don't know how it all fits together. That's what makes it brilliant to me, and it's why *Steins;Gate* will be a favorite of mine for many years to come.

Tristan "Arkada" Gallant is a Canadian YouTuber, known for reviewing Japanese animation with his video series Glass Reflection *where he explores and determines the best (and sometimes worst) that anime has to offer, all the while making outlandish expressions and gestures.*

2011 • HOUROU MUSUKO (A.K.A. WANDERING SON)

— THE PEDANTIC ROMANTIC —

"WHAT ARE LITTLE GIRLS MADE OF?"

This is the existential query made by Nitori Shuuichi as *Hourou Musuko* opens, fidgeting under the claustrophobic constraint of her school uniform.

"I asked for a baggy uniform, but it still kind of suffocates me."

Now, I relate to this plight. I, too, was a middle school girl forced into uniforms that were not exactly designed for comfort. And just like Nitori Schuuichi, I, too, was a middle school girl forced into a boy's uniform.

Yes, the most distinctive and defining feature of *Hourou Musuko*, known in the west as *Wandering Son*, is that this is an anime which deals with gender identity. However, perhaps the most remarkable aspect of the series is that it isn't primarily *about* gender identity, not really.

It's more accurate to call *Wandering Son* a study of adolescent social dynamics and to say that sexual and gender identity is a lens it equips to view those through. The anime is about the loose social circle surrounding Nitori and the many complex ripple effects that the various individual struggles of those composing that circle have on the people around them. The brash girl Chii-chan will go to school in a boy's uniform, purely because she likes the style and has no regard for social norms, frustrating her close childhood friend Momoko who just wishes they could seem "normal," while serving as an inspiring figure for Nitori and her own close friend Takatsuki Yoshino, who wants to be a boy. Upon seeing Nitori in feminine clothing, having that sight spark some romantic interest, and then learning about the identity of that pretty girl, a male classmate of hers has to reassess what he previously thought about gender and his own sexuality. Another close friend of Nitori's, Saori Chiba, goes through a universal crisis of messy romantic feelings; only, in this case, those feelings are complicated in part because she doesn't quite know if she loves a boy Nitori or also loves a girl Nitori, or if it's just that boy that she loves. Also, how she can balance supporting Nitori's gender identity while grappling with the personal romantic loss for her accepting that identity would present.

And there could've been no better seamstress to spin this fascinating web of intertwining social connections than the woman in charge of series composition and screenwriting for the anime, Mari Okada. Mari Okada is one of the most high-profile and prolific writers in the industry today, so much so that she actually got to *direct* 2018's *Sayonara no Asa ni Yakusoku no Hana o Kazarō*, which is an almost unheard-of feat for an anime writer. Some directors may write their series or films, sure, but a writer with no previous directorial experience getting to direct a feature film? That's extremely impressive.

Setting aside star power, style is what makes Okada so spectacularly suited to this series. From anime like *Kiznaiver*, to *Nagi-Asu: A Lull In The Sea*, to her breakout smash hit *Anohana: The Flower We Saw That Day*, Okada's defining specialty is in depicting large adolescent casts grappling with oftentimes somewhat convoluted Big Emotions™ to such a degree that, whether you view this as a positive or a negative, many of her anime can be accurately categorized as melodramas.

Series director Ei Aoki is a man whose style possesses a similarly large scale presence, having directed bombastic blockbuster spectacles like *Fate/Zero*, *Aldnoah.Zero*, and *Re:Creators*. This makes him a bit of an odd presence on the series at first glance, a director with a filmography full of action titles and then one, lone, subdued middle school character drama. However, in an interview with Anime News Network, he said:

> "I always loved the original manga by Takako Shimura, so when there was talk that *Wandering Son* might be animated, the president of the studio I

was working with at the time went out and got the rights settled so we could work on it."

His appreciation of the work really shines through in his adaptation of it.

As much as *Wandering Son* is not strictly about gender identity, it does feature very prominently and, with that being the case, I'm thankful that the the the best way to describe the anime's style is "delicate." From its washed-out watercolor aesthetic, content to let the edges of its background art gently fade into an abstract empty whiteness, to the prominence of light piano within the show's soundtrack—a particularly expressive and vulnerable refrain playing underneath that aching opening dialogue—in every aspect of its production this series seeks to be a place of comfort, not judgment, for both its characters and its audience. In being so delicate, it conveys the fragility of those characters; yet, in showing them endure the bumpy roads that threaten to shatter them, and that on occasion will cause some cracks to form, it also conveys the ultimate inner-strength which they possess.

While the series' de facto status as "The Trans Anime/Manga" does to some degree speak to a relative dearth of media covering the subject well, it does also earn that title through how generally well-done its own coverage is. There are some aspects of growing up as a trans person—the first time you get to gleefully watch your reflection twirl around in a skirt, the general suckiness of your period being made all the suckier with its very presence invalidating your identity by falsely insisting "you are not a boy," the sinking terror of someone (who you are not out to) walking in on you wearing feminine clothing—that are extremely specific, personal, and emotional experiences, and to see those portrayed so resonantly on screen is something which has immense value. It can validate by showing there are others like you, comfort by showing things can be okay for you if you go through this, and, in showing some experiences you are unlikely to see presented elsewhere—apprehension over the formation of your Adam's apple, or breasts—it can reveal to you what your identity might actually be, when previously you had no terms with which to describe or even conceive of what exactly you were feeling.

What makes my endearment to this series even stronger, though, is the fact that beyond the personal value it holds, it is also one of anime's greats regardless of your identity. This emotional gravity to these various experiences that will resonate with many trans people is so expertly crafted and conveyed, that every viewer will be able to understand that weight and, as a result, gain insight into this unique life experience.

Storyboarding in particular stands out as something that accomplishes so much toward that end. The framing and blocking employed throughout the series by director Ei Aoki, who storyboarded half of the episodes and served as episode director on the first and last, does a remarkable job of establishing relationships and power dynamics between characters from scene to scene, and helping to visually and almost subconsciously communicate their head-spaces. When Nitori is out in public presenting as female, elements within the frame like shop doorways will wall her in and separate her from the rest of the people walking about, infusing these scenes with a sense of isolated claustrophobia.

I'm so thankful that *Wandering Son* is a piece of media that exists, so thankful that such a strong ambassador of many of my own experiences is out there for others to consume. With so much animosity out there borne by misunderstandings, and so much harm done as a result of that animosity, art like this series, which so effectively conveys many aspects of what it's like to be transgender to a general audience, is something that does legitimate good in the world. The fact that it also happens to be a truly beautiful anime in so many regards just makes me all the prouder.

The Pedantic Romantic has been working as an anime YouTuber full-time since the age of nineteen (not particularly impressive, seeing as she is only twenty at the time of this writing, but still). She possesses a passion for anime analysis, industry research, and humbly asks people to support her work at patreon.com/ thepedanticromantic in equal measure. She thinks anime's pretty great, and you are too.

2012 • JOJO'S BIZARRE ADVENTURE

JOJO NO KIMYŌ NA BŌKEN

— GEOFFREY G. THEW —

To a casual observer, *Jojo's Bizarre Adventure* is just an oddity—a particularly out-there example of that "zany weirdness" Japan is known for. To a new anime or manga fan, it's a strange, off-putting series about burly dudes that's inexplicably referenced everywhere. To a hardcore otaku, it's legendary. One of the most influential manga ever written, second only to *Dragon Ball Z* and *Fist of the North Star*.

Really, it's all of those things, but to me, it represents something a little more personal—and this is going to sound cheesy, but I'm talking about a shōnen anime, so that comes with the territory—*Jojo's Bizarre Adventure*, for me, is all about the power of friendship. Not because of anything within the show or manga itself—although across the series' three-decade run, author Hirohiko Araki has concocted some of the best bromances to ever grace the printed page—but rather because of the way that this series brings people together.

I've made dozens of connections with people around the world—some of whom are among my best friends, and one who now lives with me—simply because of how I've expressed my love for the series. And talking about *Jojo* has also brought me closer to many of my old friends. We discuss the series every chance we get, arrange viewing parties, even plan group cosplays (though the absurd designs of the costumes make them a little difficult to actually reproduce).

People get *passionate* about *Jojo's Bizarre Adventure*. It's the definition of a "love it or hate it" show—not something you can just be a casual fan of. The strange superpowers, absurd humor, countless music references, and surreal visuals either speak to you on a primal level, or they turn you off it altogether. If you like it at all, there's a good chance you love it—and that it's one of your all-time favorite shows.

And the people who love it love it deeply ... they love gushing about the show's coolest fights, quoting memorable lines, and speculating—jokingly or seriously—about what their stands (psychic avatars with powers representing a person's fighting spirit, which are all named after music albums for some reason) would be. These are the kinds of discussions that I used to have with my friends at recess after the latest episode of *Naruto*—except now they're happening between grown-ass men, both in private and on publicly available, professionally-produced podcasts with tens of thousands of listeners.

And nobody thinks it's weird.

Well, OK, everybody thinks it's weird. Bizarre, even. But we all embrace it anyway. Because that's what *Jojo's* is about. Being your own man (or woman), asserting what makes you strong and unique as an individual—and how your individual weirdness clicks and works within your group of friends.

Well, I mean, *Jojo's* is about lots of things. With eight parts spanning wildly varying genres, from a gothic horror story (with burly men) to a Scooby-Doo murder mystery (with burly men) to a prison break thriller (with kickass ladies, and one burly man), the series inevitably touches on many different themes and ideas. And that's a big part of its appeal—if you don't like the style or tone of part one's horror story, you may very well adore the Indiana Jones adventure of part two or the Vernean cross-country horse race of part seven.

In all likelihood, Hirohiko Araki just uses the *Jojo* brand to tell different genres of stories because that's what he happens to be interested in writing at the moment. But regardless of his intent, the format couldn't be better-suited to introducing new fans to the series. Every part brings something new and fresh to the table. Almost none of them require prior series knowledge to be enjoyed. Yet, they all maintain the constants that make *Jojo* great: huge, diverse, quirky casts of heroes. Memorable villains. And crazy, inventive, super-powered battles that take cool, out-there concepts and run with them to their logical conclusions. All brought to life by Araki's bold, uncompromising imagination.

And once you find the part that hooks you, and understand what makes the series so fun, you crave more. Those parts that once bored you because of their genre, now have an iron-tight grip on you because of their place in the series. You need to know everything that happens in the crazy, unpredictable, dimension-spanning saga of the Joestar bloodline. And you need to talk to everyone you know about it, like, right now. And there's a massive community of like-minded people eager to talk back.

But unlike so many other huge fandoms, your love of *Jojo* still feels like it's yours. Because there are so many matters of individual taste involved—your favorite and least-favorite parts, your favorite Jojo. Your favorite villain and stand ... yes, everyone who loves *Jojo* loves *Jojo*. But everyone has a different thing they love most about it. You get to enjoy being part of a massive fan community, but you also get to enjoy the tight-knit, personal feeling of enjoying something obscure and under-appreciated.

I think that combination is what makes *Jojo* fans so enthusiastic and vehement about pushing their favorite franchise—too enthusiastic, sometimes. *Jojo* fans can get a little ... aggressive when they feel the franchise isn't being given its due (like when Crunchyroll didn't give part four's Kira "Best Villain" in their 2017 Anime Awards). But the other side of that is a passion that inspires people to create—to make art, stories, memes, costumes, and fan subtitles so absurdly intricate that they freeze up most computers trying to run them.

There's something beautiful about that—even more beautiful than Araki's psychedelic, mathematically perfect artwork. Even more beautiful than this duwang.

Geoff Thew, or "his divine holiness the anime pope" to his friends, runs Mother's Basement, *a YouTube channel dedicated to the meticulous dissection of small details in anime and other media. He made a name for himself breaking down the editing, cinematography, and hidden references of anime openings in his series "What's in an OP?" But he's best known for his brutal tear-downs of* Sword Art Online, *and for his family's legendary "double shill" technique.*

2012 • PSYCHO-PASS

SAIKO PASU

— VINCENT R. SICILIANO —

"IT IS NOT SOCIETY THAT DETERMINES PEOPLE'S FUTURES. IT IS PEOPLE WHO DETERMINE SOCIETY'S FUTURE." —TSUNEMORI AKANE

Psycho-Pass is a thought-provoking series of tales set in a future where technology goes beyond the role of modern day social surveillance and actually becomes the judge, jury, and executioner. It shows a future willed with good intentions, with innovation and technology as its vessel, and it backhandedly creates a new society based on psychological classism. Emotionally healthy people have the absolute upper hand over those who may be less stable in the eyes of the all-seeing Sibyl system. Appropriately, Shougo Makishima (one of the series' key antagonists) regularly cites Philip K. Dick novels. The referenced author's words, in turn, become a self-fulfilling prophet of dystopia via the antagonist's humanist and almost benevolent sense of anarchism.

Shougo is a masterful villain. A truly diabolical fiend and convincing populist, he offers the prospect of returning to a world where "ordinary things are done in an ordinary way." He's charismatically wrapped in the image of a sensible pariah longing for past liberty and sense of purpose in a society with only vestigial evidence of the once free world. He asks the really tough questions and it's those questions that drive the show's deeply reflective and thought-provoking philosophical inquiries.

He brings the viewer close to his reasoning in his evaluation of the status quo, dominant values of the social infrastructure, and each one of his often contrived— but well-placed—quotes will make you think about the meaning of judgment and the existence of universal ethics in modern society.

Psycho-Pass is full of tragedies, which are often driven by Shougo Makishima committing truly vile atrocities against innocent people. Even more tragic, he is never formally judged for his crimes; rather, the victims of his crimes, including bystanders and other observers, are routinely criminalized or demonized because of their shaken-up psychological state (or "psycho pass"). This statement about modern day victim-blaming—especially when considering the often dismissive view toward mental health issues in society—is a powerful one.

Can technology judge people? Where do we draw the line between privacy, convenience, and safety? Can morality and one's own social utility be extrapolated by an algorithm (or a single entity)? Should the quality of life be decided by an invisible digital force whose process is unknown? Are machines truly unbiased in their decision-making? Would a deferment of major personal decision-making to machines eliminate life's purpose? Or would having that improve the quality of life? It's because of these modern questions—and many more—that this anime about our present relationship with technology and ethics is stunning.

In *Psycho-Pass*, the poles of civilization's moral compass are completely reversed. Victims are the criminals, and the criminals are the heroes. This show has *grit*, and it's completely honest in its message about a dark and chaotic future. Even though this show can be somewhat uncomfortable at times, it does so to ask many of these hard questions, and it does so in a way that sticks.

"THE OPPOSITE OF BOREDOM IS NOT PLEASURE ... BUT EXCITEMENT. PEOPLE WILL GLADLY SEEK OUT ANY KIND OF EXCITEMENT, EVEN PAIN." —SHOUGO MAKISHIMA

Vincent R. Siciliano is a software developer and lover of vintage electronics, especially video games and synthesizers. He enjoys traveling to Japan, biking in the park, and playing all the JRPGs he never got around to as a kid.

2012 • SWORD ART ONLINE

SŌDO ĀTO ONRAIN

— GEOFFREY G. THEW —

Sword Art Online holds a very special place in my heart—a cold, dead part, but special nonetheless. At one point, I genuinely loved the show, but that brief affair ended pretty quickly as the first season fell apart before my eyes and the second season only got worse. But despite my waning affections, the show has given me so much—my first online death threats, for instance, which I received for bashing the *SAO* PS Vita game in a review. As well as, in all likelihood, my most recent online death threat. Which will be true no matter when you happen to be reading this, since my videos about the series draw in at least one every single day.

On that note—it's not an exaggeration to say that *SAO* also gave me my career. I talk about many different anime on my YouTube channel, but of the almost two hundred videos I've created, the six about *SAO* account for 20 percent of my total views, 10 percent of my total subscribers, and almost 163 years of total watch time. I wouldn't be doing what I do for a living—or writing this chapter, for that matter—if it weren't for the success of those videos.

But I've spent more than enough words talking about why I hate *SAO*—and I'm sure I'll spend plenty more in the future. This isn't about that. It's about why I ever liked the show in the first place.

The concept of being transported to and trapped in another world is one of the most prevalent fantasies in anime today, and it's not hard to see why. While on the surface, the thought that you might never see your friends and family ever again is scary, when you think about it, the idea of pressing a reset button on your life and starting over somewhere totally new can be very appealing. All of your debt, regret, baggage, and problems vanish in the blink of an eye, and you're free to build a new life for yourself however you see fit. And because you're trapped, because that's not your decision, you don't have to feel guilty about leaving your old life behind.

The apocalypse has a similar escapist appeal—and the zombie apocalypse gives you the added bonus of being able to bash in the heads of everyone who ever wronged you—but those scenarios are inherently frightening and dangerous. Being trapped in a parallel world has almost all the benefits with none of the risk. And if that parallel world happens to be your favorite video game, hey, all the better. Now you're not starting over from scratch—all of your knowledge of the game changes from wasted time to training.

If you're not happy with your life, the underlying concept of shows like *SAO* is incredibly enticing. And guess who has two thumbs and was absolutely miserable when *SAO* started airing!?

Oh right, you're reading this. Sorry, I'm a little too used to YouTube.

My life was not going great the summer that *SAO* started airing. I was single and jobless without many prospects, stuck living in an increasingly hostile home environment with no way out in sight. So I played a lot of video games. I watched a lot of anime. And every week, as soon as a new episode aired, I was tuning into *SAO*, finding catharsis in the underlying fantasy of Kirito and Asuna's adventures.

It's not the brightest, happiest anime in the world by a long shot. But in its own way that was kind of comforting. Misery, as they say, is best enjoyed in multiplayer. It's helpful, when your life isn't going the way you want it to, to see other people going through similar problems, it keeps you grounded.

And by the same token, it's inspiring to see someone like you overcoming that kind of adversity. It makes you feel like you can do it too. The show was never the best, but it was polished to a point that the flaws weren't too glaring, and it was what I needed at that time.

At least, I thought it was. But oh man, once that polish started to wear off, it came off *fast*. Increasingly ludicrous leaps in logic and the way that Kirito repeatedly pulls solutions to problems out of his black-leather-clad ass gradually wore down the show's believability and narrative tension. Both fairly vital elements in an escapist fantasy about a death game. Kirito stopped being challenged by the world around him, and that world stopped feeling real.

And after that came fairy dance: a poorly told, insubstantial story stretched to the breaking point and packed with tasteless, offensive moments and themes.

SAO isn't the first anime I've seen that makes the mistake of using rape for shock value while simultaneously trying to turn it into a fan-service moment—but it's the first I've seen that was stupid enough to do it twice in three episodes (and again at the climax of the next season because they ran out of ideas). And that's ultimately what broke the show's spell for me—illuminating the problems not just with the last arc, but with the whole show. Making it impossible to enjoy even the parts that I once liked.

That's probably a big part of why I'm so obsessed with *Sword Art Online*. It's hardly the only anime I've watched that's let me down—or even spat in my face for ever liking it in the first place—but it's the only one I've seen make an almost systematic effort to undo every positive thing that it does for its audience. It's the only anime I've watched that I feel left me worse off than when I started it—and that's a hell of a thing to accomplish. I've spent a good chunk of my YouTube career just trying to figure out how they did it—peeling back layers upon layers of bad filmmaking and bad writing to find where it all went wrong.

Partly because I need to know—and partly because that's the most fun that I can get out of the show these days.

Gosh, I guess this turned into another thing about why I hate *SAO* after all.

Geoff Thew, or "his divine holiness the anime pope" to his friends, runs Mother's Basement, a YouTube channel dedicated to the meticulous dissection of small details in anime and other media. He made a name for himself breaking down the editing, cinematography, and hidden references of anime openings in his series "What's in an OP?" But he's best known for his brutal teardowns of Sword Art Online, *and for his family's legendary "double shill" technique.*

2012 • WOLF CHILDREN

ŌKAMI KODOMO NO AME TO YUKI

— DOUG WALKER —

Whether you're a parent or not, everyone can agree raising a child is difficult. When factoring in the energy, patience, and communication barriers, it's not so big a leap to say that it's similar to raising a different species. Well, in the case of *Wolf Children*, they are a different species. Half canine and half human to be exact, not unlike a cuddly werewolf. Where this idea invites an '80s movie poster with a fanged Michael J. Fox holding a baby shrugging next to Steve Guttenberg, *Wolf Children* takes more of a subtle approach. There are laughs here and there—no doubt there must be with such a bizarre premise—but they are similar to how a parent laughs in a hectic household: a combination of exhausted relief mixed with nervous anxiety. This results in a unique, delightful, and refreshingly mature look at the real trials and tribulations of parenthood.

Our main character Hana falls for a tall, dark, and mysterious man. When it's revealed that he is a supernatural entity similar to a werewolf, Hana finds she surprisingly is more intrigued than frightened. She still finds him caring, supportive, and different from any other man she's ever met. Over time she gives birth to two of his children but in a tragic turn of events he dies in an accident, most likely connected to his animal instincts getting the best of him. Hana is left alone to raise two children who are half human and half wolf and can transform between the two depending on their mood. Hana knows she can't raise them in a normal environment without them being taken away from her, so she finds a secluded location in the middle of the forest where their howls and transformations will go unnoticed by others. Gone are her dreams and the bright future she planned for herself; now everything is dedicated to how to raise a species she has little knowledge of.

The two children, named Yuki and Ame, have to be raised under the guise that their mother has all the answers, but not only is she new to raising human children, but she's especially new to raising wolf children, meaning she doesn't know what behavior to encourage and what not. She juggles how much of their animal instinct is worth keeping intact while not resulting in a similar end their father met. Every day is a new discovery and every day she has no idea if she's raising these kids right or forcing them to go against what they naturally are. Any parent will immediately relate to the insecurities, tensions, and confusion of never truly knowing if what you're doing is what's best for your child.

As if this analogy isn't fitting enough, *Wolf Children* focuses on an aspect not often focused on in child-raising movies. In most films the children stay the same, they mature and sound different, but if there is a chipper child, they'll become a chipper teen, if there's a cynical child, they'll become a cynical teen. This film does a complete turnaround with one of the characters that, while sudden, is perfectly executed. Through most of the film, it is assumed who will be the dominant child, but a shift occurs that takes everyone by surprise, frightens them, and again raises questions as to how much stems from the human side or the wolf side. This isn't as simple as a timid child who must find courage and save the day at the end, this is a change that was building up without anyone realizing about it, including the child it happens to. Through a fictional situation, real fears are brought to the forefront, fears of change in a child you don't understand and are afraid to explore.

While the film does journey to these dark and difficult places, *Wolf Children* still centers around a broken family still functioning as a loving unit. There are still fun moments, silly moments, moments you may recognize in your own family. Though not everyone will connect every scene with their own encounters, they will be able to recognize the sincerity and honesty that's seen in families like this one. By placing it in this fantasy scenario, we can identify more easily with the confusion and fears our main characters are going through. This woman and her kids are very easy to like and we want what's best for them, so when something threatens them, whether it be society, aging, or even their own instincts, the turmoil feels real. Nothing about *Wolf Children* feels manipulative or dramatically convenient, it all feels as genuine as a parent and child discovering life experiences for the first time.

Wolf Children sucks you into an environment you didn't know you wanted to be sucked into, and are in a constant state of care for the characters at the center of it. Though you know the characters and situations are false, they feel more real than half of the films that come out about raising a family. The filmmakers treat this story with a level of delicacy and care that most parents would show their family, and both show the same amount of love and dedication. It is a carefully crafted film that, while is not factual, feels true. Somewhere between lighthearted imagination and honest brooding confession lies this wonderful and endearing testament of love. Though its premise might sound childish, the final product couldn't be more adult.

Doug Walker is known for his character, the Nostalgia Critic. His beloved movie reviews can be found on his YouTube page, Channel Awesome.

2013 • ATTACK ON TITAN

SHINGEKI NO KYOJIN

— J.M.G. —

Hijiame Isayama's violent war epic, *Attack on Titan*, is reminiscent of a biblical tale. His hyper-realistic titans echo the classic work of Junji Ito and his page-turning monsters, coming to rest snugly in the uncanny valley. It's body horror taken to an extraordinary extreme and it does what all great fiction accomplishes, making the horrors of the real work palatable. The mess and misery of medieval times; the crass uncertainty of some unknown steampunk past. A class system separating people by real walls, and who is expendable. Along with the ambiguous present comes a just as mysterious lore of monster creation and human isolation, leaving you also wondering if this is all there is. It mirrors the uncertainty and fear of our world, while we stay safe in theirs.

Three is a magic number in this story. Three walls, three military divisions protecting them, and three childhood friends whose synergy drives the story forward. Consider the snowball effect that found Mikasa and Armen fighting alongside Eren. Mikasa and Eren's constant tug of war between who will get to protect the other from harm echoes a deep familial bond that's developed not by their own blood, but by others. How could Mikasa let Eren fight his and humanity's monsters alone? And, as the buffer that keeps their virility from spiraling out of control, how could Armen be left behind? Apart they can be three very abrasive personality types, but together they create the perfect soldier. Cold and calculated, fearless and passionate, and righteous with a love of humanity. As the need for vindication begins with Eren's impressive balancing act on broken ODM gear and ends with his transformation into the very monster he'd been trying to destroy, Mikasa and Armen try to redeem their own inability to keep him safe by laying down their lives for the enemy in front of the entire garrison. With a lack of romantic relationships, this world survives solely on surviving. Everyone must fight, no one is safe, and every person is just as vulnerable as the next. The love in this show is the love of family, humanity, and camaraderie.

While anime is often accused of sexist portrayals of the female form and function, *AOT* and many others serve to accomplish what most western stories fall short of—strong female characters. Disregarding those anime and manga simply created for fetish purposes, creations like attack on titan give us women like Mikasa Ackerman. Mikasa manages to not only provide a maternal source of equilibrium to Eren but to also be the strongest warrior of her generation. A dichotomy that all writers strive to achieve, but that *AOT* really drives home. Mikasa is an extravagant portrayal of a modern woman's personality in an impossible world. And this, all under the wings of Commander Zoe Hange, the androgynous, genius commander of the survey corps. Between the constant and complex up-arch of character development, fast-paced battle scenes, and the triumphant music, you forget you are watching an animated story. This show has given me goosebumps countless times and I attribute most of them to the amazing score. Isayama does well with his characters' names and appearances to ensure that we stay in the gray about the nationalities living within the walls—as characters openly have Asian, European, and mostly heavily German-influenced names. He's giving us all the clues we needed along the way to be unpleasantly surprised to find out that we knew what was going on all along; however, we too were distracted by the titans.

I can't think of an anime that resonated so quickly with the west in the past few years as *AOT* has. We'd been waiting for something new and unique to fill the void that was left as all the anime from our childhood became a Sunday morning cartoon instead of a late night "Toonami" marathon. Although it's shaded in a strange mythology, it accomplishes all of America's Sweetheart—Stephen King's,—"3 types of terror." "The Gross Out" of a body bitten in half at the waist, stylistic blood splattering, "The Horror" of sexless, humanoid zombies, "The Terror" of a tree falling in the distance as it's crushed in their mindless stampede, knowing they'll be upon you soon. This show took the US like the titans took wall Maria, but it's much more than fan-fiction and end caps at Hot Topic. Judging by the lackluster reviews of the Japanese two-part, live-action adaptation, fans only want this story two ways—ink to paper or the technicolor hyperbole of anime and it's moving illustrations. With clichéd tropes that chip away to reveal deep, layered character development and surprising plot twists, *Attack on Titan* is wild, violent, fantastical, and unbelievable—a story that only anime can help tell.

J.M.G. is an avid reader, aspiring writer, and student.

2013 • SILVER SPOON

GIN NO SAJI

— MANIME MATT —

When first being introduced to a new medium of entertainment, the differences between what you expect and what you actually get can be jarring. This is especially true in the medium of anime. Anime is often associated with some negative stereotypes such as overly sexualized female characters, unusual humor, and forced melodrama. So today, let's talk about an unusual sub-genre in anime that's unique to the medium.

The slice-of-life genre is something very foreign to the western market. One of the only prominent western shows that fall into this genre is *Seinfeld*. The slice-of-life genre is almost the complete opposite of the previous works mentioned. Slice-of-life shows are usually slow paced, with little to no drama. It's extremely different from what we've come to expect from our entertainment. Most modern television shows have large stakes—saving the world from white walkers or not getting caught while making meth—but shows in the slice-of-life genre take a different approach.

There are no massive world-changing stakes in these shows, no one's lives are at risk, just people living from one day to another. These shows take the chance to dive purely into the idea of building characters and relationships in a realistic setting. Some shows prefer to do this in places we are already familiar with such as cities, schools, or workplaces. But, some decide to take the setting to places most of us have not experienced. For instance, how about a farm?

Silver Spoon in an anime adaptation from the writer Hiromu Arakawa. She's more famously known as the writer for the *Fullmetal Alchemist* series, which is perhaps one of the most popular and well recognized anime in the community.

Silver Spoon is about a kid named Hachiken. He's from the city and can't handle the pressure put onto him by his family. So, he decides to attend a high school in the country where they train students to become dairy farmers.

I know, not the most appealing log-line, but *Silver Spoon* may be one of the best slice-of-life anime out there. The show really explores life on a farm and some of the hardships one must face in these circumstances. It does have some drama, but it's never forced.

Things starts off pretty simply, with Hachiken starting his life at the new school and blowing most of the students out of the water. We quickly learn that Hachiken has a truly incredible work ethic when it comes to studying. But, unfortunately for him, this is a school where tests are only half the work. Hachiken is quickly forced into working with his hands and handling animals—something he's uncomfortable with. Slowly, Hachiken builds a network of friends who help him out in these situations until he becomes comfortable with that kind of work. He slowly becomes more athletic and learns the value of physical work.

Hachiken—along with his group of friends—are all multi-dimensional characters. The beginning of this show is merely there to set up a foundation between Hachiken and his friends. Afterwards, the show slowly breaks down each of the characters, Hachiken included, revealing their insecurities and developing them over time.

As I stated earlier, Hachiken's work ethic is over-the-top, and that too extends into his work on the farm. This is often seen as a good characteristic to have, but *Silver Spoon* explores what happens when you push yourself too far.

Hachiken ends up taking the brunt of creating a festival for the school and borrows many favors from other students. At first, it seems great because it appears as though everything is going well, but as the students come back to Hachiken and ask for favors, he becomes overwhelmed. Due to Hachiken's work ethic, he decides to power through and deal with it. As he's finishing up the last touches on the day of the festival, Hachiken passes out from overworking himself and is brought to the emergency room.

Hachiken spends the entire length of the festival in the hospital despite how much time he put into it. He ends up only seeing a few sparse photos of the event from friends. It's almost cruel, but this scene is important to Hachiken's development. It's a reminder that Hachiken is only one man and that he can only handle so much. After this point in the show, Hachiken finally learns to say no.

Another character that's incredibly important to talk about is Komaba. He is one of the earlier characters introduced in the show and is originally at odds with Hachiken. Komaba is a local who lived his whole life on a dairy farm. Komaba's arc is pretty simple. His dream is to become a professional baseball player and buy his family's farm out of debt. Komaba ends up being pretty close. He almost single-handedly won his team the regions tournament. Nevertheless, reality ends up hitting Komaba hard.

Right after losing the tournament, the debt collectors come and repossess his family's farm and Komaba is forced into making a difficult choice. Komaba decides to not only quit baseball, but also quit school and start working full-time with the hopes of one day buying back his family's farm. And that is where Komaba's arc ends. There is no real happy ending. Komaba is forced to face these facts and leave the school to begin working as a farmhand on someone else's farm. It's a tragic ending, but realistic. It's nothing the students could've fixed or something that happened because of Komaba's mistakes. It appears to have just been fate. This is what the slice-of-life genre is all about. The simple ups and downs of life.

Later, we see Komaba working, and it's not like his life is ruined. It's just something that has happened and he has to continue moving forward while trying to make the best out of it. I should mention that I am really undercutting a lot of the drama that occurs in these arcs. It's low stakes drama but since the show does such an excellent job at building these characters and their relationships, one can't help but get heavily invested.

The slice-of-life genre is really unusual and mostly unique to the anime medium. Yet, thanks to the low stakes put into these shows, it really allows the writers to heavily focus on different parts of the narrative. That mostly being characters and their relationships, creating a unique experience that can be both calming and extremely addictive.

Manime Matt has been watching anime for about ten years now. He got his degree in the art of moving images and uses it to create video essays on YouTube. He mostly talks about how anime accomplishes specific goals and evokes different emotions from its audience!

2013 • THE WIND RISES

KAZE TACHINU

— JOHN RODRIGUEZ —

Earlier in this book, I had the pleasure to discuss Hayao Miyazaki's first feature film, *The Castle of Cagliostro*, a comic caper elevated by that injection of heart only Mr. Miyazaki can provide. But *The Wind Rises*, Mr. Miyazaki's newest film (to date), is something quite different. It soars not on its action spectacle but on its story of a country coming into its own. And though its focus is in the past, it provides a timely message for today.

The Wind Rises is the fictional biography of Jiro Horikoshi, one of the legends of Japanese aviation. The film introduces mild-mannered Jiro as a boy with dreams of flight. Denied the skies by his nearsightedness, he sets his heart on designing the marvelous aircrafts he envisions in his mind's eye. And indeed, he gets that opportunity years later when he joins Mitsubishi Internal Combustion (soon to become Mitsubishi Aircraft Company).

But there's a problem. While the western world is taking to the skies in airplanes made of metal, Japan's air force is still built on rickety wooden frame planes that must be hauled to chuckhole-infested airstrips by teams of oxen. It's a gargantuan divide in military power that threatens Japan's very sovereignty. Thus, Jiro's pursuit of his dreams becomes a race against the looming threat of foreign occupation.

And the product of Jiro's pursuit? Why, the Mitsubishi A6M Rei-sen, better known as the "Zero." That's right: sweet, soft-spoken Jiro Horikoshi's labor of love opened the door to Pearl Harbor, the single most devastating foreign attack on American soil until the tragedy at the Twin Towers nearly sixty years later.

In many ways, *The Wind Rises* is pure Miyazaki. There's the sweeping vistas. The vivid palette. The familiar character designs. (Baby-faced Jiro almost looks like a longer-haired, bespectacled version of *Cagliostro*'s Lupin if you squint hard enough.) And there's that famous Miyazaki heart infusing every warm smile and shimmering tear. This is Studio Ghibli at its artistic finest, and Mr. Miyazaki at his artistic peak.

And yet *The Wind Rises* feels different from Mr. Miyazaki's previous works, too. It's warm, yes, but it's a melancholy warmth—the kind shared between lifelong friends who sense their time together is ending. In a way, it's like Jiro's wife—afflicted with tuberculosis in this fictional account—layering on rouge to hide her growing pallor. *The Wind Rises*' vistas are almost *too* bright, as if Mr. Miyazaki wants to dazzle you into forgetting that this may be your final dance together.

But if this is the final dance, what a way to go out. And what an interesting life to observe!

Jiro Horikoshi was born in the last days of the Meiji Era (a period covered in *Rurouni Kenshin*, reviewed elsewhere in this book). The Meiji Era was a study in technological contrast. Disenfranchised samurai bared their swords at rifle-wielding policemen. Steam-powered locomotives ran on tracks set alongside rustic homesteads right out of the sixteenth century.

But what really defined the Meiji Era was Japan opening to the western world after centuries of steadfast isolationism. And very quickly after that opening, it became evident that Japan's technological and militaristic capabilities lagged behind the west's. In some people, that might provoke a languid fatalism. In Japan, it sparked a hunger that fueled an industrial revolution. A revolution of which Jiro Horikoshi played a key part.

Mr. Miyazaki's version of Jiro is a man consumed by his goal of fashioning the way people fly. *The Wind Rises* doesn't delve deeply into Jiro's background, yet it's not difficult to imagine young Jiro glimpsing the splendors of western ingenuity and whispering, "I can better that." In many ways, Jiro's life is the perfect intersection of personal ambition and patriotic duty. Jiro wanted the sky. Japan needed the sky. It was a match made in heaven.

Less heavenly is the omission of the real Jiro Horikoshi's opposition to how the Japanese military used his creation, and here, I must take Mr. Miyazaki to task. *The Wind Rises* does yeoman's work chronicling the many failures and false starts on Jiro's path to the Zero, but it never goes on to show how the Zero became one of World War II's most iconic symbols of death. That seems a glaring exclusion given that real-life Jiro wrote passionately about his unhappiness with the attack on Pearl Harbor—an attack that provoked a war which Jiro steadfastly believed Japan couldn't win. Rather than address this messy portion of Jiro's history, *The Wind Rises* ends with Jiro's dream of a sky so thick with Zeroes, they look like flocks of swans. Beautiful, yes, but I would have preferred it if Mr. Miyazaki had allowed us a window into Jiro's perspective once his creation became a tool of war.

Nevertheless, *The Wind Rises* is to be commended on many counts (beyond its given Studio Ghibli beauty, of course). I found the film's exploration of the relationship between Japan and Germany particularly notable. In its eagerness to join the modern age, Japan paid fortunes for access to German technology. This drained Japan's coffers. Banks went belly-up. People ended up starving and homeless because industry lacked the funds to hire them and the government lacked the funds to care for them.

And yet it's undeniable that both Japan and Germany profited from their partnership. We know what evils 1920s Germany would spawn in the next decade, but what Germany did right—and what almost won them World War II—was to engage with Japan at a time when most of the west happily wrote the Japanese off as a backward people unworthy of respect. Yes, Germany's leaders were xenophobic, and yes, they engaged more to fuel militaristic ambitions than out of any sense of brotherhood with the Japanese people. Yet the innovations they shared helped fortify two of the era's finest militaries.

There's a lesson for our modern times here, if you care to look: engagement breeds innovation *and* understanding between disparate peoples. Keep that in mind the next time one of your elected officials turns away foreign refugees or mocks developing nations. Those refugees may be the aerospace engineers of tomorrow, and those nations may be home to thousands upon thousands of vivacious minds just waiting to harness their potential.

As for Mr. Miyazaki, consider his potential fully harnessed. It's his passion project, and the passion shows on the screen. Fitting, then, that it follows such a noted innovator, for Mr. Miyazaki himself has innovated like few other animators before him. Fortunately for us, his legacy won't be one of war but rather one of warmth.

John Rodriguez is a personal trainer whose devotion to physical fitness is exceeded only by his fervor for all things film and literature. John is currently finishing his first novel—a fantasy that's sparked fantasies of a challenging new career.

2014 • WHEN MARNIE WAS THERE

OMOIDE NO MĀNĪ

— CINDY CARATURO —

Studio Ghibli is likely the most famous animation studio in Japan. Those who may be unfamiliar with other anime classics, from *Cowboy Bebop* to *Fullmetal Alchemist*, may still know of at least one Studio Ghibli film. The films that tend to get the most attention are those directed by Hayao Miyazaki, one of the studio's founders. *Kiki's Delivery Service, My Neighbor Totoro, Princess Mononoke, Spirited Away*—these are the films that both anime fans and casual moviegoers likely know best. They're certainly the studio's most famous works. You'd be hard-pressed to find a store in Japan that doesn't carry something with Totoro or Jiji the cat on it.

Isao Takahata, another founder of Studio Ghibli, is also rather well-known, though certainly not as well-known as Miyazaki. I'd argue that *Grave of the Fireflies* is his most famous work, with the rest of his catalog known mostly to those with at least a general interest in the studio. Putting the films of those two directing juggernauts aside, even a large chunk of people who would consider themselves anime fans have seen a sporadic amount of the studio's other work. Case in point: *When Marnie Was There*.

The main character of the film, Anna Sasaki, suffers from asthma and frequently gets attacks. Her mother sends her to the countryside to spend the summer with her aunt and uncle in the hopes of helping her lungs as well as emotionally distant disposition. While there, Anna becomes infatuated with both The Marsh House, a mansion built on a cliff that overlooks a salt marsh, and the young girl who lives there, the titular Marnie.

The biggest difference between *Marnie* and Studio Ghibli's most well-known works is the film's quiet nature. The adventure in this is a small and very personal one. However, the emotional honesty that emanates from *Marnie* is the reason I connected so closely to this movie. In the first scene of the film, Anna is sketching a scene of the playground in front of her. The playground is in the middle of a circular enclosure. She thinks about how the world is separated into those who are in the circle and those who are outside of it. A teacher walks around the area, looking at other sketches. Some girls engage in a lively chat with him as Anna looks on. When he approaches her and asks to see her sketch, she blushes slightly and smiles a little. Just as she is about to hand him her sketchbook, a child falls and gets hurt in the playground area, and the teacher rushes over. Anna's expression fades, and she erupts into a coughing fit. During this, she has a single thought: *I hate myself.* I was floored by how blunt the line was. In the next scene, we learn about her asthma. It's natural to assume, then, that her thought refers to her asthma. But as the movie progresses, you realize the severity of her attitude.

I remember seeing *Marnie* in theaters twice: once at the New York Children's International Film Festival in 2015, and the other in theaters in late spring during that same year. At that time, I had graduated from college the year before and was still struggling to get my foot in the door anywhere. I was working at my friend's father's architecture firm, answering phones and doing other clerical work. He had initially asked me to help him write some things for the firm's website, a task more in line with my degree. What I thought would be a quick freelance gig transformed into more of a full-time secretarial position, and my initial writing assignment was placed in limbo. I had been working there for a number of months by the time I first saw *Marnie*. The view that I had of myself was troubling. At this stage, I lost belief that I'd achieve much of anything. I regularly thought of all the time I had wasted in college, either not doing something more productive with my time, or that I had chosen the wrong degree. My self-worth hadn't improved much from my time in junior high school. Instead, those feelings evolved from hate of my present ... to hate of my future.

There's a portion of the film when Anna goes to celebrate the Tanabata Festival in town with the other children. She's wearing a *yukata* (summer kimono), one her aunt thinks she'll look good in, though Anna herself believes she won't look good in it at all. During Tanabata, you write a wish on a piece of paper and hang it up. One of the girls grabs Anna's paper and reads her wish: "To live a normal life every day." She also remarks on Anna's appearance. Embarrassed, Anna yells at her, and the two get into a small fight. While the other girl says that they should just forget about it and move on, Anna runs away, heading toward the salt marsh. Overwrought with emotion, Anna stands on the shore, thinking about the girl's words: "After all, you look like just what you are." "Like just what I am ... ugly, stupid, moody, unpleasant ... that's why I hate myself."

I was completely taken aback by this scene. Not only were these sentiments I had never seen in a Studio Ghibli film before, but they were also feelings that still lingered within me. I remember trying to hold back my tears the first time I viewed the film, but when I saw this scene for the second time, I flat-out started crying as quietly as I could. Even after watching the movie again for this chapter, I cried. It was as if someone had taken note of the hate that I had toward myself over the years and put it into film. I thought of all the things I hated about myself: my face, my body, my moody disposition, my disconnectedness from others around me, my lack of intelligence or skill; seemingly everything I hated about myself, all at once. It was overwhelmingly painful. I'm crying all over again as I write this.

It's hard to recall how many singular moments in a story have hit me straight in the heart like this one has. It's this honesty that makes *When Marnie Was There* so precious to me. It's a children's film that isn't afraid to tackle emotions that older children may eventually come to face. There's no lack of sincerely emotional moments when it comes to Studio Ghibli's films, but *Marnie* places itself extremely close to today's real world; it doesn't take place in a fantasy setting like *Kiki*, nor is it a more historical piece like *Grave of the Fireflies* or *The Wind Rises*. That, coupled with its quiet atmosphere, is what gives the film so much power. It's the way the film allows Anna to both have and express those genuine feelings that make *When Marnie Was There* not only an important entry in Studio Ghibli's catalog, but in the animation catalog as a whole.

I don't know if I'll move past the negative feelings I have toward myself one day. But, there's nothing more powerful than knowing someone else in the world understands the way you feel. For me, that's exactly what *When Marnie Was There* provides.

Cindy Caraturo has been living and working in Japan since 2016. In her spare time, she writes and edits for the Japanese culture site Yatta-Tachi. She aspires to be both a translator and novelist, while simultaneously wondering if she's trying to wear a few too many hats.

2015 •
CONCRETE REVOLUTIO

KONKURĪTO REBORUTIO: CHŌJIN GENSŌ

— MATTHEW CARATURO —

History is extremely important because not only does it allow us to understand how things once were and how things came to be, but also how we can learn from past mistakes. *Concrete Revolutio* is a series that really uses history to its full advantage. What is right? What is wrong? Are those moral questions ever so easy to figure out?

The series takes place in an alternate version of 1940s to 1970s Japan, where all these tropes within fiction exist in real life: *kaijū* (monsters), *mahou shoujo* (magical girl), androids, etc. The show in particular focuses on Jiro who's in the Superhuman Bureau, a group that basically tries to protect superhumans and keep them in check from causing any trouble. This is especially important in *Concrete Revolutio*'s society where superhumans don't really receive any respect. They are ignored, they are abandoned, and overall just not treated well by their government and their society.

Jiro, in particular, protects them through kaijū powers he received at birth that allow flames to emit from his left arm. The show consistently uses time skips during each episode, as if jumping between multiple timelines to form one thematically coherent narrative between all of them. Many times, it is to follow a specific character within the show and their own moral struggles. Other times, it's to showcase the differences between each time period, or lack thereof.

One of my favorite episodes that does this is from the second season, titled "Iron Mask Has Arrived." In particular for its use of "past versus present" and how people's perceptions of history may be different than from what actually happened. It focuses on a girl named Koma, who lived during the 1600s and falls in love with this Dragon God named Asahi, an enemy on the battlefield. Asahi ends up sealing himself away to defeat his leader, Zess Satan, believing that if he was sealed by this greater evil, it would finally force Koma to face him in battle. Koma ends up running away from this conflict to a bitter and cold environment; she becomes frozen in time. Three hundred years later, the Japanese government finds her and unfreezes her to do their bidding. They order her to find Jiro, who has gone rogue, and put a stop to him. Koma, waking up in this new era, does listen to their orders, but she also has her own goal in mind: find those artifacts of Asahi and destroy them. She wants to, essentially, destroy a part of her past that she's ashamed of.

When Jiro and Koma finally meet up, what's interesting isn't really the differing ideologies between the two time periods, but rather the different perspectives on this past time period that Koma is from. Jiro firmly believes that it was a lot easier to tell right from wrong in Koma's time period, and that she belongs back there. Koma, on the other hand, was frozen in time, thus, to her, three hundred years ago feels like a few days ago. When many people look back on past events, they'll use the phrase, "simpler times," but Koma knows for a fact that this belief of "simpler times" just outright isn't true. If she were to return home, she would just be forced to face a bunch of different battles. It's similar to one being given the opportunity to travel back in time. Sure, one might be able to relive some good memories, but one would also have to relive all the worst parts, too.

This idea of trying to destroy one's past and trying to destroy one's past self comes up a lot within the show. Sometimes in more literal forms, such as an episode in which Hyoma—a member of the Superhuman Bureau who has the power to manipulate time—faces off against other versions of himself from other time periods. Other times, it shows up in more metaphorical terms, like in the episode where Raito Shiba, a cyborg detective, meets an alien named Washu, who shares a lot of his old ideological beliefs. The episodes that focus on this theme tend to end the same exact way.

Hyoma, Raito Shiba, and even Koma all face the setting sun. With this, they are taught a lesson: they cannot destroy the past. They can try to by killing whatever is causing them grief, but even then history itself does not disappear; all of those events still happened. They can also try running away, but they will just end up being forced to face that past eventually. The versions of Hyoma's past self aren't going to just disappear on their own. Raito can try to bury away the shame of his old ideas, but other people still may have those same thoughts, and he'll have to end up facing this shame he's buried. Koma tried to run away from her past and all that ended up leading to was more wars even after Zess Satan was defeated. All that these characters can truly do is move forward and learn from their past mistakes. Isn't that why one is taught history in the first place? So that tragedies aren't repeated?

The sad reality, though, is that history is consistently repeated within the show. The big climax of Season One is the Shinjuku Riots, in which a bunch of superhumans start rebelling at Shinjuku Station, and it leads to Jiro leaving the Superhuman Bureau. One may think, after that, the show would get really explosive and there'd be this huge war waged against the superhumans, the Bureau, Jiro's faction, and the government. None of that, however, really happens right away.

In terms of format, Season Two is quite similar to Season One. There are small episodic conflicts with a big climax near the end. This is deliberate. By having things formatted in a very similar fashion between both seasons, it adheres to the idea that, in spite of this huge conflict happening, nothing has really changed. What else can one do, then, to make sure this past is not repeated outside of remembering it?

Another thing *Concrete Revolutio* suggests is to become a hero for other people and to lead through example. This is shown many different times within the show, the big one being Rainbow Knight, a masked superhero that Jiro looked up to as a kid. Jiro considers Rainbow Knight a superhuman for the fantastic things he was able to accomplish but, at the same time, in spite of Jiro's own powers, he cannot consider himself a superhuman, believing that nothing he does is extraordinary enough to live up to that name. This changes by the end, however, when he faces off against Satomi, who wants to rid the world of superhumans by changing them into industrial energy. In other words, he wants to take that which is extraordinary and make it mundane. Through this battle, Jiro realizes that what he's facing against right now is no different than the conflicts that other superhumans faced. Satomi is the evil that, Jiro, a superhuman, must defeat. This act of heroism becomes adapted into comics and TV shows, and with that, Jiro's words are able to influence others. It's no different from how we look at fictional heroes for inspiration.

History may end up repeating itself quite often, but *Concrete Revolutio* gives us ways that it can be stopped. One major way is to not forget the past and not try to hide it; to acknowledge one's past faults and to not repeat them. Another way is to influence others through one's own actions. The search for right and wrong may never be easy to solve, but maybe, just maybe, if these ideas are taken to heart, things can continue to improve.

Matthew Caraturo is a former animation student at the School of Visual Arts. He now runs a YouTube channel on anime called RogerSmith2004, and occasionally writes for an anime satire site called Anime Maru.

2015 • MY LOVE STORY!!

ORE MONOGATARI!!

— CINDY CARATURO —

If you were to ask a wide variety of anime fans their thoughts on *My Love Story!!*, they'd likely give you one of two answers: "That's a cute show" or "Never seen it." Airing in the spring of 2015, it's very much a show that quietly came and went. I doubt very many people would consider it a modern classic. And yet, I can say that, without a doubt, *My Love Story!!* has completely changed my life.

So, what is *My Love Story!!*? The anime centers on Takeo, a bulky guy who lacks the standard good-looking features of most male anime and manga characters. Still, his heart is solid gold, and he's always looking out for others. Every time he falls in love with a girl, they end up liking his best friend Sunakawa. Unlike Takeo, he's considered handsome by practically everyone. However, when Takeo saves a young woman from a groper on the train, his love life finally begins. I know that doesn't necessarily sound like the start of a cute story, but I promise you, it is.

My "story" with this show is one of those "watched it at just the right time" kind of tales. You see, I was experiencing my own "love story." Like Takeo, I had found my first love. I know that sounds kind of cheesy, but that's what happened. Unlike Takeo, though, he didn't save me from any unpleasant sexual encounters on public transport. In a more modern fashion, we met on the Internet, in an Internet radio chat room, no less! Yes, I was worried that he was a total creep. I'm happy to report that, thankfully, he and Takeo share many qualities, and not being a crazy Internet pervert is one of them. To be honest, when I first learned about the show and saw how similar Takeo was to him, I couldn't help but want to watch it. If I was going to relate to any romance story, surely this would be it, right? I convinced him to watch the show, too, figuring it would give us something fun to talk about. The result was an absolute torrent of conflicting emotions.

Throughout the show, Takeo and Rinko, the girl he falls for, come across different issues regarding their relationship together. Because of this, I was reminded of the issues that were part of my own relationship. In one episode, Takeo is worried because Rinko seems to be hiding something from him. When Sunakawa and his older sister ask her about it, Rinko confesses that she wants to be more intimate with Takeo, but worries that he'll see her as impure since he's mentioned her pure nature a few times before. I wouldn't say my worries were exactly the same; Rinko mentions wanting to hold hands, cuddle, and maybe kiss Takeo. Still, I couldn't help but relate to the general sentiment. I often worried that saying or doing certain things would make my boyfriend think certain things about me. Even though nowadays women are more easily able to express themselves when it comes to things like sex and relationships, that doesn't mean people will always refer to those women in a kind matter. Heck, people will say certain things about women or refer to them by certain names even when there's no context for anything sexual.

I remember being upset after watching this episode because of my own fears. When we discussed the episode and my feelings around it, my boyfriend tried reassuring me: just because we might become closer and more intimate, that doesn't mean he'll suddenly think of me differently or call me any hurtful names. I was happy that we could talk about something like that. I guess it seems silly for me to worry, much like it would seem silly to the audience that Rinko would worry about Takeo thinking she was impure just because she wanted to hold hands. But, when it's your first relationship, it's hard to know how the other person will behave in a whole host of scenarios, especially if you didn't know them for that long before the relationship began. I think that's why I took the issues Takeo and Rinko face in the show so seriously. Since they start dating soon after meeting, they learn more about one another as their romantic relationship grows. It was the same for my boyfriend and me.

I think one of the biggest strengths of *My Love Story!!* as a whole is its use of reflection. Anime is known for its off-the-wall comedy, and this show certainly has its own brand of zany comedic flair. Anime, like live-action TV shows or movies, can also be extremely dramatic, particularly when it comes to romance stories. *My Love Story!!*, while having dramatic elements, never becomes bogged down by melodrama. Despite the—at times—superhuman nature of its main character, the show stays situated within a relatively realistic framework. Takeo and Rinko run into certain questions and concerns, but it's never something extremely trivial, nor is it ever anything beyond serious. That's what makes their "love story" relatable. I found myself being able to easily understand where both characters were coming from.

This goes for other characters that come across their own troubles about life and love as well. That's probably why the show hit me as hard as it did. It didn't give me pause at any point to think, *Well, now this is just ridiculous. Why did it have to fall into this stupid cliché?* The show handles the questions and themes it brings up very thoughtfully, and its sincerity both touched me and caused me to reflect on my own budding relationship.

Even if I hadn't just started dating someone when I watched *My Love Story!!*, I'd probably still have enjoyed it. I loved the characters and their eccentricities, as well as a number of little animation and art design details. It's exemplary of what animation in general is capable of: telling even an everyday love story between a boy and a girl. I think when people think about anime, a very particular image comes to mind. I have no doubts that *My Love Story!!* would knock that image on its head. I'm thankful that I watched it when I did. Though I don't necessarily look to media to determine my values or life perspectives, I'm glad this show acted as a kind of guide while I figured my feelings out during the early months of my first relationship. To all the Takeos out there: never change.

Cindy Caraturo has been living and working in Japan since 2016. In her spare time, she writes and edits for the Japanese culture site Yatta-Tachi. She aspires to be both a translator and novelist, while simultaneously wondering if she's trying to wear a few too many hats.

2015 • ONE PUNCH MAN

WANPANMAN

— CHRIS STUCKMANN —

One of the most universally popular anime genres is the fighting anime. Titles like *Naruto* and *Dragon Ball Z* are familiar even to those who aren't well-versed. Often, these shows are lovingly mocked. *DBZ* is known for endless power-ups, decibel-shattering screams, and planet-demolishing explosions. It was only a matter of time before a show came along that loved the genre while understanding what makes it hilarious.

One Punch Man follows Saitama, a regular guy who's a hero just for fun. He lives in an alternate reality where monsters, demons, and aliens constantly plague his city. Their frequent attacks are opposed by an organization called The Hero Association, which is comprised of various tiers of superheroes. The lower-ranked heroes are shuffled into Class C and often looked down upon by the celebrity heroes of Class S. When Saitama learns of The Hero Association, he joins simply because no one knows who he is. Soon enough, he becomes heralded as the hero who defeats his enemies with a single punch.

When it comes to action films, I've stated that one of the most important characteristics of your hero is that they're vulnerable in some capacity. Protagonists like Indiana Jones or John McClane reflect this trait wonderfully. The hero should feel fallible in some way, relatable. *One Punch Man* goes directly against this notion. It presents Saitama as a ridiculously overpowered hero with the ability to obliterate someone with little more than a slap. So why does he work so well? Where does the tension come from?

The answer is simple. It lies in the fact that Saitama is just a regular guy. In the first couple episodes, we learn that Saitama was fed up with the constant invasions and loss of life surrounding his city. After a face-off with a monster that left him rattled yet empowered, he decided he'd train as hard as he could every single day, and that's exactly what he did. In fact, he trained so hard that his hair fell out. Soon enough, he tapped into a bottomless pit of strength that defies all notion of believability. The series wisely plays most of this for comedy, but the underlying message is that anyone can be a hero, no matter your background. If you work hard enough, you can do anything.

Saitama thirsts for a worthy opponent and his thirst is never fully quenched. The look of disappointment on his face after annihilating a monster in one strike is priceless. All he wants is a good fight! Combine this comical teardown of hero-worship with Saitama's innate humanity and you've got yourself a delicious subversion of the genre's common tropes. It's really rather ingenious.

The show is considerably more playful than I initially expected. Saitama's character design often changes based on his disposition. Most times, he has a blissfully ignorant expression on his face, as if he's truly oblivious to the perils of the society he lives in. He wanders around the city looking for a great sale at local supermarkets, hoping to find a good deal on groceries. There could be a life-or-death battle going on a few blocks away with some other heroes, but if Saitama can't find his coupon for the supermarket, that takes precedence. In the heat of battle, however, Saitama's countenance becomes epically heroic, something akin to Tien from *DBZ*.

This is all played for hilarity, of course. Saitama will be delivering a noble speech about heroism and strength, but in the end, he comes off even sillier than his costume. It's one of the most endearing things about him. Like the best superheroes, Saitama is just a normal guy endowed with fantastic abilities. But where he differs from characters like Spider-Man is in how he fell into these powers: not by happenstance but through hard work and training.

One of my favorite characters in the show is Genos, a powerful cyborg who begs Saitama to teach him the mystery of his strength. This creates a dilemma for Saitama, who genuinely seems to have no real secret to his insurmountable power. Genos will beg for guidance and we'll hear Saitama's inner thoughts as he scrambles for some advice that sounds legitimate enough to keep Genos at bay for a while. Once the two begin rooming together, Genos often rushes to jot down instructions that Saitama rattles off in ignorance.

By all accounts, Genos is the unsung hero of the show. He knows the rank of each Hero Association member by heart, along with all their abilities and file information. But his dedication to becoming stronger isn't simply because he's a cyborg—it's a reflection of his compassion for humanity and his altruistic desire to protect them. In one of the six OVAs, Genos stalks Saitama, desperately trying to learn the secret to his power. He even goes as far as analyzing a French fry Saitama hoped to eat. This is why he's such a terrific foil for Saitama. In many ways, they're after the same goal, yet they have vastly different approaches to obtaining it.

Most fighting anime use a similar structure for building tension in battle. There's an unbeatable villain terrorizing the city/world/village and the supporting characters must fend off the villain just long enough for the hero to arrive. During *DBZ*'s Namek arc, for example, Vegeta and friends have to fend off the evil Ginyu Force as they anticipate Goku's arrival. Once he appears, he's almost immediately taken out of commission again and his friends challenge Frieza until Goku's well enough to fight. *One Punch Man* is all too aware of this common plot device and often parodies it by having a minor character like Mumen Rider throw himself into battle with a powerful villain. We know Saitama is on his way, we know he's going to win, but nevertheless, the anticipation is still palpable. That, in a nutshell, is the beauty of *One Punch Man*. It's keenly aware of its genre's clichés yet embraces them nonetheless.

2015 • SOUND! EUPHONIUM

HIBIKE! YŪFONIAMU

— THE PEDANTIC ROMANTIC —

Did you ever play in your school's band? Odd question, I know, but hear me out.

If yes, go watch *Sound! Euphonium* right now (or like, go look up one of the concert scenes on YouTube because then you'll immediately go watch it right now).

All right, that one was easy ... now onto convincing everyone else why they should watch this anime about cute girls in a high school band.

For starters, if (as someone interested in anime) you've got any passion for or interest in the art of animation itself *Sound!* is a must-watch. Its production was courtesy of the truly inimitable Kyoto Animation and it is fair to say that the series, its second season in particular, is a TV anime production with anime film production values (outside of those of Kyoto Animation's films of course, which have God creating the universe production values). The studio has achieved what nearly everyone else in the industry is currently aspiring to posses: the infrastructure to handle every facet of anime production, from the drawing of the animation itself, to the background art, to the CGI and other graphic effects entirely in-house, without having to outsource any of that work, which allows for a much greater deal of efficiency and unity of creative vision.

Strong storyboarding is something I deeply value in anime, it's a recurring feature among my favorites because, for a medium that since *Astro Boy* has been produced around an economy of motion, making your inevitable still (and basically still) frames visually engaging, something that communicates to us information about the characters or the anime's themes, is of the utmost importance. Unless you're

Kyoto Animation, in which case you get to break every rule and have constant expressive motion in your series because you're just that good.

Now, to be clear, the storyboarding for *Sound!* is pretty fantastic in its own right. The director of the series, Tatsuya Ishihara, also helmed *The Disappearance of Haruhi Suzumiya*, a film fairly renowned within the anime community for its masterful control of atmosphere and tone through that directing. The first episode of *Sound!* alone had a shot that I was mulling over for a whole week. However, as is typical for Kyoto Animation anime, the spotlight is stolen by the character animation. The studio's workflow is so efficient and their staff so talented, that there's meaningful "character acting," as this kind of animation is generally referred to, in almost every scene.

In many anime, the animation resources are stretched so thinly that the bit of flashy animation they'll have will be saved for *the* flashy action scene or *the* big dramatic emotional moment scene. In *Sound!* there are more frequent, more impressive "big" moments of animation than all but the industry's best ... and they're able to animate nuanced subtle acting and body language seemingly whenever they want outside of such scenes. Moments as simple as a character dropping into a train seat, exhausted after that day's practice, will have great fluid and weight animation of her legs falling to the floor, bouncing lightly as they splay out and come to a rest; or, even more benign, a simple regular conversation between friends riding into school will have one of them lazily swinging back and forth on the hand-hold strap, again, with a degree of fluidity and general technical excellence that most anime would love to be able to have *ever*. That was a great little moment of characterization, further enforcing that character's looser, more playful and carefree nature. You'll easily fall in love with so many of the series' characters and be easily taken in by their emotional struggles because they end up feeling so well-realized and genuine.

And *that* is where the animation appeal crosses over into relevancy to those more interested in character or narrative. Through instances like those scenes in the train, nearly ever-present throughout the series, *Sound!* has a HUGE leg up over the competition in characterizing its cast. So much about people can be communicated through body language and subtle facial expressions, and that communication can be done much more subtly when an anime is able to show it instead of having to simply tell it. The characters in this series feel so multi-faceted, so complex and human, in part because of fantastic writing, for certain; some of anime's most memorable lines of dialogue for me come from this anime, but also because the viewer can take in so much information about them before that writing even comes into play.

Recognizing this strong point, *Sound!* is a series where character drives story and, as such, the narrative is fantastic as well. Everything centers around Oumae Kumiko and her struggles with being insincere to both those around her and herself. Then, as the anime moves into Season Two with that self-deception having been largely overcome, her having to grapple with those newly-freed issues whose existence she'd been denying and repressing over the course of Season One. Insincerity, deception, and partial truths are prominent features throughout the series among many of its characters. And, of course, that subtle character animation is so valuable in giving us insight into these characters—behind the masks they attempt to hide behind, with small hesitations and expressions giving hints as to what their true thoughts may be—and creating an engaging mystery for the audience to attempt to unravel.

You might think this all sounds a bit extreme for a high school band, but as a four-year high school band member I can assure you that "band politics" is *serious* business. I only had to observe the reactions to the series from fellow band geeks to see that in this regard it definitely hit the mark. In general, it really nails the band experience, to an almost scary degree and—biased though I may be in this judgment—I think band is really cool, so it's a great insight into this little world for those who didn't experience it. In band, each instrument has an entire character or archetype of sorts that will stereotypically describe those that play them, and they tend to be pretty darn accurate. Flutists are kind of divas, trumpets, a bit brash and irreverent, and so my jaw legitimately dropped when a performance was jeopardized by a percussion player forgetting one of their mallets. Not only was the exact stereotype of percussion players one of goofy airheadedness, but *I'd experienced percussion players forgetting some piece of equipment myself during my own band years.* The understanding of bands and how they work is simply uncanny.

That faithfulness is also present in what is certainly an integral aspect of the series—the music itself. This is a high school band ... the composer couldn't just write the show's score, bring in the recording orchestra, have them play the material, and head on home. In order to give an authentic high school sound there are intentional mistakes, which can be outright bad at the beginning of the series, but as it goes on and the group becomes a competition contender things get far, far subtler. There will be an entrance that's just half a beat late, a long note that goes slightly flat at the end, an entrance from the brass that blasts a bit too hard—OH NO THE NIGHTTIME PRACTICES ARE ALL FLASHING BACK TO ME I'M SORRY MISS PRIOR! Even acoustics are accounted for, with outdoor playing reverberating as it should when compared to instruments played inside, and the pieces themselves are fantastic ... everything there is to love about concert band music, a youthful reverie in making beautiful (or not so beautiful, my band's got a few performances on YouTube) sounds.

I promise though, the bounds of *Sound! Euphonium*'s appeal lie far beyond just those that were band members or have played instruments. Through its remarkably nuanced character work, it's one of the best coming-of-age stories in a medium obsessed with telling coming-of-age stories and has some of the most striking, breathtakingly beautiful scenes anime can offer. I know multiple people closely for whom the series was a pivotal moment of self-discovery, so if your heart has ever cried out "I want to improve!" give this one a watch.

The Pedantic Romantic has been working as an anime YouTuber full-time since the age of nineteen (not particularly impressive, seeing as she is only twenty at the time of this writing, but still). She possesses a passion for anime analysis, industry research, and humbly asks people to support her work at patreon.com/ thepedanticromantic in equal measure. She thinks anime's pretty great, and you are too.

2015 • THE BOY AND THE BEAST

BAKEMONO NO KO

— ADELLE DROVER —

Mamoru Hosoda's fantastical animation *The Boy and the Beast* is an unlikely partnering of a human boy and a magical bear creature, two races, across two worlds uniting together against the odds. Their individual journey of self-discovery is complicated and testing, spanning the story's length of seven years. However, when the moment comes to finally choose between ego or family, neither hero hesitates to choose the selfless path. Themes of belonging, learning, and inner-strength delve deep into the human psyche and take their time to ponder and explore over the film's duration; expositional at times but their message is nonetheless crystal clear. On the surface, *The Boy and the Beast* is a fantastical coming-of-age adventure, but strong undertones filled with teachable lessons are the truly remarkable takeaway of this tale.

Ren is just nine years old when his mother passes away suddenly, and, with his father no longer in the picture, Ren's fate is left to the whims of his extended family. In a fit of rage and grief he runs away through the bustling streets of Tokyo, lost and alone amongst the thronging crowds. The only person to stop and notice him is not a person at all but a snarling bear. This bear invites Ren to join him. Ren, with nothing left to lose, follows his intuition into a medieval world of beasts and animal monsters. Despite protests of humans entering their concealed realm, Ren is allowed to stay under the guardianship of the bear named Kumatetsu.

Humor and charm comes from the unlikely pairing of Kumatetsu and his new apprentice Ren, nicknamed in the beast world as Kyuta. Scenes involving Ren secretly mimicking Kumatetsu's footsteps in order to learn his fighting skills are juvenile and sincere. A child wants to be like his parent and a parent in turn wants nothing more than to impart wisdom in return. Despite a growing companionship, the pair continually butt heads. Kumatetsu berates his apprentice for being slow and naïve while Ren remains mystified that such a great warrior lives so slovenly and without a sense of duty or pride. Their brimming egos and "lone wolf" arrogance would make them incompatible roommates, but at their core they are undeniably similar. This recognition is what binds them together. As the years go by, Ren matures into an adult and both their self-centered natures gradually soften. Ren becomes a warrior in his own right and finds his true challenge is still yet to come.

The true theme of *The Boy and the Beast* is of Ren's yearning to belong. Abandoned as a child and thrust into a foreign world of talking animals means his life is far from "normal," though that is his deepest desire. Ren is a human in a world of monsters, his presence is only tolerated because Kumatetsu vouches for him. His heart still searches for true belonging. Having a foot in both worlds means having a foot in neither.

The Boy and the Beast is a blending of worlds—the real world with a parallel monster world. Both worlds exist to Ren and hold different possibilities for his future. While Kumatetsu stubbornly demands he forget his human life, he cannot. The two worlds also represent the old and the new. The traditional simplicity of the animal realm where a warrior is celebrated with the right to become a grand master and reincarnate into whatever they wish. The feel of this world is like a European town with busy marketplaces and cobblestone alleyways. All this is harshly transitioned against the modern concrete jungle of Tokyo, in this world Ren has the possibility to go to school and start building connections with friends and his estranged father. Things might be more unknown, but this is Ren's path to choose.

Ren is a complex character and the film does not shy away from his flaws. He is stubborn and self-centered just like his master Kumatetsu, but his strict training as a warrior is what focuses his direction. It gives him purpose and strength. For Ren, it is many years later when he returns to the human world by accident that his true test is revealed. He is overcome with misplaced anger and self-pity at having missed out on a regular childhood. With the help of Kaede, a studious high school girl whom he meets, he develops a new training regime. This time he will become a normal everyday teenager. He has ambitions to improve his reading and writing and to someday study at a university. Ren continues traveling back and forth from the real world to the monster world but fails to communicate his new feelings to his master and surrogate father Kumatetsu. As with most rebellious teenagers, he feels isolated and unloved without seeing the true value of those around him.

Kumatetsu is likewise deeply flawed. He wears his heart on his sleeve, without composure or apology. When he first returns to the animal realm and officially names his new apprentice, his peers—along with his arch rival, Iouzen—are not impressed. They are well aware of his childish temper and rash decisions and they feel the dangers of welcoming a human into their world—but Kumatetsu will not yield. When a fight breaks out in the streets between these two great rivals, the crowds of animal onlookers cheer only for the dignified boar-warrior, Iouzen. Kumatetsu is alone and unsupported by the people. This is not a feeling unknown to him, as the story later reveals that Kumatetsu is a self-taught warrior and never had a master to teach and care for him.

Ren and Kumatetsu are two unlikely companions who eventually come to deeply respect and learn from each other in ways not even they first anticipated. The first time Kumatetsu attempts to teach his new apprentice how to be a warrior, he simply instructs Ren to grab the sword within his heart. Naturally this means nothing to young Ren and he struggles hopelessly with the metaphor—causing Kumatetsu frustration. At first, neither have the courage to admit their methods aren't working which results in a lot more bickering. After many years of living and training together they finally come to understand how deeply their fates are intertwined. Both Ren and Kumatetsu must fully embrace their own flaws and start to listen to each other with patience and respect. They let go of their fears of abandonment, uniting together to overcome a darker enemy.

The detailed world-building of the animal realm and a layering of themes and lessons all make for an enthralling fantasy film. Ren's journey to adulthood and coming into his own strength and confidence are not simple lessons to learn and, as such, the film follows several threads of conflict throughout the third act. Ren returns to the human world where he discovers a new desire to study and seek out his real father. He still wrestles with deep-seated fears of anxiety and abandonment. The growing resentment within his heart could at any point manifest into a greater threat. This is foreshadowed when the boar Iouzen warns of humanity's tendency for darkness. Overcoming this darkness within is part of Ren's final test.

Overarching themes of inner-strength, family, and choosing your own destiny are all weaved into the adventure story of *The Boy and the Beast*. A film which takes the charm of two unlikely heroes and tests them in more ways than mere physical strength.

Adelle is a movie critic and movie fangirl in equal parts. Currently working in an Australian film production house, you can find more of her thoughts on the latest movie releases and indie cinema you should be watching over on her YouTube channel, Roll Credits at www.youtube.com/RollCredits.

2016 • A SILENT VOICE

EIGA KOE NO KATACHI

— JOHN RODRIGUEZ —

Say you want to improve your standing broad jump. How would you go about doing that? I'd like to say it's easy as practicing your jumps, and sure, that's part of the process. But the truth is more complicated. If you're serious about gaining those few extra inches—inches that might be worth millions to professional sports prospects—you're going to have to dig deep. Box jumps. Backward lunges. Hamstring curls. Squats. Seriously, you'll be squatting more than you would on a camping trip with no outhouse.

But that's the discipline. That's what it takes to bridge that performance gap. It's tough. It's grueling. And yet it's child's play compared to bridging a gap more relevant to us non-sports prospects: the forgiveness gap.

Certainly, Shōya Ishida can relate. Not that he's any angel, mind you. Indeed, the young protagonist of *A Silent Voice* digs his own hole by bullying his new hearing-disabled classmate, Shōko Nishimiya. Ishida's friends initially support his bullying, which includes such mean-spirited acts as throwing the notebook Nishimiya uses to communicate into the school fountain. Yet Ishida's friends turn on him when he lists them as accomplices after Nishimiya's mother reports her daughter's abuse to school officials. The classroom atmosphere becomes so toxic that Nishimiya ultimately transfers to a new elementary school to escape it.

Five years later, Ishida is a high school pariah. Kids have long memories, and Ishida remains the big, bad bully in their eyes. And Ishida wouldn't argue. He's still wracked with guilt over his bullying of Nishimiya, to the extent that he's considering suicide. But a chance discovery of Nishimiya's old notebook inspires Ishida to visit the sign language center attended by Nishimiya in hopes of garnering her forgiveness. Thus begins a long and often painful journey of reconciliation, both without and within.

If you've passed infancy—and I'm giving you the benefit of the doubt here—then you're acquainted with regret. Regrets are very much like a bar serving nothing but sampler glasses of Bud Light. Sure, you can drink a few, and while you'd be exposing your awful taste in beer, you probably wouldn't be doing any lasting damage. But drink enough and you'll inevitably end up questioning your will to live as you wallow in a miasma of puke and self-loathing.

Regret becomes particularly problematic whenever we try to bridge that forgiveness gap we discussed earlier. You'd never catch a broad jumper competing with a big rig tire on his back, yet that's precisely how regret acts on us whenever we need to give ourselves the necessary permission to forgive. And I mean that both ways: permission to forgive the transgressions of others and permission to forgive our own personal failures.

Regret adds to the acquisition cost of permission. It makes bridging the forgiveness gap hard. Hard enough that you maybe can't manage. Hard enough that, in extreme cases, suicide begins looking like a viable out.

Which is precisely why it's so beautiful to see that gap bridged.

There's a scene midway through *A Silent Voice* where Ishida and Nishimiya are riding a train to track down a former classmate. This is still early days in Nishimiya's and Ishida's reconciliation. They're standing by the train's exit, each wrapped in their own thoughts. Light filters through the windows, shining on the space of ground between them, and for a moment you can almost *see* the gulf between them. It feels enormous. It feels terrifying.

Then Nishimiya sends Ishida a text message thanking him for joining her. There it is: a gap bridged. And nary a barbell squat required.

Why, then, does acquiring permission to forgive so often feel like a leap across the Grand Canyon? Probably because it's tangled up with all kinds of other difficult life challenges. Take friendship. You've probably got a whole jumble of acquaintances in your life. People you talk to at work, people you hang out with

... people. But how many of them are *friends*? 'Cause that's different, right? A *friend*? There's a cachet to that title, an implication of something non-superficial, something thicker than water. Acquaintances, we have in spades. Friends are precious. They're the ones who'll cross the street for us even when the traffic's heavy. They keep us wanting to breathe.

So we want friends. But friendship requires familiarity, and bridging the familiarity gap is *so goddamn hard*. It feels like a literal gap, one with a terrifying precipice waiting to gobble you up if you fall short, and, oh God, you just *know* you're going to!

In *A Silent Voice*, we see the familiarity gap through Ishida's perspective as an X superimposed over the faces of his peers. That makes sense. We're aware of the people circling us daily, but we don't really *see* them. That's doubly true when we're social excommunicates or when we're unable to obtain permission to extend ourselves the forgiveness necessary to re-engage with those we've wronged.

How, then, do we bridge the gap?

Elsewhere in this book, I mention the writing maxim "show, don't tell." That maxim applies to relationships, too. Showing ourselves is always going to get us farther than telling. And yet, people loathe to show themselves. Why? Because showing is *scary*. Telling? Not nearly so much. Telling is just narrative-building, and narratives we can control and shape to our advantage. Showing is different. Showing entails revealing the truth of us—even those parts we'd rather lose a limb than expose.

That's what makes it so rewarding when Ishida grants himself the permission to engage with an estranged classmate. The X peels away from the classmate's face, and what do you know? There's a person under there! And that's why it's so enchanting to watch Nishimiya and Ishida summon the courage to show themselves to one another. Try watching that moment when Ishida cups Nishimiya's hands on the bridge—a sign signifying a promise of friendship or a promise to remain with her forever, depending on your reading—and see if you don't cheer. Those are Olympic-sized gaps jumped with aplomb.

Maybe it's just me being on the wrong side of the aging curve, but it feels like it's harder than ever to strip those Xs from the faces surrounding us. Social media perhaps isn't helping. It provides layers of anonymity to our interactions. It practically screams for us to tell rather than show. That can become really confusing. It gets to where you're almost pasting an X over your own face, taking on a role that leaves you unable to recognize yourself.

So maybe it's more important than ever to seek role models like Nishimiya and Ishida. Here are two children accomplishing a feat that's nigh on Herculean for most adults. They're each forgiving each other for their sins, *and* they're each forgiving themselves for their own failings. That, friends, is how you kill Xs dead.

It's quite possible you'll never become a world-class broad jumper. That's okay. There are other gaps waiting to be leaped. And if ever you think the distance is too long to bridge or the burden of regret too heavy to bear, fear not: *A Silent Voice* is here to show you how.

John Rodriguez is a personal trainer whose devotion to physical fitness is exceeded only by his fervor for all things film and literature. John is currently finishing his first novel—a fantasy that's sparked fantasies of a challenging new career.

2016 • OCCULTIC;NINE

OKARUTIKKU NAIN

— MATTHEW CARATURO —

Loss of a loved one. Many times it affects us deeply, and it's really hard to cope with it. After all, this is someone who perhaps inspired us to become who we are today or, in less extreme cases, provided us company and companionship. Without that individual in our life, it may change how we act. *Occultic;Nine* manages to show how loss may affect an individual through the show's main protagonist, Yuuta Gamon, and how he managed to solve the dilemma holding him back.

Yuuta's father, Gamon Koresuke, is a radio personality. Every single time his dad performed, Gamon watched outside, and you can tell from the look on his face that he's elated to be there. It goes to show how much Yuuta looks up to his father and how happy he is just watching him perform and helping other people. Eventually, of course, we end up finding out that Koresuke was the leader of the Society of the Eight Gods of Fortune and how much he loved his son, Yuuta. He had a strong sense of justice about him, didn't want the scandium trade to even happen, and once he found out about the experiment being performed on his own son, he became extremely protective and died trying to prevent Yuuta from being a part of this plan.

Flash forward past Koresuke's death, and we see a different Yuuta. On the surface level, he's still a happy, charming, and energetic guy, but there are a lot of signs to suggest that the death of his father has led him to change. This is symbolized through Yuuta's jacket, which is a bright yellow color, yet, at the same time, he hides himself in this jacket. We see that he doesn't converse with other people in the school, really, all that often. He states that he didn't know Miyuu or Asuna were in his school, one of whom is an online psychic and the other who is a member of the FBI, respectively. You'd think that, at the very least, Miyuu would receive more discussion considering their classmates all want to hang around her in the first episode. All of this leads us to believe that he's unaware of what goes on in school because he doesn't have any friends. The first friend he meets is Ryo-tas, in the park he frequents from time to time—he doesn't even meet her in school. But what is Yuuta focusing on before he meets her? The radio.

The radio is the only real reminder Yuuta has of his father and he always carries it with him. He's still caught up in the past and his father's death still hasn't allowed him to move on. Gamon's main desire in life is to run Kiri Kiri Basara, an occult blog. He wants it to be so successful to the point where he doesn't have to work anymore; where he can just sit around, be a NEET (a person "Not in Education, Employment, or Training"), and not have to converse with anyone. When he's faced with the murder of Professor Hashigami, he's completely struck with nervousness to the point where all he can listen to is the voice in the radio. He feels as if, ultimately, that's the only device that can truly comfort him in this time of stress. That's not to say he doesn't acknowledge Ryo-tas as a friend, but rather that their relationship is very different, and not one where he could tell her about these personal problems happening around him.

For the next few episodes, we see Yuuta try his best to mentally handle what is going on, but he's not doing a very good job at it. He's looking around for the solution, the lock to the key that he found from Professor Hashigami's carcass. This situation that Yuuta is dragged into is especially difficult, because of who he is; not only because of his own paranoia and low self esteem, but also because of his age and his position. He's not an FBI agent like Asuna or even someone with connections like Toko. This really shows the difference between his character and someone like Okabe from *Steins;Gate* in the same franchise. While Okabe still had a difficult time with what went on with him in the series, at the very least he had tools that he could utilize and potentially get him out of the situation. With Yuuta, all he has is the voice on the radio, and he'd better hope that the voice isn't on the path to getting him into major trouble. To Yuuta's advantage, though, he has some room to act a bit more suspicious because the people around him still wouldn't suspect anything. Yuuta's character is one who is extremely eccentric, so if he says something crazy, then people will just assume it's as per usual and that nothing strange is going on.

A major recurring theme within the series is to stop getting too caught up in one's own struggles to the point where one starts losing awareness of those right in front of them. This is exemplified through many different characters, most notably the online fortune-teller, Miyuu, getting too caught up in Chi's death that she just sits in bed and doesn't converse with anyone. This also occurs with Aria, a black magic user, getting so caught up in her brother's death that she fails to realize her brother is actually right in front of her the entire time, just in a different form.

Gamon, in particular, gets caught up in a few struggles that ultimately hold him back; the biggest of which being his inability to accept his situation. He still hasn't accepted his own death and, because of that, he abandons Miyuu when she needs help the most. He's always been crushed by the past events in his life, but he never wanted to die. He was never suicidal, and now, because of this, he's met with another massive problem. Before it was worrying all about how he was going to avoid getting framed for Professor Hashigami's death, and in spite of that problem becoming a non-issue, another problem comes to replace it almost immediately. How can he return himself and others to the way they once were?

Yuuta later ends up being put into a situation where he has to make up for it, when Kouhei, a member of the evil organization that killed Yuuta's father, attacks the group and puts them at risk. In that instance, he's able to redeem himself, and that is where I'd say he starts to truly develop as a character. He finally not only recognizes the people around him as friends, but also protects them and keeps them out of harm's way.

There's a really nice scene at the beginning of the finale where Yuuta's in the recording room talking to his deceased father about how he even got to be a hero, something he had admired in his dad all along. This scene does a really great job reaffirming that Yuuta still hasn't forgotten what he learned from his father, even after all that's happened.

Afterwards, there's a final meeting between the entire group and we get to see Yuuta fully realize that he's more than just some loser. He has the ability to affect other people around him and to leave a good impression. Not only this, but that he's also in a position where he is the only one who can do anything to stop this great threat. This raises not only pressure, but his sense of self-worth. This is reaffirmed in the final battle, where Yuuta grows wings. Him being able to imagine anything while dead showcases that he's no longer bound by what came before him. That now, no matter what, he feels like he can do anything—which is far different from before, when he considered himself a lousy NEET that couldn't do a single good thing with his life.

The scene in which Yuuta is finally reunited with his father is the massive climax of the episode, where he finally takes everything he's learned and applies it to his mission, stopping the society from succeeding in their plans. Yuuta's body ends up frozen, with his ghost still remaining in the real world. A fake body was placed in the morgue, which would explain why Asuna is unable to read him. His friends eventually intend to bring him back when they can find a way to synchronize his soul to his body via new technology. Until then, he lives on the radio waves. Some may consider this a sad fate for Yuuta, but I consider it hopeful one. He ends up like his father, remembered as a hero, and there's still the hope that one day he can come back to this world but, until then, his messages of heroism can still be heard via the radio, much like his father before him.

Occultic;Nine teaches one to be active, and to not fall into self-doubt. It's very easy to get caught up in this sorrowful moment and it's okay to take some time to mentally cope with it, but one shouldn't get stuck in it; to realize there are people in life that you have positively affected, and to be there when they need you. It may not always be easy, but it's ultimately worth it.

Matthew Caraturo is a former animation student at the School of Visual Arts. He now runs a YouTube channel on anime called RogerSmith2004, and occasionally writes for an anime satire site called Anime Maru.

2016 • ORANGE

ORENJI

— MELISSA SEE —

I lived with my depression undiagnosed (and therefore, untreated) for most of my twenty-seven years of life. I know what it's like to feel as though you have rescinded control of your own mind to an unseen entity whose only purpose is to mentally ruin you. Sleeping until you're disoriented upon waking; feeling weighed down by seemingly unexplained fatigue; no longer loving reading and suddenly forgetting how to write stories—the two things I've loved for as long as I could remember.

I know what all of that is like.

Blessedly though, I got the professional help and medication I needed and am now living with the knowledge that my depression doesn't entirely comprise who I am.

But I love *Orange*, an anime series from 2016, because I know firsthand about what depression entails. *Orange* tells the story of a high schooler named Naho Takamiya who one day receives a letter from her future self approximately ten years into the future. Her future self tells her that a new boy named Kakeru Naruse is transferring into her class and that she wants her to befriend him. Naho's future self later admits that the reason she requested this is because she wants Naho to save Kakeru's life, as he ends up committing suicide. What follows is an anime series about the bond between friends, falling in love, and a raw, unflinching look at depression and suicide and how they impact both the person experiencing them and the ones closest to them.

I initially discovered *Orange* as a manga series in the first of its two hulking collections and instantly fell in love with everything about it. Ichigo Takano's characters, her plot that wraps its arms around you from the opening panels, and her artwork all astonished me. When I learned it was going to become an anime series soon after I finished reading it, I was so excited. And when Crunchyroll and FUNimation announced their partnership, along with announcing *Orange* was getting an English dub?

I remember bouncing up and down in my chair.

I'd watched the first episode in the original Japanese when it premiered on Crunchyroll prior to the partnership they announced with FUNimation. When the English dub started to premiere weekly on FUNimation's website via their Simulcasting service, I would watch the episodes sporadically, as I don't marathon heavy series to avoid an emotional rollercoaster. I waited until the whole series was dubbed to continue, either making a mistake or enhancing the experience by marathoning the last five episodes.

Now, about the last five episodes and my—either asinine or wonderful, I still haven't decided—decision to marathon them: while Kakeru isn't the protagonist with whom we spend the most time, he's still the main male lead—romantic or otherwise—as well as the central focus of the show, so the anime pays close attention to him. Kakeru's pain and anguish was palpable in the manga, but in the anime, with a fantastic performance by Micah Solusod in the English dub, his pain increases ten-fold. You can hear him crying, blaming himself for tragedies, and see how he crumples under the weight of his own depression. And that makes the viewer *ache*, particularly in the last five episodes. Which is why, in retrospect, it wasn't the wisest decision to marathon them. But I did it anyway.

I'm not someone who cries while watching anime—not regularly at least. But make no mistake, while watching *Orange*, I relearned that there's a difference between simply crying and openly sobbing. Because while I did get teary at points in the series, I sobbed during the final episode. Ugly tears, constricted throat, stinging eyes, foggy glasses, everything. However, I think that was what made *Orange* an even more beautiful experience.

Too often in society, we're taught that emotions are signs of weakness. We can't cry, we can't be angry. Why? Because we want to appear fine to the rest of the world to avoid being judged, no matter how harshly, for expressing our valid feelings. But *Orange*, especially as an anime, teaches us that having emotions—and having a support system to express those emotions to, as well as to confide in—is not only perfectly normal, it's something that needs to be accepted. And that's a huge reason why I love anime in general, but *Orange* in particular. It reminded me of that.

Anime has taught me more than any visual media I've consumed over the course of my life. And what *Orange* taught me is something I'll be sure to remember: even when depression has its claws sunk deep in your back, there is always hope. In Kakeru's case, Naho and the rest of his new friends want to help him through any means possible. My friends helped me too, which is why I connected with this series so much.

I know what depression does to a person. But I also know there's help out there, as well as hope. And those are the two most important things.

Melissa See is an avid collector of far too many anime, books, and manga. Her goal is to someday work in the anime industry as a director. She currently resides in New York.

2016 • DESCENDING STORIES: SHÔWA GENROKU RAKUGO SHINJÛ

昭和元禄落語心中

— THE PEDANTIC ROMANTIC —

Showa Genroku Rakugo Shinju is one of the most thoroughly "great" works of anime that exists. In every regard this series exudes excellence and class, from its subtly engrossing directing, to its meticulously-realized prewar Shôwa era setting that we see progress all the way up into the modern day—to the moody jazz underscoring the entire flawless two-season experience.

It's a period piece, an emotionally rich generation-spanning character drama, a meditation upon the fate of a traditional form of Japanese performative expression, and in turn, a meditation upon the nature of art itself and those who pursue it. Before I get swept away by a passion for the series matched only by my passion for exorbitant adjectives, though, allow me to first provide some context.

The title, mouthful that it is, provides an excellent outlining of what the series is about. The Shôwa era, as noted, is the span of time across which much of the series takes place, lasting for the reign of Emperor Hirohito, from 1926 to 1989. In spite of it translating to "the era of enlightened peace" you'll of course know that for the early stretch of this era, at the least, it was anything but. As you'd expect, setting the story during this era has huge implications for the lives of the anime's characters, everything from the duo of primary characters for the first season being separated during the war, to subtler effects of the time period like a more strict and censorious government having some suggestions about which kinds of stories they should perhaps avoid performing.

The medium in which they tell those stories is what the third word, *"rakugo"* refers to. Rakugo is a form of typically comedic storytelling which involves one performer on stage, in a kneeling position throughout the entire performance, their only props being a paper fan and small cloth, reciting stories that will typically last anywhere between ten and forty minutes, involving multiple characters—each one of them, of course, being played by this single storyteller. The art form is a fascinating exercise in minimalism, leaving the performer with just their body language from the torso up and their voice to capture an audience and resonate with them, and yet, these rakugo performers do so, brilliantly.

One of the highlights of *Rakugo Shinju* from a production and filmmaking standpoint is the anime's renditions of these performances. While the series takes a more grounded visual approach that is typically fairly reserved—with almost none of the action or expressively exaggerated character acting anime allows for—the way perspective is played with during performances, to draw the viewer in and put their experience perfectly in sync with that of the audience, is enrapturing. Even for total outsiders to rakugo and its culture, the skill of each given performer is made abundantly clear through the directing.

A floundering performance will be left on a still, dull wide shot, static, and impersonal. When one of the masters take the stage, everything changes. The shots get intensely intimate, right up in the face of the performer. The camera will cut whenever the character speaking in the story changes and their head will occupy the opposite side of the frame, a shot-reverse-shot conversation held by a single person being constructed on the back of their performative skill alone. The humor translates remarkably well, and the comedic timing is so sharp that you'll be laughing right along with the audience.

For those masters' most pivotal performances, we'll be drawn in even further. The stage fades away as the blizzard they're shivering from swells up around them, and its wind howls in the background. Of course, these performances coincide with the culmination of massive, sometimes decades-long buildups, and so the narrative and emotional weight they wield is immense.

That is part of why the final word of the title, "shinju" is so meaningful in relation to this series. It means "double suicide," and in particular is used to describe the Japanese concept of a "lovers' suicide." Fittingly for the subject matter of this series, centuries of storytelling and theatrical tradition in Japan have built up the trope of lovers whose relationship would for one reason or another be at odds with the societal order ending their lives together in order to achieve in death the unity that would not be allowed in life.

This concept is woven throughout the series as a recurring metaphorical motif, and to avoid spoilers, I'll describe one instance of it that's a part of the series' premise itself. The most central character throughout the series is Kikuhiko, who eventually becomes the foremost rakugo master. He's an immensely skilled performer, but also a man embittered by the weight of many tragedies borne throughout his life, and so, he plans for the art of rakugo itself to die with him, a lovers' suicide. For years he would take on no apprentice, in spite of the great value for the art of rakugo such teaching could hold, instead resolving that this medium which had given him everything—and taken even more away—would itself be taken away to the grave along with him.

Over the course of *Rakugo Shinju* we witness Kikuhiko's entire life, from childhood up to that decision, and then see him eventually take on that apprentice he had resolved to never accept, witnessing those decades of training and further evolution on the part of Kikuhiko's character in the process. He truly embodies much of the essence of the series, sage yet still mirthful, with his dry, bemused wit, an elegant but tortured genius.

And oh how spectacularly he in turn is embodied by his voice actor. Akira Ishida is one of the industry's most-renowned actors, with nearly thirty years of experience now and getting roles as prominent as the Japanese dub actor for Luke Skywalker in *Star Wars Episode IV: A New Hope*, and Jack Dawson in the dub of James Cameron's *Titanic*. For Kikuhiko, he gives a performance that honestly brings to mind "peerless" as the only suitable and fair descriptor. Ishida voices the man's evolution over the course of decades, from his teens to his eighties or nineties (we're never given an exact age), and gives each and every stage of his life its own distinct sound. This isn't merely a set of young man, middle-aged man, and elderly man voices. It's a rich, nuanced voicing of a man in his late sixties, and then that same man's voice once he's in his early eighties. In his sixties, his voice is a bit thinner, his breath more labored; in his late eighties, his voice is fading now, wasting away, cracking and trailing off into wispy, whispered nothingness, exactly enough so that you can definitely perceive it but never so much so that you fail to believe it for a second.

This is without even taking into account the incredibly impressive talent displayed by every voice actor of a rakugo-performing character, since that means they themselves had to perform that rakugo. While only having to perform the vocal component of rakugo, and do so in a recording booth with the ability to do many retakes instead of in front of a live audience, certainly doesn't mean that this didn't require the intensive specialized training and skill of a rakugo performer. They still had to replicate the comedic timing, the vocal distinction between separate characters, and perform pieces like "Jugemu," whose entire joke is the absurdity of the length of Jugemu Jugemu Gokō-no surikire Kaijarisuigyo-no Suigyōmatsu Unraimatsu Fūraimatsu Kuunerutokoro-ni Sumutokoro Yaburakōji-no burakōji Paipopaipo Paipo-no-shūringan Shūringan-no Gūrindai Gūrindai-no Ponpokopī-no Ponpokonā-no Chōkyūmei-no Chōsuke's name (that's his name), along with the lightning speed this confounding tongue-twister of a name is said with by those in the story.

The unfailingly smile-eliciting energy and charisma brought to the performances of Sukeroku, and his stylistic successor Yotaro, is highly praiseworthy as well. But, of course, all others are topped by Ishida's performance, tasked as he was with convincingly performing rakugo that is canonically the very peak of the art form in this series. If it had no other noteworthy qualities, *Rakugo Shinju* would be worth watching on the basis of this acting alone, for those interested in that art, because it's some of the very best you'll get.

Remarkably though, the series also happens to have some of the best storytelling, character writing, atmosphere, directing, theming, twists, and emotional punches you'll get, too. Oh, and a pair of opening themes sung by Megumi Hayashibara are what begin each episode, there to immerse you in that atmosphere before the episode proper even begins. This actress of classics like *Cowboy Bebop*'s Faye

Valentine and *Evangelion*'s Rei Ayanami is perfectly suited to the upbeat, sultry tone of the first season's opening, and also the second's sorrowful, haunting one—her voice possessing the sense of class these jazzy tunes call for. *Showa Genroku Rakugo Shinju* demonstrates a mastery of its medium no matter where you look, true artistic excellence, and is a joy to experience because of that.

The Pedantic Romantic has been working as an anime YouTuber full-time since the age of nineteen (not particularly impressive, seeing as she is only twenty at the time of this writing, but still). She possesses a passion for anime analysis, industry research, and humbly asks people to support her work at patreon.com/ thepedanticromantic in equal measure. She thinks anime's pretty great, and you are too.

2016 • YOUR NAME

KIMI NO NA WA.

— CHRIS STUCKMANN —

The city of Los Angeles. Smog, traffic, crowds, and the occasional brush fire. About once a year, I find myself traveling from my quiet Ohio town to this bustling city for an event. In December of 2016, I kissed my introversion goodbye for a few days and journeyed to the City of Angels to collaborate with pals of mine on some projects. LA is a beautiful city—especially at night—and while I have nothing against the metropolis, it's always tough for me to leave my wife home alone. Gratefully, there's something LA offers movie buffs that always softens the blow of leaving home: limited release films.

Since December is often referred to as "Oscar Season," studios go to drastic measures to get their best films noticed. This is where the "Oscar-Qualifying-Run" comes into play. Let's say a studio—in this case, FUNimation—hopes their film will be considered for an Oscar nomination. To ensure its chances, the film must play for a public audience for a specified time, and before a specified date. Usually, these "runs" take place in LA and last for one week.

Makoto Shinkai's *Your Name* had demolished records in Japan already, eventually becoming one of the country's highest-grossing films. But in December of 2016, I learned that FUNimation was hosting a special "Oscar-Qualifying-Run" of Shinkai's body-swapping romance at the Laemmle Music Hall, and believe me, tickets were already selling out.

Accessing the webpage for Laemmle, I discovered every single showtime was full except for an afternoon matinee, and I scrambled to get one of the last tickets available. Within minutes of getting my ticket, the screening was full.

Checking the map of the area confirmed it would take an hour to get to Laemmle, barring the usual unforeseen LA traffic jam. So, on the day of the screening, I found myself in an Uber, silently begging the roadways to part. I arrived at Laemmle with only minutes to spare, dashed inside the theater, and found the *one* empty seat in the auditorium.

A quick glance around the theater gave me a startling but welcome realization, *I'm pretty sure I'm the only American dude here*, I thought. How cool! To see a highly-anticipated anime with a Japanese audience is an experience I've always dreamed of, and it didn't disappoint.

There's a cultural gap between Japanese humor and American. I've watched many an anime with friends here and found my wife and I the only people laughing at the right moments. Experiencing *Your Name* with an audience that understood and appreciated the material on a personal level was a pure joy.

Your Name opens with a young girl named Mitsuha waking up in the morning to an awkward discovery. She has girl parts! But wait ... isn't that normal? Well sure, unless you're a boy named Taki that's trapped inside her body! Some distance away, Taki awakes to a similar realization, he has boy parts! But why does that surprise him? That's right, Mitsuha has switched bodies with Taki, and with the space between them, this creates a daunting challenge: can both of them survive in each other's bodies while also solving the mystery of how this happened?

Eventually, the two are able to decipher that the body swap lasts for a brief time, before giving them their true bodies back. While they're swapped, they begin to enjoy learning about the other person, their jobs, school and home life. In this truly unconventional way, the two teeter on the edge of the precipice known as love, without ever actually meeting each other.

When it comes to anime romances, there are plenty of shows and movies in the genre, yet a minute few stand out amongst the pack. The plots are so similar they appear churned from a conveyer belt: A boy joins a school, and every girl on campus falls for him. A boy moves into a harem, and every girl in the building falls for him. There's the new guy at work, and every girl in the shop falls for him. Get my point? Genuinely good romance anime is hard to come by. Often times, they sink into melodrama and unrealistic relationship tropes, coming off more like a soap opera than a legitimate connection forged through love. This is where *Your Name* shines.

Long-distance romances can be tough. Shinkai understands this, but better yet, he warps this kind of relationship into something wholly distinct. For example, everyone who's ever been in a serious partnership has likely wondered what it's like to be the other person. What does it *feel* like to be them? What unknown struggles face them on a daily basis they've never shared?

While at first, Taki and Mitsuha are both urgently searching for ways to end this star-crossed exchange, soon enough, they begin to look forward to the time spent as the other person. They become invested in the other's life and their concerns. Before long, their own lives become placeholders for the days they wake up as the opposite person. In this way, a beautiful bond is formed between the two, leading to significantly intimate discoveries for both of them.

Where stories of this nature (light, fluffy, romantic) often derail is when the plot seemingly forces the characters into grave situations. We've seen it happen many times: a film starts innocently enough, and eventually, someone checks into a hospital. To bridge the gap from light to dark takes authenticity. In life, the ups and downs come without warning, but in film, it's tough to communicate this unpredictability while still harnessing a confident tone. Shinkai pulls it off with flying colors. When the story inevitably takes a turn for the dramatic, we yearn for resolution for Taki and Mitsuha. Better still, we *care*. Their happiness and safety become a priority. *Your Name* presents a hilarious and heartwarming twist on long-distance relationships, and put simply, it's one of the best anime films ever made.

As discussed in my entry for *Sword of the Stranger*, the Academy famously overlooks anime in the Best Animated Feature category. All it takes is a glance at the 2018 nominees to recognize that (*The Boss Baby* over *A Silent Voice* or *In This Corner of the World* is laughable). So I wasn't surprised when FUNimation's "Oscar-Qualifying-Run" didn't bear fruit at the awards ceremony. That being said, in my experience, the Oscars don't choose what films become great ... *time* does. *Your Name* will be immortalized for years to come as an influential film that inspired countless people across the world to follow their dreams, even if they seem insurmountable.

2016 • YURI!!! ON ICE

ユーリ *!!! ON ICE*

— MELISSA SEE —

I'm not an athletic person by any means. A childhood spent going up and down the east coast because my older sister was on a traveling softball team squashed all hopes of even enjoying sports as a spectator. But then why did I decide to check out a sports anime called *Yuri!!! On Ice* when FUNimation started dubbing it, aside from the fact that I liked the voice cast?

I don't know. But I'm forever grateful that I did.

Yuri!!! On Ice follows a young figure skater named Yuri Katsuki who returns home to Japan, anxious and upset about what to do with his once-promising career. Inspired by his idol, famous Russian figure skater Victor Nikiforov, Yuri starts training again at his local rink, only to have his old friend record him performing one of Victor's routines. The video is uploaded and it goes viral overnight, catching Victor's attention. Victor then travels to Japan, staying at the hot spring inn owned by Yuri's family, telling Yuri that he wants to be his coach, determined to steer him toward victory at the Grand Prix Final. With a rivalry from another Russian figure skater, Yuri Plisetsky, also known as Yurio—who also wants Victor to be his coach—in addition to the stiff international competition and Yuri discovering what love is, this series is ultimately one of the most compelling shows I've seen in years.

Admittedly, I wasn't expecting to fall in love with *Yuri!!! On Ice*. At first glance, I thought it was going to be a "typical sports anime" with one-dimensional characters and repetitive episodes that rely almost entirely on the sport of choice to carry it, in lieu of an actual plot.

My perception changed immediately within the first few minutes of the show, when Yuri locks himself in a bathroom stall to call his mother and shortly thereafter starts crying because he came in last place during his competition, firmly believing that he failed. This is our protagonist. He's not confident. He's not strong. Instead, he's hiding from both his loss and those around him. (He is then scared out of his bathroom stall after Yuri Plisetsky kicks the door, but I digress.)

Clearly, *Yuri!!! On Ice* wasn't about to follow the traditional formula of a sports anime (determination, training, competition, repeat for the rest of the series). We follow Yuri from when he's at his most dejected, most lost in the world, to pursuing his dreams on the ice. And I think that's something anyone who ends up watching this show—especially those who think of themselves as the creative type, no matter the art—can relate to.

Self-doubt is a creative person's constant companion, no matter how hard we try to shake it. And that's one of the reasons I identify with *Yuri!!! On Ice* as much as I do.

We've all felt the way Yuri does at the start of the show, his anxiety leaking through. We've all had our moments of wondering just why on earth we're pursuing our passion. *I'm awful. Why am I even skating anymore?* can easily become: *Why am I even drawing anymore? Why am I even dancing anymore?* And in my case: *Why am I even writing anymore?*

I found *Yuri!!! On Ice* while I was trying desperately to rediscover my creativity after years of not writing, or even reading, consistently. And while I watched plenty of anime during that time—in retrospect, it was probably my way of surrounding myself with stories when I thought I couldn't tell them anymore—something about the way *Yuri!!! On Ice* handled its story struck me as brilliant.

We meet Yuri at one of the lowest points in his life, in an anime genre dominated by physically-perfect, determined athletes with tunnel vision of success. Yuri is upset, anxious, and seeks comforts in pork cutlet bowls, unsure of what to do when he returns home to Japan. But when he makes the decision to train again, his story isn't one of immediate gratification, even after Victor travels to Japan wanting to be his coach. He must work for his dream of figure skating and he has

Victor—who he falls in love with—by his side the entire way there. Never had I seen a sports anime handled this way.

In certain sports anime, the underdog archetype can certainly be—and often is—present, but they are almost always relegated to the roll of an endearing side character that the audience can root for. But with *Yuri!!! On Ice*, the underdog is our *protagonist*.

That's why this series meant so much to me. It taught me that, even though you can sometimes believe you'll never again be creative, regardless of the circumstances—even if those circumstances happen to be in your own mind—you still possess the potential to make art. You still have the power to be creative, you still have the power to pursue your dreams—whether those dreams are in writing, in your heart, or on the ice.

Melissa See is an avid collector of far too many anime, books, and manga. Her goal is to someday work in the anime industry as a director. She currently resides in New York.

2017 • RECOVERY OF AN MMO JUNKIE

NETOJŪ NO SUSUME

— MELISSA SEE —

Being an adult isn't an easy thing. From the time we're children, we all dream of and think about what life will be like once we're older. But when you're as much of a nerd as an adult as you were when you were a kid? That's where things get weird, and in some cases, uncomfortable. Which is why I feel blessed to have watched an anime series called *Recovery of an MMO Junkie*.

Recovery of an MMO Junkie is about a woman in her thirties named Moriko who claims she has chosen the life of a NEET, a person in Japanese society who shuts themselves away from actively participating in the world around them. Instead of working, she decides to devote her time to an MMO RPG known as Fruits de Mere. She creates a male character named Hayashi, who is taken under the wing of a beautiful female character named Lily—created by a man named Yuuta Sakurai—so that he can learn how to play the game successfully. The more time Hayashi and Lily spend together, the more the people playing them realize that they have developed feelings for each other, despite never having seen one another.

But unbeknownst to them, they have met in real life before, in a series of awkward encounters. And they slowly start falling for each other in real life as well, working up the courage to tell the other person the truth about their online identities along the way.

For the first time since I started watching anime, I saw characters roughly around my age grappling with the same insecurities I feel every day, finding solace in one of the same ways I do: by immersing themselves in video games. For Morioka and

Sakurai, it's Fruits de Mere. For me, it's *Pokémon, The Sims, Stardew Valley, Ōkami,* various installments of *Mario, Story of Seasons* ... the list goes on.

But the thing about *Recovery of an MMO Junkie* is that it goes beyond being an adult nerd with insecurities and feeling the need to hide your passions from those around you. While that aspect is explored, being an adult and being a nerd is something that is ultimately embraced. This is the show the person I am right now needed, for that exact reason.

Though I didn't call myself a nerd until college, I have been a nerd for as long as I can remember. From the summers when I lugged garbage bags full of books to my sister's softball games along the east coast; to when I received a copy of *Pokémon Red* and a matching red Game Boy Pocket for Easter; to when I was introduced to *Harry Potter* while recuperating from a leg surgery; and to when I fell in love with anime as an adult.

But after the universal obsession of *Pokémon* faded, I started to hide my nerdiness—hide my love for the things that brought me wonderful joy—from most of the people I interacted with. And the older I got, the more I hid my love for things people could deem juvenile—the exception being the friends I'd made through those things I loved. Looking back on it now, I suppose a part of me was, and still is at times, ashamed and embarrassed—at least a little bit—for still loving certain things.

However, all that shame and embarrassment goes away when I'm with other people who understand my love of things like gaming and anime. Because *we* collectively understand what it's like to hide a part of ourselves from other people, people who think adults shouldn't be enjoying anime ("It's for kids, isn't it? Animation is for kids, right?") or video games ("Shouldn't you be devoting your time to something better?"), or even young adult fiction ("Shouldn't you be reading adult books now?").

But *Recovery of an MMO Junkie* taught me something I'd unknowingly been desperate to learn for years: You can be both an adult and a nerd. You can be an adult and still be the awkward person you've always been. You can be an adult and still have your passions, even if you first found those passions when you were young. You don't need to *hide* parts of yourself, stuffing them someplace where no one can see, feeling hot and sick when your excitement for things would bubble to the surface.

My passions for things are part of who I am. I don't need to hide who I am from other people. Instead, I need to embrace who I am and the passions that make me that way. I wouldn't have been reminded of that and had it solidified were it not for this series, a series I, both an adult and a nerd, am so happy exists.

Melissa See is an avid collector of far too many anime, books, and manga. Her goal is to someday work in the anime industry as a director. She currently resides in New York.

2018 • VIOLET EVERGARDEN

VAIORETTO EVĀGĀDEN

— CHRIS STUCKMANN —

How do you know what someone else is thinking?

For young Violet Evergarden, that is one of her greatest struggles. She works as an Auto Memory Doll—a select group of ghostwriters that help customers compose letters in their stead. For some, a job like that sounds easy. But Violet comes from a traumatic background filled with violence and death, and strives to understand the complexities of human emotion. Nothing in her past prepared her for complications surrounding abstract thought, or even basic emotional reaction.

Violet was trained to operate under duress and perform her duties to maximum potential, no matter the cost. As the episodes progress, we uncover more of her backstory: one steeped in tragedy, a fact that's hinted at from the start. She has state-of-the-art metal arms—a feature that helps when needing to type fast—and isn't entirely aware of how she lost her original ones. But clearly, Violet has been through the ringer.

An old friend referred to as "The Major" is often brought up. He was the one who helped train Violet—he even named her. Through the Major, Violet found herself caught in the middle of a war. Murderous flashbacks showcase her relentlessness in battle, and soon enough, we understand why Violet has shut herself off from emotion.

Violet Evergarden is the newest anime that will be discussed in this book, and one that hasn't even completed its run yet. As of this writing, about half of the show has been released, with a total of fourteen episodes proposed. After just seeing the first half, I knew it deserved a place in these pages.

It's easy to gush about animation, especially when discussing the hand-drawn beauty prevalent in most anime, but *Violet Evergarden* is a different beast. For a television series, this is stunning. The time-consuming effort the animators are putting into every frame is nothing short of staggering. The fully-rendered movements—utilizing many frames—and the photo-realistic backgrounds create the illusion of depth, filling the screen with jaw-dropping beauty. Violet often slips off her gloves, shocking those around her by her metal appendages. Diligent care has gone into every small detail of moments like these. The gleam of light against the metal. Each individual finger twitching in a different direction. The glove going limp in her other hand. This achievement shouldn't go unnoticed.

Violet Evergarden originated as two light novels (equivalent to a novella with illustrations) written by Kana Akatsuki and illustrated by Akiko Takase. The story was the first ever to win a grand prize in three categories at the Kyoto Animation Awards. Obviously, the books were popular enough to become an anime, and anyone with eyes and a beating heart could see why. As mentioned at the outset, Violet deals with the inability to connect emotionally with others, something that many can easily relate to. But how exactly does someone like that write the thoughts of another person at their behest?

This is where the show really shines. With any character, presenting them with their greatest obstacles can be a riveting way to endear us to them. For some, it's a brutal battle with their archnemesis. For others, it could be toiling through the pressures of school. For Violet, her greatest hurdle is understanding the unspoken feelings of others. Body language is unclear to her, reading between the lines is impossible. The first letters she composes are embarrassingly frank, often stating the precise, unfiltered thoughts of her clients. Initially, this causes a great deal of strife for Violet, although you wouldn't see that on her face. Her confusion is one of complete obliviousness, but certainly not stupidity.

Up until now, Violet has known one truth: follow orders. As a soldier, her efficiency knew no bounds. She was once hailed by the nickname, "The Weapon." Bodies fell to her hands like no other. But now that the war is over, her unorthodox upbringing—or lack thereof—has never been more apparent. Gratefully, this only serves as a way to enrich Violet, her impediments in life only making her all the more enchanting.

Since she's accustomed to following orders, she excels in almost everything she does—save for communicating normally of course. Her friends offer her food and she responds by saying she doesn't require much sustenance. When a worker regrets he's unable to provide a lavish meal for her extraordinary services, she remarks that the gorgeous moonlit countryside is adequate enough for her. In reality, Violet's so unsure of how the world works ... she's better than all of us.

While Violet may not always know what people are thinking, watching her learn to comprehend these complexities isn't just satisfying, it's cathartic. Her journey is rife with stumbling blocks, but her firm resolve—and those shiny metal arms—are more than up to the task.

Netflix recently announced they'll stream the English dub around springtime of 2018, so hopefully, the entire show will be on the platform by the time you're reading this. With an engaging lead character, a fascinating backstory, and some of the most stunning animation these eyes have seen, *Violet Evergarden* is well worth your time. If the last half of the show is as good as the first, we might have a new classic on our hands.

CLOSING

Every once in a while, a letter arrives in my PO Box describing a painful ordeal one of my viewers is struggling with. Often, my videos are credited as the source of solace they turned to when in dire straits. Reading these thoughts and expressions of joy from people who've seen the darkest part of life always brings comfort to me. I'm no stranger to needing an outlet that pushes those worries away, and I'll tell you why.

If I hadn't discovered anime, it's reasonable to assume I wouldn't be here today. As detailed in my *Cowboy Bebop* entry, I may not have discovered my passion for filmmaking without that show. But even before that, Toonami entered my life, creating an unbridled yearning for unconventional animated storytelling. To say that anime became an obsession would be accurate. But it wasn't simply a search for mind-numbing entertainment. Pouring myself into these shows or movies meant more to me than just "passing the time." If you read my *Ronin Warriors* entry, you heard me describe my turbulent adolescent years. Rather than bore you by recounting those struggles, I'll just say ... it was tough, and leave it at that.

Through anime, I forged bonds with other kids who appreciated the medium, and more importantly, found something to look forward to each afternoon. Suddenly, I had an outlet: anime. When the negativity threatened to overwhelm me, I knew that turning on my favorite show would help push that away. Would the problems still be there later? Sure. But they weren't so damn loud anymore, and that was a victory.

We search for what keeps us alive. In my case, I've never given up the pursuit of my dreams, nor the desire to attain them. That wide-eyed little kid sitting on his couch—ignoring his homework for just a few more hours—would be dumbfounded if he knew what the future held.

If someone had told him that one day he'd produce a mini-documentary on Toonami, working with Steve Blum (voice of Spike Spiegel and TOM from Toonami) and

Christopher Sabat (voice of Vegeta, Piccolo, and heaps more), he'd have told them they were nuts. But what do you know? *That actually happened.*

His naiveté would never allow him to believe that one day he'd pen a book on anime, blessed to combine forces with some truly incredible people. But hey, you're reading this book right now! I guess that happened, too!

So, when I receive those poignant letters, I read them fastidiously. Those letters remind me of myself. Without something to look forward to during those restless years, I may have checked out of life for good. When we're suffering, we turn to what keeps us breathing. For me, it was anime.

In the last few months, I've watched more anime than in the *last few years.* Initially, the task seemed daunting. But before long, the rediscovery of old shows not seen in ages was a pleasure to experience. Re-watching *Ronin Warriors* was like revisiting childhood again, and enduring the brutality of *Now and Then, Here and There* reminded me that anime is capable of piercing the soul. Charting anime's path from cultural oddity to cultural staple was fascinating. Titles like *Ninja Scroll* or *Ghost in the Shell* brought back fond memories of anime pamphlets at the comics store, or covert glances at *Animerica Magazine* (that February 1996 Motoko cover ...) But above all, working on this has inspired an overwhelming sense of gratitude for my family, friends, and peers.

A major "thank you" must go to my wife, Sam, who not only composed some entries, but put up with me disappearing into the bowels of the basement to watch yet another anime each day. If you spent any time in my house over the last few months, you heard a ridiculous amount of anime Openings and Closings, and more than one occurrence of "Sorry, honey, I've got to get some writing done."

Where would I be without my great friend, John Rodriguez? Not only did he lend his seasoned voice to ten wonderful entries, but he assisted in editing, too. Keep his name in mind, for it's my sincere belief that his writing will gain legitimate notice soon.

Ernest Cline? *The* Ernest Cline? What an honor to include your work in this book! I'm still blown away that you were excited about this project and took the time to write for it. Thank you!

I'd also like to thank all the YouTube personalities, writers, and bloggers who submitted their passionate work. I'm so happy to share this with them, and it's my hope that those reading this seek out their channels and web pages. They're worth your time, so show them some support!

Acknowledgment must go to those who sent packages filled with anime DVDs and Blu-rays to my PO Box. I'm consistently taken aback by your giving nature, and I'm thrilled to have such generous viewers and readers.

And of course … you. The reader. Thank you for endorsing our efforts. It's your continuous support that keeps us going.

Our goal has been to communicate how anime shapes and moves us. How it's inspired multiple generations to appreciate a culture that perhaps they never would've known, and how it's sometimes saved us from ourselves. After reading my contributors' impassioned accounts, I believe that anime is much more than mere entertainment: it's fuel for life.

Sometimes nowadays, while looking in the mirror, that lonely kid stares back. Only now, I smile. I envision him sprinting from the bus to his tiny apartment. Mom and Dad aren't home yet, there's ramen in the cupboard with his name on it, and Toonami is about to start. That kid was searching. Searching for what kept him alive.

He's still searching.

Chris Stuckmann

January 24, 2018

AUTHOR BIO

Chris Stuckmann is a filmmaker, writer, and film critic. He's a member of the Broadcast Film Critics Association and creator of a successful YouTube channel with over one million subscribers. He's the author of *The Film Buff's Bucket List* as well as *Anime Impact*, and hopes to continue telling stories. He lives in Akron, Ohio with his wife, Sam Liz, and their dogs, Zeev and Indy.